D1601182

Rumors of Indiscretion

Rumors of Indiscretion

The University of Missouri
"Sex Questionnaire" Scandal
in the Jazz Age

Lawrence J. Nelson

UNIVERSITY OF MISSOURI PRESS   COLUMBIA AND LONDON

Library of Congress Cataloging-in-Publication Data

Nelson, Lawrence J., 1944–
    Rumors of indiscretion : the University of Missouri "sex questionnaire"
scandal in the Jazz Age / Lawrence J. Nelson.
        p. cm.
    Includes bibliographical references and index.
    Contents: "A filthy questionnaire"—Rumors of sex—"Jellying" at Mizzou—
Inquisition—"Tallow candles"—Up in smoke—What really happened—
"Facts are stubborn things"—Denouement.
    ISBN 0-8262-1449-5 (alk. paper)
    1. Sex—Missouri. 2. Sexual ethics—Missouri.   3. College students—Missouri—
Social conditions. 4. Questionnaires—Missouri.   5. Scandals—Missouri—History.
6. Missouri—Social life and customs.   7. University of Missouri—History.   I. Title.
HQ18.U5 N35 2003
306.7'09778—dc21   2002044398

∞™This paper meets the requirements of the
American National Standard for Permanence of Paper
for Printed Library Materials, Z39.48, 1984.

Text designer: Stephanie Foley
Jacket design: Jennifer Cropp
Typesetter: Bookcomp, Inc.
Printer and binder: Thomson-Shore, Inc.
Typefaces: American Typewriter, Gil Sans, and Palatino

To Verlie
to Pete, Julie, and the memory of their brother;
to my alma mater, the University of Missouri
and
to my students
who, since 1968, have made teaching a pleasure

Contents

Preface

> From the trial of Socrates to the trial of Scopes is a long time; but the story of intolerance is not yet told. It is an unhappy thought that some future chronicle may include the recent episode at Columbia.
>
> —Attorney Leland Hazard, letter to the editor of
> the *Columbia Missourian*, March 16, 1929

> . . . the older generation had certainly pretty well ruined this world before passing it on to us.
>
> —John F. Carter, Jr., " 'These Wild Young People,' by One
> of Them," *Atlantic Monthly*, September 1920

This is a story about an America long gone. The Jazz Age of the 1920s formed a sort of cultural estuary where tradition mixed with change and rumors of change, where morality and ignorance jostled with temptation and injustice. This is about an America in a cultural divide, with honorable men and women on both sides of a culture war over what was thought to be moral and right, about accepted social propriety, about free inquiry. It is a story about America's purpose, its past, and its future.

That the 1920s were marked by social change against stubborn persistence is hardly debatable. Scholars have shown convincingly that some transformation culminated in the twenties, and that it had been underway for decades. Why it occurred has been debated ever since. The minority who went to college in the twenties did so amidst the backdrop of the Great War and its intellectual backwash; residual influences of the Progressive Era, including Prohibition; the emancipation of the "new woman," armed as she was with money, contraceptives, and the vote; the democracy of the automobile; prosperity; Sigmund Freud's gospel about libidos and sexual inhibitions; mass entertainment, including college football, moving pictures, and sex and confessional magazines; the collision between fundamentalist theology and modernism; and the rise of youth culture occasioned by the commonality of the high school experience. And undoubtedly a whole lot of other things as well, including the glaring unacceptability of various aspects of Victorianism in the new century. One critic has written, "For most historians, the reaction to the war and prohibition led to a moral letdown, a debauch, as the generation of the 1920s reacted to the deflation of moral idealism and high purpose by rebelling against authority and the standards of civilization."[1]

The result was the cultural celebration of youth for the first time, witnessed most clearly on the university campus. Those who went to college in the 1920s knew there was something dramatically different about their generation and the time in which they lived. If their restless collegiate experience foreshadowed that of later generations, notably the 1960s, it also revealed, in a greater and contrary way perhaps, that in the midst of societal change, university students remained respectful of tradition and authority even as they pushed against Victorian constraints. Many sought change, but few were radicals. As one perceptive scholar argued about 1920s youth, "There was no hostility toward the world of the elders, only a sense of difference."[2]

What happened on one university campus at the end of the 1920s not only illustrates that point but also provides a window to that uneasy but exciting time. The events in Columbia at the University of Missouri demonstrated that while the youth of the 1920s eagerly embraced "modern" this and "modern" that, they were also profoundly nostalgic for a world that many feared was being lost.[3] *What was actually lost was Victorianism, not tradition, and the two were not always the same.* Despite its value for social stability, despite its many achievements in nineteenth- and early-twentieth-century England and America, Victorianism—at least that caricatured by its critics—couldn't live without dual sexual standards, hypocrisy, and limited roles for women, along with unrealistic notions of what young adults should know and when they should know it.[4] Victorians mandated an orderly culture in which its members had sharply defined roles, violations of which carried societal sanctions. One scholar of the anti-Victorian revolt in the 1920s has argued, "The assaults on Victorianism have eroded its conceptual foundations, but have left much of its structure largely intact."[5]

Maybe so, but on the other hand, traditional values antedated Victorian proscriptions of the proper society, and tradition's most basic tenets survived the 1920s. Decorum, respect for authority, sense of shame, rea-

sonable standards of social conformity, and sharply defined hues of right
and wrong, and the family (though based on greater equality between the
sexes) shook off the cultural threats that brought down the last of Victorianism as the organizing intellectual foundation of American society. In
fact, tradition in the 1920s—not radicalism—was the Victorian's greatest
and most fearsome enemy. American society was and is threatened not by
real or imagined Victorian persistence, nor even by the older surviving
structures of tradition, but by the impassioned rejection of those structures.[6] University students in the 1920s who embraced tradition while
rejecting Victorianism would have understood that. A crisis on one university campus in the heartland formed a microcosm of the culminating
and swirling changes in American life before a depression and another
world war changed things forever. But if the story of that America seems
long gone, it is also true that in another sense, except that intolerance has
switched sides, maybe this is a story about an America not so very different from our own.

Acknowledgments

This very American story could not be adequately told without the help of numerous people. I am grateful to Christine Montgomery and Peggy Platner at the State Historical Society of Missouri in Columbia, and to the staff of the Western Historical Manuscript Collection at the University of Missouri in Columbia. At the latter facility, special thanks to David Moore, who proved very efficient and helpful in numerous ways. Thanks also to John Konzal and former director Nancy Lankford. The collection is exceptionally well-organized and skillfully managed; the whole operation is simply first-class. The staff at the University's Special Collections, likewise housed in Ellis Library on the campus, also proved helpful, as did Debbie Landi and Michael Holland at the University Archives. Thanks also to Rob Hill in University Affairs and Karen Worley, editor of *Mizzou* magazine. For their assistance with other materials, thanks to the staffs of the Greene County–Springfield Public Library, Springfield, Missouri; Administrator's Office, Missouri State Senate, Jefferson City; Special Collections, Regenstein Library, University of Chicago; Special Collections, Main Library, University of Iowa Library, Iowa City; Jennifer Evans, Special Collections, University of Washington Library, Seattle; and Robert Chapel and others at the Archives, University of Illinois Main Library, Urbana-Champaign.

The story would have remained incomplete without material from the American Association of University Professors in Washington, D.C. Those materials, now in Special Collections, Gelman Library, George Washington University Archives, were made available to us while they were still housed at the AAUP's Washington offices by Jordan Kurland, associate general secretary of the association, and assistant Evelyn Miller. Jordan and Evelyn were as helpful, professional, courteous, and kind as virtually anyone I have encountered in doing research on this or any other subject.

Support from the University of North Alabama also proved very helpful. A University Research Grant and two Arts and Sciences Research

Grants provided monetary assistance; Sue Nazworth at Collier Library was uniformly patient, persistent, and successful in the retrieval of interlibrary loan material, some of it esoteric; thanks to her and to Celia Reynolds for similar help; thanks also to cartographers Angelia Mance and Kimberly McCutcheon for their work with the map included in the book, and to Shannon Wells, who again generously gave her time and photographic talent to reproducing a number of illustrations. Thanks to President Robert Potts for sustained encouragement, and to Elliott Pood, Dean of Arts and Sciences, who not only encouraged the project but also, with Kaylene Gebert, vice-president for Academic Affairs, found funds for a large number of illustration rights. Further, the outstanding and beautiful environment of the University of North Alabama, including pleasant colleagues and able students who are also among the best people anywhere, make it an outstanding place to teach, research, and write.

My thanks to the late Lewis E. Atherton and the late Walter Scholes, along with Charles Timberlake, Noble Cunningham, David Thelen, Richard Kirkendall, and other outstanding faculty of the University of Missouri who decades ago opened a world to me even while the culture of the 1960s created similar yet quite different collisions from those described in these pages. I offer my gratitude to my alma mater and to the people of the state of Missouri who allowed a non-native to enjoy the benefits and traditions of an outstanding university. To paraphrase a Missouri promo, I left Mizzou, but Mizzou never left me. I also enjoyed the vicarious company of the University of Missouri faculty and their colleagues in the American Association of University Professors of the 1920s—intellectuals who never let on that they were; those who believed what they believed deeply and sincerely but not arrogantly. Whether I agreed with them about one issue or another was aside from the privilege of looking over their shoulders at an exciting and challenging time in the life of the nation and of the American university.

Working with the pleasant professionals at the University of Missouri Press has been easy and delightful. I offer much gratitude to Director and Editor-in-Chief Beverly Jarrett for her kindness, efficiency, and ability to simply make this thing work. She made it all look easy. Thanks also to Managing Editor Jane Lago for putting this author at ease and moving the process forward; and thanks to the highly professional work of Marketing Manager Karen Renner and her staff: Jennifer Brown, Cathy Birk, and Beth Chandler. Every author's work would benefit from the sharp eye of John Brenner, whose skilled copyediting improved the manuscript, saved me some embarrassment, and left me astonished at his meticulous handiwork. The manuscript also benefited from comments by referees for the University of Missouri Press; my thanks to them for their time and insight. The press is in friendly and very capable hands.

Thanks also to friends and former students Lisa Marie Holley and Allison Ayers Weaver, who showed early interest in this project and encouraged its pursuit; and, as before, to Amy Owens Martin for editing and proofreading; my gratitude also to Dennis McNutt, an old colleague from California, who read a draft of the manuscript and gave it his usual valuable and discerning eye. The dedication includes countless students who have blessed my life and honored me more than they know; also included are my own children, who have inspired me by their talents and the integrity of their character. Their journeys have taken them miles from home, but not from my heart.

As before, as always, my greatest debt is to Verlie M. Nelson. I met her when I was an undergraduate in the 1960s, and in the years since then her encouragement and support have never wavered. She is the best and most generous person I know. Since this book is about the 1920s, perhaps I can be indulged when speaking of her to borrow Calvin Coolidge's tribute to his own wife: "she has borne with my infirmities, and I have rejoiced in her graces."

Rumors of Indiscretion

1

"A Filthy Questionnaire"

> They rather resented being asked that sort of questions.
> And the girls tell me that they put it in the wastebasket and
> would not answer such things as that. Other girls told me they
> immediately mailed it home to their parents.
>
> —Dean Bessie L. Priddy, testimony, AAUP hearing, May 18, 1929

I f anyone bothered to notice, there was something odd about the contents of the envelopes that appeared in the campus mailboxes of seven hundred or so students at the University of Missouri during the second week of March 1929. The envelopes contained a student questionnaire that asked some very personal questions, but the cover letter carried no signature and no identifying origins, save for a cryptic "Bureau of Personnel Research." Just what that was no one seemed to know. Recipients also found an accompanying return envelope that required no postage but simply instructed, "DROP IN ANY UNIVERSITY MESSENGER BOX, BUREAU OF PERSONNEL RESEARCH, 405 JESSE HALL."

It took no time at all for a copy of the female version of the questionnaire to fall into the hands of Dr. Bessie Leach Priddy, the university's dean of women. Dean Priddy had first learned of the questionnaire at a banquet on the evening of March 12 when some women students, including the president of the Women's Self-Government Association, Mary Ellen Hubbard, a senior from Kansas City, approached her and asked what she thought about "this Questionnaire." Should such a questionnaire be circulated? Should the women reply to it? "What Questionnaire?" the dean wanted to know. The following morning a copy was provided. A few of the questions on the form were, it seemed to Dean Priddy, highly personal and inappropriate. She quickly dispatched a copy to the university's president, Stratton Duluth Brooks. Mary Ellen Hubbard undoubtedly spoke for several women students who didn't like the discussions the questionnaires sparked in mixed company. Soon Priddy was fielding complaints from mothers of a couple of students, but those were merely sounds of distant thunder.[1]

Dean Priddy wasn't the only one to get wind of the questionnaires. A copy quickly found its way to Ed Watson, editor of the *Columbia Daily Tribune,* a newspaper that served the middle-sized college town in the middle of the state. The *Tribune,* which broke the story on March 13, called the survey "A FILTHY QUESTIONNAIRE," and decried its own page-one display of excerpts: "We deprecate its publication on account of its filthy, degrading, carnal, immoral, revolting and perverted characteristics and tone, but print it for very patent reasons."[2]

The *Tribune* was actually quite daring in publishing even extracts of the questionnaire. It soon became a dilemma for news editors far and wide: how to inform the public without offending either them or the law. Many readers without access to the actual document would simply have to take the word of those who had seen it, or of those who, whether having seen it or not, had no reticence in commenting on it. A rising chorus would soon demand the expulsion from the university of those responsible for offending Victorian decorum and sensibilities; others would defend the freedom of the university and of scientific inquiry itself. Few would remain without an opinion. But who could know that decisions made in the next few hours, in the next few days and weeks, would generate reactions— indeed, passions—that could not be contained on the campus of a midwestern university? None could know that before the incredible story played out, it would make news from Seattle and San Francisco to Minneapolis and New York City, and from Dallas to Baltimore and Boston and everywhere in between; that lives and careers would take bizarre and dramatic turns, and that America, engaged in a culture war, if it dared to look, would and could learn a great deal about itself in the Jazz Age.

2

Rumors of Sex

The time has come for a crusade against such discussions and such literature, for ridding our schools of those who cannot distinguish between legitimate research and cesspool delving, and for barring from local libraries volumes which reek with sex appeal.
—*Monroe County Appeal*, March 22, 1929

Some day I hope we'll be able to discuss such matters with the freedom they deserve.
—College student to Max Meyer, May 16, 1929, AAUPP

Unfortunately for President Brooks, at the very time students at the University of Missouri were pulling questionnaires out of their campus mailboxes, the Missouri legislature, thirty miles away in Jefferson City, was considering biennial appropriations for the university. In that light, the president's first response to the questionnaire unleashed a kinetic energy difficult to control.

Apparently, Brooks first learned of the questionnaire from newsmen on March 13 when they asked his reaction; in fact, they were present when Dean Bessie Priddy advised him that some complaining coeds had already brought the matter to her. That same day—the first day of the crisis—Brooks publicly disassociated the university from the "Bureau of Personnel Research," a defunct if not seemingly fraudulent body. He ordered confiscation of returned questionnaires as soon as they fell from the mail chutes and announced he would commence a probe of the affair. The whole thing, Brooks declared, was a "damn fool idea." The press graciously removed the expletive when quoting him, but privately he responded more graphically. To a concerned St. Louisan, he branded the study "sewer sociology."[1]

Early editorial opinion was similarly harsh. The *Kansas City Star* wrote, "There is cause to wonder sometimes just what the modern, intensive study of psychology and psychoanalysis is doing to some immature minds, and to minds that have more or less acute sex angles." Some of the questions were insulting, said the *Star*, "especially [to] the girls." "But we are living in an age of liberal thought and action. That is very well up to a point. The danger is when liberty is construed as license. We have those who are so enamored of our franker attitude toward many things of life that they have become obsessed with sex and sex discussion, and being abnormal, do not know when or how to draw the line between propriety and impropriety, between the healthful and the baleful. They are our prurients, and to some extent they must be tolerated; but they should not be permitted to insult or viciously influence our student bodies." No pun intended. Across the state, the *St. Louis Globe-Democrat* argued that parents didn't send their kids to school "for laboratory purposes" and called the questionnaire "a mischievous impertinence," while in southeast Missouri, the *Sikeston Standard* was harsher, decrying that "we country folks are asked for seven million dollars for educating a bunch of high brows who want to know a lot of things from young women students who do not know what they want as they have not had the experience to qualify them to answer intelligently." The paper had similar regard for the guys: "Every male student who has arrived at the age of puberty would have answered yes to the question of a trial marriage, such is the animal in them. Probably not a boy or girl in that institution but what now know more about sexual matters than do Paw and Maw. It's a hell of a mess."[2]

Pressure mounted. A prominent Columbia resident, North Todd Gentry, quickly circulated a hostile petition among downtown businessmen and university alumni. By late Thursday, March 14, the petition boasted more than a hundred signatures, with many hundreds more anticipated on Friday. Gentry's office telephone rang all day, with many callers wanting their names on the petition. One Neosho resident, apprised of the Columbia petition, wrote President Brooks on March 15 that "if my name would stop such teaching I would start tomorrow for Columbia and sign." Another constituent who read of the affair in the *St. Louis Globe-Democrat* told Gentry that his efforts to clean house "should have the hearty support of all clean-minded citizens." Resignation should not be an option, the critic added. "They should be branded as morons or imbeciles and be deprived of citizenship, or confined in a sanitarium." Bristling with indignation, Gentry's petition labeled the questionnaire "indecent and vulgar" and called on Brooks and the governing Board of Curators "to investigate thoroughly this matter and promptly dismiss" those involved, "believing, as we do, that such persons have done the university great injustice, and that such a paper will result in great harm to that institution and to the youth of the state." Gentry publicly pledged friendship for his alma mater, "but I certainly would be ashamed," he said, "if no action is taken to punish those guilty." The questionnaire, he added, "is the most insolent and indecent thing I have ever read."[3]

Gentry's name gave instant legitimacy to opponents of the questionnaire. The Gentry family had long had an intimate connection to the University of Missouri. Born in Columbia in 1866, North Todd Gentry had taken baccalaureate and law degrees from the university in the 1880s, stayed in town to practice his profession, and became a respected civic leader. His many public activities included service as city attorney, trustee for the county hospital, president of the local commercial club, president of the university alumni association, defense work during the Great War, and superintendent of a local Presbyterian Sunday school. Married to a Missouri graduate, he had two daughters, one of whom, Mary, also a Missouri alum, had been a Pi Beta Phi and the agriculture school's Barnwarmin' "Harvest Queen" in 1923. From 1925 to 1928, Gentry distinguished himself as Missouri's attorney general before Governor Sam A. Baker appointed him justice of the Missouri Supreme Court to fill an unexpired term.[4]

For more than a generation, Gentry had been the model public servant, precise, circumspect, and proper, the epitome of Victorian public morality. As attorney general he had guarded public morality when dictated by public law. When a prosecuting attorney in Putnam County, for example, asked his legal opinion about an unmarried couple cohabiting a hotel room, he cited a 1919 law wherein persons engaging in "open, gross lewdness or lascivious behavior, or of any open and notorious act of public indecency, grossly scandalous, shall be guilty of a crime." Gentry acknowledged that courts had held that occasional adulterous behavior away from public view was not criminal, but he believed that unmarried persons publicly registering at a hotel as a married couple and remaining in the same room overnight warranted prosecution under the law. A stickler, he also tempered justice with mercy, as when he personally endorsed parole for a state prisoner and, in another case, urged that an imprisoned black man convicted of embezzlement under very mitigating circumstances be granted trusty status after only a short time.[5]

After circulating his petition, Gentry soon carried copies of the questionnaire to the capital—thinking them unfit for mailing. Though he talked with Governor Henry S. Caulfield about the scandal, the governor took a hands-off approach, leaving the issue to President Brooks and the Board of Curators. Meanwhile, Gentry's campaign against the questionnaire earned him wide support. In the first week or so after the publicity, his mailbox bulged with endorsements from around the state. One Warrensburg correspondent hailed his "courageous stand," while a Holden news editor expressed "gratitude" and a Maryville attorney who was the father of a law student offered "a word of encouragement and goodwill in the fight you are making to free the University Faculty of the moral degenerates responsible for the questionnaire." Gentry's late mother would be "rightfully proud of you," said one Kansas Citian who had known them back when. One 1911 alumnus and his wife assured him they stood behind him; their daughter would attend Missouri next year, but not if "the instigators of this scandal" were not dispatched. One St. Louis alum, A.B. '09, who was a major in the army, called for expulsion of offending professors and suggested the whole business could be a communist plot. One postal clerk told Gentry he was "performing a service to the whole world," and the state president of American War Mothers declared, "If we had a few more Judge Gentrys, I think the Youth of Today would have less trouble in respecting both moral and civil laws."[6]

Brooks was also busy. The day after the questionnaire went public, he hurried off to the state capital for a prescheduled meeting on "legislative matters" with members of the Board of Curators' Executive Board. Ironically, that same evening a campus lecture featuring Harry Bone of New York, associate director of the National Council of the YMCA, was scheduled for Jesse Hall auditorium. Sponsored by the Student Religious Council and the University YMCA, Bone's topic was to be on "youth and sex life—for men only." Spooked by the rising crisis, Brooks summarily canceled the lecture before leaving town.

Of course, the controversy preceded Brooks to the capital. In Jefferson City, a group of state legislators, led by Robert F. Miller of St. Louis, stood poised with their own call for an investigation of the university. Constituent mail ran heavily in favor of doing something about the ruckus on the Columbia campus. Brooks's prompt response may have preempted legislative action. Frank M. McDavid, chairman of the university's Executive Board and vice-chairman of the full Board of Curators, was a Springfield attorney and former state senator. According to Brooks, McDavid asked him what he "had done about" the questionnaire business and suggested a prompt meeting of the three-member Executive Board. Asked later if he didn't think that the controversy might be contained without such a meeting, Brooks replied that the issue "was already a matter of widespread publicity all over the state." Brooks had his ear to the ground. The meeting of the Executive Board was slated for the following Tuesday afternoon, March 19, 1929, ostensibly, according to the press, to consider the Gentry petition.[7]

2

Missourians, loyal taxpayers all, wasted no time in supporting Brooks. The first letter the president got congratulated him for having "scotched this new morbidity called psychology." Another supporter was glad the president had "the backbone to stand up for the protection of the morals of our state institutions." One 1909 alumnus applauded Brooks for preventing "the perverted minds . . . [from] using the young boys and girls as laboratory experiments." If those guilty of the outrage were not expelled, he said, "parents will look with horror upon our University."[8]

Some saw the questionnaire as an affront to chivalry. One St. Louisan told Brooks that the questionnaire was an "insult to the womanhood of America. . . . There is entirely too much of this sex sewerage being broadcast through the movies, magazines and other channels, and it is high time something drastic was done to curb it." The "morons" and "degenerates" responsible should be slapped and hissed by the offended young ladies who had received the insulting document. A circuit court judge from Lancaster, Missouri, whose daughter was a senior at the university, looked for a "decided stand" against those responsible. "I am perhaps old fashioned," he said, "but such things are, to me, entirely inconsistent with the requirements of common decency." The postmaster at Powersville, Missouri, another parent of a female student at the university, regretted "very much if she should of been one of those who received the disgraceful questionnaire which has a tendency to create a distrust in our state school institutions or their efficiency." And the editor of the Mexico, Missouri, *Ledger* wired Brooks that "SEX MINDED TEACHERS AND STUDENTS MIGHT BETTER GO TO RED LIGHT DISTRICTS FOR LABORATORY EXPERIMENTS."[9]

One group close to home and quick to comment publicly was Chi Omega sorority, which thought the questionnaire was "an insult to every university woman who received one." In a statement to Brooks that was also made public, they said they appreciated the protection offered by the administration, friends, and alumni, but they appealed "to the chivalry of the men and good taste of the women in the university to join in this protest." The sorority didn't want anyone fired or hurt in the aftermath, but the women urged that a policy be developed "which will protect us from such salacious exposure in the future." Reportedly, Chi Omega's "severe condemnation" was unanimous.[10]

Inevitably, there were cranks. Those responsible were "wicked and depraved," said one such critic from Oklahoma. Problems with education in America resulted, he said, from "Women teachers" who were "usually short of broad education" and were "merely large children"; also to blame were poor trustees and especially Catholics hired to teach Protestant youngsters. He added, incoherently, "The evolutionists in your school are behind the questionaire [*sic*]."[11]

Irresponsibility wasn't limited to letters from cranks. This was the era of questionnaires, of finding out what people thought by scientific or semi-scientific methods. A questionnaire had been circulated at Fort Scott High School in Kansas a year or so earlier. The *Fort Scott Tribune-Monitor* suspected that it might be the same as the one on the Columbia campus, and asked President Brooks for a copy to compare. They weren't even close. The Kansas version was not only quite innocuous but might even have been helpful for research if sent to an appropriately targeted group. But no matter. Before the paper learned that the questionnaires were miles apart, the editor blithely published his suspicions anyway, including that both "are promoted either by some person with a fiendish lust for sex subjects or by a social anarchist."[12]

What could possibly stir such passion in Middle America, such outrage? The questionnaire tucked in those envelopes contained eleven questions, but even the document's introduction drew attention:

> Dear University Student:
>   During the last several decades it has become increasingly apparent that there is something seriously wrong with the traditional system of marriage in this country. But, unfortunately, the whole matter has been so inextricably bound up with religious dogmas, moral sentiments, and all manner of prudish conventionalities as to make it exceedingly difficult to ascertain with any degree of accuracy the precise reasons for this situation. The present investigation represents an attempt on the part of this Bureau to discover, by the direct questioning of several hundred men and women, the real causal factors which lie back of the widespread dissatisfaction with the prevailing institution of marriage, and to determine, at least in part, those elements in the present social regime which are today so profoundly affecting the American family.

As an intelligent, modern woman, you are kindly requested to read through the questionnaire on the succeeding pages and then, but not until then, to answer the questions. When you have done this, place the entire leaflet in the enclosed, self-addressed envelope, seal the envelope, and then drop it in a University mail box, one of which you will find in every University building on the campus. If you do this, a stamp on the envelope will not be necessary.

This investigation is statistical rather than personal. Therefore, *do not sign your name or give any other indication of your identity.*

Some of the questions, you will find, pertain to rather intimate, personal matters; yet, in view of the anonymous nature of the replies, we feel confident that you will consider each of the inquiries carefully and conscientiously and that you will answer each of them with the utmost sincerity and frankness. If you care to elaborate your opinions concerning any of the questions or to qualify any of your answers, we hope you will by all means do so; the blank space on the second page of this leaflet is specifically meant for that purpose.

Finally, allow us to thank you for your cooperation in this matter and to assure you of our genuine appreciation. If you are especially interested in either the purpose or results of this investigation, we shall be glad at any time to confer with you.

THE BUREAU OF PERSONNEL RESEARCH

So much for the introduction. Then followed eleven groups of questions, with sufficient space provided for answers where warranted. Most public attention would eventually focus on the first three questions in the female version:

1. (a) If you were engaged to marry a man and suddenly learned that he had at some time indulged in illicit sexual relations, would you break the engagement? (b) Would you break the engagement if you learned that he had so indulged frequently and indiscriminately? (c) And if, after marriage, you were to find that your husband was sexually unfaithful to you, would you terminate your relations with him?

2. (a) Would you quit associating with an unmarried woman on learning that she had at some time engaged in sexual irregularities? (b) On learning that she had so engaged often and promiscuously? (c) On learning that she had accepted money in return for her sexual favors? (d) Would you quit associating with a married woman on learning that she engaged in extra-marital sexual activities?

3. (a) Are your own relations with men restrained most by religious convictions, fear of social disapproval, physical repugnance,
fear of pregnancy, lack of opportunity, fear of venereal diseases,
or pride in your own ability to resist temptation? (b) During your
childhood, did you ever engage in mutual sexual play with another individual? (c) Since sexual maturity, have you ever engaged
in specific sexual relations.

Some of the remaining questions were mild, such as the size of the community where the respondent was born, size of family, intentions to marry
and at what age, vocational expectations if married, plans for children,
and so on. Others got closer to the edge: "Are you in favor of family lim-
itation by means of birth control?" Question five went over the edge:

(a) Would you favor the establishment of a legal system of "trial
marriage" wherein a man and a woman would be not only privileged but expected to live in sexual intimacy for some days or
weeks prior to their definite marriage in order to determine
whether or not they were sexually compatible? (b) Would you
favor the establishment of a legal system of "companionate" marriage, which would require for its dissolution merely a public announcement made by mutual agreement of the parties without
any appeal to the courts?

Question six began a bit better: "Do you believe in easy divorce?" followed by several more questions relating to alimony and finally whether
the female chose her husband because of money or personal characteristics. Question nine asked about the woman's economic dependence or
independence if she married and whether she intended to pursue a vo-
cation aside from housekeeping and if so what it would be. The next one
dealt with equality of intelligence between men and women and if women
were physically able to compete in the world of business, and whether the
female's monthly cycle would prove to be a liability in her chosen profession, business, or industry. Lastly, the questionnaire asked whether she
would favor sharing expenses equally on "dates" and, "If such a system
were in vogue, would you consider it as proper for a woman to ask a man
for his company as for a man to ask a woman?"[13]
    What shadowy figure stood behind this document deemed "filthy, de-
grading, carnal, immoral, revolting and perverted" by a local newspaper? On March 13, the first day they communicated about the issue, Dean
Priddy dispatched a copy of the female version to President Brooks and,
among other things, claimed, "There is a rumor current that it comes

from a man student engaged in thesis work but I doubt if such an elaborate printed questionnaire would so originate." Despite that otherwise reasonable assumption, the rumor was mostly true. The prime author of the questionnaire was an enterprising yet innocuous-looking student, Orval Hobart Mowrer, a twenty-two-year-old senior from Unionville, Missouri. The press identified him as the questionnaire's author from day one, though he was mislabeled as a *graduate* student in psychology. Further, he was a paid assistant in the psychology department, which implied official connection to the university beyond his student status. In any case, the origins of his creative document sprang from several sources, but primarily it was a means to fulfill partial requirements for a class known as "The Family," taught by Dr. Harmon O. DeGraff, an assistant professor of sociology. Three months or so away from scheduled graduation, Mowrer was about to become infamous, and early press assessment was decidedly unkind. The local *Tribune* wondered "who told this . . . student, hardly dry behind the ears, that there is anything wrong with the 'traditional system of marriage?' Marriage is not a 'system'; it is a sacred institution that has from immemorial time been the foundation stone that has upheld society and maintained principles but for which the whole human race would in all probability long ago have been perverted. . . . Even asking an opinion, and this of 500 girls, as to trial and companionate marriage, is a desecration and an outrage."[14]

On the day the story broke in the press, young Mowrer spoke openly about the questionnaire and his activities. At that time about two hundred of the questionnaires had been returned from students and remained in his possession. Next day, as the story spread, the *Kansas City Star* reported that "fathers and mothers discussed with disgust the sending of 1,000 questionnaires to University of Missouri students, inquiring into their beliefs regarding sex problems, trial and companionate marriage, divorce and alimony." Mowrer claimed results from the replies would never have been publicized, but that he was looking for graduation with distinction. However, a widely circulated story claimed he also looked to get money by publishing his findings in a magazine, an idea soon seized on by Brooks and other critics.[15]

3

Meanwhile, frightening noises came out of the state capital. The day after the story broke, State Representative Robert F. Miller of St. Louis talked about the Missouri House authorizing a three-member committee

charged with investigating the propriety and usefulness of the questionnaire. Nothing much came of that, but the following day, the *St. Louis
Globe-Democrat* reported that Kirk Jones, the house appropriations chairman from Jefferson City, warned darkly of funding cuts unless Brooks
and the curators took decisive action. The timing of the questionnaire was
bad, he said. He feared his committee membership "may be led to whittle
appropriations for the university unless it is straightened out before we
make up the budget for that institution." Calling the affair a "sex questionnaire scandal," he thought only summary dismissal of the professors
involved and expulsion of culpable students would stave off heavy budget cuts.[16]

Such talk resonated with a segment of the public, though it's difficult to
know just how much. One Sedalia attorney who wanted to keep "rot and
trash" away from students, for example, supported Gentry's intimidat-
ing efforts and petitioned his county's representative, J. Fred Williams, to
keep appropriations cuts in mind in order to bring the university around.
Williams agreed. Within days of his first pronouncement, however, Representative Jones, speaking on the house floor with personal privilege,
urged his colleagues not to allow the affair in Columbia to negatively impact university funding. His earlier comments had been misunderstood,
he said. He was merely reading the committee, not threatening the university. In fact, the day his comments appeared in the *Globe-Democrat*, he
fired off a letter to the editor challenging the paper's spin on his remarks.
He never said the university would suffer funding cuts without summary
dismissals. Loyal to the university, he would neither predict the decisions
of more than forty members of his committee nor dictate to university
officials what action to pursue.[17]

Representative C. E. Clowe of Stoddard County went beyond threats.
He introduced a resolution in the house damning the questionnaire and
ordering Brooks and the curators to take prompt action, including preven-
tion of similar developments in the future. Clowe hadn't seen the questionnaire himself, but no matter, he'd heard enough. Representative Eli
Wherry of Kansas City, chairman of the house committee charged with
university affairs, announced a prompt meeting that same night. Cool
heads prevailed and the resolution was tabled pending the curators' Executive Board meeting the next day. Even Clowe didn't push the matter,
acknowledging that he had been "all worked up" at the time he introduced it. "You had a right to be worked up," replied Representative W.
R. Logan of Carroll County. "I'll bet that's not all that has gone on over
there either." That brought a retort from J. S. Rollins of the university's
own Boone County: "They are our sons and daughters over there; some

of them are sons and daughters of members of this legislature and I resent any insinuations against them." Logan said he wasn't referring to the students, just "some of the things that are being taught." Chairman Wherry added: "We must face the fact, gentlemen, that there are things creeping into the teaching. Why, there are even cliques among the high school teachers of Kansas City where this Russian bolshevism and communism is being discussed. They even hold meetings." Charles L. Woods of Phelps County claimed the problem rested with Ben Lindsey, a controversial Colorado judge who advocated companionate marriages and who had generated considerable publicity on the issue. He started this mess, said Woods, and "some one ought to go out to Denver and deal with Ben Lindsey." Very likely, the Associated Press was referring to Woods when it cited an unnamed legislator who said "Judge Ben Lindsay [sic] ought to be shot." The same lawmaker also, said the story, "accused the Denver judge of turning the thoughts of youth prematurely toward sex matters."[18]

Shoot Judge Lindsey? And shoot him because he got kids thinking about sex? Benjamin B. Lindsey had been a reformer since the turn of the century. A native of Tennessee, he eventually migrated to Denver, where he established a juvenile and family court and got himself elected judge repeatedly, a Democrat in a largely Republican domain. Believing the cause of adolescent crime was nurture not nature, he advocated a customized legal system for youthful offenders. A high-profile progressive, he lectured on the Chautauqua circuit as well as to state legislatures, wrote muckraking exposés of alleged corruption between utilities and Colorado politics, and won the admiration of many Americans, including Teddy Roosevelt, Robert LaFollette, George Creel, Hiram Johnson, and Missouri's own progressive governor, Joseph W. Folk. In 1915, he even cruised on Henry Ford's quixotic "peace ship" seeking a negotiated end to the European war.

Lindsey became a lightning rod for critics of social change—over the years he took fire from everyone from Victorian censors to the Ku Klux Klan. But nothing earned him more scorn than his alleged assault in the 1920s on traditional marriage and his expectation that modern youth could lead civilization toward that brave new world of what he popularly called "companionate marriage." *The Revolt of Modern Youth*, published in 1925, was followed by *The Companionate Marriage* two years later, the former volume encapsulating what magazines, Sunday newspaper supplements, and moving pictures had all detected: something culturally dramatic was going on. No end of social observers cited numerous reasons for the seismic changes of the decade, including the aftermath of the Great War, proliferation of the automobile, post-suffrage economic emancipation of women, and the influences of Freudian notions of sex and life.

Lindsey's ideas about companionate marriage were elucidated in his book of that name as well as in other publications and in debates during a tour of numerous U.S. cities in the late twenties. According to Lindsey, companionate marriage was what was actually going on in America already, simply without legal sanction. Its components included birth control, mutually agreeable divorce for couples without children, alimony only when warranted, and rigorous government-sponsored sex, marriage, and family education. Lindsey was a bit fuzzy around the edges, unclear about the specifics of such education. He also teetered on favoring eugenics and a scary part of progressivism that gave power to experts to determine biological fitness for parenthood. Much as he denied it, companionate marriage in pop culture was associated with easy divorce and even free love. Though some of the wildest allegations may have been untrue, Lindsey's books exaggerated the dysfunction of family life in America and seemed particularly concerned with liberating sexual behavior from the constraints of the past.[19]

Missouri's criticism of Lindsey was nothing new. The day after the verbal barbs, he replied to the United Press that "Most of these legislators are living companionate marriages now and don't know it. Companionate marriage is modern marriage." Marriage needed help, said Lindsey, and if he roused some lawmakers to do something about it, then he would be "happy to assume the blame." Another advocate of companionate marriage, Emanuel Haldeman-Julius, whose daughter had just such an arrangement with a University of Kansas student, also came in for a tongue-lashing in the legislature. The well-known Kansas writer, essayist, and publisher might have earned scorn for his socialism alone, or for his agnosticism. But he promptly inserted himself into the breaking controversy through an open letter to University of Missouri students wherein he accused the questionnaire's critics of Babbitry, after Sinclair Lewis's best-selling novel about self-absorbed businessmen. He called on the students to exercise their right to freely discuss morality, and even offered his publications as a forum.[20]

4

The state of Missouri by no means stood in harmony on the hot controversy that was growing by the day. The letters in Brooks's mailbag decrying the questionnaire and demanding the ouster of those respon-

sible jostled with those supporting free inquiry. Some thought Brooks's
response did more damage than the questionnaire. One 1921 alumnus
living in Kansas told him the issue should have been handled internally:
"Your press comments remind one of a cheap reformer and are too sensational for academic dignity." One Kansas Citian wanted to send his
daughter to Missouri someday and claimed the questionnaire seemed "an
intelligent effort to get at the roots of a problem that has been 'silently'
discussed." One DeGraff supporter, a 1927 journalism school graduate
living in Madison, Wisconsin, ridiculed Gentry and tweaked Chi Omega,
the sorority that had initially reacted in horror to the intimacy of the questions. At times during his student days, the alumnus said, Chi Omega
"was generally conceded to be most eminently qualified to furnish valuable first hand information such as might be [elicited] through a sex questionnaire[.]"[21]

One couple from Kansas City told Brooks the crisis would be a test of his
leadership, whether or not he was up to the job. They urged him to "save
Missouri from joining the ranks of Tennesee [sic] and Arkansas." Better to
"have our University with only one professor and have him free to teach
as his judgment tells him than to have it full of lackies that are the tool
of sensational newspapers." The Tennessee-Arkansas connection, a reference to the debates over teaching evolution in the public schools, was a
frequent refrain with critics of administrative action. One three-time Missouri alumnus, a Kansas City school principal who feared such a connection, told Brooks he had attended one of Kansas City's biggest churches
on the first Sunday evening after the publicity had broken. The capacity
crowd of well over a thousand people listened to the questionnaire read
from beginning to end, and he was sure the great majority favored free inquiry and wanted no dismissals. "Surely the great state of Missouri does
not want to be classed with Tennessee and Arkansas in its intolerance,"
said another Missourian. Don't link the university with those "who believe a rainbow never existed before the flood." One letter to the editor
of the St. Louis Post-Dispatch claimed that "Tennessee had its Scopes trial,
Arkansas imprisoned her evolution teacher; I suppose it's Missouri's time
to show that we are not to be 'bested' by our neighbors. Whipping posts
and the 'ex cathedra' attitude go hand in hand." A Kansas City physician
who had two sons at Missouri—one had already taken DeGraff and the
other he hoped would be able to—claimed Columbia's mayor and other
local professionals and businessmen who signed the protest petition were
"makeing [sic] a mountain out of a mole hill." He saw lots of matrimonial
problems and youthful venereal disease in his practice and was convinced
90 percent were ignorant not only of how to pick and properly relate to a

marriage partner but also of illicit sex and sexually transmitted diseases. One Missouri alumnus, a 1912 journalism school graduate with the *St. Louis Post-Dispatch*, condemned Gentry and accused Brooks of exacerbating the problem. "Did you act with the dignity expected of a university president? You waved aloft a piece of lingerie and defamed the university with the cry of 'sex,' scandal,' [and] 'sewer sociology.' " If appropriations were reduced, so what? "Why should the State continue to maintain an institution of higher learning when manifestations of mental activity on the part of its students are greeted with a pitchfork and a bucket of tar?" A leading alumnus from St. Louis, who had taken the pulse of alumni in that city, told Brooks bluntly that he and others believed the only one who deserved dismissal was the guy who let the problem get out of hand.[22]

Many opponents of administrative action against the professors urged Brooks to stand up to legislative intimidation, notably that inaccurately ascribed to Representative Jones. Even parents of students at the university supported the professors, as did the mother of a woman who had received one of the questionnaires. Herself a Missouri graduate and president of the Clay County alumni association, this mother recalled her own days at the university when "a great cry" arose from local married women after a home economics instructor provided tutoring on bottle feeding of babies—no fit subject for unmarried women. "The University is no kindergarten," she said, "nor should we expect its activities to be limited to the standard applicable to the weakest student." A Kansas City woman familiar with the questionnaire told Brooks she "heartily approved," and that only " 'ignorance and prudery' " prevented good results: "I think the professors who worked the questionnaire out were humanitarians." One telegram from a father of college-age children was likewise blunt. He and his wife had read the questionnaire, supported the professors, and hoped their own children would "NEVER BE HAMPERED WITH SUCH IGNORANCE AND SUPERSTITION AS WE ENCOUNTERED AT THE SAME AGE STOP." Times were changing, the editor of the *Tulsa Tribune* told Brooks. "Don't be afraid of some hillbillie legislator down in Jefferson City."[23]

If the U.S. mails were hot with the questionnaire controversy, the issue was also being debated on campus. North Todd Gentry's early petition had helped the controversy reach critical mass. Now students resorted to the petition process themselves, and within a few days the press reported on the war of petitions raging in the city. No fewer than eight student-generated petitions were soon making the rounds—the largest of which boasted about six hundred names—most or all of which had the goal of staving off the feared ouster of one or more professors, most notably

DeGraff, the sociologist at the center of the storm. "We, the undersigned students of the University of Missouri," read one petition, "believing that the purpose of the sociological questionnaire, issued in the spirit of scientific investigation, has been misunderstood and perverted, do hereby express our loyal co-operation with and our support of those professors and fellow students who have formulated and circulated the questionnaire." Another petition, generated "in the interest of fair play," deplored "any and all blame that may seemingly attach to Dr. Harmon O. DeGraff." Still another petition threatening a boycott of downtown merchants who had signed Gentry's earlier petition garnered about fifty signatures by noon on March 16. Later, students in pairs reportedly visited merchants threatening the boycott. The *St. Louis Post-Dispatch* claimed Gentry matched the boycott petition with one among Columbia women, although that may have been the one circulated by a Columbia physician, J. B. Cole. Dr. Cole had signed Gentry's petition but thought local women should also have a role. After Gentry reproduced a few copies for both men and women, Cole took charge of the women's petition. Reportedly, forty-five signed it at a Methodist women's luncheon on the same day, with further circulation expected. According to the *Kansas City Star,* President Brooks showed no alarm when advised of the eight student petitions bouncing around town. He told the press, "The right to petition is the inherent right of the American people." By noon on Sunday, March 17, more than a thousand students had exercised that right.[24]

The women in Greektown were also busy. On Sunday, two days before the Executive Board meeting, five of the most popular sororities on campus, in polite and measured statements, declared their support of the faculty involved, isolating Chi Omega as the lone critic. Pi Beta Phi thought the questionnaires aimed at "constructive education, and not to be morally injurious," adding that "we are not in favor of the dismissal of valuable faculty instructors." Kappa Alpha Theta believed the whole mess "originated through a misunderstanding," while Alpha Phi agreed, and called for "a fair and unbiased hearing for those accused." Kappa Kappa Gamma said the instructors were "valuable . . . and that student sentiment is against their dismissal." Tri-Delts thought the same.[25]

By Monday morning's light, even campus sidewalks had become a part of the heightened sense of theater, having been marked in bright red paint with slogans pleading for "free thought" for the students and professors. In comparison to their counterparts who four decades later would paint campus sidewalks to protest the Kent State shootings, the painters were polite, even making a poignant statement at the Memorial Tower, dedicated at homecoming in 1926 to honor the university's war dead.

Fashioned after the memorial at Oxford's Magdalen College and majestic in its splendor, the tower and its grand arch provided entree to the university's white-stoned East Campus. On normal days, students might reverently linger within the arch with its inscribed names of 116 university men who had paid the full measure of sacrifice. This time, on the floor beneath the names, the living had painted several slogans, including "Keep Faith," and "We Died for Light." The *Missouri Student*, a generally harmless rag that had provided a forum for student views in the past, was energized during the crisis, endorsing the propriety of the scrawlings at the sacred site. Those in the war generation may have "died for light," said the paper, but "little more than ten years later we are striving to return to ignorance."[26]

Meanwhile, the investigation, such as it was, produced several faculty members scheduled to appear before the Executive Board on Tuesday afternoon, March 19, though not all were publicized. Early on, Brooks had asked DeGraff for names of those connected to the questionnaire, and DeGraff had dutifully submitted a list containing the names of four students and six faculty. One name on the list and eventually linked to the rising scandal—and reportedly scheduled to appear—was that of Professor Howard Jensen, professor and chair of the department of sociology. In fact, Jensen's name appeared in the *St. Louis Post-Dispatch* on Monday and Tuesday, much to his surprise. According to the paper, "The names of two professors hitherto not mentioned in the investigation were revealed today. They included Prof. Jesse Wrench of the History department, said to have approved and read the replies on the questionnaires, in addition to acting in the capacity of 'adviser' to the self-styled 'Bureau of Personnel Research,' which issued the literature; and Howard Jensen, assistant professor in the department of sociology, who is said to have aided in the drawing up of the questions that have been considered objectionable and 'insulting.'"

Jensen scrambled to cover his base that same day, desperately trying to reach President Brooks at his home and office to explain his innocent and distant relationship to the unfolding story. The next day, the very day the Executive Board met, he wrote Brooks again, detailing his relationship to the questionnaire. A month earlier, he told Brooks, Hobart Mowrer had come to his home to discuss a civil service exam and wanted to know what to prepare for the statistics portion of it. Specifically, Mowrer wanted to know how large a statistical sample of university students would need to be to satisfy professionals. He told Jensen he was working on a questionnaire involving "the Economic Independence of Women" and wanted to have Jensen's opinion when it was finished. Jensen agreed, but, as he told

Brooks, the meeting didn't happen and he "had no knowledge whatever of the contents of the document until I was shown a copy by a student after distribution."[27]

In his first year on the Missouri faculty, Professor Jensen was running scared, and the atmosphere on the eve of the Executive Board meeting seemed to justify his concern. Talk about town suggested that the curators' knives would be out and that jobs were in jeopardy. Even "The Family" appeared headed for the curricular dustheap. The press reported that on the morning of the Executive Board meeting some curators had told Brooks they wanted to oust the professors responsible. Publicly, Frank McDavid, chairman of the three-member panel, was more circumspect, telling the press that morning, "We shall do our talking after the meeting and also take what action may be necessary."

Meanwhile, the faculty's public silence was conspicuous. The university had able spokesmen for academic freedom—at the moment watching events unfold by the minute—but none wished to worsen the atmosphere in the critical days leading to the Executive Board meeting on March 19. There would be much to say later, but even then, professionalism dictated that most of it would be out of public view. For whatever reason, Jensen ultimately was excused from attending the meeting, but five other faculty members and seven students were scheduled to appear, along with North Todd Gentry and J. B. Cole from Columbia, the latter of whom had petitions to present. Gentry, Cole, and the students would appear by choice; the faculty were so directed by President Brooks.[28]

Prime attention focused on a few of those faculty members, notably the instructor of the course at the center of it all, Dr. Harmon O. DeGraff. DeGraff had come to the University of Missouri in 1926 in midcareer. Born in June 1886 in a small town in Iowa, he graduated from high school in 1903, attended a small school in Mason City, and became a high school principal at age nineteen in Burr Oak, Iowa. The following year he served as superintendent in Linn Grove, Iowa, and, in 1907–1908, attended Iowa State Teachers College where he picked up a diploma. For the next decade or so he produced a checkerboard résumé of superintendency, small-college teaching, private business, study, and army service in the Great War. Along the way he earned baccalaureate and master's degrees from the University of Iowa in 1916 and 1918. He continued advanced study at Iowa, serving also as an instructor in sociology and economics; he began doctoral studies at the University of Chicago in 1923, completing the Ph.D. in 1926 with a practical dissertation on juvenile delinquency. At age forty, DeGraff was ready for a serious academic position. Some recommendations in his portfolio were tepid about his academic and mental prowess, but others were enthusiastic about his people skills, teaching ability, maturity, and sterling character. One of his professors at Chicago who knew him well thought him "above reproach in character," and believed "He works well with other people, [and] is pleasant and attractive in personality." He added that DeGraff was "especially desirable as a college teacher because of his motives for influencing young people. He will make an excellent teacher in a college where he can establish personal contact with the students in an intimate way. I think a college will be fortunate to secure Mr. DeGraff as a teacher." The University of Missouri, in the market for a new sociology instructor in 1926, was that place.[29]

The course in "The Family"—Sociology 114w—had been offered without any great sensation since the spring semester of 1925. Professor DeGraff, a gifted communicator with a passion and respect for students under his charge, rapidly turned the course into a campus phenomenon. Starting with less than two dozen students, enrollments ballooned to more than 120 by the spring of 1929—all the more remarkable since it was an elective course with a reputation for difficulty. The subject matter, word of mouth, and DeGraff's abilities and personality had done their job. During that spring the class met in Jesse Hall room 123 on Mondays, Wednesdays, and Fridays at 8 A.M. One student in the course, senior Mary Ellen Hubbard, president of the Women's Self-Government Association who had been among those who first alerted Dean Priddy to the questionnaire, had taken Professor DeGraff twice before and liked both him and the courses. Other students told her that if she didn't take the Family she'd be missing a real campus experience. She signed up. So did others—lots of them—wanting "to find out what was really taught." One later called the course material "hot stuff" though not easy to understand.[30]

The Family focused on a wide range of topics, including marriage and divorce, varieties of love, and the issues arising from increasing emancipation of women. Included in Professor DeGraff's very frank lectures were contrasts between androcentric and gynacentric theories of the family. The former, viewing the male as the dominant element of the family and the edifier of the weaker woman, was the theory of modern culture. The latter view held that modern culture's viability and virtues flowed from the woman's choices about who would be the fathers of generations to come. However simplistic that may seem, there was no doubt that the 1920s had seen a shifting of attitudes regarding the status and role of women in all parts of American life. DeGraff also lectured on four phases in the life of a family, notably courtship, marriage before and after children, and finally, the family with adult children. Courtship phases embraced vision—including "making eyes"—verbal expressions,

and physical contact. To DeGraff, romantic love was a psychic experience and preferred above others, including "natural love," which was
simply possession of one by another. The latter was an expression of the
much-bandied "companionate marriage," the basis of which, ironically,
given the sensationalism resulting from the questionnaire scandal, De-
Graff vehemently criticized. Companionate marriage or natural love—by
either name—ended in divorce, argued DeGraff. Actually, divorce occupied much of the discourse of the Family, with DeGraff pointing to arguments over church affiliation and doctrine, rural-urban conflicts, and
differences in class, status, health, money management, cultural refine-
ments, sexual appetites, and the like. Divorce resulted from a "process
of summation" wherein problems accumulated over time. According to
DeGraff, "The smaller factors of aggravation pile up and eventually the
climax comes. The process may 'hang over,' with one person remember-
ing all the little incidents for years."

Sociology 114 necessarily went where many classes in the academy
feared to tread—discussions on relationships between the sexes. DeGraff
had no time for the professoriate that eschewed any study of the subject.
As he told his Family class, "Students study all physiology except sex,
and when they get to that point they find that the textbooks have nothing about it and that charts are blank." But DeGraff also had no time for
the sex-study zealots either. In reality—and with irony approaching wry
amusement—Harmon O. DeGraff was a conservative who knew that society rested on the family, and that complete emancipation of the woman,
something discussed intensely since the Great War, threatened the very
structure of that family. In that, he wasn't alone. One very successful professional woman, having abandoned the workplace she had mastered
to raise her kids, wondered in a national magazine, "What About the
Children?"

Another irony was that even in the deepest slough of controversy and
accusation, no one who knew anything about the facts of the case ever—
not even once—impugned the character of "Doc" DeGraff. Just the opposite. While DeGraff could be candid in lectures, one student argued
that "his delivery is very conservative." The student added, "Many times
we disagree with him because we think he is a little too moralizing." A
bachelor all his life, students were DeGraff's surrogate family. A familiar
figure at virtually every Greek mixer or dance, a confidant to hundreds
of students on a myriad of issues or problems, a beloved figure on campus in such a short time, DeGraff remained conscientiously professional,
never obtrusive, never crossing the line that was at once imaginary and
real. "Perhaps one of the best compliments that can be given Dr. DeGraff

is to say that he applies his classroom studies to the life about him," said the campus paper in the fall of 1928—months before the questionnaire mess developed. "The result is that he is in closer touch with the actual tempo of campus affairs than perhaps anyone else." No great athlete, the 5'7", slightly built DeGraff nevertheless was often seen on Rollins Field's cinder track south of the central campus. But he was also a regular at the university hospital, visiting students who were ill, a sort of celibate priest whose lack of biological children left time for ministering to others. That ministry continued on Sundays at the local Presbyterian church, where, while not a Presbyterian, he taught Sunday school. In fact, on the Sunday before the Executive Board meeting, DeGraff carried on his normal activities, teaching his Sunday school class in the morning, visiting students in the university hospital in the afternoon, and attending prayer meeting at night. He seemed relaxed, unmoved by the prospects awaiting him on Tuesday. Reportedly, he even told close friends he could find another position but might lecture and write instead. That morning, Rev. David R. Haupt, one of DeGraff's admirers and rector of the downtown Episcopal Church, deviated from his prescheduled message on "The Meaning of Marriage" to commend Stratton Brooks for his handling of the questionnaire. A good man and a trusting soul, Rev. Haupt was in for a disappointment.[31]

While the Family course retained a lecture format, Professor DeGraff had the students form committees of four students each to work on a substantial semester project relating to the subject. But the professor was no guru; DeGraff wanted students to arrive at independent judgments based on real-world research, and their research tools and methods could be worked out in the four-member committees. The large class size in the spring of 1929 meant the creation of a couple dozen or so committees that were supposed to meet once a week. Only time separated one of those committees from disaster. The restive mix of sociology, youth, and reckless investigation put the whole operation on a collision course with Victorian decorum. The fatal combination coalesced that spring in the committee made up at first of Orval Hobart Mowrer, a senior from Unionville, and Clarence Ferguson, a thirty-three-year-old married graduate student from Illinois; they soon recruited Howell Williams, a junior from Columbia, and then added Alberta Davis, a nineteen-year-old from Kansas City. Mowrer had the initiative, drive, and presence to emerge as chair of the committee, quickly setting the agenda for the semester project. Their original topic submitted for DeGraff's approval seemed a natural at the end of a decade that had celebrated both youth and the growing emancipation of the American woman: "A sociological study of the effect of the economic independence of women on married life."[32]

5

The focus was on Jesse Hall. A beautiful, sprawling red-brick building topped by a white dome and originally by a balustrade and statues, Jesse Hall housed the campus auditorium, administrative and faculty offices, and numerous classrooms. Built in the eclectic style popular in the late nineteenth century, Jesse was flanked by other red-brick Victorian structures housing several academic departments and schools, each unique, but displaying Missouri-born architect Morris Frederick Bell's touches of Romanesque and Beaux-Arts Classicism and free use of asymmetrical, octagonal, and square towers. The new buildings joined Switzler Hall and the president's house, two older structures on Francis Quadrangle. Standing in the middle of the quad were six ionic columns left after a fire destroyed the original Academic Hall in 1892; the columns quickly became a campus centerpiece.

At eight o'clock on Monday morning, March 18, 1929, in room 123 of Jesse Hall, the Family class met amid an air of expectation and uncertainty. Everyone knew about the curators' meeting scheduled for the same building on the next day. Not that the professor and the students weren't prepared. Actually, DeGraff picked up his lecture of the previous week on his "process of summation," those conflicting issues between married couples that build up over time and culminate in divorce. Monday's topic centered on children who can sometimes disrupt the flow of family life and stimulate jealousies between their parents. Witting or unwitting, sons looked for marriageable females who exhibited qualities like their mothers, while daughters looked for fatherlike qualities in potential mates.

At the request of his students, DeGraff shortened his lecture—delivered, said the press, "in his customary friendly manner." In fact, he seemed immune to the tension. The students wanted a few minutes to talk over the issues swirling around their class and so asked DeGraff to leave the room. He complied, but asked that the chairs of the committees remain after the class dismissed. Whether DeGraff returned to his office, or idled in Jesse's hallway, is unclear (as was Mowrer's whereabouts), but with the professor out of the room, tension filled the air until a young woman took charge and eased the anxiety. She asked those in the class who fully supported their professor and the scientific work of the student committee to rise. If the rousing response of the 120 or so students wasn't unanimous, it certainly seemed so. She excoriated the press for its inaccuracies and berated those members of the class who served as correspondents for various newspapers. She even noted several visitors in the class and wondered if they were in support of DeGraff. Apparently, she didn't know that the older women visitors were members of the Women's Christian Temperance Union, who made their appearance for reasons one could only guess. At least one petition supporting DeGraff was circulated, and some students criticized the press for elevating tensions. An older woman student objected to the class petition, believing it might be seen as instigated by DeGraff himself. Regardless, the petition passed quickly from row to row, picking up more than 90 percent of the students' signatures. C. Franklin Parker, a class member who also served as executive secretary of a student religious group, praised his professor and sharply criticized those in the press who didn't have the university's best interests at heart. Two other students, including Lawrence Laupheimer, a journalism student from Sedalia who told the class a petition among St. Louis alumni was doing well, and another student who gave a "eulogistic and fiery speech" prompted more applause throughout the room.

DeGraff returned to the classroom, but no one seemed in a hurry to leave; groups of students milled about, chatting excitedly while DeGraff met with the committee representatives. He explained that President Brooks had asked for any questionnaires from committees, and DeGraff wanted as many as possible collected from fraternities and sororities and turned over to the sociology department. Some of the class committees had been working on problems relative to broken homes and divorce, and DeGraff wanted those questionnaires immediately.[33]

Professor DeGraff wasn't the only faculty member scheduled to appear before the Executive Board on March 19. Professor Max Meyer, whose service at Missouri stretched back to the turn of the century, was one of a handful of faculty members who had achieved international acclaim. Meyer had chaired the psychology department for years and was respected within the discipline for his laboratory work and extensive publications. Alumni who had passed through his classes over the decades mentioned Meyer as exemplifying the best of their university experience. While the exact nature of his relationship to the questionnaire remained unknown, his primary link came through discussions with his protégé Hobart Mowrer, who served as his paid laboratory assistant in psychology. Further, Meyer had given Mowrer the old envelopes from the "Bureau of Personnel Research" for use in facilitating the project.[34] But there was more here than met the eye. Lurking in the shadows was a controversial lecture Meyer had delivered over several semesters to female members of his course in "Social Psychology." What influence would that play in the hearing with the Executive Board or with the full board?

The remaining three faculty members were closer to the periphery of the questionnaire issue. Jesse E. Wrench, an associate professor of European history, had long been a campus icon. A friend of students, he too had an advisory role as the questionnaire was fleshed out. One critic who later decried the radical influences on impressionable youngsters under the guise of free thought told one of the curators that "there is entirely too much tendency on the part of a large number of professors in leading educational institutions to expound radical and undesirable influence on young minds. They do this under the caption of free thinking and similar titles to cover up radical theories." He added: "I note with particular interest professor Jesse French [sic] is mixed up in this affair. I am not surprised."

Jesse French? The critic was wrong about the name, but right about his involvement. To anyone familiar with the University of Missouri, Professor Jesse Wrench standing in the midst of controversy would be no surprise at all. In his eighteenth year at Missouri, Jesse Erwin Wrench had long been a campus phenomenon. To his critics he was a source of consternation; to outsiders a likable curiosity; but to students and others the bearded historian was a living legend. Over the decades his eccentricities became the stuff of banter and myth: how he would take walks or bike rides at 3 A.M., rolled his own cigarettes in class, and got arrested after mowing the lawn in his skivvies. The lawnmowing legend wasn't true; most likely neither was the nocturnal bike riding. He did ride a bike to school in the daytime but gave it up in the 1920s, as he said later, because there were too many woman drivers. Such sexism raised no eyebrows then or later when the story was told, and he was pretty much universally loved on campus.

One of the biggest Jesse Wrench legends, however, grew out of his graduate education. He had taken a Phi Beta Kappa baccalaureate at Cornell in 1906—sandwiched around a year in Palestine—then returned for another eighteen months at an archeological dig. His studies in Jerusalem were augmented by graduate work at Syracuse and the University of Wisconsin. But Wrench never got an advanced degree because he refused to type out his Wisconsin thesis, which was scribbled on—depending on who told the story—toilet tissue or scraps of colored paper. Truth was he never wrote any thesis at all. Though he had most of his residency completed for the Ph.D., he never got around to writing a thesis. Too busy. At least that's what he said decades later.

Affectionately nicknamed "Monkey Wrench," or simply "J.E.," Jesse needed no apocryphal stories to embellish a clearly eccentric life. He fondly recalled three nights in jail—once when he was arrested in Palestine for having no passport, then in Turkey for riding a freight train hobo-style, and then for celebrating too loud and too late in graduate school after a friend's wedding. He volunteered for summertime war-related work in Iowa and Kansas during the Great War. (With a goatee and swept-back hair, he was later mistaken for the exiled Leon Trotsky while in Mexico City—Trotsky was assassinated while both were in the city in 1940.) For the rest of his life he continued his youthful passion for archeology at home and abroad.

At Missouri, Wrench proved no less intriguing. Long a campus favorite, he chaperoned fraternity parties, served as bouncer for those too rowdy, and cheer-led the so-called "Thundering Thousand" at football games. After dances at Rothwell or the Women's Gymnasium, he was the last one out the door. On one occasion he reportedly halted fisticuffs between vocational tech and academic students over campus elections and counted the votes himself. He devised a secure method of ballot counting for student elections. "As a result," one graduate student reported in 1926, "the day of the stuffed ballot box at M.U. is gone forever." Students wanted the administration to make him dean of men, but "Prof" was all he ever wanted to be. Impeccably attired in bow-tie, tweed jacket, flowing cape, and knickers (supposedly until a doctor warned him they hindered circulation), he looked the part. He wore a beret and said he used a hairnet to control his flowing mane because he had so little left. His reputation for hard teaching and "heavy assignments" deterred few from signing up for his filled classes. According to one report, "Some take his courses because they want additional knowledge of history, while many others say that a class under 'Doc' Wrench is something one can't get any place else in the world." His obvious respect for students, which they reciprocated, reflected some variation of his oft-repeated motto: "Treat 'em like grownups. But remember they're nothing but kids. You've got to be as young as they are."[35] Every campus needed a Jesse Wrench, and Missouri seemed to have the original. Controversy? Of course J. E. was involved.

To a lesser extent, perhaps, Russell S. Bauder, an instructor in economics, also figured in the questionnaire. Bauder was young, with an undergraduate degree from Knox College and a master's from the University of Wisconsin in 1925. In fact, he joined the Missouri faculty straight from Madison in the spring semester of 1927, had befriended students, and had a role in the questionnaire's development. The curators wanted to know what he knew. Dorothy Postle, a new assistant instructor in the psychology department, was the only woman faculty member summoned before the committee. What would she tell the inquisitors?[36]

The meeting of the Executive Board was set for 2 P.M. in Jesse Hall on Tuesday, March 19, 1929. It had been a mere six days since the controversy stormed into the public consciousness. With breathtaking speed, modern communications, including wire services and other media outlets, along with telephone and telegraph, had taken the great questionnaire scandal statewide and beyond. Debated from one end of the state to the other in crossroad villages and in boardrooms of the state's two great metropolises, few Missourians were without an opinion.

3

"Jellying" at Mizzou

Men and women—yes women—always eat. The Thetas take breakfast enroute, the crowds jelly in the morning at the Palms, flirt college girls in the afternoon at Jimmies', and are attracted by the orchestra to Sampson's at night. And if she's a good date—it's Harris' for Sunday dinner.

The old bell in Switzler Tower signals relief from one more class, the buildings are relieved of their human content, and the walks of the campus are again thriving with students. Some hurry to another class, some go to study, and others jelly in Jesse Hall—the favorite Haunt.

—*Savitar*, 1927

Maybe our parents didn't have petting parties but they played "postoffice." Maybe they didn't run out of gas but they stopped to rest the horse.

—"E.W.S." to editor, *Missouri Student*, March 29, 1927

Alumni have debated the origins of the term for decades, but every student at the University of Missouri in the late 1920s knew what it meant. Some have claimed that "jellying" arose when students without much money lingered over coca colas so long that the drinks became jelly; others believe it had something to do with jelly on toast or bread. Probably the term originated when Jimmie's College Inn, a local hangout, served jelly rolls to students, who soon made it a campus custom to order them up while listening to live music. Whatever its origins, the word seemed to mean inexpensive dates, shifting into the campus pastime of shooting the bull or simply into a rendezvous between or among friends, or perhaps with one special friend. One could jelly anytime—between classes, after hours, on weekends—and anywhere—in Jesse Hall or any of the campus haunts around town. Harris's Cafe was a spot for that special date, but then in the 1930s so was Gaebler's Black and Gold Inn, a jelly hangout of choice at Gentry and Conley Avenues across from Jesse Hall. Dinner, dancing, and black bottom pie were staples at Gaebler's, but so were twenty-cent jelly dates.

A few doors down the street students could jelly at the Davis Tea Room, a ramshackle place featuring a full menu. The story is that one day in 1921 Chandler Davis drove his truck into town from California, parked across from the administration building, and began selling sandwiches to hungry students. A structure soon developed, wings were added, and a shabby chic tea room emerged. The odd angles of ceiling, floor, and walls, the patchwork construction that stood aloof from building codes, and the ceiling sockets, bare bulbs, and carved initials only added to the charm. In the mid-twenties the tea room had become Jack's Shack and, later still, simply the Shack, a favorite beer joint for generations of university students. For years Gaebler's and the Shack competed for the hottest "night spot of Campustown." Mort Walker, creator of the "Beetle Bailey" comic strip and a Missouri graduate, worked the Shack into his very first strip. By the time the Shack went up in flames decades later, jellying had long since passed into lingo lore. Before it did, *Life* noticed it, as did the *Saturday Evening Post, American Speech,* and syndicated columnist Damon Runyon, who mastered his own special slang. Said *Life* in 1937: "Yale goes to Morey's to hear the Whiffenpoofs sing. Wisconsin goes to the Union to beer and bowl. Missouri goes 'jellying' at Gaebler's." That same year another observer claimed, "The ability to 'jelly' skillfully is a sure sign of the experienced campus campaigner." Unique to the University of Missouri, the slang lasted for a generation or so, joining contemporary imports, some recognizable even decades later, such as "blotto" (an unconscious stupor after heavy drinking), "honk-out" (a failure), "bust a course" (failed a class), "bagdaddies" (escorts for a dance or whatever), "flat tire" (dull company), "give 'em a lot of house" (lots of attention), along with the more familiar "cribbing" (as on an exam), "purple passion" (a sort of unrequited love), and of course "cat's pajamas," "hang a pin," and "bull session"—all illustrations of youth speaking to itself in an age of transition.[1]

2

   Student life at the University of Missouri in many ways mimicked not
only the experiences of their brothers and sisters in public institutions
elsewhere, particularly in the Midwest, but also the stereotypes long held
about the collegiate experience of the twenties. Like sleepy college towns
nationwide that came alive each fall, Columbia swelled by thousands at
the start of fall classes, some students coming by Ford or jalopy, most
swarming the bus depot or the MKT or Wabash rail stations downtown.
Columbia, the seat of Boone County and incorporated a century before,
had grown to mid-size and was exhibiting a patina of progressivism that
belied its quiet and conservative tastes. Light industry supplemented its
primary service as a platform for Missouri's flagship university and two
small women's junior colleges, Christian College and Stephens College.
Columbia and Boone County had wanted the university since well before
the Civil War, and put up sacrificial money to get it. About 15 percent
of Columbians were black, including a professional class. Though a 1917
academic study of black public schooling found Missouri dramatically
leading all former slave states in per capita spending for black children,
and though the 1910 census showed Missouri had proportionately fewer
illiterates than all other former slave states, no blacks yet entered campus
except as custodians or service workers.[2]
   Most arrivals in town each fall in the 1920s dispersed to boarding and
rooming houses cheek-by-jowl with the university. Some headed for
Greektown, but a number of females found nice accommodations in ivy-
covered Read Hall, opened in 1903 and named for the president who
admitted women to the university in the nineteenth century. Then followed pink cards and registration, listening for the bell that tolled from
old Switzler Hall (until it fell silent in 1936), donning close-fitting beanies
if a freshman, and rules upon rules, with lighthearted summonses and
a paddling gauntlet on the Quad for those who broke them. Academics
were reasonably stressed, with appropriate warnings from the dean, who
had statistics of those who fell by the wayside. But the varsity spirit of the
twenties was no myth. The days of fall belonged to the gridiron, the more
so with the inauguration of Memorial Stadium on the south edge of campus in the middle of the decade. Missouri claimed to have originated the
merger of football and Homecoming in 1911 when Chester Brewer, the
athletic director, called on alumni to return for the big game with arch-
rival Kansas, scheduled for the first time on either campus. Thousands
did, and the tradition was born. Homecomings became a big deal, with
lots of preparations, competition among Greeks for the best decorations,

and a big parade through town—seventy-five floats in 1923. There were Tigerettes, a pep talk at Rollins Field by President Brooks at Homecoming 1924, and a packed beat-Nebraska rally in Jesse Auditorium that same year (Nebraska won that year, but not the next). Winters meant tuxedos and fancy dresses. Every organization had a "formal," fifty-one in 1924 alone. Two years later the *Savitar*, the student annual, called it "The season of Tuxes, flowers and fine dresses—of Formals. It was there that he met that girl—the one he remembered—he would see her again—too bad she had a pin—how perfume and sweet music will haunt a man—sometimes for years."

Of course, the campus social tone was set by the Greeks, without which any campus would be a much duller place. So it was at Mizzou, the affectionate nickname hooked on the university long before. Gradually, the Greek system displaced the old nineteenth-century literary societies. Women had been admitted to the normal department in the late 1860s, and with some trepidation by the authorities, were admitted on regular status the following decade. At the time they were segregated in chapel and the library. By the 1920s all that was amusing ancient history. Forty-three fraternities and sororities dotted the community by the end of the decade, many with impressive houses—a bunch of new ones were chartered during the twenties. Kappa Kappa Gamma had been chartered as early as 1872, Pi Beta Phi before the turn of the century, and Alpha Delta Pi, Phi Mu, Chi Omega, Alpha Phi, Kappa Alpha Theta, Delta Gamma, and Delta Delta Delta before the world war. The twenties saw dramatic expansion, with the number of sororities nearly doubling. After all, this was the decade of the woman: Alpha Chi Omega, Alpha Gamma Delta, Theta Phi Alpha, Gamma Phi Beta, Alpha Epsilon Phi, Chi Beta Epsilon, and Zeta Tau Alpha. In addition, numerous professional houses dotted the landscape.

Sorority rush at Missouri would be recognizable both on other campuses and to generation after generation of rushees. "The poor, innocent lass fresh from high school, with all her sweet ideals," said the *Savitar* in 1924, "never knows what is in store for her." One rush party looked like all the others: "Spasms of tittering and giggling, and dancing that is merely a prolonged struggle to see who will lead. Towards the end of the week all of the members begin to look haggard, and occasionally some sister cannot wait until all of the rushees are out of the house before she drops her sweet smile, which really wasn't so sweet anyway, and finds grateful relief in horrible profanity."

Then the rushee had to make her choice. Would she choose the best-looking sorority house with "the largest stock in the cellar"? That's her first choice. Second on her list was the sorority that broke the rules and had men over during its rush party. Third on the list were "those women whom she really liked."

"Rush week with its galaxy of automobiles and trail of pledges and pathos has come and gone," announced the campus newspaper two years later. "The Greeks have dated, danced, dined, and placed their ribbons." What about the frosh who didn't get a bid? "The boy who forgot his date, spilled gravy or otherwise made himself apparently unacceptable socially, has poignant thoughts as he watches his fellows pass by with the insignia in their button holes." He had become an independent by default, a "barbarian" or "barb" for short. Cheer up, said the paper. There was still a chance, and if it never happened, it wasn't the end of the world. A cynical senior offered advice to his fellow students a year later: "If you haven't made the frats or sorats yet, do so immediately. It's easy. If a boy, have dad buy you a hippet and a Galloway bull coat, say 'Howdy, old man—glad t' see you,' and loudly toot your horn. If one of the more rabid sex, kindly camouflage all rough spots, exhibit a well-chewed neck, exhibit all you can, and you'll make the grade. In case you don't, for goodness sake don't eat peas with a knife, smile at the waiter, let your trousers get baggy in the knees, write your own themes or go to 'sup-per' instead of 'dinneah.' "

Each sorority and fraternity had a house mother, and a campuswide position of women's adviser had been established shortly after the turn of the century, which became a deanship of women in 1923. The university even made unusual strides in women's health issues with a program developed in 1921–1923 by Dr. Edith Matzke, a medical doctor who got considerable cooperation from campus sororities. "The college girl problem," said Dr. Matzke, "is not a problem of the flapper, of the social butterfly, high heels, powder, paint, and the lip stick; it is not concerned directly with bobbed hair, abbreviated skirts, elongated skirts, or the knickers, but it is vitally concerned with the mental attitude toward life and toward all educative, constructive, and progressive factors that dominate and influence sane living in a clean, wholesome, academic environment." It came down to a regimen of exercise, hygiene, diet, and lots of sleep. Delta Gamma sorority, for example, followed a strict program, eliminating "the usual burning of the midnight energy with a wet towel tied around the head and coffee to serve as a stimulant." Phi Mu and Alpha Delta Pi prescribed milk for undernourished coeds; others considered ventilation and calorie intake. The program recognized the emergence of women's issues on the modern university campus and compensated somewhat for the small role for women's athletics.

Body, mind, and spirit merged. Courtesy of the Women's Self Government Association, coeds arriving in Columbia in the fall of 1925—members of the Class of 1929—were greeted with a pamphlet, "Around the Columns," containing, among other things, a homily from Dean of Women Bessie Leach Priddy, lots of friendly campus information, and rules for proper behavior. Priddy stood squarely with the Victorians, seeing women as the builders of home and society, as she told the local press after her arrival in 1923. Two years later, she argued that a woman subsumed herself in the identities of others. "May neither fashion nor folly ever tempt you to vulgar and vicious social customs, and unseemly conduct," she advised. "Leisure and recreation are your servants. Compel them to bring you the sweetest, purest, finest gifts of life." She added, "A woman walks on holy ground. She moulds the future of the race. . . . Through all the ages the wife, the mother, the daughter, the sister and the sweetheart have comforted, counselled, guided and guarded man in his spiritual struggles. Woman must not fail him now." Not unmindful of the recent emancipation of women, Priddy urged female students not to miss their role "in the divine plan."

For those young women tempted to stray, the Women's Self Government Association had some rules. Organized in 1909, the group had been empowered to develop social regulations governing all female students in the university. None of them were outrageous. Be in by 12:15 A.M. on normal Fridays and Saturdays, 10:30 P.M. all other nights, approved functions excepted. Recommendations included chaperons everywhere: no "automobiling beyond the city limits after 9:00 P.M." without an approved chaperon; no afterdark "picnic parties" without one. The university added its own requirements: no receiving gentleman callers, and no activities with both sexes without a chaperon on the premises. The university also mandated residence in approved housing, no living where there were males, and no leaving town without permission.

The decade emphasized the automobile and all the freedom it offered. For Missouri students, however, "automobiling beyond the city limits" was difficult, night or day. Students with cars of their own were rare, especially earlier in the twenties—only about one in every twenty-eight or so students had a car in 1923. Some cars were expensive, but most were in "the 'whoopee' class," said the *Tribune* that year. There were lots of cars for the first couple of weeks each fall, but once the fraternity rushees had been impressed, the vehicles went home. Still, the administration was sufficiently alarmed by the number of cars on campus that President Brooks wrote a letter to parents discouraging their use and pointing out their detriment to collegiate success. *Columbia Tribune* editor Ed Watson agreed:

"Automobiles and proper attention to college duties are entirely antithetical propositions." Despite such concerns, the number of cars registered with the Dean of Men's office climbed to five hundred in the fall of 1928. More than half were Fords and Chevrolets, but virtually every nameplate roamed the campus, including Dodge, Buick, Lincoln, and Chrysler, along with exotics such as Auburn, Jordan, Paige, Wolverine, and even a couple of Pierce Arrows.[3]

Cars or no cars, the postwar generation that arrived at college in the 1920s wasted little time showing things were changing. Clothing styles on and off campus underwent such dramatic change that early in the decade, some states—Virginia, Utah, and Ohio, for example—even toyed with legal regulation: nothing inappropriately accenting the female form, falling so many inches from the ankle, and so on. The flapper girl, noted by H. L. Mencken before the war, arrived at Missouri with skimpier dresses and shorter hair. Said the *Savitar* in 1921: "A year ago bobbed hair on a girl announced that she had had the flu; now it indicates that she has social aspirations." "On the whole," said the *Savitar* of the new female attire, "the styles this year have been more than satisfying to anyone who came to school for the purpose of seeing all angles of society. Verily have we here an institution of higher education!" The guys also sported new hairdos as shiny as their shoes. In a blatant display of anti-Victorian independence, coeds had even learned to roll their own cigarettes, though the practice among guys seemed on its way out—save for Professor Jesse Wrench, who liked his Bull Durham. Checkbooks were also replacing rolls of cash. "When you're broke," said the *Savitar*, "all you have to do is to whittle one off." And music, that was changing too. "Dancing has developed new styles," said the yearbook, "and they in turn have developed gray hairs for the referees who sit on the sidelines and say what is naughty and what is nice. The shuffle is over-developed. Just when everyone learned to put their feet down flat the chaperones came out with a flat-footed statement that it was taboo!"[4]

What were rules but to be broken, and gauging the twenties by the written code would miss reality. Speaking of "lines" used to lure the opposite sex, the *Savitar* in 1921 claimed they were "like sorority house rules—everyone must have them but no one pays any attention to them." College life meant parties and hanging out, all supposedly chaperoned. But the rock quarry a mile or so from campus was a favorite getaway for couples. And lights on Ninth Street stifled romance. Said the *Savitar* in 1926: "College life, it is alleged, leaves one with dear memories of studies, Profs, and other things. These are things that the Columns, the Moon, and the night watchman see but do not speak of. It is said that the first two do not care, and that the latter was not always old and gray as he is now."

Mostly, however, a tour of the campus would find balls, follies, plays, debaters (entry into the League of Nations, opposition to Prohibition, etc.), weenie roasts, roller skating, the annual College of Agriculture's Barnwarmin', Jesse Wrench's cheering Thundering Thousand at the stadium, athletics—a huge mixture of goings-on. Greek or independent, no one could be bored on campus. A visit to Delta Delta Delta—"the Columbia Insane Asylum" according to one observer in 1923—might find a pool game, the table loaned by the Phi Gams for approval; on the divans sat numerous gentleman callers; at the Phi Mu house there was a couple on the porch, another—with a Pi Kappa Alpha—in the Ford parked at the curb. The walls of the Pi Phi house were plastered with pictures of guys; the Pi Phis reportedly had money—even a car in 1920—and there were plenty of local alumni to boost them credit. They had lots of clothes and fraternity pins too. At the Alpha Delta Pi house there was an Alpha Tau Omega brother with his lady friend playing marbles on the floor; a visitor to Alpha Chi Omega could get a free meal; at the Palms or Jimmie's the meals weren't free but if one could get a table or a booth the food was as good as the gossip. A guy might even find a date with a girl from Stephens College, the two-year women's school not far from the university.

The typical Mizzou coed? "A shock of red, blond or brunette hair; a lip stick, powder puff and a box of rouge; a maximum of eight ounces of concealing revelation encasing sensuaus [sic] figure and you have a picture of the average University of Missouri girl," claimed one male student in 1927. "Then put her in a car (anything that runs will do), a country road, any male and what have you? A long distance 'petting,' 'necking,' or 'courting,' or anything you wish to call promiscuous osculation."

Hyperbole for sure. But for those Missouri parents concerned about the moral tone of campus and community, Miss Jessie L. Burrall was there to help. Director of religious education at Stephens College, Burrall organized and taught a Sunday morning Bible class for Stephens' women beginning in February 1921. The class proved so popular that men were soon admitted, along with students from the university as well as from nearby Christian College, another two-year women's school. Affiliated with Columbia's First Baptist Church, Miss Burrall's class was quite ecumenical, and attendance ballooned to a thousand students within five years, packing the Stephens Auditorium each Sunday. Well organized with numerous officers, class members got behind a drive to build a radio station at Stephens, where the class was broadcast to the larger community. A class paper grew to eight pages a week.

Away from parents, perhaps for the first time, students at the university did what college students usually did: made their own decisions. Some of those choices were poor, and scandals were staples on every college campus. Despite Miss Burrall's Bible class, Mizzou in the twenties was no exception. The scandals could be trivial, as were the brief suspensions of numerous women in 1922 for performing bits of a play, "Ninth Deacon," at a frat house after midnight; so also were the arrests several years later for gambling. Aside from the two quiet but traditional campus sins, alcohol and sex—subjects of innuendo and sophomoric humor—were out-of-hand transgressions, as, for example, the dozen suspensions for intoxication at a Gamma Phi Beta dance in a downtown hotel in 1924. That made headlines from Omaha to New Orleans, and rumors on campus claimed that one of the chaperons—a mother of one of the students—had supplied the illicit alcohol. Often Kansas City and St. Louis bootleggers filled the need, and students would mix the alcohol with a near beer called Country Club. More serious was the suspension two years later of H. R. "Pete" Jackson, the popular captain-elect of the football team—the quarterback hero who had engineered Missouri's gridiron conference championship in 1925—amid allegations of cheating and drinking as well as talk of an assault on a female student. Further, a couple of good-looking St. Louis women either withdrew from the university or were suspended, the result of an unchaperoned party gone bad. Even before the local prosecutor probed the matter, fraternity leaders, in concert with the administration, vowed a war on violations of the drinking code. The men also endorsed the Women's Self Government Association's condemnation of drunken males at dances and other socials. The women warned that such students would be reported and blacklisted. "It is said that it is better not to wash your clothes in public," said Dr. Albert Heckel, the university's generally well-liked dean of men, "but the clothes have been washed and they are clean. We want the public to know that drinking at the university is on rapid decline."

Heckel was probably right; such peer-driven resolutions to student behavior were probably more effective than heavy-handed administrative crack-downs. Interestingly, male authorities took women's charges of male aggression seriously, whether out of Victorian chivalry or more likely out of the simple credibility of those charges and administrative unwillingness to tolerate such behavior. Feminist charges against male cover-ups of alleged violations against women wouldn't have applied to Dean Heckel, nor to the University of Missouri. But violations of the law didn't mean students had no moral code. Sororities in particular provided peer-developed parameters of social and sexual behavior among their mem-

bers. The editor of the University of Michigan student daily, who claimed
students should be left to work out the drinking issue themselves, would
doubtless have agreed. While the head of Michigan's Student Christian
Association argued that drinking would go on as long as there were bootleggers, the president of the student council thought drinking on the Ann
Arbor campus was on the decline, and claimed that "The novelty of defy-
ing the prohibition amendment is wearing off." And in Columbia, athletic
director Chester Brewer declared publicly that student morals were never
better. He'd been around colleges for a quarter century and he recalled
open saloons and flowing liquor; then there were the wild and disorderly
crowds of students clogging Kansas City streets for the Kansas-Mizzou
football games. Things were better, he was sure.[5]

Students developed a moral code and upheld collegiate traditions in
the 1920s. Simple gestures such as men respectfully removing their hats
as they strode through the Memorial Union archway were instituted after the tower was dedicated in 1926; similarly, lighthearted paddlings by
engineering and agriculture students for those walking on the Quadrangle grass were minor parts of role and order. "If you are a Missouri man,
you must do as Missouri men do," the campus paper warned freshmen
in September 1927. "The saying about Rome and the Romans has become
quite trite but still contains much truth. Freshmen, the way for you to get
along here is to make your self a part of us." That same year one nondrink-
ing student urged the Women's Panhellenic organization to use moral
suasion on the boors who drank at parties and danced with women who
didn't have enough backbone to refuse. After all, chaperons couldn't be
expected to be breath police. Peer pressure would probably prove effective, he argued, but if not, then regulations with the force of those governing Greek rush could be instituted. One obviously disappointed Mizzou
male student was a bit more cynical. "The average college girl is down
here for a good time," he said. "She thinks you are a flat tire if you do not
have a car and a silver pocket flask."[6]

While tradition thrived, some women students complained about Victorian in loco parentis. They chafed at needing parents' permission to
leave town or requirements for signing this or that. For example, regardless of age, female students heading for Chicago on the special Pullman
for the football game with Northwestern in 1927 needed not only to file
permissions but also a detailed day-by-day plan, including chaperons at
their place of lodging. One acerbic woman asked the *Missouri Student:*
"Might it also not be proper to demand that no girl can leave town to
attend a football game unless she has with her her high school diploma
and also an Award of Faithful Attendance at Sunday School for the past

five years? Mr. Editor, what manner of girls are these that we have here at Old Mizzou? Are they grown ups or are they still tied to Mamma's apron strings? Are they able to care for themselves or do they need a wet nurse?" The retort from a law student was, "Did not your parents send you to Mizzou to abide by rules and regulations? If not, you are in the wrong place."[7]

Parties gone bad were sad affairs, but some of the most tragic scandals never made the newspaper at all, and sometimes eluded even the Dean of Women. In the cultural estuary of the twenties, what students knew and didn't know was often a matter of speculation. Several years before the sex questionnaire scandal exploded, for example, an eighteen-year-old woman arrived on the Mizzou campus to begin her studies. By her own admission, her all-female preparatory education had been sheltered, carefully disciplined, and completely devoid of the facts of life. Exceptionally intelligent but hopelessly naive in the ways of the world, the young woman encountered a fraternity man, a senior, the kind upstanding folk would approve of. In the spring of the year they began living together and continued to do so after he graduated and left Columbia. Still a virgin, the naive woman nonetheless feared she was pregnant and so married the young man secretly. Since her husband had no job as yet, they parted for the homes of their parents, expecting to link up again in the fall. Bizarre as the case may have been, the young lady and some of her friends entertained exotic ideas about marriage, notably that sex alone shouldn't hold couples together and that experimentation with others was preferred. Real marriage, in that view, would be more pure than those of their parents' generation. At her husband's suggestion, she tried out some of his fraternity brothers and discovered she had been a virgin all along. She sought advice from an older female, a mother, in her home community. The older friend advised divorce but asked if there was someone else she could talk to. By the time she returned to the university for the new academic year, her husband had a teaching job in another community and the marriage was still a secret. That year she took one of Professor Max Meyer's psychology courses. But there was no discussion of sex at all. Nothing. "We students had come there for instruction," she said later. "We thought that we might learn something about sex, as we really wanted to know, and we had often seen the word 'Psychology' coupled with articles about sex." The same thing went for interest in sociology courses. The young lady feared that Professor Charles Ellwood, who chaired the sociology department, would think of her as "a bad girl," so she didn't seek him out; nor did she confide in Professor Jay William Hudson, who taught philosophy. Hudson said in class he didn't know why students brought their problems to him, so that ended that. "Of course," she said, "I could not consider the Dean of Women, as that would mean expulsion, and I did not tell any other woman because I feared they would tell her, as I have heard that girls can[n]ot keep a secret."

She finally got up the courage to talk to Max Meyer. She was disappointed. Meyer told her to do the moral and traditional thing—go back to her husband. She didn't follow his advice, divorced somewhere along the line, and ended up in several more affairs, one of which left her pregnant. "There are, in cities, such people as abortionists, and not unknown to University girls," she said. That's all she would say about it. That didn't end her illicit behavior, but by the end of the twenties she had married an older man, "intelligent and kind," established in his profession. Whether she loved him was unclear, but she had no regrets, or so she said. Her ethics class with Professor Hudson taught her that morality was not found in self-absorption, but rather in looking at life from the interests of others. That, she thought, was what she had begun to do. She did say she wished there had been a sex questionnaire on campus when she was at Missouri. "It might have given me courage to go to the head of the Psychology department, or to the Sociology Department, and to have asked them, 'What is potence? What is impotence? What are men like? Is sex the really so important thing as I have judged from literature and art? Why do our elders keep so silent about it?"[8]

The young woman's lurid wanderings were surely atypical, but her curiosity about biology and human behavior were shared almost universally by her peers. In one respect, university students in the 1920s were like other generations since. They were works-in-progress, a mixture of developing sophistication and lingering naivete. But in the twenties both society and universities were of two minds on how they might treat this brave, new, and much-celebrated rising generation. Were they boys and girls, or developing adults? What did these youngsters know? What should they know? The generation that came to maturity in the 1920s seemed to contemporaries different from any other, quicker to cast off Victorianism, more willing to question received cultural norms. Sexual behavior among college students in the twenties represented no all-the-way revolt against Victorian practice, but both dating and petting seemed like compromises. F. Scott Fitzgerald, himself not long out of Princeton, published *This Side of Paradise* in 1920, telling all who dared to look that a new day had arrived, even though "petting parties" had been underway since before the war. Citing a study at the University of Pennsylvania charting the rising incidence since the war of pyorrhea, or "trench mouth," Ed Watson at the *Columbia Daily Tribune* saw a link with widespread "petting parties."

Dating and the search for privacy was at once far removed and yet a logical step from the rigid Victorian experience of a young man "calling" on a young lady where they were never far from their elders' prying eyes. University life simply accelerated the process. Robert and Helen Lynd, in *Middletown*, their classic social anthropological study of Muncie, Indiana, in the 1920s, found the "heavy taboo" against illicit sex wavering a bit among youth, but still quite strong. In a 1929 poll of seniors at New York's Columbia College about three-fourths admitted to necking, a bit more than half acknowledged drinking, and not many supported Prohibition. But the guys liked the Republican party, and most planned postgraduation careers in law, medicine, and business—pretty traditional stuff. A survey at the end of the 1920s of the Seven Sister colleges—Radcliffe, Wellesley, Bryn Mawr, Barnard, Vassar, Smith, and Mount Holyoke—found more rumor and loose talk than reality about immorality. Bad manners? Smoking? Drinking? Petting? Not much, if the survey published in the *New York Herald Tribune* magazine is to be believed. The poor manners charge was a bad rap, and fewer than twenty cases of drinking had surfaced in the previous three years among eighty-three hundred women students at the Sister colleges; none of those interviewed had even witnessed drinking at school, though quite a few had heard tales. True, smoking regulations had been relaxed here and there, but it still wasn't much of a problem for administrators. And while some admitted mild petting with a special guy, they didn't do so promiscuously, nor did they think that went on very much in college. The respondents thought that was more characteristic of noncollege girls. One anonymous University of Missouri student who admitted petting claimed in 1927 that not all girls would pet and that none "will indulge in it excessively or indiscriminately." She did so because the guy demanded it, even though paradoxically the guy was "like so much clay" to be molded by the girl. "The keynote of the whole situation," said the student, "lies in the judgment of the girl for though her dates may be numerous she never allows them all the same familiar privileges. Why, you ask? Because she realizes that the characteristic of personal conquest in a boy is very strong and when he learns that his competitors have been enjoying the same privileges he'll stop dating her unless he can secure exclusive rights."

Of course, not all illicit behavior drew the attention of college authorities, and sometimes problems were handled discreetly, such as having an offending student not return for the next semester. And then, the Seven Sister colleges were not coed, and females weren't thrown together every day with the opposite sex. But the survey among them is still impressive, the more so when combined with other evidence. There were lots of rumors. It was all a curious mixture of what everyone knew was a new era, but one in which change blended with tradition. One scholar who surveyed "Undergraduate Attitudes Toward Marriage and Children" at the University of Pennsylvania in 1928–1929 concluded, "Evidences of the 'modernistic' attitudes with which the younger generation of to-day is sometimes said to be imbued occur occasionally, though rarely." While one young woman in the survey said she'd "go against public opinion" and have kids without marriage if she could do so financially, another coed expressed the more common attitude: "It is every girl's ambition to be married," she said. "Marriage is the culmination of the heart's desire."

As the twenties wore on, students at the University of Missouri debated the idea of the modern emancipated woman. A survey by the *Missouri Student* in 1928 showed that Mizzou men seemed about evenly divided on whether they wanted an old-fashioned girl or a modern, aggressive one. It was similar to the confusion in the early wake of the feminist movement nearly five decades later. One journalism senior didn't want the old girl back. "I think it is better to have the freedom of thought and actions of the modern girl," he said, "rather than the meek, shy demeanor of the girl of Grandmother's era." A senior in business and public administration disagreed—the demure ones were "so scarce." An Arts and Science student claimed the old version "was a staid, straight-laced, prim thing with no mind of her own. She believed what she was told and had no way of reasoning things out for herself. It would be the hardest thing in the world to fit the so-called 'Old-fashioned' girl into the modern scheme of things." He thought the old-fashioned girl "would be completely at sea with modern relationships" without knowing why. Another journalism student liked his women feminine but thought the modern girl was too masculine. "Long hair and a gentle manner are two-thirds of a woman's charm," he said. "I want and appreciate intelligence in women, but I also want to be able to love and protect my ideal girl and who would even dream of offering a suggestion of any sort to your typical 'mannish' woman?" Others went further, saying they wanted women in the home where they belonged, and didn't want to challenge tried-and-true customs. For them, a woman's duty was to provide refuge for her man in a hostile world. But for those who had reconciled to the new woman of the 1920s, perhaps the views of a couple of other students were more typical: "I want my wife—and she is, or always should be, a man's ideal girl—to be my companion and equal, both mentally and socially," said one Missouri male. "I would prefer a girl with a University education and one with some business experience. If my wife wishes to work, it is her privilege and her own business. She can smoke if she wants to; that is also her own business. I want a companion, not a defenseless chattel." A graduate student thought much the same thing: "I like the modern girl because she is what she is through choice. The old standards of sweetness and a gentle demeanor need not necessarily be lost because a girl professes to be modern. . . . The old-fashioned girl was what she was because she had no other choice. The modern girl observes and chooses, therefore she is more worthy of praise and admiration." The next year, one forlorn, old-fashioned Mizzou male had a different view. He asked the women if they wanted a guy who'd kissed every girl in sight, "and whose idea of happiness is a car and two quarts? And boys, do you want to take 'for better or worse' one whose petting was learned long before she met you?" Too many girls, he thought, had their "faces painted hideously," and smoked cigarettes, "holding them between dainty fingers which should never feel the touch of a disgusting cigarette. Those of us who stick to the old thought, 'I want a girl just like the one that married dear old Dad,' will be disappointed if matters are not changed." Another disagreed, claiming the Missouri female student was just as good as she'd ever been. So what if she pets and smokes, he said. She had to learn the facts of life sometime. A frustrated Mizzou female echoed that claim, lamenting that the guys dated women on the edge. "We all know," she complained, "that it is the old-fashioned non-petter, non-smoker, and non-drinker who stays at home on Friday and Saturday nights reading the Saturday Evening Post, or worse still, buying her own ticket to the movie." "Inconsistency," she protested, "thy name is man!"[9] Despite the division, in the debate over the modern woman at the University of Missouri, one thing was clear to all the guys: since the war, there was a new member of society, and she had to be reckoned with.

Winterton C. Curtis, a zoologist who came to teach at Missouri in 1901, noticed the change in students over the years. Before the Great War, the Curtis house, about a dozen blocks from campus, was a favorite port of call for students looking for food and simple pleasures, including listening to a victrola or, more often, to one of their own at the piano or other instrument, staples of Victorian life. Mostly, however, they liked Mrs. Curtis reading stories as they sat around the alcove and the fireplace in the living room. The twenties changed everything. Then came "the flappers and the jalopies," recalled Curtis decades later, "and the kind of entertainment that we had to offer became old fashioned." Students still came, usually those involved in zoology, and often they rolled up the rug and danced, but things had changed.[10]

3

One student who figured in those changes was Orval Hobart Mowrer. Outwardly, Mowrer fit the standard eighteen-year-old profile when he arrived in Columbia in 1925 to begin his studies at the University of Missouri. But Mowrer's enrollment in the university, let alone in DeGraff's Family class, had been by no means certain. Born on a farm in January 1907 in rural Putnam County near the Iowa border, Hobart was doubtless a surprise to his forty-five-year-old father, John, and thirty-nine-year-old mother, Sallie, a couple who already had two older children (a third had died as an infant). A delight to his parents, the boy's childhood of pleasant memories was marred by his mother's frequent unexplained illnesses—something known as "nerves" and "depression," as he later learned.

Hobart's father, John Andrew Mowrer, managed only a few terms of rural schooling and watched his dream of becoming a lawyer dashed by demands of family and farm. Any educational hopes for his two eldest children likewise went aglimmering—they completed rural school, but that was the end of it. Then, in middle age, the farmer got a reprieve: an active, intelligent little gift from God, one in whom the frustrated hopes of the father might yet be realized. The "PLAN" emerged. At age fifty-one, the elder Mowrer, after a life of diligence, hard work, and now reasonable prosperity, would leave the farm for Unionville, Putnam's county seat of nearly two thousand souls. There, urban advantages awaited, including "town schooling." If all went well, the youngest Mowrer might even become a university man. Somewhere, a sort of understanding between father and son developed, a "contract" in which the younger, as a steward of these opportunities, would fulfill the ambitions of the elder.

Accordingly, after a taste of rural schooling, the family moved to Unionville in the summer of 1913. Normal boyhood pleasures filled his days, usually centering around the pond near his house, including ice skating in winter and fishing, swimming, and boating in summer. Most of the time, only church and school took him to the center of town, precluding community assimilation and thus denying him entrée to the homes of Unionville's "better" families. Though church formed a big part of community life, Hobart seemed only remotely interested in religion. Biologically Protestant, Hobart took some interest in the religion book in the family's parlor bookcase—complete with visions of hell and the devil—and would listen to his father talk with friends after Sunday dinners about the wonders of heaven. Normality filled his life. In fact, one day when he was about twelve, Hobart experienced a moment he would recall all his life. Standing under an elm tree in his yard and holding on to his "beloved bicycle," he said to himself: "My life is *good,* and I always want to remember *this moment."*

Unfortunately, the idyllic repose of family life was soon shattered. As Hobart remembered it, in "the next two or three years I was to move, psychologically, from Paradise to Purgatory." After a very short illness and failed surgery, John Andrew died suddenly in March 1920. Hobart was thirteen. The family was crushed and the father-son contract might have been jeopardized save for a trust fund established for the youngster. Sallie lived another twenty-seven years as a widow but never really recovered, and Hobart's life changed dramatically as he moved from place to place.

Nothing would be normal again. During Hobart's freshman year in high school, after aborted attempts at Latin, algebra, and football, he fell into a melancholia, not "abnormal" really, but unpleasant just the same. "Then came a morning," he recalled later, "when I got up with a mysterious and quite disturbing feeling of unreality and 'strangeness'—about my environment and, worst of all, even *about myself."* He had few reference points for what had happened to him. Over the next while, nothing helped. After the onset of this "depression," young Mowrer found sympathy in his family but no effective therapy. He dropped out of school for the balance of the semester and, with his mother, herself an occasional victim of the same sort of malady, sought medical assistance of one sort or another. All such efforts ended in failure, including that offered by a doctor-relative in a distant city, who, as Hobart remembered it, "slapped me optimistically on the shoulder and predicted that I would soon 'outgrow it.' " The doctor also recommended a tonsillectomy, the shop-worn cure-all for a variety of toxicities. Neither that nor a special diet and bed rest provided relief.

At age fourteen, young Mowrer had his first serious bout with what later generations would call "clinical depression." Unfortunately, the small northern Missouri community had no help to offer. Of course, everyone knew that on the other side of the state, in St. Joseph, stood Missouri's "Insane Asylum" and that sometimes people known in the community wound up there. "Sometimes they came back," recalled Hobart, "more frequently they didn't; and in neither case did you ever know *why."* Even Sallie, mired in her own depression, kept her own counsel, probably not wishing to burden her son further. About so many other things, it seemed, Unionville, like small towns everywhere, could be candid, but about this, said Mowrer, "there was certainly a 'conspiracy of silence'— and, I may add, a concentration of ignorance." Fortunately, Mowrer's last two years of high school were at least tolerable, thanks in part to his good academic performance and to the support and kindness of his classmates. He even served in class offices and as coeditor of the school yearbook.

If nothing else, Mowrer's brutal experiences had sharpened his life goal. "When I was graduated in the spring of 1925," he wrote decades later, " . . . it was a foregone conclusion in my own mind what I must do in the fall, when I got down to the State University: I was going to have to study this thing called Psychology and find out, if I could, what had been and in some degree still was 'the matter' *with me."*

Newly arrived from Unionville, young wide-eyed Hobart saw the university world through a rosy lens. In a letter published in his hometown paper, he reported that all was well, that commonly held fears that the campus encouraged atheism, sacrilege, irreverence, and materialism weren't true. This was, after all, less than two months after John Thomas Scopes, amidst circuslike media coverage, had been convicted of teaching evolution to his high school students in Tennessee, contrary to state law. Mowrer's exuberant confidence overflowed: "We read so much," he said, "about the radical conflicts between the theory of Organic Evolution and the Biblical account of Creation, of the antagonistic attitude of modern science to all forms of religion, we hear such a fuss about the 'mad pace of Modern Youth' that we hastily conclude that all forms of higher education are an abomination to civilization and that the students attending institutions inculcating such knowledge are degenerates, a disgrace and a scourge to humanity." None of that was true, he said. Freshman assembly opened and closed with "devout invocation," and President Brooks "strongly admonished" that the newcomers get into a church and Sunday school of their choice. His first Sunday in town he'd even been to Miss Burrall's, where it was standing room only, with others unable to get in. Mowrer didn't even find any "hazing" at the university, only lighthearted sophomore rules for the frosh. It was a wonderful world, this university town, and if Columbia had a bad neighborhood, he hadn't seen it.

Unfortunately, Mowrer's hometown assurances, just six days after his arrival, proved the collegiate high-water mark of his religious faith. A psychology course here, a biology class there, with a class in rhetoric taught by an East Coast–educated atheist thrown in as well, and at the end of the first semester Mowrer's fragile Christian faith was in tatters. Science, he thought, despite its failure to help him in his depression, was the future. He pledged Lambda Chi Alpha his second semester, had already gotten in the university's band and orchestra and, on weekends, played his horn in a small student band for dinners and extra cash. He experienced no alcohol, no tobacco, and not much dating that first year, but intellectually he busted out, reading beyond class assignments, grappling with independent thought, and reveling in campus bull sessions.

That first summer a dance band gig in Colorado took him on his first long trip since his folks had taken him to the San Francisco World's Fair in 1915. In that Colorado summer, he got drunk for the first time, didn't like it, and, though he imbibed from time to time, alcohol never occupied a satisfactory part of his life. Free time between band performances led to his brash grading of psychology papers at the University of Colorado—he, an overly confident nineteen-year-old, marking papers of graduate students, schoolteachers twice his age. He also got into his first real love affair, which lasted a couple years before it fizzled, bought a topless Model-T for twenty-five dollars, and, after advertising for riders, carried an elderly gentleman and his four-year-old grandson back to Missouri, his passengers paying for gasoline and oil and all three of them generally sleeping under the night sky. Music also took him to Europe the following summer, where he enjoyed the British Museum and marveled at the wonders of Paris, notably its parks and gardens. He also saw disorderly and violent communist workers march in the backwash of Bastille Day. Overlooking the city one day when the sun and clouds played a drama in the sky, he had what he recalled was a near-mystical experience, closer "to 'knowing God'" than at any other time in his life. It never left him.

During his last two years in college, Mowrer got up his own dance band, played student parties and local jelly joints, and took his entourage to Kansas City in the spring of 1928; during his senior year he pinned a talented and musically inclined young lady. He also served as vice-president of Lambda Chi Alpha, ensuring he would remain active on campus. Even though the desk in his room was piled high with heavy treatises on philosophy, psychology, and sociology (Bertrand Russell, Oriental philosophy, etc.), his fraternity brothers valued him as a member of their bull sessions—the subjects of which, for anyone who ever went to college, covered anything and everything. A motto in his room:

> "Don't feel afraid of anything;
>   Through life just freely roam.
> "The world belongs to all of us,
>   So make yourself at home."[11]

One other highlight of Hobart's senior year: he enrolled in Harmon O. DeGraff's popular class in the Family.

4

The questionnaire problems in the spring semester of 1929, Mowrer's last at the university, were not meteors across the Missouri sky. What happened that spring was part of the American experience. Granting its own features distinctive to its time and place, the University of Missouri was like many others in American higher education in the nineteenth and twentieth centuries. The Northwest Ordinance of 1787 had encouraged educational development, and in 1820 the federal government gave the new state of Missouri two townships of land for such an institution. Benefiting from the sale of those townships, the University of Missouri— carved out of Thomas Jefferson's Louisiana Purchase—became the first land-grant state university west of the Mississippi River. (As if to underscore the Jefferson-Virginia-Missouri affinity, Jefferson's original tombstone from Monticello graced the university grounds before the century was out. And Winterton Curtis recalled meeting new people after his arrival in 1901: "I'm a Missourian," they would say, "but my father came from Kentucky, and my grandfather, suh, was a Virginian.") Boone County, in the middle of the state, pledged the most money in competitive bidding to land the school in 1839, and the governing Board of Curators selected a site in the county's seat, Columbia, for the new university. The cornerstone of Academic Hall was laid July 4, 1840, and classes began in a borrowed building the following year. The first two graduates completed their studies in 1843. Unfortunately, no glory attended the university's earliest days, as the school struggled against virtually every insult visited upon any such institution. Underfunding, political interference, sectional jealousies, and neglect were warm-ups for the trauma of the Civil War. While Missouri never left the Union, secessionists made havoc in the state for years. Meanwhile, the university's buildings were exploited by Union troops who even housed war prisoners in the Athenaean Society's quarters on the third floor of Academic Hall. The indignities of vandalism, fire, and the stabling of horses in campus buildings added to the mess, and for a time in 1862 the university shut down.

Fortunately, brighter prospects awaited the university in postwar Missouri. The revival included new facilities, unprecedented growth, and, for the first time, limited funds from the state. President Daniel Read, a Union loyalist who eventually ran afoul of local Southern sympathizers, oversaw much of the development, including an educational department along with schools of agriculture, law, medicine, engineering, and, in Phelps County, mines and metallurgy. While a real educational institution took shape, for decades the University of Missouri unfortunately illustrated the generally checkered history of American higher education in the nineteenth century. That ambivalence characterized the administration of President Samuel Spahr Laws, who replaced Read in 1876. In the 1870s and 1880s, the university witnessed capital improvements and growth in enrollments, though Laws's responsibility for such improvements is debatable. Well regarded as president of Presbyterian Westminster College, Laws was well-read, sharply intelligent, and self-sacrificing, but he seemed to lack vision and held outmoded ideas of the university curriculum. Further, students balked at the autocratic legalism of his administration, which prohibited profanity, campus smoking, hanging out in pool halls, and sleeping in on Sundays, and ultimately drafted criminal statutes that appeared in the college catalog. Before he resigned in 1889, Laws had also run afoul of the state legislature.[12]

Two acting presidents followed as the Board of Curators cast a wide net, including contact with presidents from, among others, Yale, Harvard, and Cornell, for suggestions on Laws's successor. Richard Henry Jesse emerged as the leading candidate. With a tidewater heritage, Jesse had been educated at the University of Virginia, held a deanship at the rejuvenated University of Louisiana, and was a major and successful advocate of that institution's merger with the newly organized Tulane University in New Orleans. At the time of his recruitment for Missouri's top spot he had been professor of Latin at Tulane for seven years.

Richard Jesse's seventeen years at Missouri's helm marked the arrival of the modern university in Columbia. At age thirty-eight, his youth signaled a new day, and his inaugural address as Missouri's eighth president in 1891 carried no rhetorical flourishes characteristic of nineteenth-century oratory. Possessing vision and energy, Jesse didn't want the top educator in the state to be a political lobbyist, but he was a realist about politics. Louisiana had taught him that. In his first year Jesse oversaw changes already in the works, including filling faculty vacancies and reorganizing the course catalog into something that would be recognizable to later generations.

The most dramatic development of that first year, however, was not in the curriculum but in the physical plant. On a Saturday evening in January 1892, a meeting of the Athenaean Society was interrupted by a fire in the chapel of the university's columned main building. Probably generated by an electrical malfunction, the blaze could not be contained. Students, faculty, and others helped salvage some items, but the building, including the library, was a complete loss, save for portions of the law library as well as loaned-out books. Classes were dispersed to various churches and other sites throughout Columbia, but despite the moral support offered by the new president and Governor David Francis, a genuine friend of the university, the future looked bleak. Forces that had never accepted Columbia as the home of the state university now worked to move the institution elsewhere, with Sedalia and Independence, in the western part of the state, as contenders. Ultimately, alumni, Columbia itself, and friends of the present site beat back the surprisingly strong challenge, and a crash rebuilding at Columbia moved forward. A protracted fight ensued over the fate of the surviving and imposing six ionic columns that had graced the main building before the fire. Under pressure from alumni, the curators reversed an earlier decision to have them removed and instead let them stand on a small ridge amid the developing construction on what became Francis Quadrangle, appropriately named for the governor. The columns became a centerpiece for the modern university and eventually one of the most visited sites in the state.[13]

The fire, along with Jesse's arrival, marked a major division in the university's history. The new president oversaw a major building program, including dedication in 1895 of a new administration building that later bore his name, most of the "Red Campus"—so named for the color of the bricks—which flanked the old columns, and, by the end of his tenure, the architectural development of the limestone Gothic revival "White Campus." But Jesse made his greatest contributions in administrative, curricular, and intellectual developments, the latter of which included the appointment of a large number of stellar faculty. Further, entrance exams were stiffened, graduate programs professionalized, and, with enhanced high school curricula, the university's preparatory department was abolished. Jesse and members of the faculty toured the state's high schools repeatedly, elevating the visibility and prestige of the university. In fact, within a few years of Jesse's arrival, the University of Missouri shook off its perceived localism and actually became, in the minds of most residents, the state's higher educational institution. The university joined the flowing mainstream of higher education in America.

By the turn of the century, the slow but palpable pace of modernization accelerated with the proliferation of new departments and energetic junior faculty. Political economy and history, for example, founded in 1891, eventually became four separate departments: history, economics, political science, and sociology. These and other departments were soon staffed with able young men sporting prestigious degrees, lured in large measure by Jesse himself, who often violated protocol in bypassing department chairmen. Assembling an outstanding faculty attracted Jesse's intense interest, and he developed personal links to established eastern institutions, including Johns Hopkins and Harvard. He overcame the university's relatively low salaries, institutional youth, and remote location to attract a surprising cadre of established and potential scholars. Some of the recruits left after a while but others stayed the rest of their lives, with buildings bearing their names. George LaFevre, for example, a longtime professor of zoology with a doctorate from Johns Hopkins, came in 1899 and stayed until his death in 1923; so also Herman Schlundt, a Wisconsin Ph.D. who arrived in 1902 to teach chemistry and over the next thirty-five years became one of the university's most acclaimed teachers. He also gained national renown as a scholar in both physical chemistry and radioactivity. Four appointments—Merritt Miller, Frederick Mumford, Henry Waters, and J. C. Whitten—enhanced agricultural education; the latter three had buildings named for them, despite Waters's departure in 1909 for the presidency of Kansas State College of Agriculture. Another Johns Hopkins Ph.D., Henry Belden, came to Missouri in 1895—the same year he got his degree—and stayed for the balance of his long career, earning wide recognition for his work on frontier literature. Missouri's prestige within academe rose. Not surprisingly, the university's application for a Phi Beta Kappa chapter won approval and was established in 1901; a charter for scientific honors, Sigma Xi, followed four years later. According to historian Jonas Viles, who came to the university during the transition and stayed for decades, the optimism, zeal, and enthusiasm proved virtually immeasurable.[14]

In this milieu, natural and social sciences flourished, as did the professional schools, including engineering and agriculture. Faculty at Columbia more than doubled during Jesse's tenure, while enrollments ballooned from 681 in 1895 to nearly 2,100 by 1906–1907. The percentage of graduate students showed even greater growth, up to 138 during the latter year. Even intercollegiate athletics flourished, including football games with Vanderbilt, Northwestern, Iowa, Purdue, Kansas, and others, moving inexorably toward standardization and regulation. Rothwell Gymnasium, completed in 1906, brought better facilities for intramurals and physical education.

Modern amenities still eluded Columbia, but pressure for appropriate living quarters was relieved not merely by new student housing but also by the growth of fraternities (and eventually sororities) that often offered their own facilities. The Wabash Railroad helped break the isolation in the nineteenth century, as did the arrival at the turn of the century of the Missouri, Kansas, and Texas Railroad—the "Katy" to generations of students. Max Meyer arrived in Columbia in August 1900 to find board sidewalks and unpaved streets with flagstones placed strategically in the dirt at intervals to allow both passage of wagon wheels and walkways for pedestrians. Winterton C. Curtis, the promising zoologist from Johns Hopkins in Baltimore who had met George LaFevre at the prestigious Marine Biology Lab at Woods Hole, saw pretty much the same thing the next year when he came to interview for a faculty position. Despite dust, mud, horses, mules, hitching posts, and tobacco juice on the wooden sidewalks, President Jesse made the turn-of-the-century outpost of learning—"The Athens of Missouri"—attractive to some of the best young minds in the nation. If most left for more money and prestige after trying their wings, others stayed and made the university a good place for research and learning. That was true of Curtis, who, after being wined and dined for three days by faculty as well as by Curator Walter Williams and President Jesse himself, took the job as soon as it was offered. His mother was horrified at the prospects of her boy—only twenty-five at the time—heading for such a forlorn place, the wild west of Jesse James. (Even a generation later, an observer claimed Mizzou "owes much of its rah-rah charm to the fact that its connections between the campus and St. Louis are so difficult.") But Curtis just knew the University of Missouri was on it way up and he never looked back. "I said for years afterward," he recalled of that first visit, "that never in all my life did I have so much good time packed into so few days."[15] He stayed sixty-five years.

Jesse's tenure might have lasted longer had it not been for the unfortunate breakdown of his health. A pair of sabbaticals, including one in Europe, failed to restore physical vigor and he had no alternative to resignation at the end of 1907, effective the following year. Despite his immeasurable value to the university, Jesse had not always been popular with students—they didn't like compulsory chapel for one thing—nor had he been fully appreciated by junior faculty, who, coming as they often did from avant garde institutions, chafed at archaic vestiges of a changing system. Little did they nor many of the tens of thousands of students who passed through Jesse Hall during the next century fully appreciate Jesse's contributions. One longtime Missouri veteran, Isidor Loeb, who saw much of Jesse's presidency firsthand and who later served briefly as acting president himself, thought students were awed by the president, though "he was a charming man when they met him." To Loeb, Jesse's upgrade of faculty was his "greatest achievement." Frank Thilly, who had left for Princeton in 1904 and later went to Cornell, recalled that the school "had the spirit of a real university" at the time, something echoed by Max Meyer a quarter century after his own arrival. Jesse, said Meyer, had "transformed a small and local institution into a real university of the State, unlimited in its possibilities of growth and future usefulness."[16]

Fortunately for Missouri, his successor as president, Albert Ross Hill, recruited in 1903 as professor of education and who became the inaugural dean of the university's teachers college the following year, restored the vitality of the best years of Jesse's tenure. A Cornell Ph.D. prepared as an educational psychologist, Hill had filled the void left by the acknowledged intellectual leader of the university, Frank Thilly, who had come to Missouri in the 1890s as the first full-time professor of philosophy. Thilly departed for Princeton in 1904 but the faculty warmed to Hill's leadership, groomed as he was for the presidency in the face of Richard Jesse's declining health. Jonas Viles, never blind to Missouri's shortcomings, claimed years later that as far as the faculty was concerned, Hill's selection as president in 1908 completed the process "in making the University of Missouri the most attractive and promising in the country."

Nevertheless, Hill's thirteen-year stint at Missouri's helm was a mixed bag. The Hill era witnessed boundless energy and enormous vision for an expanded and greater university. As such, the nation's first school of journalism was founded in 1908 as a legacy to both Jesse and Walter Williams, its dean and a future university president. But Hill carried forward the development of both the School of Commerce and the Graduate School as separate entities. The "White Campus" expanded dramatically, and the university acquired an impressive library building. High academic standards for appointment and promotion marked Hill's tenure—as it had Jesse's—and the roster included, for seven years, Professor Thorstein Veblen in economics, one of the most renowned academics in America. Ultimately, Hill grew frustrated at the slow pace of change, had conflicts with the faculty, and resigned in 1921. But his failures were largely self-perceived. As Viles pointed out later, lesser executives content with merely marking time would not have held the university to Jesse's high standards. In any case, until the appointment of Stratton Brooks in 1923, Missouri benefited from two able caretaker regimes led by university veterans John Carleton Jones from 1921–1923 and, for a short time, Isidor Loeb.[17]

As a result of the emergence of the modern university, the University of Missouri offered serious academics along with the collegiate mix of fraternity fun and the occasional drunken scandal. Graduates made their mark across the nation, and in the professions and cultural life of the state. If racial segregation denied equal access to black Missourians throughout the decade, the university welcomed a motley number of foreign students from countries including India, Japan, China, and the Philippines. Among the handful of Chinese students at Mizzou in the early twenties was K. C. Hsiao, who took a baccalaureate and a master's in philosophy. Hsiao later earned a Ph.D. at Cornell, then taught in Chinese universities until the communist revolution in 1949, and then at the University of Washington until his retirement in 1968. Acclaimed as "The world's foremost expert on Chinese political thought," he reveled in his studies at Missouri. He admiringly recalled Robert Kerner's packed lectures in modern European history. Philosophy professor Jay William Hudson explained "profound concepts in simple terms," while Walter Williams, "the 'doyen' of American journalism . . . provided us an endless array of profound ideas" in his principles class. Hsiao studied sociology and anthropology with Charles Ellwood, who, despite being "a famous sociologist," "devoted much attention to educating the younger generation." Aside from his major professors in philosophy, Hudson and George Sabine, "the most memorable and to whom I owe the most gratitude" were Max Meyer and Hermann B. Almstedt, who taught German. Meyer's "famous dictum," "Emotion is wasted reaction," Hsiao long remembered, along with his embrace of a physiological approach to psychological analysis. Almstedt taught with great enthusiasm and also befriended Hsiao, inviting him to dinner and accompanying him at the piano while he practiced for a public recital of the Chinese national anthem. "I lived in Columbia for three years, and when I first arrived I was a stranger to the people and the place," said Hsiao when it was all over. "But within less than a year, whether in the downtown streets or the residential areas, people all greeted me. When I left this hospitable and friendly 'college town' in the summer of 1923, I could not help but feel some reluctance to say goodbye."[18]

Despite Columbia's happy embrace of well-mannered foreign students, darkness lurked just beneath the community's surface. It erupted violently in April 1923 when a mob using an acetylene torch raided the local jail and lynched James T. Scott, a black custodian at the university. He had been accused of assault on the fourteen-year-old daughter of Professor Almstedt more than a week before. Governor Arthur Hyde reportedly was mobilizing a battery to protect Scott but it all proved too late. While the mobsters took Scott to a railroad bridge in the southwestern part of town, the crowd grew by hundreds and became more boisterous, including the addition of university students, some of whom were in the parade of fifty or so automobiles. Professor Almstedt was himself threatened after he pleaded for law and order; evidently, no students— including women at the scene—participated in the lynching, something Acting President Isidor Loeb declared in a statement to the press and that was confirmed by Missouri Attorney General Jesse W. Barrett several days later.

The lynching was front-page material for the *New York Times* and symptomatic of the racism that afflicted America in the decade, one of nearly thirty such murders of blacks in 1923. That was down from more than fifty the previous year, and way down from a high of more than two hundred in 1892. The killing was also the sole lynching in Missouri in 1923, though there was another the following year in Charleston, and still another near Kansas City the year after that. But unlike most such lynchings, there was an attempt at justice. The angry local prosecutor, Rubey M. Hulen, later physically threatened by the Ku Klux Klan from Arkansas, announced boldly, "We know the leaders. They were rough-neck men from out[side] of Columbia." Whether or not that was an effort to shift blame from the city, he got an indictment against one of the alleged mobsters for first-degree murder but no conviction, even amid speculation that Scott had been guilty of nothing.[19] The whole affair proved difficult for a purportedly progressive community to overcome, and even the passage of decades could not erase the scar.

5

Despite the city's violent aberration, the University of Missouri offered students a good education in the 1920s. Such was the legacy of the Jesse and Hill regimes. Unfortunately, those gains stalled in the twenties. Save for rural Missouri, indeed rural America, the nation's economy enjoyed unprecedented prosperity under the presidencies of Warren Harding and Calvin Coolidge. Unfortunately, such prosperity didn't extend to appropriations from the Missouri legislature. Though biennium requests from Columbia regularly topped $6 million in the decade—more than $7 million in 1929—the actual appropriations never matched even half those amounts. Two years before Stratton Brooks's arrival as president, the legislature did appropriate funds for nine new buildings or portions thereof, all of which were eventually completed. Two years later funds were passed for four more. But the appropriations for one never materialized and funds for the other three lapsed, leading to reappropriations in 1925 followed by the governor's veto of funds for two of the buildings. Money for the fourth, Tate Hall, new home for the Law School, was released only because such was required to match private gifts in the early twenties from a St. Louis couple who wished to memorialize their late son, Lee R. Tate, a law school grad. In 1929, the legislature also rebuffed the curators' plea for a long-term building plan. Regardless, two major capital improvements by 1926, funded by private subscription, were the imposing Gothic Memorial Tower, which formed the focal point of the "White Campus," and the Memorial Stadium, which rose dramatically on the south end of campus and kept the university apace of the national rise of big-time collegiate football. Each fall, final scores formed large page-one headlines in the *Tribune* whether Mizzou's Tigers won or not.[20]

The Missouri legislature's failure to appreciate the value of their flag-ship educational institution wasn't the only negative in the 1920s. The leadership established by Jesse and Hill faltered with the appointment of Stratton Duluth Brooks as new president in 1923. Initially, Brooks's ap-pointment was viewed positively. While a number of able candidates had been passed over in the lengthy search to replace Ross Hill, and while re-peated attempts to lure Frank L. McVey from the University of Kentucky had been unsuccessful, Brooks's résumé carried some positives. A native of rural Missouri, fifty-three-year-old Stratton Brooks had graduated from the University of Michigan, had taken a master's at Harvard, and had taught at the University of Illinois. But his primary emphasis had been as a public schoolman. Principal of several high schools, he had risen to the superintendency of public schools in Cleveland and Boston before being named president of the University of Oklahoma in 1912. Brooks had over-seen the development of that institution from small-time status to grow-ing university, complete with a major building program and expanded student enrollments. Unfortunately, he had run up against politicos who reportedly wanted the professoriate subject to political spoils, a develop-ment he vehemently opposed. Oklahoma's governor wanted him ousted; he might be open to feelers from his native state. The bespectacled Brooks even looked the part—distinguished, sartorially correct, with white hair and mustache. After meeting successfully with the search committee in St. Louis in May 1923, he was introduced to the full board the next day, which named him president at a $12,500 salary, not counting use of the even-tually renovated president's house on Francis Quadrangle, along with a monthly $50 automobile allowance.[21]

Brooks took office in July and was officially inaugurated in November amid much fanfare, including an address by President Marion L. Bur-ton of the University of Michigan, an ROTC review on Francis Quad-rangle, a student torch-light parade at the columns, and a late evening reception. Representatives of more than 130 colleges and universities at-tended, and the curators' Executive Board chairman, E. Lansing Ray, af-ter reviewing the history of the university, introduced Brooks, anointed him as "the chosen one," and praised his record and temperament. "We expect this institution to go forward and upward under your administra-tion," he charged. "We expect to see it become greater, more honored and more loved. Our faith in your fitness assures us these expectations will be realized."[22]

It didn't happen. University chroniclers have either panned or largely ignored Brooks's administration. In his centennial history, for example, Jonas Viles devoted slightly more than half a page to Brooks's seven-year tenure, and deemed it inadequate, "an interim," "A period of quiet." And Frank Stephens's 1962 *History of the University of Missouri* titled the relevant chapter, "The University Falters in the Twenties."[23] Some of the criticism may reflect Brooks's role in the questionnaire scandal, but the consensus remained that his selection had been unfortunate.

6

Regardless, several other interesting personalities and characters added to the making of the culture war of 1929. Like so many things good and prestigious about the University of Missouri, Max Friedrich Meyer was a product of the Richard Henry Jesse presidency. Meyer fit the profile of Jesse's recruits: young, able, energetic, and sporting a prestigious degree, in his case a Ph.D. from the University of Berlin. Although psychology and philosophy doubled up in the early years, Meyer founded the serious study of psychology at Missouri, becoming the first faculty member of the new department.[24]

Born in Danzig on June 15, 1873, Meyer early on showed academic prowess. A life in theology attracted him, but he felt stifled by the state church; he likewise rejected philosophy as lacking relevance "to the biological necessities of the human race." After studying quantum theory with Professor Max Planck and hearing theory under the legendary Carl Stumpf, Meyer, at twenty-three, earned the Ph.D. at Berlin in 1896. Against Stumpf's wishes, Meyer published findings contrary to his mentor, leading to not only personal and professional estrangement but also his departure from Berlin. Lack of satisfactory employment opportunities drew him to America by way of London before the turn of the century— nudged in part by Professor Hugo Munsterberg of Harvard, who noted Meyer's work. Meyer demonstrated both ability and willingness to participate vigorously in the discipline, carving a life-long independent role within the academy. He rejected "gestalt" theories long before they were formally articulated, focused on sounds and auditory theories, and presented himself as a physicist.[25]

Meyer had been lured to Missouri by Walter Williams, a newspaperman who chaired the university's Board of Curators' Executive Board. Williams worked in tandem with Jesse's ambitious goals and later founded the first school of journalism in the United States. Meyer may also have been attracted to the university by its consensus intellect, Frank Thilly, a German-American who had matriculated at Berlin and had taken a Ph.D. at Heidelberg. Before Woodrow Wilson, president of Princeton, enticed Thilly to leave Missouri for New Jersey in 1904, Thilly shared the philosophy department with Meyer, after which Robert M. Ogden, who held a Cornell baccalaureate and a German doctorate, served as Meyer's assistant.[26]

At Missouri, Meyer's publishing continued apace, with most attention focused on hearing functions and music theory, but he also wrote a number of textbooks, including *The Fundamental Laws of Human Behavior* (1911), *Psychology of the Other-One* (1921), *Abnormal Psychology* (1927), and *Elementary Laboratory Psychology* (1927). He soon added *The Musician's Arithmetic* (1929). Though some of his writings were esoteric, his work enhanced his growing reputation—if only among a rather narrow band—even as he rejected the developing emphasis in the discipline on behaviorism. Meanwhile, he carried a heavy teaching load in all his years at Missouri, including conducting a number of courses required in some of the professional schools as well as in the College of Arts and Science. Almost from the beginning, he made use of a string of able assistants, starting with Robert M. Ogden, who years later in his book *Hearing* (1924) credited Meyer with starting him out on the subject. One Meyer assistant, German-born Albert P. Weiss, became not only Meyer's disciple and lone Ph.D. but also a significant contributor to the profession in his own right, spending several years at Ohio State University and ultimately producing twenty-five doctoral students. "I have had very little—almost no—influence on American psychology *directly*," reflected Meyer later, "but perhaps a good deal through mediation by students of Weiss." Meyer also took a pair of sabbaticals, one in 1909–1910 and another a decade later. In the first, he spent considerable time in Paris writing *Fundamental Laws,* though he gave two papers at the Sixth International Congress of Psychology in Geneva, Switzerland. Looking for cultural diversity, his second sabbatical took him to Cuba, Spain, and Morocco. Some of his observations of an Arab religious dance rhythm found their way into his *Psychology of the Other-One,* published in 1921. Meyer's return to the United States in steerage by way of Bordeaux, France, provided another opportunity for his eclectic writing, this time resulting in a pair of articles describing the journey in *Survey* magazine.[27]

One personal by-product of Meyer's work at Missouri led to his marriage in 1904 to Stella Sexton, a freshman in one of his psychology classes. Intelligent and strong-willed, she proved a match for her older German-born husband, eventually earning both baccalaureate and master's degrees, and teaching Spanish and eventually serving as acting dean at Christian College before losing the permanent position to a male. The marriage lasted more than three decades and produced five children between 1904 and 1914. Stella later suspected that her lack of sophistication led Meyer to believe he could turn her into a submissive *hausfrau*, and cultural conflict surfaced over the years. His intelligence led to impatience, though those who knew him admired his commitment to family; his manual skills produced significant renovations to his home, nicely landscaped grounds, and play equipment for the children.

Home life was neither normal nor particularly happy. Meyer had educational ambitions for his children, and in fact had little patience for the untutored mind. He encouraged no levity, and dinner conversation tended to the cultural. A dictionary or encyclopedia settled arguments, though Meyer usually encouraged no opinions contrary to his own. Stubborn, remote, and absorbed with his own work, he also had little time for his growing family, leaving even discipline to Stella. The children mostly developed stronger relationships with their mother. The brood stepped lightly when "Father" was home, but played popular music on the victrola in his absence. They rarely entertained in their large Columbia home, save for out-of-town visiting colleagues or an occasional faculty group. While growing up the children became familiar figures on campus and sometimes hung around Jesse Hall's fourth floor. Meyer worked there on research, experiments, writing, and lecture preparation and teaching from early morning till late afternoon or early evening, sometimes returning after supper. Stella had her own professional duties but still managed to stop by Jesse to help her husband, particularly with editing his writing, which had a tendency to German structure. He respected her abilities in this regard but typically had to argue it out anyway. In his long labors and achievements, Meyer earned the respect of both Stella and the children—respect without warmth.[28]

Meyer enjoyed similar respect in his profession, though his gentlemanly reputation and erudition was mitigated by impatience and temper. A bit of a perfectionist, his contempt for what he regarded as shallowness in American psychology showed at meetings of the American Psychological Association. His biting criticism and polemic style earned few friends. His intellectual biographer regarded his "bluntness, tactlessness, eccentricity, etc." as a by-product of his Prussian training, a view shared by others. He behaved similarly among colleagues at the university. By reputation, he was a bit of a loner, at home with his laboratory equipment, or muttering to himself as he wandered the campus. Colleagues regarded him as a gentleman, but knew he had a temper, a sort of German-bred contempt of American superficiality in the profession. Everybody knew him, but he counted no one as a soulmate, the more so in the 1920s, after he singlehandedly developed a fine-tuned and sophisticated statistical grading system for the campus that many likely resented and rejected. (He also developed a grading system eventually implemented in the Missouri school system.) His work was his life and none could name a single vice, save for his love of concert music.[29]

So Max Meyer was a bit eccentric. Not a few students must have thought so in the early years when he often rode his bicycle to school, then carried it up to his office on the unfinished fourth floor of Academic Hall, later named for President Richard Jesse. The top floor, mostly unpartitioned at the time, served not only as Meyer's office and laboratory but also as a great arena for cycling when the mood struck him. Anyone who ever climbed to the top of Jesse Hall knew what a hike it was, and Meyer did it for nearly three decades, happily ensconced at the top of the campus. More than once Hobart Mowrer recalled Meyer's "good-natured little joke he once made when somebody arrived one day and, between gasps for breath, remarked on what a dreadful place this was for the Department to be located. 'No,' replied Meyer, 'this is quite a proper place for psychology to be, for it is, as you know, the science of the 'upper-story.'" Legend also had it that one day he came to class and, apparently wishing to make a point, entered the classroom "on all fours barking like a dog." Mowrer heard lots of such stories and didn't believe most of them, but admitted the one about the barking dog might well be true. Mowrer found him a gifted pedagogue, "dramatic, exacting, and on occasion, amusing."[30]

One reporter for the *St. Louis Post-Dispatch* who visited the campus when the questionnaire blew up talked to students and others who knew him and visited the professor himself in his lab. Meyer proved to be a sympathetic character. "His courses were never popular at the university because they were difficult, and Meyer himself was eccentric," said the reporter:

> He was blunt and ruthlessly sarcastic. . . . The more timid students usually dropped out after the first course, but those hardy ones who came back for more came to know Dr. Meyer as the most kindly of men beneath his blunt exterior. To them psychology courses were a delight, because he made them so interesting and so amusing. He had a sly sense of humor and enjoyed himself never so much as when clowning. Up and down before the class he would pace with hands behind him, lost in deep thought. Then,

suddenly, he would pause and fire at a startled student some apparently irrelevant and foolish question. Whether the student gave a canny answer or not, Meyer usually succeeded in tangling him up and provoking a laugh at his expense. But when the comedy was over everybody had something to think about and mayhap had learned a thing or two about psychology.[31]

Many of Meyer's students swore by him. One of them, Merrill E. Otis, a two-time Missouri grad, including the law school, had acquitted himself well, rising to U.S. assistant solicitor general, then a Coolidge appointee to the federal district bench in Kansas City. In the rising furor over the questionnaire, Otis publicly declared his fidelity to his old prof in the *Kansas City Star:* "As a student I took every course he offered. My views concerning him were those of all who sat at his feet. He was and is a great teacher, a great lover and exponent of truth, who inspired all who heard him with the scientific spirit. He not only illuminated the subjects he taught, but he planted in his students a deep and earnest desire for real light and truth. . . . Today he is one of a handful in the faculty at the university who rank as world famous scholars." Paul Farnsworth, who spent time working with Meyer in the summer of 1923 and later enjoyed a career at Stanford University, noted that Meyer quickly determined which students "were dumb or lazy and hammered them until they left his class in disgust or began to do real work." Farnsworth, a student of Albert P. Weiss and nurtured on Meyer's textbooks, years later dedicated *The Social Psychology of Music* (1958) to Max Meyer—"one of the most brilliant theorists and experimenters in the field"—from whose writings he had obtained the requisite inspiration.[32]

Many of Meyer's women students felt the same. One of his students, Josephine Smith, who briefly returned to teach at Missouri, reportedly "idolized him," and Mary Paxton Keeley, who took Meyer's basic psychology course nearly two decades earlier, recalled him as "brilliant," "fascinating," "probably the most talked of professor on the campus." She added: "He was by far the most outstanding teacher I had at the University. He was pleased when any student showed evidence of thinking." Dorothy Postle, an instructor in psychology who was with Meyer in the questionnaire storm and went on to a career at the University of Michigan, said later she thought she might be able to write a book on Meyer. Her single semester associating with him "was worth two years of the ordinary graduate work."[33]

In one respect, Meyer was a misfit not only at Missouri but also in the discipline of psychology. His life-long passion was acoustics and hearing theory, yet he spent many of his best years developing a series of psychology courses for undergraduates. Nor did he encourage promising students to remain at Missouri for graduate study, arguing his style was out of favor within the discipline. Yet he seemed to have no desire to significantly expand the field at Missouri, perhaps because he would rather work harder himself to cover the bases than share his domain with others who might not see things his way. Eccentricities and isolation constituted the baggage of a brilliant scientific mind. Hobart Mowrer used to recall a Meyer anecdote about some scientific conference where the media "asked him if he was a 'behaviorist.' He said: 'Behaviorist? the only kind of an *ist* I am is a scien*tist!*' " Whether because of culture or temperament or whatever, Meyer sometimes became his own worst enemy, but he was also a remarkable and pathbreaking scholar. One of his colleagues, the highly respected Winterton C. Curtis, claimed the faculty knew Meyer was "a man of unusual ability," if a bit eccentric. "In my opinion," said Curtis when it was all over, "Max Meyer was one of the most competent scholars we ever had at the University of Missouri in my time."[34]

7

The development of psychology at the university paralleled the growth of other social sciences, including sociology. The Progressive era provided a natural environment for such growth, even as it pursued efficiency, uplift, the cult of the expert, and the professionalization of the social sciences. In fact, the first several decades of the twentieth century nurtured the rise of those disciplines that flourished despite the decline of progressivism. That all required data and its analysis. Social scientists—psychologists, sociologists, anthropologists—wallowed in data.

The serious study of sociology at the University of Missouri mirrored the national trend. Yale's William Graham Sumner was long credited with offering the first sociology course in the United States in the 1870s. But Missouri's president, Samuel Spahr Laws, offered a "Social Science" course the year before Sumner's, and continued to offer it for a decade, using as a text a book by Herbert Spencer, the noted Social Darwinist. That course flagged in the 1880s, but for one year only, 1896–1897, the political economy department offered "Introduction to Social Science." Finally, the Board of Curators, led by President Richard H. Jesse, established a chair in sociology in 1900 and appointed Charles A. Ellwood as its first occupant. A promising career lay ahead for young Ellwood, who had taken a bachelor's of philosophy at Cornell in 1896 and the Ph.D.

three years later at the University of Chicago, which had pioneered sociological study. President Jesse charged Ellwood with fulfilling the standard goals of teaching, research, publication, and public service. Further, some members of the Board of Curators, including Walter Williams, told Ellwood, as Ellwood himself recalled it, "that they hoped that the Department would undertake to apply the principles of Christianity, in a scientific way, to the solution of social problems." The department debuted in the fall of 1900 with thirty students. The following year additional offerings included "Ethnology," "Race Psychology," and "Psychological Sociology." Over the decades, Ellwood, a student of John Dewey and a disciple of William James, grew along with his department, keeping faith with Jesse's academic charge and winning moderate distinction for sociology at a midwestern university.

In that regard Ellwood was more than successful. Over the years, able additions were recruited to the faculty. Baccalaureate graduates could be found in endless social service, and advanced master's and doctoral grads eventually entered open doors in academe. Ellwood himself found significant distinction nationally, partly through his prolific and well-received publications. He resisted trends in the discipline toward behaviorism, noticeable even before the world war. Numerous publications reflected such resistance, including his reworked *Introduction to Social Psychology*, published during the war and later translated into Japanese and Chinese. An ardent supporter of the American Sociological Society from its inception in 1906, Ellwood became its president in 1924.

Ellwood proved to be an effective organizer. He helped foster sociology in Missouri high schools and by the early 1920s the state stood second in the nation in percentage of such students taking sociology courses. Generating sociological study in Missouri's churches proved more difficult, however, though it remained one of Ellwood's abiding interests as evidenced in a lengthy article in the *American Journal of Sociology* in 1913 and *The Reconstruction of Religion*, published by MacMillan in 1922. That in turn led to lectures at Yale later that year, published in 1923—also by MacMillan—as *Christianity and Social Science*. During Ellwood's presidency in 1924, the American Sociological Society instituted Sociology of Religion as one of its sections. Theological liberalism, promoted by Ellwood and by sociologists generally, collided dramatically with Christian fundamentalism in the 1920s, though fundamentalism suffered a severe blow in the public spectacle of the Scopes Monkey Trial in Dayton, Tennessee, in 1925.

Sociology as an academic discipline also was on a collision course with the Victorians. Ellwood never looked for that, although President Richard

Jesse, who had hired him, claimed that "a Department of Sociology which did not stir up any fuss was no good." In early 1902 Jesse urged the department to conduct a scientific study of Missouri's county jails and alms houses, which the president deemed were in sad shape. Question-naires returned from superintendents and law enforcement officials in 1902 confirmed deplorable conditions. President Jesse and the Board of Curators pushed for a more thorough investigation. Students working on the project visited the jails and poor houses in their home counties, newspapers were perused, and the head of the State Board of Charities and Corrections opened his files for investigation. Compilation and inter-pretation of the data led to Ellwood's report to the convention of the State Conference of Charities and Corrections in Kansas City in 1903. Ellwood's chapter-and-verse indictment of the state's charitable and correctional in-stitutions was picked up by the media and carried nationwide.

Despite society's embrace of progressivism with its attendant exposés and remedies, a number of local newspapers argued that such informa-tion should have been suppressed and decried Missouri's public humilia-tion. One "prominent public official," destined for higher office, publicly told professors at the university to leave if they didn't like the state. Recall-ing the affair decades later, Ellwood argued that challenges to academic freedom were not the property of the postwar generation alone.

Fortunately, neither President Jesse nor the curators were intimidated by the controversy and instead urged that the investigation proceed, as-suring full dissemination of the findings. The result was two university bulletins on conditions in the respective institutions, both of which were widely circulated to various boards, academic libraries, and selected so-cial workers. All that led to Ellwood accepting an invitation to speak to the National Conference of Charities and Corrections in Atlanta in May 1906. Even if the investigation led to no corrective legislation, the whole business revealed not only the zeal of a young and aggressive sociology department but also the integrity of a university administration unwill-ing to be cowed by public pressure. Two decades later Ellwood's depart-ment again found itself in controversy, this time over race. In early 1925 a young instructor, Herbert Blumer, gave an informal speech to a small group on what Ellwood called "the negro problem" that got splashed in the press. The Ku Klux Klan, though declining in influence, pressured Stratton Brooks and the Board of Curators to demand the instructor's res-ignation. The faculty stood firm against the pressure even if Brooks didn't, and the incident passed. There were lessons to be learned in such contro-versies. Ironically, Ellwood said in 1927 that following the race incident, "the department has not been troubled by outside interference."[35]

8

Among the research methods of choice for generating usable sociological data was the questionnaire. Americans in the 1920s were awash in questionnaires, which burst into the national consciousness when they were given to every male subject to the draft in the world war. Early on nobody even knew for sure whether "questionnaire" had a single "n" or two. Prepared well or poorly, most questionnaires raised no attention at all, and many were simply tools for forgettable research projects. One wag even publicized a "questionnaire" that allegedly surfaced in connection with the formation of a bicycle club in the university's School of Journalism and which spoofed the sex questionnaire controversy. The club had but one bicycle for its 160 cub reporters—"strong communist tendencies"—so a questionnaire asked some pointed questions of its users:

1. Do you think it degrading for a boy to ride a girl's bicycle?
2. Do you prefer a masculine or a feminine bicycle?
3. If both boys and girls pay for the bicycle, do you think it good form for the girl to ride on the handle bars?
4. Would you ride on a bicycle that ever had a flat tire?

Such spoofs were inevitable, but a few questionnaires managed to raise eyebrows and generate controversy. One reportedly very explicit sex questionnaire surfaced at Pennsylvania's Bucknell University in 1926, others at Union Theological Seminary and Columbia University in New York, and still others elsewhere.

Until Hobart Mowrer's questionnaire at Missouri, however, none had created more controversy than one at Smith College in Northampton, Massachusetts, a member of the so-called Seven Sister colleges. Subliminal stories about some kind of questionnaire given to Smith girls made the rounds for years. In 1927, for example, a member of the National Security League spoke in Northampton about campus radicalism, including that of Smith professors, and about a questionnaire asking about companion marriage, out-of-wedlock children, and the like. "If I gave you the lowdown of some of the college professors in this city, things that they stand for, too immoral to circulate," he said, "I am sure you would drive them out of town before the clocks struck midnight tonight."

Such attacks on colleges and universities proliferated in the 1920s, paralleling changing attitudes toward sexuality and fears of postwar radical ideas pervading the classroom. After two Smith students disappeared with hardly a trace, one in 1925, another in 1928, probably drowning victims, officers of the alumnae association dispatched a letter to the sisterhood clearing the air about wild allegations of goings-on at the college, including dark charges that President William A. Neilson wasn't even an American citizen (he was). The facts about the notorious questionnaire, said the alumnae officers, were these: back in the 1924–1925 school year, some senior students in an advanced sociology section gave a questionnaire to themselves. President Neilson didn't learn of it for months, and when he did he disapproved; the professor in whose class the incident occurred regretted allowing it and gave assurance that such would not happen again. "It would have been a dead issue at the college long ago," they said, "if certain organizations had not kept it alive by sending thousands of copies through the mails accompanied by distorted and misleading statements as to its origin and use."

Noting the sisters' public plea, the *New York Times* rejected the notion that high school and college campuses were "Sodoms," and agreed with the point of Miriam Van Waters's *Parents on Probation*, which blamed elders for thinking the worst about the young. Drinking and sexual misbehavior were not as rampant as widespread rumors claimed, and empirical analysis in one community showed it: "All the ugly stories of habitual drunkenness and wild living were 'utterly without foundation.' "[36]

Meanwhile, the department of sociology at Missouri that had commenced with thirty students in 1900 swelled to more than five hundred each semester in the 1910s and to almost seven hundred each semester in 1926–1927. Two hundred more took courses in the summer. At the outset Ellwood stood by himself, but by 1927 there were three sociologists in the department and four more in rural sociology within the College of Agriculture. That didn't include a variety of graduates, fellows, assistants, and adjuncts. In 1900 the catalog boasted nine courses, though the department taught only five; in the mid-twenties, there were more than twenty-five classes, all taught. Ellwood believed the faculty was "considerably strengthened" in 1926 with the arrival of Professor Harmon Opdyke DeGraff, a forty-year-old, newly minted Ph.D. from the University of Chicago. DeGraff's responsibilities guaranteed wide student exposure since they included General Sociology with its large enrollments each semester.[37] He also took over the Family course and immediately turned it into a talked-about campus experience. Questionnaires became a staple of students in their class projects, and it was only a matter of time until one of them crossed the line of perceived propriety and frightened Missouri's public about what was going in their university and in American society. In the spring of 1929 that time had come.

4

Inquisition

> A flourishing middle western village and a modern State University have assumed the aspect of a medieval monastery overnight with a youthful Savanarola and an elderly Galileo as the objects of an inquisition fully as deadly as any persecution of the middle ages.
>
> —*Missouri Student*, March 19, 1929

> The Inquisition is with us again in the twentieth century.
>
> —*Savitar*, 1929

For one awful week in mid-March 1929, an air of inevitability gripped the state of Missouri and its columned university. The three curators who constituted the Executive Board of the full Board of Curators converged upon Columbia on March 19 for their rendezvous with President Brooks, two local townsmen, seven students, and five members of the faculty. There were no kleig lights, but inquisition was in the air as they assembled in the president's office in Jesse Hall. One might only imagine what the late President Richard Jesse might have made of the spectacle taking place in the building that bore his name. After all, he had thought that a sociology department which didn't stir things up a bit wasn't doing its job. And Max Meyer, now on the short end of his career, had been one of his star recruits in Mizzou's "Golden Age."

Board members Mercer Arnold, a Joplin attorney, and Frank M. McDavid, also a lawyer and a former state senator from Springfield, arrived in Columbia by early afternoon on Tuesday. The scheduled 2 P.M. meeting was pushed back an hour to accommodate the late arrival of board member H. J. "Jack" Blanton, a newspaper editor from Monroe County.[1]

2

Two Ozark lawyers and a country editor would decide what to do next. But Missouri was no isolated backwater. Since its territorial days Missouri had looked outward, from its fur traders who plied the great river to the northwest, to the merchants who looked to Santa Fe for lucrative exchange, to the agricultural exporters who reached out from central Missouri's "Little Dixie" where slavery, hemp, and tobacco flourished before the Civil War and livestock production after. The Ozarks, however, were a place where folkways and suspicion of outsiders dominated, and the region stood aloof from the flow of Missouri's commerce and intellectual life. If, on the verge of America's plunge toward urban industrialism, Mark Twain had enshrined the virtues of small-town Missouri in the American imagination with *Tom Sawyer* and *The Adventures of Huckleberry Finn*, the hollows and gentle mountains of the Ozark backcountry had been celebrated in *The Shepherd of the Hills*, Harold Bell Wright's wildly successful 1907 novel heralding the region as a place of renewal while warning of the dangers of encroaching modernity.

Missouri as a whole stood near the epicenter of sectional strife in the nineteenth century, but, though torn by Civil War, it remained in the Union. Its urban progressivism at the turn of the twentieth century was real, but tradition and folkways persisted, determining much of the cultural and political landscape. The mutual contempt of cross-state rivals St. Louis and Kansas City increased the political potency of the rest of the state, including Little Dixie, the Ozarks plateau, the Bootheel in the southeast, and the prairies of western and northwestern Missouri. That potency was often displayed in the legislature. But like America itself in the 1920s, Missouri was a mixture of continuity and change, fertile ground for cultural conflict.[2] There was no better place for such conflict than at the state's flagship institution of higher learning, smack in the middle of Little Dixie.

3

All eyes were on Columbia. Few could have been surprised at a report on Tuesday in the *St. Louis Star*, true or not, that each of the three members of the Executive Board had told President Brooks they favored ousting all faculty with complicity in the questionnaire's circulation. The same day, a mysterious report floated out of Jefferson City that the state attorney general's office had been investigating the questionnaire issue. Also, for whatever reason, the Rev. Earl Blackmon, the so-called fighting parson from Kansas City, dispatched his own watchdog to Columbia to observe the proceedings.

Actually, the whole state of Missouri awaited the outcome, as did four thousand students in Columbia; only the more naive among them could reasonably hope it would have a happy ending. Nonetheless, that morning several students offered petitions to President Brooks, who promised they would be presented to the curators. One petition supposedly measured eighteen feet, and all of them boasted more than eleven hundred names. And Chi Omega sorority had felt the heat from their early protest against the questionnaire. At their chapter meeting Monday evening, members of the sorority signed the general student petition favoring retention of the professors—something their earlier statement had favored all along. Even an officer of the Women's Christian Temperance Union on Tuesday claimed its members who had attended DeGraff's Family class the day before had done so on their own, without any representation or authorization from the organization. Word also came from the Linwood Boulevard Christian Church in Kansas City that their pastor, Rev. B. A. Jenkins, whose Sunday evening message was on divorce, had read the questionnaire to his large flock and defended its authors. Kansas City's All Souls Unitarian Church went one better. Its pastor, Rev. L. M. Birkhead, polled his liberal congregation, which unanimously opposed expulsion and then approved dispatching a telegram to Frank McDavid, Executive Board president, urging a halt to the investigation. That stood in contrast to Representative William Freeland of Taney County, majority floor leader, who charged on Tuesday that the questionnaire was "sewer psychology," a reminder that the legislature, momentarily awaiting action by the curators, hadn't gone away. "If a college professor wishes to organize a class in 'sewer psychology,'" he argued, "the Legislature has not only the right, but a duty, to say whether public funds may be used for such a purpose." That same principle would apply if the class was in arson, anarchy, or treason, he said, and the questionnaire issue was even more serious than that. But on Tuesday also the United Press reported that "a sharply-worded" editorial in *Student Life*, the official student paper of Washington University in St. Louis, feared, like so many others, the linking of Missouri with the intolerance of Tennessee's lawmakers, and begged its legislature to leave its sister institution alone. The paper scored the public and its legislators for always looking to verify long-held suspicions about the immorality of American college students.[3]

The curators, meeting in the president's office in Columbia, were in for a long day. They transacted normal business, then turned to the questionnaire issue. Executive president Frank McDavid asked most of the questions, although Mercer Arnold posed a few and, on very rare occasions, Jack Blanton joined in. North Todd Gentry led the parade, with McDavid wanting to know what he knew, and whether or not he knew of others who might be called in. As it turned out, Gentry didn't have much firsthand information, and his appearance before the curators was brief. His sleuthing had revealed that the infamous questionnaire had been produced locally by Herald Statesman printers "and paid for by a gentleman named MOWRER." He knew "nothing personally about this Bureau of Personnel Research"; he had heard that Professor DeGraff was a member, but didn't know for sure. Such misinformation by a former attorney general and state supreme court justice was embarrassing, and one might wonder if Gentry's prestige and known bias got him on the witness list in the first place. As for his petition, he had mostly carried it around himself, had several hundred signatures, and had been turned down only twice. Dr. J. B. Cole followed Gentry, with McDavid asking the physician what he knew directly, not hearsay, about the origins of the petition. Dr. Cole didn't know anything about that either, but wanted to talk about how he found out about the questionnaire in the press, had been aroused by Chi Omega's protest, and how because he didn't think local men should shoulder "all the responsibility of the University," he developed a petition to get women involved as well. Cole seemed to think of the university as a local affair. In any event, he thought one function of the petition would be to generate an investigation of the questionnaire mess.[4]

The two locals hadn't been much help; maybe the students would be better. Alexander Heiken, a senior journalism student from St. Louis, led off, presenting a petition with about six or seven hundred names favoring retention of the professors. Heiken, who had taken DeGraff's Family class the previous year, believed the questionnaire had been misunderstood, and that in fact it was scientific. McDavid grilled Heiken on how it could be misunderstood: "Do you approve of a professor or anybody connected with the University sending to any one a miscellaneous questionnaire asking these specific questions concerning sex[?]" Was it proper to send it to girls?

"A. I can only answer qualifiedly.
"Q. Answer directly.
"A. I cannot answer that 'yes' or 'no.'
"Q. You have said this questionnaire has been perverted, misunderstood. It could not be perverted—could not be misunderstood.
"A. According to who read the question.
"Q. You understand this to mean just what it inquired about?

"A. I do not know sir.

"Q. You look like a pretty intelligent fellow. You tell the Board you signed this petition and circulated it. We want to be perfectly fair!"

McDavid may have wanted to be fair, but his badgering and patronizing had an inquisitor's tone about it. No, Heiken didn't approve everything in the questionnaire, he said. But its purpose was still scientific, he believed, and those behind it were sincere. Heiken refused to answer whether he approved the questionnaire's purpose.

"Q. Would you ask a young lady these questions—yourself?

"A. If she had no objection.

"Q. Would you ask her first if she had objections?

"A. I do not know, sir.

"Q. Do you have a sister?

"A. A small sister—five years old.

"Q. Do you think that a question of that kind should be asked a young lady whether it is done personally or anonymously?

"A. It all depends on the case.

"Q. Take 500 girls who are not given any choice. Do you think it ought to be asked indiscriminately[?]

"A. They have their choice in answering.

"Q. Who gave them their choice? Don[']t you think it would be a piece of impertinence for an individual to ask such a question of any young lady?

"A. I do not know. I do not think you can generalize it.

"Q. Is it not the purpose to get a better understanding of the moral tone?

"A. Perhaps you had better ask the people who sent the questionnaire.

"Q. As one of the circulators of this petition, express student opinion as to whether you think a question of that kind asked of any particular lady friend of your acquaintance would be impertinent.

"A. I think that would rest with the young lady.

"Q. Would you first ask the question and then find out her reaction[?]

"A. I do not know—I have never been placed in that situation.

"Q. Would you personally, as a gentleman, ask a respectable young lady a question of that kind?

"A. I do not know, because I have not been faced with this situation."

Confusing an impersonal and anonymous questionnaire with a face-to-face individual questioning of a lady friend constituted a serious error in logic, of course, but no matter. Attorney McDavid's fierce defense of womanhood's purity surfaced more than once during the whole affair. But for now he also wanted to know who had gotten up Heiken's petition, and who had written its preamble—might there be any nonstudents involved? Implicitly, might any faculty be behind it? It was spontaneous, said Heiken, and several had a hand in drafting its preamble.

Did the petition indicate approval of the questionnaire?

"A. Approval was not involved.
"Q. Do you think the general public might interpret it that way?
"A. I do not know what the public approves."[5]

Heiken was excused. Next was Lucille Dorff, a twenty-one-year-old journalism student from Dallas, Texas, who was a member of DeGraff's class in the Family. Senator McDavid read her petition, signed by every member of the class, she said, except ten. As an added bonus to her testimony, she had gotten a questionnaire herself. McDavid wanted to know if she appeared before the board to indicate her approval of the questionnaire, or did she merely wish to support those behind it? Primarily, she said, "to uphold the sincerity of the people who prepared it." McDavid, a gentleman, wouldn't subject her to an unchivalrous specific examination about the document's questions. Dorff brushed the chivalry aside and said she didn't mind. Her mother was "very broad-minded" and Lucille, having read all the questions, had no personal objections.

"Q. Do you approve of them?
"A. I do not know. None of them insulted me or any of my girl friends, and I have many girl friends. The questions may have been ill-advised, but certainly not insulting[.]
"Q. Why ill-advised?
"A. Ill-advised because it was made public and may affect legislative appropriations. But it was a not a political matter with us.
"Q. I hope not, it is not a political matter with us."

When Dorff lamented, "This is one of the things that makes us all feel that a mountain may be made out of a molehill," McDavid retorted: "Dismiss that from your mind."

McDavid's staple repartee usually turned on the insult to girls receiving the questionnaire, and whether or not the student approved all the questions on the document or just supported those involved. The students pleaded for the sincerity of those developing the questionnaire as well as its scientific value. For her part, Dorff stood her ground and gave little quarter, and McDavid applauded her forthrightness but made it clear his mind was made up on the whole questionnaire business. Like most students, Miss Dorff remained quite conservative; she defended traditional marriage and Professor DeGraff's desire to see it improved. She also wanted to see the inaccuracies swirling around him corrected, such as the media story alleging he had joined a circus to research sociological material.[6]

When Dorff was excused, Dr. Cole reappeared, leaving the women's petition he had forgotten. Jack Turner, a junior journalism student, was next in line, bringing his own student petition containing about five hundred names. McDavid posed the same litany of questions about asking girls intimate things. The senator couldn't seem to get clear the difference between a purportedly scientific inquiry using a questionnaire and a personal—even intemperate—question asked by a young man to a young lady. Young Turner didn't make that mistake. McDavid abruptly diverted his questioning: "Where are you from[?]" he asked.

> "A. Texas.
> "Q. How long do you think a man would last in Texas who sent out 500 of these questionnaires to women in Texas? How many bullet holes would be in him before night?
> "A. I have not been in Texas for the last five years."[7]

If McDavid's fellow curators didn't blanch at such questions, they should have. McDavid claimed they were trying to find the questionnaire's source but he seemed immune to alternate views on its value. Nor could he get past what he genuinely thought were inappropriate questions for "girls," as he called the female recipients.

Maybe Hobart Mowrer could help. The twenty-two-year-old told the investigators that he had drafted the original version of the questionnaire and submitted it to both his committee and various faculty members. The committee had debated several methods of investigation on their topic of women's economic independence before deciding on the use of questionnaires. Mowrer had several discussions with Professor Max Meyer, who was both Mowrer's mentor and chairman of the psychology department. Meyer played the normal role of instructor—criticizing, suggesting, improving—but apparently never questioning the general propriety of the whole thing. Each questionnaire, one male, one female, went through about half a dozen rewrites, with both Meyer and DeGraff urging that the questions be less opinion-oriented and more "yes"-and-"no" specific. It turned out that part of question three about illicit sexual relations was suggested by Russell Bauder, an instructor in economics in the College of Business and Public Administration. Mowrer agreed, with Meyer then suggesting a subdivision of the same question. Before the questionnaire went out, Professor Jesse Wrench in the history department had seen it, as had Meyer and DeGraff; Bauder didn't see the final version, but Dorothy Postle, an assistant instructor in psychology, had some unclear role in question three. Mowrer couldn't remember specific roles in the development of that question.

Only naïveté prevented Mowrer from realizing what the curators could reasonably expect: out of all the questionnaires mailed, didn't Mowrer expect one would find its way to a newspaper office? No. Mowrer guessed that most were mailed—about seven hundred of the thousand prepared. Others were hand-delivered to friends by committee members who had used the student directory to select recipients at random. McDavid pressed the issue of sending out question three to students who had no connection with the study. Mowrer took the same position as others: there was no obligation for recipients to answer. Would he ask it of a girlfriend? Mowrer wouldn't say.

"Q. Do you make a distinction between asking thru the mail and personally?
"A. I really fail to see the point of that question.
"Q. I am to be the judge of the point.
"A. I refuse to answer.
"Q. The only interest we have in this investigation is as to the University. We do not want to be unfair—we want you at the same time to be fair with the Board. You had some reason for sending this questionnaire out. I am trying to get your reaction. You decline to answer it.
"A. As I understand your question, it was not as to my motive for sending out this questionnaire.
"Q. You understood when you sent this that you had the final approval of Dr. DeGraff and from Dr. Meyer?
"A. Yes."

One of the nagging issues about the questionnaire was how an inquiry into "A sociological study of the effect of the economic independence of women on married life" had drifted into matters of sex. Mowrer explained that he wanted to find out what impact the trend toward women's economic independence had on society, morality, and marriage and the family. That's what he had in mind when he drafted the questionnaire in the first place. The committee proved pliable, had not questioned the relevance of the questionnaire, and since Mowrer bore the expense of producing and mailing the document had acceded to his request that he have exclusive rights to the material for his later use. In all, the project cost more than fifty-five dollars: twenty-nine dollars for printing and $22.66 for a thousand prestamped envelopes, plus three dollars for adding the return address. That's where the infamous "Bureau of Personnel Research" came in. Professor Meyer had some old envelopes from an agency that Mowrer wrongly thought was still part of the psychology department's special testing. President Brooks interjected that in 1925 Meyer chaired the Committee on Personnel Research and Vocational Guidance but that he, Brooks, had dissolved the committee later that year. The only tangible legacy of the defunct committee were all those envelopes with "Bureau of Personnel Research" on them. Since the envelopes were no longer of any value, Meyer offered them to Mowrer to save return postage.

Some of Mowrer's views would have easily marked him as a radical. But such ideas flowed from a developing young man with a probing mind. Mowrer's youthful naïveté may have prompted McDavid to unexpectedly ask his age, year in school, and whether he or someone else was paying for his schooling. Other questions ran the gamut. Mowrer defended the preamble's indictment of marriage as well as the first three questions. He thought about whether or not to include question three on sexual relations but deemed it had relevance; no one ever cautioned him about the decency of the questions nor did adverse parental reaction occur to any of them. Rising divorce rates validated his view that family life was falling apart, and that "irrational" sentiment flowed from religious dogmas. Mowrer claimed high ideals, but believed traditional marriage shouldn't be maintained if it enslaved humanity rather than served it. And yes, issues of sex had been frankly discussed in DeGraff's class, but not often.[8]

Another member of Mowrer's committee, Howell Williams, followed him to the witness chair. A junior in arts and science and journalism, Williams had already logged five credits under DeGraff, and took the Family because of his interest in both the instructor and the subject. He agreed that the questionnaire was designed to assess the impact of economics on moral standards. Mowrer did most of the work, with Williams helping more than any of the other members; in fact, Alberta Davis was least involved although they wanted her to look over the questionnaire "to get the women's view." According to Williams, it never occurred to any of them that the questions might be in bad taste. As far as he knew, DeGraff saw no impropriety in the questions and, frankly, Williams's committee thought they were no more important than the two dozen or more other committees in the class.

McDavid repeatedly pressed the issue of scientific value, particularly the relevance of the first three questions to the issue of women's economic independence. To Williams that seemed clear, with question one on illicit sexual behavior related to a single moral standard in which a woman "would not have to depend on her sex nature for her very livelihood." The second question gauged attitudes of respondents toward those of their own sex engaged in certain behaviors, and the third sought to discover what restrained people in their intimate relationships, how childhood and adolescent behavior impacted later attitudes. "Perhaps a person who had indulged in sex irregularities would or would not wish to have economic independence. We included this question to see if such a thing existed."

Whether or not that made any sense to McDavid and his colleagues is aside from a larger issue. Here was the specter of a nonacademic governing board not merely inquiring into the scientific value and procedure of academic work but also perhaps censuring such work. The board seemed unrestrained in probing the matter, something that would later bring them grief. Such administrative arrogance even prompted McDavid to press students, including Williams, about the efficacy of the selection process. Why indiscriminate polling? Why not survey statewide? Did DeGraff think it was scientific? And why the prejudicial preamble letter about the breakdown of the institution of marriage?

Williams wouldn't speak for Mowrer's motives about the introductory letter, but the recipients were handy and, yes, there was clear "dissatisfaction" with marriage.

> "Q. You would not believe in free love?
>
> "A. I think that in the institution of marriage at the present time there is something wrong.
>
> "Q. As we understand it, the institution of marriage is an agreement between one man and one woman, generally solemnized by a minister of religion. Are we to understand that you believe in an arrangement by which one man married several women, or one woman married several [men], by which they lived together without any marriage ceremony? Tell the Board just what your committee had in mind.
>
> "A. So far as my own personal views are concerned, I believe that monogamy is the best type, but it does seem that in individual cases things are wrong and that people might solve their problems and make a better arrangement. That would be the case of the individual.

"Q. Has it been suggested in your class in 'The Family' that
there was such a breakdown in the marriage relations as to become
alarming and needing a change in the scheme?

"A. I am expressing only my views. Dr. DeGraff in his delivery
is very conservative. Many times we disagree with him because
we think he is a little too moralizing.

"Q. Some of you are broader-minded?

"A. While young, our ideas are rather uncertain. We do not have
the stability that Dr. DeGraff has."

Williams got the standard questions. Didn't they know this questionnaire would become public? No, and in fact, sex wasn't the big issue with
the committee anyway. Didn't they contemplate injury to the university?
No again. This was a sociological inquiry, and they didn't foresee any
unfortunate results accruing to the university. They all admired Professor
DeGraff both as a person and as an instructor, said Williams, and they
found his teaching stimulating and not harmful at all.

Attempts to implicate Professor DeGraff in radical theories, suggestive
doctrines, or dangerous influences on the children of Missouri uniformly
failed. In the final analysis, his greatest sin, indeed his only sin, lay in not
halting such pernicious activities of those under his charge. It seems not
to have occurred to the Executive Board the dampening effect the present
spectacle might have on academic inquiry at the University of Missouri.
Williams was excused.[9]

The remaining two members of Mowrer's committee stood on the periphery of the questionnaire and made brief appearances. Alberta Davis,
a nineteen-year-old from Kansas City, was the only female on the committee. Her father, a Kansas City physician, had angrily written President Brooks demanding ouster of those responsible, only to reverse himself days later—obviously after learning his own daughter was on the
committee. He needn't have worried. Alberta's fingerprints on the document were few. She joined the class more than a week late after dropping
another class and picking up the Family. She likewise joined Mowrer's
committee late, after the economic emancipation topic had been selected,
and then attended committee meetings sporadically after that. She even
missed an important discussion session. A week before the first questionnaires went in the mail, they all went over it. She thought the recipients
should not be chosen at random nor did she think the first three questions were relevant to the topic. She raised such issues but didn't object.
In fact, she seemed to be along for the ride, and she typed addresses on
only twenty or thirty envelopes.[10]

Clarence Ferguson also stood a bit aloof from the goings-on. A thirty-three-year-old married graduate student from New Lenox, Illinois, near Chicago, he hadn't really gone over the questionnaire. "I figured this way—," he said, "if bigger men than I am passed on them, there could be nothing wrong, and I understood there were some of the instructors around."

> "Q. As a married man did you not see enough in the first three questions particularly to arouse in you some feeling of repugnance?
> "A. I thought maybe I was behind the times."

The board, again undeterred in its intrusion into both the propriety of the course's activities but also its relevance, asked how all this knowledge would apply to Ferguson's work when he graduated. He could use it in teaching, he said, in cooperative extension, home demonstration, and in the schools.[11]

Student witnesses were only a warm-up for the main event: the examination of the faculty. First up was Russell Bauder, fairly new on campus as an instructor in economics, having come from the University of Wisconsin in the spring semester of 1927. Still in his twenties and not very much older than those in his classes, Bauder was a pleasant fellow, easy to know, and socialized with students. If he had any fear for his position it didn't show. "Well," he told the board, "I was invited to attend a social dinner of the fraternity in which one of the students making this investigation is a member, a man whom I have known to be a capable and serious student. After dinner he asked me whether I had any knowledge concerning the making out of questionnaires and asked if I would help him in this particular set of questions. I am an economist—not a sociologist. I know however that the formation of a questionnaire is a difficult thing because the questions have to be so stated that the answers may be tabulated. I looked these questionnaires over and made some suggestion as to re-phrasing."

Bauder didn't have anything to do with the first three questions, nothing materially anyway.

> "Q. Do you approve them as they stand?
> "A. I am not a sociologist. I only re-phrased them."

But what was his reaction to such material "being sent out indiscriminately to young men and young women in this University?" That wasn't the issue, he replied. He was concerned with phrasing, and there could be no ambiguity in wording. McDavid again pressed the propriety of such material being sent out. Didn't Bauder think it improper? Yes, it occurred to him, but that wasn't his place. But wouldn't he be interested in content, not merely form? "Not necessarily." But then why did he agree to look it over?

> "A. I have friends, and when a friend requests me to help him I am accustomed to do so if I can. I do not consider that anything I did was as a member of the faculty. It was during a social engagement. I was merely asked to do a favor—and complied.
> "Q. You did not have any thought at all as to the content of the questionnaire?
> "A. It seems to be the kind of thing that is being done. I have read in Harpers concerning questionnaires. And I have been very much interested in noting in Current History that the church has also begun an investigation into the institution of marriage. Since so many people are making such investigations, I supposed it was not up to me." [12]

Bauder was right about questionnaires. In fact, one wonders if the Progressive era's commitment to uplift and efficiency, to the rise and professionalization of the social sciences before the Great War, was not reflected in the 1920s' obsession with "scientific" inquiry into society's motivations and behavior. The questionnaire was a means to the end, and questionnaires littered the decade. Inquiry that was random within a given group, inquiry that probed things regarded as personal, even intimate, could come close to the line of social propriety. In fact, in an age of transition, it's no surprise at all that some, a good many indeed, believed the line had been crossed. Given the dynamics of the decade, it was only a matter of time.

Like Bauder's appearance, that of Dorothy Postle, an assistant instructor in psychology, was brief. She too was asked by Mowrer to look the thing over, and she also made suggestions about a comma here or there, but nothing about content. She didn't know anything about distribution, and couldn't remember whether that part of the third question relating to sexual relations was in the document she reviewed. Mowrer had told her he was investigating attitudes about marriage "—this thing started by Judge Lindsey." And no, she didn't see the relevance of question three to the independence of women. But nothing surprised her. "I was not shocked with the questionnaire when he showed it to me. I have seen questionnaires that are far more personal than that. I have been in courses and have always worked with girls, and we were more or less wont to speak of those things frankly. I have seen questionnaires that were sent out to social workers but not to students. Not to freshmen and sopho- mores."[13]

Jesse Wrench, Harmon DeGraff, and Max Meyer were next. Wrench's name had been tossed around in the press and on campus. Since he was involved with students generally, it was no surprise that he got caught up in this issue. The curators wanted to know what he knew about the questionnaire's preparation and distribution. Wrench served as adviser to Mowrer's fraternity, and early in the semester the pair had discussed the topic, including the use of questionnaires. They even routed through some magazines in the university library. Mowrer occasionally advised Wrench of his progress. "Finally one day," said Wrench, "he brought it down to me to look it over. He asked me if I thought anything should be added and I said it looked kind of strong." Mowrer told him he wanted anonymity, and thought they might use "bureau" or "committee" to a- chieve it. Wrench didn't recall much about the questionnaire, didn't give it complete attention: "I have plenty of my own troubles." Because it was under another professor, Wrench didn't want "to pass judgment" on the document when Mowrer brought it to him. Mowrer was "one of those cu- rious cases," said Wrench, "—played around for several years and then discovered there was something worth studying. He has since been get- ting down to business and working hard. They 'kid' him around the [fra- ternity] house about holding lectures at the dinner table."

McDavid asked Wrench to look over the first three questions.

> "Q. Pretty intimate sort of questions?
> "A. Yes, but from a scientific standpoint I cannot see that there is anything extraordinary about the thing. But in this day and age young people are fairly frank in their ordinary conversation.
> "Q. Bearing in mind the situation this faces, and the duty we owe to the public, what would be your idea as to the effect of ques- tions like that, calling for answers as are called for, if they fall into the hands of fathers and mothers in this State.
> "A. Hard to say, because I have so many reactions from fathers and mothers in the State that my judgment would not be clear at the present time. In a good many cases, girls have sent these questionnaires home and parents have written back 'What is all the excitement about?'

"Q. Have you received some communications from parents approving.
"A. Yes—unsolicited."[14]

The board had recessed over the supper hour even before it began its
inquisition of students, but after they reassembled the evening wore on.
For obvious reasons they lingered longest, about an hour and a half, with
Professor DeGraff, under whose charge the whole thing had exploded.
After a few preliminaries, the board let him speak.

DeGraff explained the procedure of his course in the Family, how
groups of four students formed committees, each with wide latitude to
develop a topic for a term paper, and that how the committees formed,
whether through acquaintances or common interests, was left to the students, as were the methodologies they employed. DeGraff approved the
use of a questionnaire for Mowrer's group and told Mowrer to bring it
to him when it was ready so they could look it over together. Mowrer
later reported that Professor Meyer would grant credit toward graduation with distinction in his major of psychology if a satisfactory subject
could be developed. That was fine with DeGraff. He thought the resultant
questionnaire was actually in two parts, one part dealing with Mowrer's
work toward graduation with distinction in psychology, the other for his
paper in sociology. DeGraff thought the expense for postage, about ten
dollars per committee member, was steep, that it made for an expensive
term paper. Some days later Mowrer reported that the postage expense
was taken care of because Meyer made the defunct "Bureau of Personnel Research" envelopes available. "The questionnaire was sent out and
I knew nothing more about the matter," said DeGraff. "Parties reported
once or twice that they were coming in—until last Wednesday when the
break came. So far as I am concerned it came out of a clear sky. This is
the situation as far as I am concerned. I am in no way attempting to shift
responsibility."

DeGraff thought the questionnaire had two things going at once, one
for Mowrer's work with Meyer, the other for the Family. That's what he
thought until Sunday, March 17, when Eugene Morgan, professor of rural
sociology, talked things over with him, and then, that same day, conferred
with Mowrer in DeGraff's office in Jesse Hall. The three of them carefully
reviewed the questionnaire. What part was for Meyer, and what part was
for the class in the Family? Mowrer said it was all for DeGraff's class.
Well, that changed things. Though DeGraff saw no relevance of the first
question to the topic, nor much for the third one either, he said that he
would assume full responsibility. In fact, he admitted to the board that

he had slipped up on the issue of random distribution. He offered no ex-
cuses, and didn't know why he had not dealt with that issue, unless it was
because of the divided nature of the project. "The thing did not dawn on
me," he said, "until last Sunday morning—that was the situation. I do
not want you to think that I am trying to shift this at all. I do not want the
blame to fall upon any one else because this all came out of my class in
the family."

What emerged from DeGraff's testimony is that because Mowrer was
straddling two disciplines, working two angles at once, and that the questionnaire ostensibly was doing double-duty, that responsibility was likewise divided. That led to the "mix-up," as DeGraff called it.

> "Did it not strike you in reading those first three questions that to
> a large measure very bad taste was shown in sending them out to
> a large number of young men and women?
> "A. No, it did not, for this reason. In the contacts with the young
> people on a university campus the conversation about matters of
> sex and about the relationships is not nearly so unrestrained as it
> is out in the State, and these young people talk about these things
> very frankly—more so than people on the outside.
> "Q. Is there any distinction between those who approve and
> those who disapprove?
> "A. I have not talked with very many of the students about how
> they felt about this thing, except as they voluntarily came to me
> and there was not any feeling of that sort. I do not believe I was ap-
> proached on the way this thing had been received, until it 'broke'
> last week."

At that point, Mercer Arnold announced that he hadn't seen the questionnaire until that very day. That in itself should have been a shocker, that
a member of the board of inquisitors would pass on matters of importance
in such a short time after seeing the document. In any case, as an alumnus of Missouri, he felt he knew with what freedom students discussed
such matters a generation or so ago. "I have a daughter who is not in this
school," said Arnold. "It seems to me that if my daughter received a paper
sent anonymously thru the mail, no matter what bureau name might be
signed to it, asking questions of that sort, I would resent it as a piece of
impudence more or less insulting in its nature because of the implication
which must necessarily follow when a woman is asked a question of that
kind, and it seems to me that would have been the reaction of any one
reading the questionnaire."

"A. Well, I thought those things thru to a certain extent. I perhaps should have talked with Professor Meyer and some other people, but my reaction was that when this young man told me he had taken this up with Dr. Meyer and people of that type, my feeling was that those were men of judgment and in the department of psychology who were more able to judge than I am.

"Q. Did you ever talk with Dr. Meyer about this?

"A. No."

The inquiry eventually turned to companionate marriage, a source of consternation to the traditionalists of the 1920s. Ben Lindsey, the judge in Colorado, had spoken and written of it, and it became the subject of discussion in the university. Would not a university sociology course on the American family that avoided the subject constitute a dereliction of professional duty on the part of those responsible? The difficulty for the University of Missouri in 1929 was that curators wanted to tamper with the classroom not merely on grounds of public propriety but also on the scientific value of that instruction. It became clear in the hearing that one or more members of the Executive Board simply didn't want certain issues discussed in the university classroom. They didn't even want students thinking or talking about such controversial issues.

The Executive Board examined Professor DeGraff on the matter of companionate marriage. He made his position clear: "In my course in 'The Family,'" he told the board, "we do not advocate trial marriage or companionate marriage. In the papers, I understand I have been quoted as advocating companionate marriage. I am strongly opposed to that sort of thing and in every lecture I have given, I have registered my opposition to it." But weren't those subjects on the list from which students might choose their term paper topics? One was, said DeGraff. "One on companionate marriage and birth control."

"Q. Suppose you knew that some student was going to prepare a document advocating strongly trial marriage. Do you think that is a good thing to have in this school or anywhere else?

"A. I believe this—that if there is any place where a young man or young woman should receive as nearly as it could be given, correct knowledge concerning companionate marriage, trial marriage, etc., it should be in the university. Of the type of companionate marriage, meaning divorce by consent—I have hit those things as hard as I could hit them."

Senator McDavid's response betrayed the huge chasm between the governing curators and the professoriate: "What is the value of the discussion?"

> "A. The value of it is this. In my contacts with the young people of the University, I find that literature and magazines with no rating and some with better rating, may be obtained in which these subjects are played up in the most sensational form. In many cases I do not think these lecturers and writers know what they are talking about. Now I think our young men and young women should be protected against this sort of thing. I think they should know what is really meant by companionate marriage and should know the social dangers which would come to society as a result of such a practice on society.
>
> "Q. Is it your understanding that the way to regulate the irregular things in life concerning relations between the sexes, is first to get them to thinking about it and second to get them talking about it?
>
> "A. No.
>
> "Q. Don['] t you know that talking about it leads to the things you desire to avoid?
>
> "A. My attitude is that if you were to talk to the young men on this campus who have talked with me about these things, it would present a different viewpoint."

McDavid acknowledged DeGraff's value and his great popularity on campus. But he was up against the mothers and fathers of southwest Missouri, where he was from, and they were outraged that their children were subjects of a sexual clinical study. That's what curators had to face. DeGraff replied that he never would use the student body for lab work. For a moment during the hearings, at least one of the curators—it is unclear as to which of the three—seemed to get it. There really wasn't any exploitation here, he said. This was an attempt to help.

Unfortunately, the questioning drifted back to the efficacy of classroom discussions on apparently taboo subjects. Even if DeGraff's opposition to companionate marriage was established, even if his conservative credentials were clear, wouldn't discussions of this sort get students "talking and thinking and deciding in favor of those things?" DeGraff, ignoring the fact that the subject appeared on the approved list he gave to students, said he didn't get them to do that. Students essentially did that themselves. Repeatedly questioned on the issue, DeGraff replied that "Companionate marriage as I understand it is a marriage relationship in which a man and wife are legally married and live in marriage relationship, in which you voluntarily have some sort of birth control. Now the history of the thing goes back to the primitive people. There are three phases, infanticide, abortion, and companionate marriage—as I talk it or teach it to the class in 'The Family.' I oppose companionate marriage. I teach that the purpose of the family is to transmit our civilization to the children and that this purpose of establishing the family group is this transmission to the child."

4

DeGraff didn't say so, but young men and women knew something was amiss in the culture. They knew more divorces littered the cultural landscape than ever before, up more than 6 percent in 1927 alone, according to the Commerce Department. Divorces had topped 100,000 per year before the war, and would reach 205,000 for 1929. Robert and Helen Lynd's *Middletown*, published that same year, found women's economic independence a factor in divorce. One Middletown lawyer claimed, "If a woman has ever worked at all she is much more likely to seek a divorce. It's the timid ones that have never worked who grin and bear marriage." What was acceptable in the 1890s was simply not tolerated in the 1920s. The liberal *Nation* saw no reason for alarm, wanted the stigma removed from divorce, and argued that people were just "more honest" and that "if they honestly and deliberately reach the conclusion that divorce is necessary we believe that the state should help them to part with dignity and friendliness." The magazine even snorted over a committee report of the Federal Council of Churches that condemned companionate marriage and reaffirmed traditional marriage values. "To suggest this supremacy of institutional duty over human happiness to a generation raised on Freud shows surprising—shall we say?—temerity." The *Nation* further ran a series of articles on divorce, one of them, "What is Happening to Marriage?" published the very day the curators back in Jesse Hall rendered their verdict in the sex questionnaire case. Writer Charles Wood argued that the machine age began the institution's downfall, and was the great destroyer of the necessity and dominance of the family. The woman now chose her own mate for a life of wedded bliss, something that didn't work out. "Then," said Wood, "came the automobile and the war, and psychoanalysis and the knowledge of birth control. The automobile made it impossible to chaperon the youngsters any longer. The war destroyed their respect for the alleged wisdom of adults. Psychoanalysis encouraged them to be curious as to matters which had aroused fear and trembling theretofore. The knowledge of birth control completed the revolution. It made virginity a problem to solve instead of a precious mystery to guard. To be sure, the solution has not yet been found, but the younger generation is on its way."

That's what a social liberal thought. But an established Middletown clergyman was sure he knew why there were so many divorces: secular ceremonies without "the sanctity of the churches." The traditional Victorian family's social and economic functions now had outside competition. Amusements, nurturing, education, and the like now challenged the hegemony of the home and family. Liberal Christians seemed prepared to yield societal nurturing to newer outside forces, while conservatives steadfastly regarded the Christian home as the only answer to social disintegration. As one material culture scholar has argued, in the first three decades of the twentieth century "parlor piety came to reflect the general split in American Protestantism." In 1929, Arthur Garfield Hays, a left-wing activist attorney with the American Civil Liberties Union, citing what he thought were outdated divorce laws that worked a genuine hardship on mismatched couples, publicly called for "Companionate Divorce." Meanwhile, Reno, Nevada, retained its distinction as America's premier divorce mill, dropping its residency requirement to just three months.

Everybody knew there was something going on in American society, something frightening and exciting at the same time. In fact, the more one was exposed to the literature of the decade, whether it be H. L. Mencken or Ben Lindsey or Sigmund Freud or F. Scott Fitzgerald or popular magazines (*True-Story*, started in 1919, boasted nearly two million readers by 1926) or, for that matter, to the records in the county courthouse, the less Hobart Mowrer's brash questionnaire preamble about "something seriously wrong with the traditional system of marriage" seemed an effrontery from a precocious youth. The president of Vassar College flatly told *Harpers* readers in 1927 that "The family, as an institution, needs overhauling and repair, or it may break down completely." Noting the rise of divorce in the twenties, Frederick Lewis Allen claimed "There was a corresponding decline in the amount of disgrace accompanying divorce."

Some radicals even forecast the eclipse of marriage before the century was out. One serious book, *What Is Wrong With Marriage?* by psychiatrist Gilbert V. Hamilton and journalist and stage producer Kenneth Macgowan, was published virtually during the Missouri crisis. Even while Hobart Mowrer's completed questionnaires lay unanalyzed in the university vault, one could read the results of Hamilton and Macgowan's questions posed to two hundred married men and women, all living in New York. Generally well educated and well off, the target group was far from those of Mowrer's committee, but the results made interesting reading anyway, and illustrated the persistent inquiry into marriage and family in the 1920s. Some items: lots more women than men thought marriage was in trouble; more than a third in each category would terminate their marriage if they could simply push a button; almost all had employed contraception at some point; those without college educations were more likely to have a successful marriage; women who earned their own living were less satisfied in marriage than those who were dependent; and a mere 29 percent of men and 21 percent of women claimed their marriage was an unqualified success. Noting both the new book by Hamilton and Macgowan and the proliferation of questionnaires since the war, one writer facetiously claimed, "Sex came along after the war, too. Probably it was known before then, but it wasn't talked about. Maybe it came from France. . . . Or from Vienna, along with Sigmund Freud's books on psychoanalysis. Freud said that sexual unrest was at the bottom of a lot of our troubles and ought to be investigated scientifically." He added: "Conservatives said the more you talked about it the worse off you would be and the more people would do the things they read about."

That all sounded familiar. Hamilton and Macgowan weren't worried about marriage, but they remained less sanguine about the repeated failure of parents to nurture their young in a healthy manner. Since the culture corrupted discussions of sex, open and factual approaches to education in the home were required. No less an authority than John B. Watson, the acknowledged founder of behaviorism and a true threat to absolute moral standards, wrote the book's introduction and defended sex questionnaires. "The study of sex is still fraught with danger," he said. Almost prophetic of the Missouri controversy, he added: "It can be openly studied only by individuals who are not connected with universities." But sex was crucial in life, he argued. "And yet our scientific information is so meager. Even the few facts we have must be looked upon as more or less bootleg stuff." [15]

Maybe there was nothing wrong with marriage at all, as Ed Watson at the *Columbia Daily Tribune* argued, but then the problem lay in people themselves, or in a changing culture. But if the family seemed imperiled in modern culture, Professor DeGraff's course didn't promote the notion that it had failed. Not at all. On the contrary, the course, taught by a high-minded traditionalist, was designed to strengthen the traditional family. Victorianism was in its death throes, not tradition.

5

In his summary, DeGraff wanted his interrogators to know he took full responsibility for what went on in his class. "In the two and a half years that I have been here," he said, "the interests of the student body have been the thing that has constituted my whole concern and I would not willingly bring discredit or disgrace upon the student body."[16]

On campus, interest in the proceedings at Jesse Hall grew more intense all afternoon and well into the evening. While the testimony droned on inside the president's office, students milled about in the outer office, filling up the corridors, with others spilling outside. Interest momentarily climaxed about midevening, when several men hoisted a woman up to the sill of an open window of the president's office. From there she relayed DeGraff's testimony verbatim to the eager crowd. After a night watchman discovered the spying and broke it up, the testimony inside resumed.[17]

Finally, after ninety minutes or so of courteous, gentlemanly exchange, Professor DeGraff was through, in more ways than one.

The evening was long, and the only witness remaining was Max Meyer, chairman of the psychology department. In the space of an hour, Meyer was cavalier, combative, and apologetic. He wasn't prepared for what awaited him, and, as one who normally went to bed early, was tired. "On entering," recalled Meyer, "I found the President of the University sitting on my right at the corner of the table, in an attitude rather different from his usual one when he has the whole machinery of the big office table symmetrically in front of him. The next day the idea came to my mind that he had been playing the medieval role of the executioner lurking in the background, for the whole grouping had a stage effect." McDavid sat facing him, with Arnold and Blanton to the left. The secretary of the Board of Curators, Leslie Cowan, sat behind him, and on each flank, "like guardian angels," sat two stenographers.[18]

Meyer said he had been busy with other matters, had paid the questionnaire only the slightest attention, would tell what he knew, and yes, he was versed in the document's contents.

"Q. Do you approve of the questions as set forth?
"A. First tell me what you mean by 'approve.'
"Q. Do you approve the idea of sending a questionnaire of this kind to a miscellaneous group of students, a thousand in number, without regard to the course they were taking, and without regard to ages?
"A. I see nothing wrong in it.

"Q. Will you please give your attention to question 3. [Sections
(a), (b) (c) are read.] You see nothing wrong with that?
"A. With what?
"Q. With the question I have just read.
"A. I do not not see how any question in itself can be wrong.
I think any intelligent person has a perfect right to answer or to
leave it unanswered.
"Q. Do you approve?
"A. I do not know what you mean by 'approve.' "

Meyer acknowledged his mistake about the "Bureau of Personnel Research" envelopes. He had seven or eight hundred left over and wanted
to save the students money. They were worthless anyway, and it wouldn't
cost the university anything. "It seemed perfectly legitimate to offer these
students the old envelopes," he said. "I realize now that I made a mistake,
because these envelopes could easily give the person who wanted to drag
the University into the public for the purpose of defiling it, a chance to say
that this questionnaire was sent out by the University administration." He
just didn't think about it.
     Some details Meyer couldn't recall, and he appealed more than once to
distraction or overwork. Nor could he recall promising Mowrer psychology credit for his work with DeGraff. If he did make such a promise it
was given absentmindedly. But Meyer defended the questionnaire, "that
perhaps it was a serious effort to find out what kind of ideals intellectual
young people in our colleges have with respect to requirements which
they make on other people of the opposite sex, with respect to what ideas
they have about the roles which in the opinion of the young women and
young men in the future would have to play in the economic and general
civic life of the State and Nation." He agreed that sending out the questionnaire randomly could be debated, but had made suggestions about
its wording. If a student in his class had been constructing it, some questions might have been phrased differently or left out altogether. But he
also defended the inclusion of the sexual relationship question from an
interdisciplinary approach. After all, Mowrer was approaching the sociology issue as a psychologist.
     So much for all that. The questioning took a different turn. There was
more than either the public or the campus knew about Meyer's appearance before the Executive Board. Late in the evening, the stenographers
were excused, but Professor Meyer remained, as did President Brooks.
According to Meyer, McDavid's nod to the stenographers "must have
been a prearranged sign," and they left. "And I, still quite naive, thought

everything was over. But it came otherwise, for now I was placed before a tribunal which embodied virtually all the infamous methods of those tribunals common in the sixteenth and seventeenth centuries . . . which are known in history as the procedures of the Inquisition." There was no formal indictment, no confrontation with the accuser, no proper defense, and no "public record." "Of such a medieval brutality," said Meyer later, "I was the victim in the dark hours of the evening of March 19th, 1929, in Columbia, Mo., the 'Athens' of Missouri. However, it is flattering to me that some progressive men of the state recalled that it was also an Athens, in Greece, where Socrates had to drink the poison given him by his superstitious countrymen."

If Meyer flattered himself with such references to Socrates or the Inquisition, it was true that the Executive Board now fell into a sort of executive session. A couple of weeks before the questionnaire scandal went public, Meyer had been subject to administrative scrutiny for a lecture he had given in a class in Social Psychology over several semesters, including the current one. The lecture, given to students preparing primarily for social work, scientifically objectified the biological reflexes involved in insemination during the sex act. To spare women students any embarrassment, Meyer gave the lecture only to them. Apparently, a tabulation handout from the lecture inadvertently fell into other hands and eventually raised administrative eyebrows. Briefly, quietly, and satisfactorily investigated, the matter was thought to be closed by both Meyer and President Brooks. Now, however, it was reopened, albeit behind closed doors and without benefit of stenographers' shorthand. At some juncture during Meyer's testimony, newsmen spying from a monument outside Brooks's office reportedly saw the beleaguered professor throw a book on the table and stalk out of the room.[19]

Whatever happened, when Meyer's testimony had concluded the board privately debated what, if anything, should be done. The consensus favored disciplinary action of some sort, including sanction for Meyer for his Social Psychology lecture. When asked, Brooks said he favored firing both Meyer and DeGraff. More discussion followed, including whether those on the periphery should also be punished; they also debated the Executive Board's authority to deal with the matter or whether this was for the full board alone. By 12:30 A.M., after deciding nothing officially, the board adjourned for eight hours, after which the whole matter was hashed out again. Before noon on March 20 they had decided on not only their course of action but also the specific wording of the statement to be released to the public, something that would soon cause comment around the state and across the nation. The statement constituted a recommendation to the full board and, following by-laws which provided that any three curators could call a meeting of that board, they did so, scheduling it for 9 A.M., April 6, 1929, in Columbia. The Executive Board also authorized the president to release the statement and explain it to the university faculty.[20]

"Whatever a university may be," said the board's official public statement, "it must be a place to which parents may send their children with full confidence that the surrounding moral atmosphere will be sane and wholesome." That was true at the University of Missouri; everything was fine. The suppressed questionnaire resulted from no "morbid or unsatisfactory condition affecting the whole student body." But students were not subjects for experiments, the more so "when such investigation by its very nature tends to create the condition it is alleged to correct." The questionnaire had no scientific validity, and those responsible for it "have a radically mistaken conception of the essential conditions which must prevail in order to establish and maintain public confidence in the university." Despite the abilities of those involved, their usefulness to the university had been "seriously impaired" and they had to be terminated. The result: Max Meyer and Harmon DeGraff were dismissed from the faculty, Hobart Mowrer, while permitted to remain a student, was relieved of his lab assistant duties. The Executive Board merely expressed "regret" that Jesse Wrench and Russell Bauder didn't intervene in the questionnaire's creation and dissemination. Finally, credit would be available for students affected by the faculty dismissals.[21]

That was it. An internationally renowned scholar with nearly three decades of service and one of the most popular and effective professors on campus had been summarily fired by a country editor and two Ozark lawyers. The official statement contained no mention of the Social Psychology lecture. In any case, having committed themselves to some sort of sacrifice on the altar of either public appeasement or more likely their own sense of outrage, the trio of curators trooped out of Columbia. The full board would meet in eighteen days to either ratify, modify, or undo the work of the Executive Board. Given the excitement of the previous week, and given the predilections of those in authority, was there ever any real hope of reversal? Meanwhile, what of the students who had eagerly awaited word? What of the faculty? What of the academic community in universities nationwide in a time of cultural shift? And what did it all mean for Richard Jesse's careful handiwork, the University of Missouri?

Jazz Age, University of Missouri, *Savitar,* 1927. Courtesy of University Archives, University of Missouri–Columbia.

President Richard Henry Jesse, University of Missouri, 1891–1908. Jesse's energy and vision led to expanded curricula, facilities, and faculty, and marked the birth of the modern university. Courtesy of University Archives, University of Missouri–Columbia.

Academic Hall, 1892. The destruction of the university's main building challenged the entire community, including the new president, Richard H. Jesse. From the ashes rose the modern university. Courtesy of University Archives, University of Missouri–Columbia.

University of Missouri, 1910, during the administration of President A. Ross Hill. The "Red Campus" around Francis Quadrangle is in the center, including the columns from the old Academic Hall. Domed Jesse Hall is in the upper right. Courtesy of University Archives, University of Missouri–Columbia.

Signifying the University of Missouri's upward reach, five Missouri natives who made a mark in the world receive honorary degrees in 1902. Included are two cabinet secretaries, one assistant secretary, the founder of the Brookings Institution, and writer Mark Twain. See James and Vera Olson, *The University of Missouri: An Illustrated History* (Columbia, Missouri, 1988), 46. Courtesy of University Archives, University of Missouri–Columbia.

Jimmie's College Inn. Jimmie's became a favorite campus hangout and, in the late 1920s, a "jelly-joint" of choice. A live band appears on the mezzanine at upper right. *Savitar*, 1924. Courtesy of University Archives, University of Missouri–Columbia.

Attired in their collegiate best, students enjoy a campus mixer in Rothwell Gymnasium. *Savitar*, 1928. Courtesy of University Archives, University of Missouri–Columbia.

Rainy day on Francis Quadrangle. The landmark columns are at left. *Savitar,*
1922. Courtesy of University Archives, University of Missouri–Columbia.

Happy collegians. *Savitar,* 1929. Courtesy of University Archives, University
of Missouri–Columbia.

Mizzou football. *Savitar*, 1929. Courtesy of University Archives, University of Missouri–Columbia.

St. Pat's Ball. *Savitar*, 1929. Courtesy of University Archives, University of Missouri–Columbia.

Memorial Tower. Dedicated in 1926 to honor the university's dead in the Great War, the floor of the tower became a canvas for student protest slogans during the sex questionnaire controversy in 1929. *Savitar*, 1929. Courtesy of University Archives, University of Missouri–Columbia.

Orval Hobart Mowrer as he appeared in the student annual. The brilliant, sober-looking twenty-two-year-old senior who set off the great sex questionnaire controversy later rose to the pinnacle of his profession. *Savitar,* 1929. Courtesy of University Archives, University of Missouri–Columbia.

Mowrer, fifth from left, played with the College Inn Band in the late 1920s. Photo courtesy of the University of Illinois Archives, Urbana-Champaign.

Well-dressed University of Missouri students jam Jesse Auditorium to protest
the ouster of professors in the wake of sex questionnaire controversy, March 20,
1929. This photograph appeared in several state newspapers and later in the
student yearbook. *Savitar*, 1929. Courtesy of University Archives, University of
Missouri–Columbia.

The Board of Curators just prior to their meeting to consider the ouster of Professors Max F. Meyer and Harmon O. DeGraff. From left: A. A. Speer, Charles F. Ward, Milton Tootle, Jr., H. W. Lenox, President James E. Goodrich, H. J. "Jack" Blanton, Mercer Arnold, George C. Willson, Frank M. McDavid. *St. Louis Post-Dispatch*, April 7, 1929. Courtesy *St. Louis Post-Dispatch*.

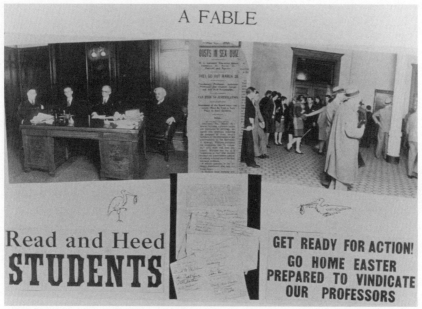

A FABLE

Read and Heed
STUDENTS

GET READY FOR ACTION!
GO HOME EASTER
PREPARED TO VINDICATE
OUR PROFESSORS

The University of Missouri student annual included a collage of the sex questionnaire controversy. At upper left are the university president and members of the Executive Board of the Board of Curators. From left: Mercer Arnold, a Joplin attorney; Jack Blanton, a Paris newspaper editor; Frank McDavid, a Springfield attorney; and President Stratton Brooks. Students in the photo at right mill about Jesse Hall, probably waiting for official word from the curators. The trio voted to oust the professors, but final word rested with the full nine-member board. *Savitar*, 1929. Courtesy of University Archives, University of Missouri–Columbia.

Dr. Bessie Leach Priddy, dean of women. Holding both a Ph.D. from the University of Michigan and strong Victorian views of proper relationships between male and female students, Priddy was probably the first among the university's administration to learn of the sex questionnaire circulating on campus. *Savitar*, 1928. Courtesy of University Archives, University of Missouri–Columbia.

University of Missouri Professor Max F. Meyer, internationally renowned psychologist near the center of the sex questionnaire controversy. Photo courtesy of the University of Illinois Archives, Urbana-Champaign.

University of Missouri Assistant Professor Harmon O. DeGraff. After his arrival
at the university in 1926 with a fresh Ph.D. from the University of Chicago, the
gifted teacher soon became one of the most popular professors on campus. The
controversy over the sex questionnaire that originated in his "Family" class led
to his termination by the Board of Curators. *Savitar*, 1929. Courtesy of
University Archives, University of Missouri–Columbia.

Jesse Wrench, associate professor of history. A favorite campus legend
during his forty-two years at Missouri, the eccentric yet well-respected
professor was reprimanded by the Board of Curators for his marginal role in
the sex questionnaire episode. "Monkey" Wrench, as he was affectionately
known, urged caution at a student protest rally in Jesse Auditorium during
the controversy. When he retired in 1953, he was honored by the Missouri
Legislature and serenaded by students. *Time* was there to cover it. *Savitar*,
1928. Courtesy of University Archives, University of Missouri–Columbia.

Stratton Duluth Brooks, president of the University of Missouri, 1923–1930. By all accounts, the university stalled during Brooks's tenure as president. His early decisions in the questionnaire crisis exacerbated a difficult situation and probably contributed to the decision of the Board of Curators to oust him in 1930. *Savitar,* 1928. Courtesy of Archives of the University of Missouri–Columbia.

EDUCATION IN THE MISSISSIPPI VALLEY.

Critics of the Board of Curators' action in the sex questionnaire controversy often drew a comparison with the evolution controversy in Tennessee. With the columns on the Missouri campus as a focus, political cartoonist Daniel Fitzpatrick ridiculed the board's action in the *St. Louis Post-Dispatch* during the controversy in March 1929. Used by permission, State Historical Society of Missouri, Columbia, all rights reserved.

Recall St. Pat

The oft-cited connection between the sex questionnaire controversy and the perceived educational censorship in Arkansas and Tennessee was noted in this cartoon in the *Missouri Student,* the university's student paper. March 19, 1929, AAUPP. Courtesy of University Archives, University of Missouri–Columbia.

Professor A. J. Carlson, 1941. The diligent and distinguished scientist from the University of Chicago headed the investigation of Missouri's sex questionnaire controversy by the American Association of University Professors. His renowned scientific career placed him on *Time*'s cover in 1941. Courtesy of TimePix.

REPORT
OF
AMERICAN
ASSOCIATION
OF
UNIVERSITY
PROFESSORS
ON
SEX QUESTIONNAIRE

A NEW PILLAR FOR UNIVERSITY OF MISSOURI CAMPUS

In early 1930, after the American Association of University Professors issued its report critical of the action of the Board of Curators, political cartoonist Daniel Fitzpatrick added another column on Francis Quadrangle with his cartoon in the *St. Louis Post-Dispatch*. Used by permission, State Historical Society of Missouri, Columbia, all rights reserved.

Professor Orval Hobart Mowrer, research professor of psychology, University of Illinois, and president of the American Psychological Association, mid-1950s. Photo courtesy of Illini Studios and the University of Illinois Archives, Urbana-Champaign.

University of Missouri-Columbia. The modern "Red Campus" with Jesse Hall
and the famed columns is at center. Courtesy of the Office of University Affairs,
University of Missouri-Columbia.

Missouri route map, 1929, from *Seventh Biennial Report of the State Highway Commission of Missouri* (Jefferson City: State Highway Commission, 1930); adapted by Cartographer Kimberly McCutcheon; edited by Angelia Mance. Used by permission, State Historical Society of Missouri, Columbia, all rights reserved.

5

"Tallow Candles"

Missouri owes no thanks to the people who put on this unholy show. They put her in a class with Tennessee, Arkansas, Mississippi and those other benighted states which abhor nothing so much as truth.

—*St. Louis Post-Dispatch*, March 21, 1929

They are the kind of men who if their neighbors went back to tallow candles would follow rather than go against convention.

—Critic of Executive Board of Curators, March 21, 1929, UMPOP

S hortly before noon on March 20, 1929, reporters milling around Jesse Hall got what they had been waiting for. Estelle Hickok, secretary to President Stratton Brooks, handed out the statement of the Executive Board of the governing curators. Unlike the previous evening, not many students were there, but word traveled fast anyway. During the afternoon, notices of a student protest flew up on bulletin boards around campus. The anonymous flyers called for students to meet at the columns on Francis Quadrangle that night to protest the action of the Executive Board earlier in the day.

The six ionic columns left standing from the old Academic Hall fire thirty-seven years before had become a magnet for campus activities over the decades. The columns' shadows had long fallen on graduations, tap day ceremonies, and all manner of solemn proceedings, so it was natural for students to gather at a campus shrine to vent their frustrations. Generations later the columns would witness angry protests over issues surrounding the war in Vietnam; now, however, it was a protest about a matter close to home: the ousting of two professors over a questionnaire on sex and economics.[1]

The meeting at the columns never happened. Perhaps to get out of the way of the juggernaut, or maybe to ensure more orderly behavior, the administration offered Jesse Hall's auditorium instead. The press labeled both the disturbance and the meeting over the firings the biggest in Mizzou's history. Whatever was happening on campus got shelved; personal plans got canceled. This was big, and the university converged on Jesse for the mass protest. Newsmen outdid each other. One paper claimed twenty-five hundred students were in the hall, which could seat fewer than fourteen hundred, "while scores of others choked the entrances." The Associated Press said Jesse "was jammed to the topmost balconies . . . with 3,500 students" who had come to protest or simply out of curiosity as to the outcome, while many more were denied entrance. Not outdone, the *St. Louis Times* under bold headlines trumpeted that "The entire student body" turned out. At least two papers treated doubters to an impressive photograph of the sea of faces in Jesse Hall.[2]

The biggest gathering in the ninety-year history of the University of Missouri had all the makings of a raucous student protest. Angry rhetoric, threats of a boycott, student walkout, convergence on the legislature, and passage of resolutions marked the evening. Several students led the procession of speakers, including Lucille Dorff, the twenty-one-year-old student who had sparred with Curator Frank McDavid in the Executive Board hearings. Dorff quickly emerged as a leader of the protest, telling the crowd in Jesse Hall that the firings constituted "medieval injustice." Another student leader, C. Franklin Parker, executive secretary of the Student Religious Council, told the students that the decision wasn't final, that they could petition the full board, then consider legal action. He urged campus leaders to offer temperate action. The crowd could have been demagogued into frenzied protest; every time Parker mentioned Meyer, DeGraff, and Mowrer, cheers echoed through the hall. Frank Knight, president of the student government association, took the chair, pleaded for calm, and called on the crowd for suggestions. What about the status of Professor Jesse Wrench, whose protest resignation, among others, had been rumored all day? The press had reported the potential loss of an unnamed "veteran history professor, one extremely well liked by Columbia residents and equally popular with students." President Brooks's secretary knew of no such resignation. In any case, the popular professor was in the crowd, and he took the stage and scotched the whole idea: "First, I want to say the reports that I have resigned are grossly exaggerated," he told the cheering crowd. Wrench's normal attire, along with mustache and beard, reinforced his eccentric persona: blue coat, white knickers, and a net for his flowing hair. Wrench eccentric? Of course. Wrench resign? No chance—he had it good at Missouri, was respected, even loved, and frequently went out of the lines. But he was no radical. In fact, he decried suggestions of violence and urged a rational response. "You must be careful," he warned the crowd. "You are facing the force of bigoted public opinion. It cannot be ignored, but must be endured—up to a certain point. The president and the curators are not to blame for what has happened. They are the innocent agents of public opinion."

Wrench's spin was far too generous to the governing authorities, but he likely had a soothing effect on the meeting. Harsher measures were considered, including a student strike reportedly proposed by Gerard Singleton, editor of the *Missouri Student*. The call for a walkout struck an enthusiastic chord with the crowd, and other speakers urged its adoption. Moderate voices, however, claimed such radicalism would defeat their cause. Likewise, lawyers in the audience said a concerted boycott of downtown merchants who had signed North Todd Gentry's petition was illegal. A resolution proposed by Herbert Hoffman, a law student from Peoria, Illinois, met with scattered calls for harsher language and underwent slight revision. Free and open discussion marked the event, but in the end the well-groomed, well-dressed crowd opted for moderate action. By rising votes, the mass meeting approved two resolutions, one to the full board of curators protesting the injustice of the firings and pleading for review, the other to the locals "heartily" condemning their signatures on the hostile petition.

Resolutions aside, the evening's most poignant and dramatic moment centered around the absent star of the show, Harmon O. DeGraff. The crowd demanded his appearance, a search was instituted, and he was brought to the stage amid applause rarely equaled in Columbia's history, or so said the press. The cavernous hall immediately fell silent, but the gregarious, mild-mannered professor who rarely missed a Greektown dance was virtually unable to speak. "There is only one thing I can say now," he said with choking voice, "and that is, thank you." Tears filled his eyes and he quickly left the building to thunderous applause.

Despite the angry rhetoric, the proceedings were both democratic and orderly. The student body had spoken, and moderation had carried the day. Underscoring campus tradition, the students capped the evening with a rendition of "Old Missouri" and "Varsity" before dispersing. True, 150 or so students congregated downtown in front of the Missouri Theater and merchants feared retaliation, but police were out in force. Nothing happened, not even when a sizable and disapproving crowd drifted to the offices of the *Columbia Daily Tribune,* whose hostility to the questionnaire had set off the tumult a week before.[3]

2

The Executive Board's ousting of Meyer and DeGraff ensured that the questionnaire fiasco would occupy the university's attention for a long while. It set off more than just student anger. In the short term, it initiated a whole new round of public comment, subjecting the school to unwanted controversy. Newspapers nationwide weighed in on the issue. Ohio's *Cleveland Press* said President Brooks and the curators had brought more harm to the university than had the questionnaire. Could anyone really imagine the students of Missouri hadn't thought of these things? Alabama's *Birmingham Age-Herald* reasoned along similar lines: "Surely the time has come, even in Missouri, when the subject of sex can be approached candidly and scientifically, whatever hysteria may be shown among people who regard virtue and ignorance, truth and suppression, as interchangeable terms." The *Milwaukee Leader* argued that if the instructors weren't reinstated, "the university will step down a notch in the estimation of advanced thinkers." The "great fuss" was "a tempest in a tea pot." "The deplorable thing about this situation is this," said the *Omaha World Herald,* "that if the university is to be governed to satisfy every temporary outburst of public indignation, then independence of thought and action by its faculty are at an end." Ultimately, professors "tend to become mere classroom proctors with parrots for pupils." The *Nation* thought everything would have been fine had the president just let the questionnaire take its course, but speculated that Brooks was "evidently a man of action rather than thought; or perhaps he is a politician, or a publicity expert, or a promoter." The Dayton, Ohio, *Daily News* called on Missouri to "rectify its sorry blunder. Like the man from Missouri, we've got to be shown. There's only one way for Missouri to prove she doesn't belong in the category of the dark minded. Show us, Missouri."

Missouri *was* showing them. That was the problem according to the *St. Louis Post-Dispatch.* "Missouri could not be the backward State she is without reflecting it in many ways, and she did it in this matter with an emphasis that has not escaped the eyes of the country." It was all a "barbarous absurdity." The *Baltimore Sun* carried Max Meyer's picture above the fold on its front page under the caption: "Victim Of 'Sex-Canvass' Row Is World-Famous Professor." The *Sun*'s morning edition snorted, "It is appalling to think that a serious scientist, who has spent his whole adult life in one college, should be dismissed merely to serve the small ends of political meddlers." Closer to home, the *Kansas City Star* was subdued, noting that the discipline of psychology had pressed the envelope and that what had once seemed "shocking" had become routine. Censure might have been better, but public confidence in the university had to be maintained. Across the state, the influential *Post-Dispatch* would have little of that argument. Sure, maybe the questions "were injudiciously bold," but certainly they were not worthy of such draconian punishment. The paper instead reached for metaphors, calling the whole business "a tempest in a teapot" (like the *Milwaukee Leader*), a "witchburning," a "public lynching staged by the university and its irrational home guard." Both the university students and the newspaper knew cultural problems abounded. But the paper thought that "The State Legislator who charged that Judge Ben Lindsey of Denver is at the bottom of all these new-fangled ideas about sex furnished the rest of the country with a sufficient index to the status of civilization in Missouri. Neither he nor any of the people who lynched the university psychologists know how far the institution of marriage has fallen in Missouri or what can be done about it. They can only plead ignorance of their time and abuse those who seek to make suggestions."[4]

The curators' action also set off another batch of letters. As before, competing and jostling opinions symbolized a culture at war within itself. One Philadelphian sarcastically congratulated Brooks on getting the university a full column in the *New York Telegram,* while across the country, an alumnus living in Seattle who approved of the firings noted that since 1920 only two things had put Columbia on that city's front pages: the lynching of James Scott in 1923, and the current sex questionnaire. Letter after letter supported university authorities in the firings, many moderate in tone, such as that from the father of an eighteen-year-old woman who had received the questionnaire. He knew university funds were short, lamented the bad timing of the problem, and thought the ousters were required to restore public confidence.

Other critics weren't so genteel. A Hannibal businessman, for example, told Brooks the "filthy," "foul," and "bestial" questionnaire "originated in the brain of a degenerate or pervert," while a mother from Liberty now felt "much better over the safety of my daughter in the university." A Sedalia father thought the questionnaire "vulgar and having a tendency to be very harmful," and approved the board action, as did a judicial circuit judge and alumnus who thought the offending document was "as filthy and slimy and disgusting a paper as young people ever were called upon to read." One Kansas City attorney told Curator Frank McDavid, "If anyone would address to my daughter the queries that were contained in this questionnaire and I could get my hands on them, I would feel like using physical violence." The female students were "young girls" and the offending professors should "be tarred and feathered and ridden out of town on a rail." The action of the Executive Board would constitute "a wholesome warning to other Professors that such conduct will not be tolerated." Violence even crossed the mind of one clergyman.

Some saw the battle in global terms, the ultimate stakes being the very survival of civilization. The Kansas City attorney who wanted to reach for tar and feathers claimed, "Whenever the modesty of womankind is broken down and invaded, the morals will be the next thing that will be invaded and broken down and with that will go the family and marriage and ultimately the Republic." Another Kansas Citian thought that if the university's morality wasn't protected, "we are headed for the rocks," while a Moberly pastor asked Brooks: "Shall sex life be no longer sacred and safeguarded?" And in his "candid judgement," said a Sedalia pastor, "I believe the inspiration for all of this comes from Soviet Russia and is a studied effort to undermine four of our basic corner stones—the home, the school, the church and the state." Whatever the origins, the problem would earlier have been met with a shotgun and horsewhip, said one Columbian to North Todd Gentry: "If these questions are proper to be discussed in writing or in the class rooms then why not in private conversations or on the street—and then in the auto parked on the roadside in the darkness of the night? Is not this the natural result of familiarity thus encouraged? [A]nd may it not account for many of the things observed on the roadside and also for the great increase in Drugstore preventives?"[5]

Some of the cultural divide could be explained by how society viewed the students at the University of Missouri. Were they boys and girls, as some called them, whose immature minds needed protecting, or were they developing adults whose time to handle the big issues of life had come? In the 1920s that constituted a societal question on which reasonable people could disagree, although the former idea struck at the very integrity of the modern university. A former student and father of three living in Illinois claimed, "You cannot convince a young man or woman at the university age that the stork or even Sears-Roebuck brings babies into this world." If they didn't yet know about sex organs, he said, then they needed to learn. A Phi Beta Kappa and two-time alumnus living in a Chicago suburb who claimed she was "no radical" seemed to agree: "A university to be worthy of the name must give its students an opportunity to consider the problems of the day. If M.U. ceases to do this it loses its right to the name." Such matters raised by the questionnaire were being talked about by young people all over the nation, she said, and the harsh reaction would suppress free thought.[6]

One alumnus living in Kansas acknowledged that Meyer might have been ahead of the times, but told Brooks that "history books are full of instances of men who were made martyrs by one generation only to have a monument erected to their honor by the next." Another former student claimed Brooks couldn't hold back enlightenment forever, that it was coming, and that no subject should be forbidden to anyone over fifteen years old. "To think such a disgrace must descend upon Missouri University," he said, "because a politically minded president and Executive Board must toady to a legislature and backwoods voters!" But not everyone from the backwoods concurred with the curators. One person from a tiny village in the Lake of the Ozarks had no college education but wanted to learn as much as possible, including the tabulated results of the questionnaire. He didn't want faculty or students dismissed "on account of their opinions" either. "It will look too much like the sixteenth century." A Kansas Citian thought along similar lines, claiming, "The only interpretation possible is that the rack and thumbscrew of the Dark Ages will be applied in the future to any professor who has the intellectual honesty to teach the vital, fundamental facts of human life and relations." Run "by a coterie of hypocritical pecksniffs," the university was an institution of "cultural atavism and intolerance." One St. Louis critic claimed modern university students didn't fear discussions of sex as did generations past but regarded it in physiological terms like the beating of the heart. Times had changed, but most of the Executive Board suffered from "mid-Victorian prejudice." And of course, the old anti-evolution link came up again more than once. A St. Louis school principal lamented to the curators: "Poor old Missouri is tottering on the brink of the Pit of Ignorance, which swallowed up Tennessee and Arkansas." That was Daniel Fitzpatrick's theme in his cartoon in the *St. Louis Post-Dispatch* on March 22. Labeled "Education in the Mississippi Valley," Fitzpatrick drew a monkey sitting atop one of Mizzou's columns on the Quad, while a stork with a new baby in swaddling clothes stood on another. Across the country an alumnus living in California read of the ousters in the *San Francisco Examiner* and dispatched the clipping to Brooks, hoping the president would deny the awful story. "If it is true," he wrote, "then this is the first time that I have had occasion to be ashamed of my Alma Mater."[7]

Other alumni were more than merely ashamed. Some were prepared to act. A. B. Knipmeyer, a leading Memphis attorney and head of that city's 150-member Missouri Alumni Club, stood ready to call a meeting after polling colleagues. He had read the questionnaire, thought the whole thing was "much ado about nothing," and failed to see how such subjects could be adequately studied without confronting questions of sex. In Kansas City, after talking long-distance with Max Meyer, Dr. Isadore Anderson busied himself telephoning fellow alumni about the course they should pursue to get the revered professor reinstated. And the president of the Central Ohio Alumni Association, E. L. Dakan, a professor at Ohio State University, wired Brooks asking for "full information" about Meyer and claiming "YOU OWE ALL ALUMNI A FULL EXPLANATION OF YOUR ACTION." When Brooks's nondescript reply proved unsatisfactory, Dakan chastised him, claiming reports they were receiving were none too kind to the university. He recalled that he and his high school friends looked forward to studying with Meyer, then took his classes and relied on his advice throughout college, then told their children yarns about their unique professor. Surely something must be wrong—the university couldn't dismiss such a great man. With a swipe at Brooks, Dakan added: "The most disappointing part of it all is that no where have we read that the President of the University has raised his voice to prevent this hasty action."[8]

Unquestionably the most concerted effort centered among alumni in St. Louis, where a concerned and influential group looked to chart the most judicious course. John D. McCutcheon, Jr., an investment broker in St. Louis who had taken an A.B. from Missouri in 1920, had expressed concern to President Brooks about potential ousters as early as March 18. But events moved rapidly. Well connected with numerous influential alumni throughout the city, McCutcheon and his friends soon contemplated not only exerting pressure to get reinstatements but also circulating a petition among alumni throughout the state calling for the ouster of Brooks himself. But these were mature people, not wanting to take precipitate action without verified information. Two days after the firings by the Executive Board, McCutcheon took his case to his friend Dr. Jonas Viles of Missouri's history department asking for details and chronology.

Viles had become one of many pillars of the faculty, having come to Missouri in 1902 with a doctorate from Harvard and staying for his long career. Rumored to have contemplated his resignation over the questionnaire disaster, a highly dubious prospect, he languished over the damage to the university and speculated that unless the Executive Board's decision was reversed, the school would be set back three decades. McCutcheon wanted to know if Brooks had sacrificed the professors to head off negative publicity that would play into the hands of the university's enemies. He held out the possibility that Brooks made a mistake, but an honest one. The issue got a bit fogged because some among the St. Louis

alumni wanted Brooks ousted for reasons quite apart from the questionnaire that remain unclear. McCutcheon may have been among them; he
even told Viles he'd be willing to spend his own cash to consolidate what
he sensed was rancor among alumni toward Brooks. But he'd do nothing
without facts.[9]

Meanwhile, some of the faculty thought the world beyond Columbia
had forgotten them, and for his part Viles was delighted to get McCutcheon's inquiry. But Viles pleaded to not turn their idealistic battle "into
a personal attack on the President." He could take Brooks or leave him,
but that wasn't the point. The fight was, or should have been, over the
integrity of the university, and Viles was sure that personalizing it would
not only forfeit any hope of the full board overriding the executive decision but also fragment those who had coalesced on matters of principle.
Viles urged the St. Louis alumni to send a group to Columbia to meet
with Brooks and a loosely organized faculty committee distressed by the
whole thing. He thought such an alumni delegation should possess no
open enemy of Brooks and have at least one woman. "I have in mind as
the type one out about ten years," he said, "with the reputation of being rather conservative and old fashioned on sex questions. If she ma-
jored in science, fine; if she has a daughter, still better." Viles wanted all
bases covered and no mistakes. These alumni had to be able to handle
sensitive material with discretion—material the press should never see.
Viles and everybody else knew the critical role of the press in the whole
matter. Viles blamed editor Ed Watson and his *Columbia Daily Tribune* for
publicizing the questionnaire "with characteristic comments." But while
that was bad enough, it was no big deal. In fact, Watson's *Tribune* was
hardly beloved by local correspondents of metro papers, most of whom
were in the university's journalism school. The real problem came when
North Todd Gentry hooked his famous name on his petition demanding
removal of those responsible for the questionnaire.

What Viles had in mind was the story most of the public knew nothing
about and what he didn't want the alumni to have "sprung" on them.
Beneath the surface lurked the nagging problem of Max Meyer's Social
Psychology lecture on the physiology of sex. Viles and more than a dozen
other faculty had tried hard to develop the facts surrounding "this supposedly shocking material" and wound up "heartily" approving it. Whatever his idiosyncrasies, Meyer was a scientific professional and the faculty
knew it.[10]

While the St. Louis group worked through alumni president J. Wesley
McAfee, an attorney who communicated diplomatically with both Brooks
and board president James Goodrich, the Columbia faculty group was

busy on a couple of fronts. Made up of some faculty stalwarts, several recruited during Richard Jesse's "Golden Age," the group dispatched a carefully worded letter to Brooks and the curators three days before the meeting of the full board. They pleaded for the reputation of the university and its ability to recruit and retain able faculty. Such now stood in jeopardy. "The academic interest has no insistent spokesman," they wrote. "But if, for lack of vigorous expression, its requirements are disregarded, the result rests like a veritable blight upon the institution." They urged the curators to not sustain the Executive Board's decision on two bases: the punishment was unjustified and too severe; and the Executive Board's recommendation "would do a serious injury to the university from which it would not recover within the lives of most of the present faculty."[11]

The anguish of these men is impressive, many having devoted much of their professional lives to the university. Spread around campus, no group dominated. Included were men such as James Harvey Rogers and Harry Brown in economics and Henry Hooker in horticulture, all from Yale; Henry Belden in English and Herbert Reese in physics, both from Johns Hopkins, as was W. C. Curtis in zoology; Herman Schlundt in physical chemistry from Wisconsin; Addison Gulick in physiological chemistry from Wurzburg, Germany; E. B. Branson in geology and geography from Chicago; and from Harvard, A. C. Lanier in electrical engineering and of course Jonas Viles in history. There were no radicals among them, none given to flights of fancy. And despite rumblings from some faculty who thought the questionnaire was out of line or that Meyer and DeGraff should have better gauged public response, the Viles and Schlundt group likely spoke for many if not most faculty. Frank Stephens, with a Ph.D. in history from Penn and whose service reached back to 1907, was not a signer of the faculty group's letter, but said privately he thought the faculty stood virtually united in believing the curators' action had been draconian. He also thought the questionnaire was well-meant but "undoubtedly too rash"—also a view shared by many faculty—but Stephens believed it had been horribly misperceived by outsiders.[12]

Some outsiders were perceiving the matter very well, and the university's reputation suffered among other professionals. Dr. Stuart Queen, chairman of the sociology department at the University of Kansas, a longtime Missouri athletic rival, declared publicly that "Missouri has been made ridiculous through the stirring up of an apparent trivial affair." Missouri had "slapped her own face in ridding herself of one of the most able psychologists in the country and an intelligent sociologist." The university suffered the dictatorship of "drug-store cowboys and others who know nothing of science" and had degenerated "from an educational institution to an institution of propaganda." His colleague at Kansas, Professor Donald Marsh, argued that no subject should be off the table of scientific investigation and that movie houses offered up the same subjects. At Johns Hopkins, renowned psychologist Knight Dunlap told the *Baltimore Sun* that he suspected something more than just the questionnaire had stirred up "all this fuss." He knew Max Meyer well (ironically, young Mowrer had gotten hooked on one of Dunlap's textbooks) and couldn't believe—even if the research was "clumsily carried on"—that Meyer would be deliberately involved in anything sensational. "You can light a match in many places and nothing will happen," said Dunlap, "but if you light it over a gas tank there's bound to be an explosion." Missouri was a gas tank in the spring of 1929, and probably lots of other places where lots of harumphing and pontificating went on were gas tanks too, but nobody lit any matches.[13]

3

The curators' action embarrassed the university even further. The Southern Society for Philosophy and Psychology had never met in Columbia in the more than two decades since its creation. A year before the questionnaire scandal, Max Meyer wanted to bring the twenty-fourth annual meeting to Missouri, what Meyer called "this northwestern corner of the southern territory." President Brooks agreed, as did the society, which met in Lexington, Virginia, in 1928. The group scheduled its next convention for March 29–30, 1929, in Columbia, with the fairly new downtown Tiger Hotel as the host facility, while all sessions were slated for Jesse Hall on the campus. Meyer planned for Brooks to welcome the convention, then have Professor L. R. Geissler of Randolph-Macon Woman's College give the outgoing presidential address in the hotel's banquet hall. Meyer also looked to broaden the university's interaction with instructors from statewide senior and junior colleges who would attend the convention; he further tried to line up members of the Missouri faculty to act as chauffeurs for conventioneers wanting to tour the campus and community. "A little hospitality shown to our visitors," he told his faculty colleagues, "may greatly increase the feeling of good will with which we hope they will depart from our campus."[14]

It didn't happen. The day after the Executive Board relieved Meyer and DeGraff of their duties—effective March 23—Meyer thought Brooks should invite someone else to host the upcoming convention, the program for which had gone in the mail the morning of the curators' action. Brooks, however, wanted Meyer to continue to host the affair: "From my point of view I see no reason why any change should be made, and I hope that you will share this opinion." Brooks's schedule even permitted him to deliver the official welcome. The whole thing was bizarre. The next day, however, everything changed. The society got wind of the firings at Missouri and promptly canceled the meeting in Columbia, transferring the convention to the University of Kentucky in Lexington. ("This will relieve both of us from a situation which might be slightly embarrassing," Meyer told Brooks.) Despite the short notice, the twenty-fourth convention met at the relocated site at the end of March. The Associated Press reported that Meyer, a member of the society's three-member council, "was accorded a rousing applause when he entered the meeting." It's tempting to suppose that it was a slap at Missouri's administration and curators for the convention to elect Max Meyer, now without institutional portfolio, as its president for 1929–1930. Some of that may be true, but Meyer was in line for the honor and was so regarded by his colleagues.[15]

Closer to home, the professional embarrassment touched everyone, or nearly so. Even President Brooks knew that Missouri's repeated classing with Tennessee and Arkansas proved humiliating to faculty; W. C. Curtis, Missouri's eminent zoologist, didn't look forward to seeing colleagues during his summer research at the scientific lab in Woods Hole, Massachusetts. Even those no longer at the university felt the sting. Dr. Isidor Loeb, a Missouri graduate who took a Ph.D. at Columbia University in New York, had devoted thirty years to the University of Missouri as professor of political science, aide to President Richard Jesse, and various deanships, including faculty, School of Education and, for a long time, the School of Business and Public Administration. A gifted executive, he even served as acting president for a few months in 1923 before Brooks came on board. A decade later he would serve as president of the American Political Science Association. In 1925 Loeb became dean of the School of Business and Public Administration at Washington University in St. Louis but of course remained vitally interested in his old alma mater. The questionnaire fiasco and attendant injustice appalled him: "distressed beyond measure," he told Frederick Middlebush, current dean of Business and Public Administration. Scheduled to appear at some conference in Columbia, he didn't even want to be publicly associated with the university if he could avoid it, and had reached the same conclusion Jonas Viles had about the damage to the university. Discreet about airing his own views, Loeb had been on a recent trip during which, he said, he "heard almost universal criticism, and the matter has done and will do the University incalculable harm."[16]

4

The other front occupying some of the Missouri faculty involved others who were monitoring developments in Columbia, namely the American Association of University Professors (AAUP). A curriculum-wide professional organization, the AAUP always stood alert for real or potential infringement on academic freedom and inquiry.

Founded in 1915, the organization arose in the milieu of the gentility of the Progressive era, the increasing professionalization of the academy, and the expansion of higher education. Learned scientific societies had long since coalesced, as had barristers and physicians, and—at the turn of the century—scholastic accrediting agencies. Believing the need existed for a unified organization of faculties, a number of leading academics across the nation issued an organizational call in late 1914 that resulted in more than 250 gathering in New York City in January 1915. Welcomed by John Dewey, the controversial education innovator at Columbia University, the association not only elected him its first president but also embarked on an impressive agenda of unifying the professoriate and, before the year was out, enunciating principles of academic freedom. The latter issue, without clear definition but which nonetheless lay at the core of teaching and research, had been a topic of discussion within several disciplines. A committee appointed to look into the matter, whose membership included luminaries such as economist Richard T. Ely from Wisconsin and Roscoe Pound from Harvard Law School, issued its report at the end of the year.

The AAUP also created numerous committees, designated by letters of the alphabet, to work on varied problems within the academy, including those on ethics, research, standards, pensions, and insurance; "Committee A" was of course the one on academic freedom and tenure. The organization tried to promote advanced education and research in American collegiate and professional institutions, and to help elevate and secure professional standards even as it expanded the utility of its constituent disciplines. But this was no "trade union," as some critics might charge, even if monitoring alleged violations of academic freedom became a function of the organization. In its fourteen years, the AAUP had investigated several such allegations in a variety of institutions. Moderate in approach, respectful of each institution's tradition, as in the case of religious denominational colleges, the association moved with the circumspection and cautious dignity befitting a professional organization. Some administrators resented what it believed was biased meddling and interference on the part of the professors association, and the agency repeatedly had to prove its good intentions. It often found that allegations against administrative bodies were groundless. Such was the case at the University of Colorado in 1915, where its president anxiously looked for an AAUP inquiry into the dismissal of a faculty member lest the university's reputation suffer. That same year, however, the investigating committee looking into the case of the dismissal of Scott Nearing, a left-wing professor at the University of Pennsylvania's Wharton School of Business, found a violation of academic freedom. In the backwash of the investigation, Pennsylvania's governing board established new procedures for tenure and dismissal, always a goal of the AAUP. In early 1924, the chairman of Committee A reported that charges of restrictions on freedom of teaching were rare, but that most referrals to the committee involved dismissals from faculties without hearings or other due process. The association struggled to achieve dignity and fair treatment for the professoriate against often arbitrary administrative rule, which itself could be subjected to outside pressures. Aside from the tenuous nature of the professoriate, a changing culture inevitably produced conflicts in the academy and among the public. In the 1920s, the crusade against teaching organic evolution, for example, had prompted creation of a special AAUP committee to deal with that issue alone.

The idea of permanent tenure developed slowly. Some institutions regarded reappointments at the full professor rank—and some even at the associate professor rank—as constituting a sort of permanent tenure, though removals could be made for cause. But, as one observer noted in 1924, "For the most part, regulations regarding tenure resemble the British constitution in that they are mere understandings or customs." Of course, administrators resisted a system that limited their options, while professors disliked the lack of dignity and "casual laborer" treatment occasioned by the tenuous nature of their appointments. Many institutions, such as the University of Tennessee and others, recognized no appointment as permanent: all appointments were for a single year only. However, those faculty who held professor rank needed no formal reappointment year-by-year on good behavior, although the administration could, should it so decide, terminate anyone. Tennessee did just that in 1923, for several reasons dismissing seven faculty, including a dean and five full professors. Some of the dismissals apparently resulted from protests related to the nonrenewal of two faculty members. The ensuing AAUP investigation, at first resented and then welcomed by an administration early on convinced of the association's pro-faculty bias, found no legal or contractual violations by Tennessee authorities, although it did find intolerance and lack of fair play.[17]

The genteel and generally harmless reprimand of Tennessee's arbitrary ousters of seven faculty anticipated the problems of the AAUP in the Missouri case several years later. The association opened itself to second-guessing and charges from the left that its investigation was ineffective, as the *New Republic* alleged in May 1924. "The public . . . is not interested in piddling points of law, with the standards of etiquette of the committee on academic freedom and tenure," charged the magazine. "What has happened? it asks. Is the ship being lightened of bilge, or has the cargo been jettisoned?" The point was well taken, but so was that of the defenders that the association was no anti-administration agency invariably taking the side of its members. Critics who wanted the association to do more in defense of the professoriate, such as the *New Republic*, could readily interpret the AAUP's Tennessee report. As the association's president, A. O. Leuschner put it, "The facts should speak for themselves." Ultimately, the AAUP had to rely on publicity and moral suasion.[18]

Within a decade of its founding, the organization had members on more than two hundred campuses and by the time of the Missouri crisis counted upwards of eight thousand members nationwide. Even more impressive, however, its membership counted distinguished professionals in research, teaching, and in the intellectual life of the nation. Its leadership in the spring of 1929 included Henry Crew of Northwestern University in physics as president, Howard C. Warren of Princeton in psychology as vice-president, and H. W. Tyler in mathematics of the Massachusetts Institute of Technology as secretary. The University of Missouri's Isidor Loeb had been on the Committee on Organization, as had former Missouri faculty Arthur Lovejoy and Frank Thilly, and its chapter had long been one of the largest in the AAUP, boasting fifty-two members in the first such listing in 1916. By 1929, that number had reached ninety-six, twelfth largest among all institutions.[19]

The AAUP soon learned of the unfolding drama in middle America. With alarm, Vice-President Warren read in the press of the faculty ousters in Missouri and rapidly fired off a letter to Secretary Tyler at the AAUP offices in Washington, D.C. If the accounts of the firings, including that of "my friend Max Meyer," proved true, he said, "the action is the most flagrant violation of academic freedom that has occurred since our Association was founded." Warren granted that Missouri officials could curtail research because "of old-fashioned notions of propriety," but if that was the case, warning or censure would be the proper course. In any event, Warren wanted the association's academic freedom committee to look into it "without delay or hesitation."[20]

That Warren and others yielded to governing officials the right to proscribe research is itself remarkable. But the firings seemed an affront to reason. The same day Warren wrote to Secretary Tyler, Ellsworth Faris, a member of the AAUP and a professor in the Department of Sociology and Anthropology at the University of Chicago, alerted a member of the association's Committee A to the problem. Faris had likewise read of the firings in the press as well as in a letter from an unnamed Missouri faculty member, but the unnamed person was neither Meyer nor DeGraff.[21]

The AAUP's interest was clearly aroused. At Johns Hopkins, Arthur O. Lovejoy told Secretary Tyler he thought the association should wire Missouri's chapter president about possible AAUP intervention, something Tyler did on March 26. He also alerted Professor H. C. Fairclough at Stanford University, chairman of Committee A. Meanwhile, Lovejoy heard from an unnamed "old friend" at Missouri who told him, "Of course, you have heard of the catastrophe and no doubt you are wondering whether the faculty will lie down under it. I think I can promise that we shall not." He mentioned the faculty group working for reinstatement of the two professors, alluded to unpublicized underlying details, and didn't blame Brooks and the curators wholly. The problem was really some legislators, along with North Todd Gentry ("a presbyterian fundamentalist"), and locals, some of whom—not Gentry—regretted their action.[22]

Lovejoy's correspondent was naively optimistic, but he was right about a faculty group working quietly to overturn the firings. Not surprisingly, Professor Herman Schlundt, the chemist, served as Missouri's AAUP chapter president. Schlundt had been a Jesse recruit, enjoyed wide respect, including for his brilliant classroom performance, and was a person of diplomacy and tact. Referring to "the critical situation," in Columbia, he told Tyler that students and a number of faculty were working on the professors' behalf and that the local leadership counseled a wait-and-see posture by the national association until after the curators' meeting in April. Schlundt was hopeful.[23]

Less sanguine was AAUP president Henry Crew. "As to the affair in Missouri," he wrote on March 28, "I feel almost outraged that the trustees of an institution feel like coming in and interfering in a matter of this kind which, seems to me, ought to be handled entirely by the faculty." Leave issues of propriety, morality, and even the value of questionnaires aside; the solution should be faculty-driven. Fortunately, Crew had great confidence in the local chapter president, "a distinguished chemist and a man of great ability."[24]

Within days, the press got word of the AAUP's inquiry. In a prepared statement, Schlundt said that officially the matter was still undecided, that he didn't want to embarrass the curators, and that he wouldn't release his reply to the AAUP other than that he had recommended delay pending the outcome of the meeting of the board. Still, the statement recognized the gravity of the moment. "It is felt, in fact, that, although nothing short of the academic future of the University of Missouri is at stake, no interference from outside sources should be tolerated until after the full board has had an opportunity to pass upon the incident in the light of all the facts."[25]

5

While the local professors worked quietly out of sight, and the national organization anxiously but diplomatically watched developments from afar, life went on at the University of Missouri. Eighteen days separated the recommendation of the curators' Executive Board and the meeting of the full board on April 6. Even on the morning of March 20, before the curators' announcement, Meyer and DeGraff were back in their classes. At 8 A.M., the Family had its normal quiz followed by DeGraff's lecture on family strife and divorce. He hoped students would practice what they had learned when they went home for the Easter holidays. When the class ended, sympathetic students surrounded the professor's desk. At that moment the curators were elsewhere in the building doing what they were doing. At 9 A.M. Meyer entered his "Employment Psychology" class and received cheers and a standing ovation from the thirty or so students. He thanked the class, particularly the females who had expressed no offense at the questionnaire, and got down to the day's business. Later, after news of the firings, Meyer expressed some relief and didn't say much, except that he was finished at Missouri and had no intention of seeking a teaching position elsewhere. He'd probably write. "The mentality of the state legislature and not the action of Dr. Brooks or the executive committee is responsible for my dismissal," he said. He later discounted a report that he might return to his native Germany. Professor DeGraff said simply that he was sorry. What were his plans now? "I'm not going to die." He wanted to finish a book he was writing and didn't know whether he'd remain in Columbia. "It is no use talking about something that can't be helped," he said. "One simply accepts it."[26]

Meanwhile, the *Kansas City Star* reported impending resignations of two lab assistants, an unnamed woman and Howell Williams, one of the four members of Mowrer's committee, who said he was going to resign out of sympathy with those deposed by the curators. Reports of Williams's withdrawal from school also surfaced, as did rumors that Otto Meyer, Max Meyer's son who had been a lab partner with Hobart Mowrer, would also withdraw. Williams apparently changed his mind, and Professor Meyer dissuaded his son from quitting, leaving only Mowrer, who followed through, in part because of his protest but also because of "unpleasant notoriety." Following official notice of the dismissals, including his own as lab assistant, Mowrer issued a lengthy public statement, remarkably articulate for a twenty-two-year-old. He was surprised that he hadn't been removed, so he himself would "relieve the administration of that task"; he would voluntarily quit. "I have no desire to graduate from any university which does not respect the principles of freedom of speech, freedom of thought, and freedom in the pursuit of the truth wherever or however it may be sought, and which is dependent for its support upon a legislature such as is now convened in Jefferson City." He didn't know what he'd do now, except that he'd give his story and articles about the issues raised by the questionnaire and about student sexual morals and ideals to any courageous publisher who would have them.

So much for brave talk. In fact, Mowrer had kept a low profile during the controversy for fear of exacerbating the problem, though he noted that the public remained divided. The crowd had demanded blood, from either the administration or some of those involved in the questionnaire. Mowrer thanked the students and those public men who had stood with them. And he could hardly praise Meyer, DeGraff, and other faculty members enough: "Not only did they manfully assume individual responsibility, but they also tried to relieve the students of whatever opprobrium might seem to attach itself to us." Sarcastically, he hoped the local *Tribune* along with the anti-university politicians would get back to their routine trivialities "and that the public will survive the dreadful shock its modesty has suffered, and that it will experience no regret as the result of its exceedingly prompt condemnation of a matter concerning which it had only the most superficial knowledge." [27]

The serious also blended with the bizarre. On March 20 one paper even reported an incredible story that the president and curators were "expected to investigate the report of a coed 'bull club,' the meetings of which are given over to discussions 'which would make the sex questionnaires sound like mild queries,' it is reported on the campus." Such a group did exist, but mercifully there was no investigation. That kind of talk ranked with a later report that Max Meyer had a lucrative offer to join a vaudeville troupe. Fortunately, that wasn't true either.[28]

Monitoring bull sessions may have been out of reach for college administrators, but that didn't stop campus paternalism. Missouri's dean of women, Bessie Leach Priddy, present at the origins of the questionnaire crisis, was a point person for such in loco parentis approaches. Possessing a broad education, she had been at Missouri for several years but had also served as a dean of women at Michigan State Normal School in Ypsilanti before that; her appointment at Missouri also carried an associate professorship of history. She had taken a bachelor of philosophy at Adrian College in Michigan in 1891, a bachelor of arts twenty years later, and then, at the University of Michigan, a master's in 1913 and a Ph.D. four years later. But Priddy demanded orthodoxy in a changing culture and easily vindicated the *Columbia Daily Tribune*'s pronouncement that she was "not of 'the new woman' type" upon her arrival in 1923. She had told Brooks at the beginning of the crisis that "such a questionnaire is to be deplored in its social effects on account of its unpleasant and in some cases, antisocial suggestiveness." In announcing university social rules to house presidents, Priddy warned that low grades after six weeks jeopardized social privileges. No problem there. But outdoor parties, picnics, and hikes required chaperons after dark, and men had to be out of women's housing by 11:30 on Friday and Saturday nights. Nor could any female attend dances who exposed bare legs between hem and stockings.[29]

If nothing else, such rules assuaged the fears of some anxious mothers whose daughters attended the university, as did the curators' decision in the questionnaire scandal. The mother of senior Isabel Baker, president of Pi Phi sorority, for example, figured that if Dean Priddy had rules about bare knees and chaperons it seemed "rather inconsistent that a questionnaire like the one which I have heard should be circulated in an institution that guards its girls as our state university does." She thought the professors were over the line. Mrs. Baker, from Kansas City, had visited her daughter's sociology class and decided the subject was out of bounds in mixed company. "In mixed classes a young girl delicately brought up may be seated next to a boy quite a different type. With such discussions as are the custom in sociology classes, I feel that the sexes should be separated in class." And Mrs. Andrew Young, also of Kansas City, obviously wanted protection for her daughter Alice, a sophomore who lived in Pi Phi sorority house. The curators were right, she thought, a view shared by others. "There is entirely too much talk about such things nowadays," she said. "I believe it might suggest the conduct it discusses so freely. It would be an act of weakness for the board to allow it." Amazingly, at the apex of the questionnaire crisis, when students and all Missouri could speak of nothing else, Mrs. Young had talked long distance with Alice and the subject never came up. "I hope," said Mrs. Young of the questionnaire, "that my daughter did not receive one." A Kansas City bank president thought along similar lines, demanding protection for the "children" and expressing the Victorian notion that "There are questions there that no refined mother would even think of discussing with her daughter, and the guilty professors should not only be expelled, but should be barred from the University grounds." Not outdone, a father from Macon with a son at the university told Brooks that the questionnaire "could not be read and discussed in a mixed crowd of *parents* even."[30]

On the other hand, culture wars always had at least two sides. Mrs. Arthur C. Brown, who had three daughters, two of whom had gone to Mizzou, told the *Kansas City Star* that her daughters talked to their parents "freely of practically everything," and that she and her husband "allowed them a great deal of liberty and I believe this liberty and the freedom of the home talk has been of great benefit to them." Her children, including a younger son, hung out with "modern" friends, and their friends' parents were likewise "modern," and that was just fine. Mrs. Brown had even taken one of her daughters to the risqué *Strange Interlude*, Eugene O'Neill's contorted play about infidelity and insanity, and had no regrets.[31]

Within days of the curators' decision, the deposed professors' classes were being divided up or canceled. Dr. Frederick M. Tisdel, dean of the College of Arts and Science, announced that Howard Jensen would take over the Family starting on Monday, while Charles Ellwood and a graduate student would share DeGraff's remaining courses. Instructor Dorothy Postle, very bright but only twenty-three, would assume one of Meyer's classes; the others would be canceled, half credit would be given, and affected students would be permitted to enroll in specially developed classes to ensure full credit for the semester.[32] Max Meyer met his Friday classes—the last before his dismissal took effect—and ended his 11 A.M. class with "Good Luck." Harmon DeGraff told his final Family class that healthy inquiry would produce no harm and that he believed collegians worked not to erode societal principles but to strengthen the family. "We criticized the family in transition but not as to its fundamental purpose," he said. "We make suggestions as to how its fundamental purpose may be carried out. This purpose is the handing on from parents to children all that is good and worthwhile in customs, standards, 'mores' and traditions."

Much of DeGraff's success as a teacher and counselor rested not merely in his enormous human decency, but in his genuine respect for his young students. And they knew it, sensed it, and sought him out repeatedly for advice. He gave it liberally, informed as it was by honored values and deep religious faith. "Twenty-five years from today," he predicted, "you are going to be the conservative element in the society. Youth is dynamic. The dynamic personality is youth. Youth in its impetuous haste and its desire to help does things in a mistaken way. You need your parents to act as a balance to your impetuosity; parents need you to soften their conservatism." [33]

Not surprisingly, emotion filled the room. Professor DeGraff, courageous in public but personally crushed by the developments, couldn't finish the class. No angry rhetoric this day, just solemnity and tears from both DeGraff and a number of women in the class. The course he had developed from a relatively few students to a campus phenomenon had come to its last day, and now emotion got the best of him. He left fifteen minutes early. [34]

By the weekend, a metro reporter found the campus "calm," with students partying and dancing like normal, and talking of plans for the spring break scheduled to start on Thursday. The administration said little after the announcement of the dismissals, other than Brooks's remarks about his delight in the orderly manner of the student protest at Jesse Hall, that a restructured Family class would continue, and that rumored faculty resignations had not developed. Protest letters continued to pour into his office, but that was to be expected. Privately, Brooks had boilerplate spin about the healthy morals of the student body, and that student loyalty to a popular instructor—not to an onerous questionnaire—dictated their behavior. Talk of a student strike had waned, and reportedly both Meyer and DeGraff stood vigorously against the idea. While members of DeGraff's Family class remained upset, the matter had about been talked out. [35]

Something might be done, or at least there was more talk about doing something. After DeGraff had left his class on Friday, students used the remaining time for more eulogies and loose talk of assessing each member a dollar to rent space in Pemberton Hall across from Jesse Hall for Professor DeGraff, where they could see him for conferences and where he might complete a book. Bred of frustration, such naive gestures remained the province of youth faced with things they couldn't change. More realistic was the proposed dinner in DeGraff's honor at the Tiger Hotel, with plans carried forward by Lucille Dorff, the student leader from Dallas, Texas, and several of her classmates. On Wednesday, March 27, just a week after the big rally in Jesse Hall in which DeGraff could hardly speak, and the day before spring break began, about eighty of his former students crowded into the hotel's ballroom for the testimonial to their favorite professor. His class was like a real family, he told them, and he couldn't leave or betray them, regardless of the final outcome of his case. Proud of his former students, pleased with what he had done at Missouri, he said he would carry on the same wherever he taught in the future. "This dinner is my one big challenge to go on," he said. "In years to come it will be one of the bright spots in my whole career, and I am at your service always."[36]

6

The controversy that started with a class project under Professor De-Graff set a new standard of sorts in Columbia. The local Western Union Telegraph office, whose normal business might include word-stingy messages from students needing money from home, broke all its records for total words sent in any one week. From Friday, March 15—day three of the controversy—to Friday, March 22, the office clicked and clacked more than 108,000 words to the outside world, with another 6,000 added on March 23. Nobody counted the words dispatched by telephone and by air and regular mail. Aside from students freelancing for various newspapers, correspondents from the *Baltimore Sun, St. Louis Star, Kansas City Star,* and *Fort-Worth Star-Telegram* hurried their own correspondents to the scene—all that in addition to normal reports from the Associated Press, United Press, International News Service, and the NEA Feature Service. Columbia became media central. Not since the tragedy of Floyd Collins's lingering death in a cave in rural Kentucky and the anti-evolution trial of John Thomas Scopes in Dayton, Tennessee, had American communications technology converged on such a relatively small place.[37]

With all the coverage, the questionnaire that rocked Missouri couldn't be contained on that campus alone. A new anti-fraternity student paper at the University of Texas in Austin, the *Texas Barb,* created a brief stir when it pledged to print Missouri's offending questionnaire in its March 28 edition. The idea was to get six thousand Texas students to fill it out, publish the tabulations, and pass on the results to the deposed professors in Columbia. Scientific research might continue after all! One suspects the real idea also included selling a few copies of the *Barb* while tweaking convention in the process. Texas authorities, not wishing to be sucked into the black hole into which Missouri had fallen, acted quickly, threatening "summary action" should the unauthorized paper carry out its plans. *Barb* editor John Woodruff, who weighed the matter, claimed the authorities wouldn't even read his copy of the troublesome questionnaire. They didn't need to. Texas President H. Y. Benedict and Dean V. I. Moore argued that if it was a problem at the University of Missouri, then it would be an unwelcome problem at the University of Texas. Woodruff was told frankly that if the paper published the questionnaire he'd be expelled, and all earned credit erased. Woodruff understandably caved. "The questionnaire is dead," declared the *Barb*'s lead editorial on March 28. "Dean V. I. Moore killed it with his veto and President H. Y. Benedict laid it beneath the sod with his confirmation of action of the dean." Woodruff said he deferred to authorities in the best interests of the University of Texas.[38]

That didn't end the problem for Texas, however. If the anti-Greek *Barb* wouldn't publish the questionnaire, the underground *Blunderbuss* would. And did. University of Texas authorities had been plagued for years on April Fool's Day, when the forbidden paper reared its anonymous and un-conventional masthead. In the past, when authorities learned the editors' identities, they received rebuke, one year even expulsion. This year, how-ever, the timing couldn't have been better. The April 1 edition, reportedly going for a dollar a copy, contained not only the forbidden questionnaire but also bristled with assorted remarks about student life at the Univer-sity of Texas, some deemed scandalous by Dean Moore. Austin's police chief, R. D. Thorp, had his officers hot on the trail of the perpetrators of the *Blunderbuss*, claiming it was "the rawest thing I have ever seen," and threatening obscenity charges against those responsible. Meanwhile, five hundred copies of the March 29 *Texas Barb*, with its editorial about the sup-pression of the Missouri questionnaire, showed up at Peck's Drug Store in Columbia; about four hundred flew off the stands at a dime apiece by early the next day. The edition carried what it claimed were excerpts of twenty-two telegrams and letters received from the University of Mis-souri, along with, apparently, a letter from a member of DeGraff's Fam-ily class. By April 6, the very day the full board of curators convened in Columbia to begin its hearing on the questionnaire scandal, the Austin po-lice had their man—or one of them at least. They charged Horace Walker, a former University of Texas student, with criminal libel for allegedly par-ticipating in the *Blunderbuss* scandal.[39]

There was money to be made and fun to be had in those questionnaires, as the editors of the *Blunderbuss* found out. Students in Columbia already knew that, at least the money part. The confiscated questionnaires proved scarce in the early days, driving up the street price. Early on they went for $2.50 and up, with one news correspondent reportedly paying a stu-dent $10 for an original. The Associated Press claimed the market for the sex questionnaire mimicked the ups and downs of the New York Stock Exchange after an enterprising university sophomore from Moberly, Missouri, Roy H. Heimen, broke the bull market. Heimen appeared in front of the Tavern Drug Store in Columbia with a heavy supply of "original uncensored copies" of the questionnaire. His price: thirty-five cents. Not a bad profit from what Hobart Mowrer claimed cost about two and a half cents each. Unfortunately, the English major from Moberly soon learned that Texas authorities weren't the only ones with heavy hands. After selling about one hundred copies to students headed for spring break, Columbia police arrested the student-salesmen on Thursday afternoon, March 28. Columbia's city attorney, Howard Major, deemed the infamous questionnaires "souvenirs," sale of which required a city license. Of course Heimen, whom the *Columbia Daily Tribune* claimed was "an unsophisticated youth of apparently about 19 or 20 years old," didn't have one, and didn't know he needed one. Heimen said he had had the questionnaires printed privately in Kansas City, but authorities were suspicious, since Heimen's copies were on the same paper and had the same typographical error as in the original. They reasoned that a printer would have corrected the mistake. Actually, the city attorney wasn't sure that the questionnaires didn't fall under obscenity laws, but in any case they were souvenirs and the law was clear about selling without a license. All the young capitalist wanted, he said, was bus fare to Moberly for the Easter holidays. After confiscating the remaining questionnaires and warning Heimen not to repeat the offense, the authorities sent him on his way.[40]

With questionnaires in short supply, the university was besieged with requests for copies from all over, and even curators scrambled to get their own. The requests started early and continued for weeks. Some had no opinion one way or the other but were curious to see what the fuss was all about, while others wanted it for legitimate inquiry, such as the student at the teachers college in Florence, Alabama, who wanted to look at a copy of the questionnaire in connection with her class on Adolescent Psychology. A sociologist at Trinity University in Texas wanted one too, as did a physician-editor in Kansas City, a workman's compensation administrator in Jefferson City, a general merchandiser in Minnesota, a Madison Avenue type in New York City, and assorted others, including a Utah resident who had read of it in the *Salt Lake Telegram* and elsewhere. Even the *Columbia Missourian* got requests, as did North Todd Gentry, including, in Gentry's case, from the chief justice of the Missouri Supreme Court, as well as from A. A. Speer, one of the university's curators. Stickler for the law, Gentry wouldn't send the documents through the mails, evidently concerned they constituted obscene materials. It was an issue that came up more than once, such as when a Shelbyville minister asked Gentry to dispatch a copy to him "if the mails will carry it." It was not an idle concern. Fred Reuter, St. Louis postal inspector, declared publicly that under court decisions "the circular might be construed to be unmailable matter, in that it has a tendency to raise impure thoughts in the minds of those in whose hands it may fall." Perhaps less concerned about legalities, the *Kansas City Star*, in a Victorian display of self-restraint, said it had not reproduced the questionnaire because of material "not suitable for use in a newspaper going into thousands of homes." President Brooks apparently didn't have any such qualms, but his answer to almost all requests to the university for the questionnaire was the same. None was available—except, of course, when he really wanted someone to have one, but that was rare.[41]

7

A quirk of the calendar had put the university on a collision course with the biennial legislature. Before the Executive Board met on March 19, there was a lot of silly talk about resolutions and budget cuts and general interference with university governance. The prompt dispatching of Meyer and DeGraff and the defrocking of Mowrer had preempted further action by legislators demanding blood. In fact, the Executive Board's resolute action was quickly hailed in Jefferson City. Kirk Jones, house appropriations chairman, for example, delighted in the news because of its calming effect on certain members of his committee. For his part, the house majority leader now predicted the end of further action from the legislature.

And hardly a minute too soon. Sadly, an Associated Press story claimed that sentiment in the capital required such strong action on the university's part in order to head off likely budget cuts. Blood had to be shed. Evidently, that seemed to be the view of Dr. Roy M. Cater, mayor of Marceline, Missouri, who also served Linn County in the Missouri General Assembly. A physician, Cater spoke informally with colleagues in Jefferson City on a bill calling for legal sterilization of epileptics, certain criminals, and those with mental defects. Inevitably, the sex questionnaire surfaced. Cater thought such things were scientific and valuable, and that if all house members had been college-educated, there would have been no threats to the university's appropriations. So far so good. But then eugenics got in the way. Dr. Cater didn't think Missouri was ready for a law providing for sterilization and which approved marriages only for the strong. Such talk was a scary holdover from the building-better-men-

and-women debates of the Progressive era, but Cater thought the time was coming when society would prohibit marriage for defectives.[42]

Eugenics talk aside, some legislators thought the curators feared legislative cuts. Several days later, Representative Charles Clowe's tabled resolution critical of the questionnaire was reincarnated in the form of a report by Eli Wherry, chairman of the university affairs committee, which recommended praise for the university's official actions. The university was "in safe hands," claimed Wherry's report, and the morals of the state's sons and daughters "will be protected while their intellects are being developed." Perhaps sensing that the horse was already dead, the house shipped the report back to the committee, wishing to hear no more of it.[43]

Unfortunately, Missouri's Fifty-Fifth General Assembly wasn't quite finished embarrassing itself. This time, however, it was the other side's turn. Representative Carl P. Werner, from Missouri's ninth district in Kansas City, dispatched a letter to the president of the Board of Curators, James E. Goodrich, with copies sent to the other eight, nakedly warning of budget cuts if those deposed by the Executive Board were not reinstated. The letter claimed Brooks was "unreasonable" and "incompetent," Missouri had been made "a jackass," and that no "human sacrifices" were required for a fair share of state appropriations. Werner allegedly got more than twenty of his colleagues, mostly urbanites, to sign on to the letter, deemed by one critic "crude and abusive." Werner's letter was certainly that, along with being inarticulate, naive, and unbecoming of a member of the legislature. As soon as the letter and the story played in the press—including, eventually, in the *New York Times* and elsewhere—protests mounted. The *Columbia Daily Tribune* later called Werner's behavior "cheap political meddling." One legislator after another—more than half—claimed he hadn't seen the whole text of the letter, had been tricked into signing, had his name forged, and so on. One alleged signer, George Williams of St. Louis, whose brother served as director of the university's Extension Division, was surprised to learn he was among the dissidents and assured Brooks of his confidence that university officials could handle the problem. And Representative Louis Hehl told Brooks he signed "under misapprehension," and berated the questionnaire and the faculty involved.

Sadly, Werner kept the story going. In coarse language, he publicly and angrily charged his colleagues with lying, adding further to the circus atmosphere. James Goodrich refused public comment on the letter, but said that copies would be sent to all of the curators and that official word would come from the full board, not individuals. He did say, however, that he had not made up his mind about the ousters, that he had gotten fifty or sixty letters, split fairly evenly on the issue, but that the merits of the case would dictate the outcome. Mercer Arnold, a member of the Executive Board contacted by the United Press, said he had received a copy of the letter but likewise declined comment on its substance. From his hometown in Springfield, Executive Board president Frank McDavid, who had also gotten his copy, was a bit more expansive to the Associated Press, defending Brooks and the budget process. He refused to predict whether the full board would endorse the Executive Board's action, but added that it usually did. For his part, Brooks escaped much of the embarrassment by going fishing in the Ozark Mountains over the Easter break. Tracked down by reporters on long-distance telephone, he declined to defend himself and said he would withhold any statement until after the full board meeting on April 6.[44]

In the end, the appropriations committee shook off the extremes and came through with a budget exceeding three million dollars, a bit larger than in the previous biennium. While no mention of the sex questionnaire scandal surfaced during the deliberations, the correspondent for the *St. Louis Globe-Democrat* reported the general view that only firm action by the Executive Board assuaged the hostility of rural legislators angry about the goings-on at the university. The university had actually requested more than seven million dollars, though more than three million was slated for new buildings. Instead, the committee recommended a bit more than one hundred thousand dollars for medical and home economics buildings, some equipment for the latter, and completion of a fourth floor for Jesse Hall. Even at that, however, subsequent cuts took total appropriations under three million dollars, and money appropriated was further trimmed by veto or withholding. When it was all over, total expenditures for the biennium stood under a mere $2.95 million.[45]

Unfortunately, questionnaire or no questionnaire, Missouri suffered the torpor of underfunding throughout much of the 1920s. Rural Missouri suffered financially during the decade, as did rural America generally, but otherwise times were good, and with aggressive leadership other revenues might have developed. It didn't happen. As a result, in fiscal terms, the university stagnated when it might have advanced. In his workmanlike 1962 *History of the University of Missouri*, Frank F. Stephens, who was there through it all—some of it in administration—later blamed the board for "a paucity of that aggressive leadership" shown at other times. "Missourians, as represented in their state government," he wrote, "were not convinced of the merits of higher education. All of this may have been due to Brooks's dearth of inspirational leadership, his lack of fitness to head a great institution of higher learning, but this checks back again to the Curators who were responsible for his election. It is difficult to distinguish between cause and effect in assessing the total situation." In any case, Stephens thought the inertia reflected poorly not only on the legislature but also on those constituents they represented—Missourians who simply failed to see the full value and ideals of the university. One Jefferson City woman expressed that idea even before the curators acted, telling Stratton Brooks she had "long since wanted to enter a protest against some of the teachings in 'Sociology[']" in the university. If high standards "and a proper *attitude* toward *law enforcement*" couldn't be achieved, she said, "then the University as a state institution should cease to exist." That was echoed by another constituent who told several curators to "Close up the University rather than have Paganism taught or our girls exploited."[46]

The university was still open, but it had been wounded. In Jesse Hall's labyrinthian fourth floor, Max Meyer picked among the artifacts of his decades of thinking, tinkering, and inventing, showing a visiting correspondent this apparatus or that. He said he wasn't emotionally settled enough to play his personally developed quarter-tone reed organ, but quickly changed his mind and played it anyway. Obviously too close to the bitter disappointment to make sound judgments about his future, he nonetheless spoke of holding no grudges, of his disgust with teaching, and of leaving Columbia forever. Harmon DeGraff talked of hanging around for awhile, writing, and not forsaking his students. On March 24 he spoke to two thousand people in a huge forum at the Linwood Boulevard Christian Church in Kansas City, explaining the conservative arguments of the Family class, receiving "thunderous acclamation" and not mentioning the infamous questionnaire, nor allowed by the moderator to answer questions about it. He did much the same thing at the noon City Club in St. Louis on April 3, during which he damned companionate and trial marriages and defended American youth. The problems were always the same, he said, except that parents approached those problems from a "horse and buggy" mentality, while the sons and daughters had an "automobile" mind. He predicted that the present generation's sons and daughters would likely use "the airplane technique." After the St. Louis meeting he would make no plans until after the full board met on April 6.

And what of Hobart Mowrer, the fellow at the source of the crisis? Reportedly, he had received publication offers, didn't know whether he would take them, but expected to head for Detroit within days, apparently in connection with that civil service position that he had talked about with Professor Jensen. Having quit the university just eleven weeks to the day before his scheduled graduation, he had no clear plans to continue his academic career.[47]

With all the comment in the public arena about the questionnaire, one editorial from Monroe County might have been overlooked. It shouldn't have been. While Paris, a small farming village that served as the county seat, was not forty crow miles from the university, Monroe County might have easily been a thousand miles away instead. In an editorial in the *Monroe County Appeal*, Jack Blanton felt the administration and the university couldn't be blamed for the doings at Columbia any more than Missouri's William Jewell College could be blamed for the controversy that arose some years earlier after a faculty member taught "things that are contrary to all orthodox doctrines." Blanton raged against unorthodoxy. "With so many local newspapers and magazines stressing very intimate sex matters," he said, "with practically all writers of books including more or less sex filth as a means of promoting sales, and with public libraries putting out literature reeking with sex appeal, there is little wonder that old ideas of modesty should be broken down or that those with abnormal interests in sociological matters should take advantage of any opportunity to pursue the subject, regardless of the harm that might result, as was undertaken at Columbia." Blanton applauded university officials for "wielding baseball bats on the offenders" and for giving wide publicity to the controversy. In fact, he wanted unorthodoxy banned. "The time has come," he said, "for a crusade against such discussions and such literature, for ridding our schools of those who cannot distinguish between legitimate research and cesspool delving, and for barring from local libraries volumes which reek with sex appeal. The University of Missouri is taking the initiative for such a crusade." He was sure President Brooks would enjoy the "undivided support from the Board of Curators."[48]

Such rant from a country editor might merit scant attention amid the cacophony of voices surrounding the controversy. But Blanton was a member of the Board of Curators, and it appeared he would be right. Chances of reversal did seem dim. Two days before spring break, even the *Missouri Student* lamented that "it looks dark" for reinstatement of the ousted professors, but it noted that "there will be practically nothing else talked of at home." "Go home students," urged the paper, "and when you get there tell the folks not only of the injustice that is being done these men, but of the other inadequate conditions that we are faced with and that the legislature refuses to take cognizance of. Tell of the injustices that are done both to students by lack of equipment and to instructors by lack of adequate salaries." The editorial matched placards which appeared on university bulletin boards that week urging students to turn the tide of public opinion, to create a powerful taxpayer demand on the legislature and Board of Curators to reverse the Executive Board's decision.[49] These were hopeful signs of youth not yet hardened to stubborn realities.

6

Up in Smoke

We are all agreed, I think, that the problem is many-sided and difficult.

—Henry Crew, President, American Association
of University Professors, August 3, 1929, AAUPP

T hirty-five-year-old Leland Hazard wasn't sure why he took the case at all. Why, indeed, would an able attorney in a comfortable Kansas City law firm offer his legal services without fee to a beleaguered university professor under siege throughout the state? As he told it, maybe he remembered the advice of Whittier: "Young man if you would get on in the world, select some worthy but unpopular cause and oppose it with all thine heart." Maybe it was also because his well-educated wife, Mary, who headed a prominent girls school, had publicly decried the firings and ridiculed President Brooks and the curators. Maybe there were other explanations, including his recent reading of Hendrik Van Loon's *Tolerance*. But if for no other reason, he respected teachers. A graduate of the University of Missouri, where he had studied with no less than Thorstein Veblen and Herbert Davenport, and a matriculant at Harvard Law School, Hazard never shared what he thought was America's low regard for teachers. "If a new martyr was coming up," he wrote later, "I wanted to know why. I soon found out."[1]

Hazard, in fact, had wasted no time in publicly rendering a verdict in the case. In a letter to the *Columbia Missourian* just days after the story broke, he argued, "Society for some reason has built a wall of silence and ignorance around a very vital part of life. Psychology is engaged in an effort to open a way for objective study. Naturally resistance is great." As in Socrates's day, youth had to be protected, he said, so Socrates had to go. He conceded that the students' method may have been flawed, and that Brooks depended on public funding, "but of what use is more money if the scientific pursuit of truth must be sacrificed?" Hazard even invoked Galileo and his problems with the Church, as well as the travails of early scientists who had to snatch bodies from gallows for anatomical research.[2]

The young lawyer returned to his alma mater in the company of Professor James Harvey Rogers, who had gone to Kansas City to get him. As they drove the 120 miles or so back to Columbia, Rogers, an economist with a Yale Ph.D. and one of the most respected members of the Missouri faculty, filled Hazard in on the case. Hazard had happy memories of his prewar days at Missouri—almost wistfully he remembered how the pedestals of the old Greek columns on the quad had formed the perfect site for Puck's gymnastics in *A Midsummer Night's Dream*. He loved his alma mater, but was sure his alma mater was wrong. He had not been Meyer's student, had never met him before, but Judge Merrill E. Otis, a Phi Beta Kappa and two-time Missouri graduate, including the law school, had recommended him to Meyer. Judge Otis was a straight-arrow in a corrupted city under the thumb of the Pendergast machine. The notorious big-time Kansas City gangster, Johnny Lazia, gunned down mobster-style in 1934, once appeared before Judge Otis on some federal charge. Said Lazia later: "That sonofabitch almost makes me respect the law." Now, in the rising uproar over the questionnaire, Otis publicly defended his old professor in the *Kansas City Star*, likening him to Socrates and saying he was certainly no threat to campus morals. Did anyone really think students had not thought of the issues in the questionnaire? It was "scarcely thinkable," said Otis. The judge assured Meyer he could trust Hazard.[3]

Hazard found his new client "alone in his bleak laboratory" high up in Jesse Hall. He formed an early impression of Meyer: "shy but unafraid; surprised at the furor; distressed that academic work had been so ignorantly misrepresented. He was a good client." Perhaps Meyer's limited expectations made him a good one. "He avoided general questions," said Hazard later. "How will it come out? Will we win? Am I in trouble?" According to Hazard, "An engineer can give categorical opinions: 'The bridge as I build it will stand.' With rare exceptions it does. Or the doctor: 'You will not die of this'; or sadly, 'You have six months to live.' But when an issue is to be decided by judges, juries, or anybody with the power of decision, the lawyer can only say, 'You must let me try the case as I see best; the outcome cannot be predicted with certainty.' Lawyers often say, 'Every lawsuit is a horse race.'"[4]

This race had lots of horses. A continuing flurry of letters and remonstrances bulged the file waiting to be presented to the curators: among them the letter from the businessman in St. Louis, A.B. '05, whom DeGraff had impressed at the City Club and who had taken the pulse of other alumni in the city and pleaded for reversal; a similar plea for Meyer from ten school men in the same city; another from a St. Louis medical doctor on behalf of DeGraff; a telegram from Ohio warning Missouri "WILL BE THE LAUGHING STOCK OF THE EDUCATIONAL WORLD" without reversal; fourteen alumni in Schenectady, New York, graduates from 1910 to 1928, all wanting the men reinstated; an alumnus teaching at the University of Wisconsin wanting the same; so also a two-time alumnus teaching at Cornell University in New York ("The students of today are an alert inquiring lot. They wish to know the answer to the ages old question, what is life?, and they are asking for an answer in frank terms. But knowledge does not mean corruption"); and so also the superintendent of the Jewish Hospital of St. Louis ("The present generation is seeking after truth in a perfectly dignified way and any attempt at covering up the facts only tends to make the youth of today lose respect for those who hamper them in their efforts at honesty and truth finding"); a letter from Student Government President Frank Knight conveying the resolution passed by the mass student rally in Jesse Hall directed to the curators; and of course the carefully crafted letter from the loose faculty group in Columbia making their final plea.[5]

One letter that shouldn't have been overlooked was by the Reverend David R. Haupt, Episcopal Rector of Calvary Church in downtown Columbia, just a couple of blocks from the university. In a reflective, agonizing, and personal plea, Haupt appealed on behalf of Meyer and DeGraff, the former a "Godly" man of enormous respect, the latter, only in his third year at Missouri, beloved and respected by students more than any other on the faculty. "Furthermore," said Haupt of DeGraff, "to many of the young men he has been the greatest influence for decent, upright and manly living in their lives here. A Christian man of excellent habits and the teacher of a Sunday School class, he has spoken frequently, in public and private, for those things which make up what we call The Christian Way of Life. He has addressed the students under my own pastoral charge and inspired them with a deeply religious message. He is a man of genuine reverence for holy things, and most of all for the souls of his students. Withal he knows more about where students really live than probably any other man in Columbia, and is better qualified to give students the help they need in intimate matters than many well-meaning parents who are naturally shocked by this publicity."[6]

Of course, where one parent of a student wanted the professors reinstated, another wanted them out. Contrary messages urging support of
the firings awaited the curators, including recurring agitation from J. B.
Cole of Columbia and a gaggle of protests from two women's clubs along
with the Anne Helm chapter of the Daughters of the American Revolution
from Macon, Missouri. Those matched the letter from the vice-chairman
of the same group in Danville, Indiana, who warned darkly of threats
to America's foundations, including marriage, by "the great army of so-
cialists and communists who are spreading their insidious propaganda
everywhere throughout the land."[7]

Would any such pleadings make any difference? The gap in understanding was wide, but the hearing on April 6 took on the trappings of
a legal proceeding. Several days before the meeting, in very lawyer-like
language, Meyer and DeGraff, along with Hobart Mowrer, were served
notice of the impending meeting of the curators in the president's office in
Jesse Hall and informed that they could make a statement if they chose. In
identical but separate statements, all three men authorized Leland Hazard
to legally represent them without cost at the hearing. The United Press
claimed the community looked for no reversal of the Executive Board's
decision. In fact, it reported "that failure of university authorities to 'go
down the line' might react unfavorably on appropriations." Even Hazard
knew his clients weren't the only ones in the dock; the trio of curators who
had recommended the action in the first place were also on trial. Reportedly also, after three weeks of mulling it over, students who had mounted
a spirited defense had now resigned themselves to their own impotence.[8]

2

The full Board of Curators convened in President Brooks's oak-paneled
office in Jesse Hall at 9 A.M. on Saturday, April 6. Old business was soon
dispatched and the "trial," such as it was, commenced. As students and
reporters milled around Jesse Hall and in the president's ante-room wanting to know the latest, the board first called attorney Hazard, representing his three clients. While the session proceeded behind closed doors,
the *Columbia Missourian* raised the specter of the issue spilling into the
courts, something on which Hazard refused comment until the board had
rendered its decision. Hope for a quick verdict faded when Hazard produced a long list of witnesses he intended to call, all to the consternation
of some of the curators who thought the proceedings were unnecessarily protracted. The aura of legalities reportedly prompted the presence of

the university's attorney, Orville Barnett, who had been at the morning session on other business before the board.[9]

The curators received the Executive Board report of March 20, as well as the most recent batch of communications petitioning the board one way or another. They decided to renew the inquiry into the controversy and called Leland Hazard, who made his preliminary presentation. The questions before the board, said Hazard, included whether the sex questionnaire lowered morality among Missouri students; whether it contained any scientific validity; whether the three affected parties possessed fundamental misapprehensions of the requirements of public confidence in the university in both the academic and nonacademic worlds; and whether the trio possessed moral fitness to hold their positions at the university since the Executive Board had implicitly deemed them unfit. Hazard also inquired if any other charges were outstanding against Meyer and De-Graff since their defense rested on knowing them all. After discussing the matter privately, the board advised him that no other issues were pending, that Meyer and DeGraff could remain in the room, that Mowrer would not be present, and that he should proceed. With the transcriptionist present, testimony commenced about 10:15 A.M. and continued throughout the day, with appropriate breaks for lunch, supper, and so on. Hazard dominated the hearing, posing questions to his two clients, while the president, the board, and the university attorney looked on. None offered any questions, and attorney Barnett objected only when he thought testimony strayed too far.

Although Hazard had spent the day before working with Meyer, the heart of his defense eluded him. Hazard said later that the stresses of his life had not interrupted his sleep and that rarely had professional matters kept him awake. But the subconscious—that was another matter. Whatever happened the night of April 5, the young lawyer awakened with a clear sense of his client's defense. He would have Professor Meyer deliver the controversial Social Psychology lecture to the full board. And he would have him do so in front of the female students who had heard it originally. It was a great scheme, one he had to work up to, to be sprung at just the right time. Hazard had debriefed all former women students in the lecture who were available. "They were a somber lot," he said later, "as social workers are likely to be. All affirmed an understanding of the reasons for the so-called sex lecture and all were willing to testify on behalf of Dr. Meyer." So far, so good. But Hazard's preparations were clouded with doubt. Social work was new, and Hazard figured eight of the nine curators had never heard of Jane Addams or her work in the settlement house movement. There were taboos that could not be violated. Those included prohibition against placing obscene materials in the U.S. mails. In the 1870s, Anthony Comstock, a conscientious moralist appalled at the lewd goings-on in New York, had lobbied an anti-obscenity statute through Congress and had become a special agent in the U.S. Postal Service, where he helped protect the nation's morals until his death in 1915. Though definitions of obscenity were coming under increasing scrutiny by that time, Comstock's success placed strictures on the national dialogue about sex and struck terror in many a publisher's heart.

At the time Max Meyer underwent his travail—"kicked out of the University of Missouri by the Comstocks" said one critic—the infamous case of Mary Ware Dennett was working its way through federal court in Brooklyn, New York. Dennett had found a dearth of material for instruction on the facts of life for her two boys and so wrote an instructional manual, *The Sex Side of Life*, a pamphlet used by the YMCA and other organizations, including the Bronxville, New York, school system. The pamphlet had been banned from the U.S. mails in 1922, the order for which was signed by Postmaster General Will Hays, who later went to work for Hollywood to police the morals of motion pictures. A few weeks after the curators mulled over Max Meyer's fate in April 1929, Dennett was convicted of mailing the material to a married woman in Virginia. Protests, testimonials, and a defense committee to raise funds for her appeal followed her conviction, as did stirrings in Congress, led by New York Senator Royal Copeland and Congressman Fiorello LaGuardia, to exempt such instructional materials from federal prosecution. Max Meyer hadn't mailed anything obscene, but the Victorian mind-set that had hauled Mary Ware Dennett into federal court had brought Max Meyer to his own trial in Jesse Hall. Dennett wanted instruction for the young, Meyer for the potential social worker. The arguments were already old in 1929, that of the protection of society's morals versus unwarranted censorship. Jack Blanton repeatedly claimed the sex questionnaire was unmailable, but Hobart Mowrer must not have thought so when he and his colleagues brashly or naively popped about seven hundred of them in the mailbox a few weeks before.[10]

Testimony continued throughout the evening. The time was right. Hazard referred the curators to the ending of the Executive Board's minutes, which indicated that "Dr. Meyer's inquiry continued further by the Board." The only record of that further inquiry belonged to Meyer himself, who said it was about the appropriateness of the sex lecture in his Social Psychology class. The attorney now announced Meyer's willingness to rehearse that lecture, after which the women students who had heard it would testify about its faithfulness to the original version. The board hashed the matter out in executive session, after which Hazard reentered the hearing room and was advised to proceed. Meyer's women students filed in, one even on crutches. "The lawyers on the Board, four of them, knew what I was doing," said Hazard later. "Two showed well restrained approval. Two were unhappy. There was tense silence."

What had brought these men and women to this point in a long evening had been a single lecture in a normal psychology class. But exacerbated by reckless talk from Brooks ("sewer sociology," for example) and others, the lecture had spawned ugly and utterly outrageous rumors, including one about Meyer using the questionnaire to compile a list of "easy girls." If the issue over the infamous sex lecture was actually reasonably well concealed from the press and the public, it weighed heavily on the minds of the curators. Actually, Meyer had given the Social Psychology lecture on the physiology of sex only four times to a total of about twenty women students, most preparing for social work. The point of the lecture, Meyer would say more than once, was to prepare such professionals for their own safety as well as for field work with prostitutes or other unmarried women who might be in danger of unwanted pregnancy. While Meyer despised the term behaviorism, he did use reflexology to describe mammalian physical responses to sexual stimuli. In a Victorian gesture designed to not embarrass the women by discussing such intimate matters in mixed company, Meyer engaged in some deception, telling the male students there would be no class. With the lecture he included a tabulated summary of the reflexes, again saving some embarrassment; alert to untutored outside reaction, Meyer cautioned care in handling the tabulated summary.

Evidently, a copy of the scientific document got out. In early March, Brooks had summoned Meyer to his office to discuss the lecture because of complaints about it from unnamed individuals. He was reportedly teaching how to engage in sexual intercourse. Of course that was not true. In fact, it was absurd, but the president wanted Meyer to "talk it over" prior to giving the lecture the next year. According to Meyer, Brooks told him he shouldn't "enter into any detailed discussion of sex functions. That is too risky." Fine. Meyer would talk with him next year. For now the matter seemed closed until it was reopened—to Meyer's great surprise—at the Executive Board meeting after the stenographers had been excused. Meyer speculated that one of his current students "who had a certain neurotic tendency" might have taken offense and said something about it. But she ended up joining the entire class in signing a statement complimenting Meyer's instruction. Later, Meyer guessed that the copy of the tabulation might have been passed along by the father of a young woman who had taken Social Psychology the year before, who liked medicine and social work but had differed with her parents in her desire to study medicine. An able student, she decided to major in psychology and also asked to serve as Meyer's assistant beginning in the fall of 1928. That was fine with Meyer, as he had been impressed with her laboratory work. Before school started, however, the young woman wrote Meyer that she would not be returning to finish at Missouri, but was transferring to a small southern college that her father preferred. Meyer thought that possibly the father had discovered the tabulation among her things, prevented her return to Columbia, and passed the document along to Brooks or to someone else who passed it along. For his part, Brooks wouldn't say who complained, and the origins of the issue remained a matter of speculation.

Ironically, Meyer had asked Dorothy Postle, an instructor in psychology, to sit in on the sex lecture that spring, thinking she might take on that course in the future and wanting her to see how he handled it. After the complaint, Postle was debriefed about Meyer's conduct of the lecture, and she spoke of it in professional terms. In an added irony, Postle had an outstanding academic career ahead of her, but it wouldn't be at Missouri. Instead she finally wound up at the University of Michigan, her talent lost to Missouri, possibly another casualty of the questionnaire fiasco.

During the Executive Board hearing on March 19, or perhaps the small hours of the morning of March 20, Meyer had to explain a matter he thought the president had already closed. Obviously briefed by Brooks, the Executive Board possessed the reflex tabulation and wanted answers from the weary and ambushed professor. Was he teaching students how to have sex? Was he teaching them how not to have it? As Meyer remembered it, Jack Blanton declared, "Well, now, don't you realize that when one of these young ladies wants to have sexual intercourse with a boy she will just take that sheet of paper and silently slip it to him as an indication that—an invitation that she would like to have sexual intercourse with him?" Recalled Meyer: "That question so completely overthrew me I didn't know what to answer." "Those women were known to me as respectable women. I cannot dream of anything as silly,—by that, I mean absurd, utterly absurd. I cannot understand how a man can ask that question, and I answered to that, 'No, I certainly have too much respect for American womanhood to dream of any such thing as that, that women taking an advanced science course will use a series of biological functions, shown them for their information for such a purpose as that.' "[11]

No wonder Meyer's attorney wanted to make the Social Psychology lecture the centerpiece of his defense. For his part, Blanton later emphatically denied making the statement about a young woman using the tabulation as an invitation for illicit behavior. McDavid supported him. Unfortunately, such collision of memories only pointed up the foolish danger of sending the stenographers out of the room. In any case, whatever was said or wasn't said, Meyer himself thought his dismissal by the Executive Board was due more to the lecture than to the questionnaire. When his rehearsal of that lecture began amid the tense atmosphere in the president's office on the evening of April 6, Professor Meyer gave no hint of being "on the defensive." He was "in full command of the scene, making a classroom of the courtroom, students of his accusers," said Hazard later. "I shall not be able to put on paper his high pitched but not unpleasant voice, or the character of that voice, which made of every taboo word a sharp cutting tool to excise mystery from the subject and to expose the clean, bare bone of scientific fact."

Meyer explained the societal requirements for food and for the perpetuation of the species. Eleven physiological reflexes fulfilled the latter, but just three were essentially sexual. Skillfully, Professor Meyer took his listeners through each of the eleven with scientific discussion of fluids, body parts, biological responses, and the like. Less than two weeks earlier Meyer's sex reflex tabulation had been audited by two distinguished scientists on the faculty, Professors Addison Gulick and Winterton C. Curtis, and endorsed by fifteen additional faculty members. "The content of this paper is scientifically systematic," Gulick and Curtis wrote at the time, praising the document and citing its necessity. There was nothing tawdry or cheap about it. Now, while his client lectured, Hazard watched the curators. He thought Mercer Arnold and Frank McDavid, both from the Ozarks, probably wanted to stop the lecture, but they were lawyers and their profession prevented them. "Seven centuries—since the barons wrested from King John in the meadow of Runnymeade the right of due process of law—stood in their way," said Hazard. "They had had the 'Sex Lecture' in hand when they suspended Meyer three weeks earlier. They had inflamed the people of Missouri without telling them all the facts. Now when those facts fell from the serene lips of the accused, they sat abashed. Where was the indecency, the unspeakable vileness? Had their own pitiable inadequacy supplied it? In any case the lawyers, all of them, knew that no one dare deny me the right to have my client repeat at the hearing the very matter for which he was on trial."[12]

It was a brilliant coup for the young lawyer, though his characterization of the curators inflaming the public is a stretch. In any case, when Meyer finished, "There was a hush which I did not hasten to break," recalled Hazard. "One of the Curators [bearing all the marks of McDavid] had a back as stiff and straight as that of his fellow Missourian, [General]

John J. Pershing. Presently he fixed me with a fiery, frustrated eye, and said, nodding in the direction of the students, 'Mr. Hazard, I will never cross-examine a woman on this subject.' I waited. No other Curator spoke. The women students filed from the room. Chivalry for the ladies. Would there be justice for my client?"[13]

The generally cordial and sober proceedings were interrupted by the day's lone entertainment late in the afternoon, at least for those milling outside Brooks's office. As Hazard built his defense, State Senator Carter M. Buford from southeast Missouri suddenly appeared, wanting to be heard by the curators. He got in, spent a few minutes telling them to throw out the offenders, and emerged on the steps of Jesse Hall, surrounded by students, reporters, and the just plain curious. Seeing the crowd, he raised his fists, claiming, "You can stand 40 deep and I can still fight my way out, but if you want to know what I told the Board, I told them that if Meyer and DeGraff are reinstated the whole institution might just as well be rented out to DeGraff and his gang so he can carry on his teachings among these students whose parents are willing to send them here." That was red meat to the heckling crowd, who taunted him mercilessly. He said he'd employed a stenographer who reproduced the questionnaire for his constituents who asked for them. "Down in the Ozarks, where I was born and educated," said the unshaven senator, "we didn't need high salaried professors to discuss sex problems with us."[14]

Such buffoonery only highlighted the serious cultural tensions unleashed by the questionnaire controversy. But the other end of the witness spectrum included distinguished men of science and learning, notably Edwin B. Branson in geology, James Harvey Rogers in economics, and nationally renowned Winterton C. Curtis in zoology. After midnight, the respected trio filed into the hearing room and spoke for the larger faculty group protesting the executive decision. "We were really refreshed to know that we had in our college men of that standing and caliber," said Curator George Willson later. "Their opinions were heard with respect." No stranger to high-profile controversies, Curtis had been called by the American Civil Liberties Union as an expert witness for the defense in the trial of John Thomas Scopes in Dayton, Tennessee, in 1925. Accused of teaching evolution contrary to Tennessee law, the high school teacher had been prosecuted by frequent presidential candidate and former secretary of state William Jennings Bryan, and defended by Clarence Darrow, the well-known agnostic "attorney for the damned." Found guilty, Scopes had his conviction overturned on a technicality. More significant, the unfortunate case inflicted a serious blow to fundamentalist Christianity in its war with modernism and labeled Tennessee as a cultural backwater. The linkage of Tennessee's case with Missouri's by critics in editorials, letters, and political cartoons became shorthand for the grave error the curators had made in ousting a world-famous scientist and an energetic and popular sociologist.[15]

With all the direct testimony heard, the curators debated their next move. At 2:15 A.M., having reached no decision, they adjourned until morning, resuming at about 10:15. Hobart Mowrer, source of the questionnaire, waited all day and evening for his summons to the president's office. It never came. Decades later, Leland Hazard claimed the session with the curators that first day was the longest of his very long career. On Sunday, round two, the curators took no testimony, save for that of Walter Williams, founder and dean of the School of Journalism. Williams commanded more respect among the faculty and administration than anyone else on campus, as well as from among a good number of highly respected professionals. A world-traveling journalist who devoted his life to professionalizing his craft, Dean Williams brought competence and quiet dignity to any task he assumed. Not surprisingly, the board had sent for him, as James Goodrich explained, to provide his view of the faculty reaction to the recommendation of the Executive Board dismissing Max Meyer. His answer: the recommendation was too severe. The facts didn't warrant dismissal of Professor Meyer. Williams was excused.[16]

With Williams out of the room, the curators debated the relevance of testimony about Meyer's Social Psychology course. Frank McDavid offered a motion to eliminate from the charges against Meyer all material related to the class; A. A. Speer seconded, and the motion carried. That's what the minutes said anyway. Then the hard work began. For several hours the curators hashed out whether to endorse the Executive Board's decision or to modify it. There seemed no significant debate about Professor DeGraff. He was probably gone. In fact, Dean Tisdel and Professor Charles Ellwood, chairman of the sociology department, had discussed between themselves the wisdom of his reappointment for the following year even before his ouster by the Executive Board, essentially because of the questionnaire fiasco. But curators Speer, George Willson, Milton Tootle, and James Goodrich wanted to condemn the questionnaire, punish the culpable faculty, but soften the severity of the Executive Board's dismissal of Meyer at least. He was a scientist of renowned standing after all; his moral character had been exemplary; and didn't his lengthy and faithful service to the university count for something? Look at all those letters from people outside Columbia that pointed out those things again and again.

Even though Leland Hazard wasn't privy to these proceedings, he had been right all along. The three members of the Executive Board were also on trial, and all three stood by their original recommendation of dismissal.

Eventually, Mercer Arnold and Jack Blanton relented, at least in the case of Max Meyer, but McDavid, ever the true believer, held on to the end. And what about President Brooks? The record is clear: no other course was open than to approve the firings, and he hoped the action of the Executive Board would be sustained. There was more debate, including the language of the communiqué to be released to the public and those involved. As the afternoon wore on, the words fell into place and the document was approved unanimously.[17]

In proper and semi-legal language, the curators' order declared its approval of and concurrence in the Executive Board's report of March 20, 1929, including its statements and recommendations relative to "certain questionnaires" circulated among students at the university "except that the recommendations and statements therein as affecting Dr. Max F. Meyer be modified as hereinafter ordered, in view of his long service to the university and our conviction that the offense for which he was suspended will not be repeated." Instead of dismissal, Meyer would be suspended from his university duties without pay for one year commencing Monday, April 8, 1929. The order sustained DeGraff's dismissal effective April 8—no surprise there—and made no mention of Hobart Mowrer. The order also incorporated into the full board's report the niceties from the Executive Board's March 20 statement about the nature of the university and its morality, wholesomeness, and sanity, and the confidence that parents could place in it; it also embraced the same statement's condemnation of unwarranted questionnaires, and that "students should not be made subjects of investigation by other students, particularly when such investigation by its very nature tends to create the condition which it is alleged to correct." The kicker in the whole statement was the issue of scientific validation, an issue that would plague the curators no end: "Neither can we find any justification for an inquiry that from its very nature could not produce any scientifically valid conclusions nor any facts likely to be of substantial value." Further, the perpetrators had no good sense about the requirements of getting and keeping the public's trust. The curators also ordered their secretary, Leslie Cowan, to destroy the completed questionnaires, which had been sealed in the university's vault. They concluded with a call for reform: "In order to protect the University from a recurrence of similar indiscretions, it is recommended that the general faculty establish, by committee or otherwise, some system of providing for the careful supervision of all investigations affecting students."[18]

The deed was done. Whether McDavid saw any wisdom in his colleagues' arguments or not isn't clear; more likely he looked around the room and saw himself as a minority of one. For those on the outside at

least, the sheer length of the debate suggested integrity in the process. After all, reasonable men could disagree. But would time betray leaks from
the oak-paneled office?

Word of the curators' action traveled fast. By Sunday night the board's
decision formed the single topic of talk over dinner in frat houses, sororities, restaurants, and hotels throughout the city. But three weeks had
numbed even the young, and the campus had seemingly resigned itself
to the heavy hand of discipline for their professors. Except for the spate
of "did you hear?" discussions after the curators' announcement, talk on
campus had moved to upcoming student elections, dances, and normal
jelly dates. In fact, spring was in the air as the temperature climbed toward
90 degrees on Saturday. The heat left sweaty brows on the somber men in
the president's office while stockingless women bounced through solemn
Jesse Hall. Rouge between knees and shoetops, which defied midwestern propriety, had made a brief entrée a year earlier, but now the fad im-
ported from California—even then a trendsetter—seemed here to stay for
a while. Change was coming.[19]

3

By Monday morning quiet had settled on the campus, with students
picking their way to classes through a drizzling spring rain. Neither De-
Graff nor Meyer had any public comment on the curators' action, though
Meyer reportedly had been pleased with the outpouring from supporters far and wide. He wouldn't discuss his plans, but speculation ran the
gamut, some saying he'd be back while others claimed he'd be elsewhere
when his year of suspension was lifted. A reporter found one unnamed
dean who claimed the decision would placate both parents and scientists, while an unnamed professor criticized the curators, speculating they
feared reversing the Executive Board while still wishing to save Meyer.
For his part, James Goodrich called the decision a compromise, which it
obviously was. The board had shed some blood—not its own—and people were punished. If everyone wasn't satisfied the curators would simply
have to ride out the storm.[20]

Though the fight had been lost, a few days after the hearing Jonas Viles
told alumnus John McCutcheon that the faculty group didn't regard the
matter finished. Indeed it wasn't. With Meyer in his fourth-floor office
the day after the hearing, President Brooks was closeted for several hours
with Herman Schlundt, head of the local chapter of the AAUP. Brooks
had little regard, perhaps even contempt, for the American Association

of University Professors—"The Professors-Union," he reportedly and repeatedly called it—but he had to respect its membership on campus, including its local president. A gentleman of great competence, Herman
Schlundt had been at Missouri for twenty-seven years—another President Jesse recruit—and had long established himself as one of the outstanding instructors on campus. When it was all over there would be a
building named after him. Schlundt was no hothead and had urged patience from the national organization, but now the issue seemed drawn.
Arthur O. Lovejoy, having taught a couple of years at Missouri but lately
a member of Johns Hopkins University's philosophy department, had noticed the goings-on at Missouri in March and had correctly speculated to
AAUP secretary H. W. Tyler the day before the meeting of the full board
"that the Missouri people would probably prefer to play a lone hand for
the present; their position, in any case," he thought, "is in some degree
strengthened in that they are enabled to say to the local authorities that
the Association has already manifested an interest in the case, and that an
investigation is likely if the Board of Regents should sustain the recommendation of its committee."

If Lovejoy hoped the early AAUP interest might influence the curators
toward leniency, such hope was unfounded. It's unknown whether the
curators even discussed the AAUP's likely reaction among themselves.
But action was clearly called for. Schlundt wasted little time, dashing off a
letter to Secretary Tyler along with pertinent enclosures, including copies
of the female version of the questionnaire and the orders of both the Executive Board and the full board. "The hope expressed in my former letter
of a happy solution of the situation has not been realized," Schlundt said.
He offered a fair summary of the hearing and alerted Tyler to the hot Social Psychology lecture issue; he claimed it figured in Meyer's suspension
even though it had been peer reviewed. Schlundt invited a quiet, firsthand
visit to the campus to gather material and issued a Macedonian call to the
national organization: "PLEASE COME ON."[21]

Such a call also came from others, just as Schlundt predicted. On the
morning of April 8, the wires were hot between Columbia and AAUP
headquarters in Washington. Addison Gulick in physiological chemistry
and James Harvey Rogers in economics sent separate telegrams urging investigation of the Social Psychology issue, with Rogers claiming the matter required on-site investigation and Gulick promising cooperation from
faculty leaders. That afternoon, Jack Turner, a student leader and member
of DeGraff's Family class, sent his own wire to Tyler with the desperation
of outraged youth: "TURNING TO YOU AS LAST RESORT TO EXON-
ERATE MEN SO RUTHLESSLY EXECUTED BY AGRICULTURAL MIND

OF MISSOURI WE THE STUDENT BODY UNIVERSITY OF MISSOURI ASK THAT YOU DO EVERYTHING IN YOUR POWER TO FREE OUR LEADERS IN ACADEMIC FREEDOM FROM MORASS OF IGNORANT INTOLERANCE WE OFFER ALL OUR AID." Two days later, Turner and more than forty of his Family classmates again petitioned the AAUP "to take some action to vindicate the characters of Dr. DeGraff and Dr. Max Meyer, so foully maligned in the recent so-called 'sex scandal' at this institution, and to investigate the details of a situation that has become unbearable here." Of course Lucille Dorff's signature headed the list, which also included Mary Ellen Hubbard, the outgoing president of the Women's Self Government Association, who had been among the first to bring the questionnaire to Dean Priddy's attention; and Alberta Davis, whose father had at first protested to Brooks about the questionnaire and then recanted when he learned his daughter had been on the issuing committee. The students understood the stakes involved, and feared the chilling effect on academics and the loss of Missouri's educational stature if things continued as they were. The next day, Professor Jonas Viles, part of the faculty group intimately involved in the crisis and who had been communicating with St. Louis alumni, assured Tyler of the necessity of the AAUP's investigation and that it had to be principled—all without the petty fighting and personality conflicts that could plague such cases. He too saw big issues at stake. While he found no fault with the curators' procedures, he argued that "the final action was not only an injustice to the men involved but strikes at the very roots of some of the ideals most essential to the profession."[22]

Students and faculty weren't the only ones petitioning the professors' association. On Monday afternoon, Stratton Brooks sent his own wire to Secretary Tyler, likewise calling for an investigation and promising full cooperation by the university. Further, he would be in Washington, D.C., later in the week and offered to confer if so desired, an offer Tyler quickly accepted. For his part, Tyler wasted no time either, quickly arranging for members of the association to meet with Brooks in Washington and apprising Henry Crew of Northwestern University, the AAUP president, of developments. Crew was also on the move, endorsing Tyler's activities and exchanging names of those who might serve on the investigating committee. In fact, in the days after the request for the probe, a flurry of letters and telegrams bandying candidates for a potential roster went in and out of the Washington office. Professor Albert Weiss at Ohio State, Meyer's doctoral student at Missouri and eminent in his own right, made such a suggestion and called on the association to quash what he mistakenly thought was the university's attempt to side-step investigation by merely suspending Meyer. It amounted to dismissal, thought Weiss, and was "considerably more humiliating." Tyler worked to smooth out the organizational and jurisdictional problems occasioned by distance and other matters. Did the Missouri situation call for an investigation by the association's Committee A on Academic Freedom and Tenure, or was this a matter for the Executive Committee? Could a special committee be quickly appointed and report directly, or did it need to go to the Executive Committee through Committee A? To outsiders these might have seemed arcane and inconsequential matters, but they had to be resolved, and Secretary Tyler did so quickly and professionally. He hoped to put some sort of statement in the association's May *Bulletin*, knowing there wouldn't be another issue until October.[23]

Things were still very much up in the air when Stratton Brooks, in Washington to attend the Gridiron Club dinner on April 13, met with five AAUP officials for two hours at the association's headquarters on Friday—just five days after the curators' decision. The five came from American University, Penn, MIT, and Johns Hopkins, and represented both the Executive Committee and Committee A, as well as one who attended without portfolio. "The occasion was I venture to say something of a landmark in the history of the Association," reported Secretary Tyler to President Henry Crew. "It has been sometimes alleged that we were ready to use a club on small and weak institutions, but rarely willing to tackle large ones. This time the President of a large state University appeals to us to help him save the University from disaster, urging that unless a report can be prepared by a competent outside body, he is in great danger of losing his faculty." Tyler thought the threat to Meyer's Social Psychology lecture posed the most severe challenge to academic freedom in the whole Missouri case, but listening to Brooks it sounded as if that had been handled properly. After all, Brooks said the curators had stricken from consideration everything associated with the lecture, and that Meyer could teach it again. Further, while the president thought Meyer guilty of a mistake in judgment, he nonetheless spoke well of him and looked forward to his remaining in the university. Brooks didn't know for sure the curators' attitude toward the investigation but would gamble they'd accept it. He didn't care, he said, whether the investigation supported his and the curators' position or not. He wanted the investigation no matter what. At least that's what he said.

After Brooks departed, the group decided that the association should act quickly and that Professor John M. Maguire of Harvard Law School, who had been closely watching the Missouri case, would join the committee or serve as legal adviser. Still, the group deferred final decisions until the AAUP's Council met in regular session on April 20. The favorable impression Brooks left suggests a good deal about his abilities to smooth things over. Of course, Tyler hadn't been privy to the curators' minutes of the previous Sunday, which showed that Brooks urged firing both Meyer and DeGraff, and apparently Tyler took at reasonably face value the president's call for an investigation. Did Brooks think he could both mask his hypocrisy and influence the investigation by getting ahead of it? His motives may have been clouded, but what is clear is that April 12 was the apex of the relationship between an increasingly beleaguered president and a professional organization dedicated to the noblest ideals of American higher education. The days ahead wouldn't be so smooth.

The file in the AAUP's headquarters soon bulged with letters and telegrams from around the country as the procedure and committee took shape. At Missouri, Winterton C. Curtis represented the faculty group defending Meyer and DeGraff. Always deferential, Curtis still had his own suggestions and even visited President Crew at Northwestern before traveling to Washington, where he talked by phone with Tyler. He wanted the best committee possible, with no radicals to obscure the crucial issues. On the train east from Chicago he read the article by Lillian Symes, "What Shall We Tell The Children?" in the April issue of *Harpers*. Symes argued for a situational ethic, and thought that people who lived "in a state of happy certainty about God and man" were a shrinking minority. The old mores, morals, and taboos betrayed serious fissures and proved inadequate to a culture in the grips of change. Impressed, Curtis contemplated sending copies to the curators.[24]

Herman Schlundt had ideas about committee membership also, as did just about everybody else. As an added twist, AAUP Vice-President Howard Warren of Princeton University had been at a conference of psychologists in Washington the day after Brooks's visit, and found some who thought joint action by the AAUP and the American Psychological Association might be feasible. "Dr. Meyer is held in great esteem by the psychologists in this country," Warren told Tyler. "All those with whom I have talked are very indignant at the treatment accorded him, and want the Psychological Association to take some action." He wasn't sure joint efforts were best, but believed that the psychological association could do something on its own if it wished.

Both before and after the AAUP Council authorized the creation of an investigating committee, wire services and other sources took the story of the probe nationwide—which brought another round of unwanted publicity in Tulsa, Shreveport, Wichita Falls, Little Rock, Louisville, Lancaster, Lincoln, Long Beach, St. Paul, and everywhere else. Early on Secretary

Tyler announced that the association had investigated numerous dismissals but never one over a questionnaire; and that elsewhere, such documents had been aimed at targeted groups. He also pointed out the discretionary latitude of the committee. Meanwhile, names fell off the potential committee list almost as fast they went on, all for one reason or another. Work, family illness, and the like forced some of the invitees to excuse themselves. It came as no surprise that it might be difficult to persuade hard-working academics at a crucial time of the year to travel to Missouri, conduct an investigation into a distasteful matter, draft a report, and stick with it to the end, all without reward except for the satisfaction and the discharge of professional obligations. Professor Caswell Grave, a zoologist at Washington University in St. Louis, offered the most telling reason for declining the chairmanship of the committee. The issue over Meyer in Missouri was too hot, notably in St. Louis, said Grave, and he had to decline. President Crew lamented to W. C. Curtis that it wasn't "nearly such an easy matter as one might think to get together a committee, its membership of which will command respect everywhere and the members of which can spare the time and energy to serve."[25]

Finally, by the end of the month, the visiting committee membership took shape, and it proved to be a good one. The trio included Percy Bordwell, acting dean of the Law School at the University of Iowa, and Louis L. Thurstone in psychology along with Anton J. Carlson in physiology, both of the University of Chicago. Carlson accepted the chairmanship, while J. H. Gray in economics at American University became one of the original nonvisiting members. Arthur O. Lovejoy in philosophy at Johns Hopkins, a Missouri faculty member from 1908–1910, came on board in May only to drop out later. Since final examinations began May 25, with commencement set for June 5, some of the faculty group in Columbia wanted an early on-site visit and certainly did not want to delay it until fall. Herman Schlundt, checking dates and trying to coordinate things to make sure everyone and everything necessary to the investigation would be available, was in Brooks's office when Carlson's telegram arrived. Fortunately, May 17 and 18, Friday and Saturday, emerged as the consensus for the visit, and all concerned parties prepared for what could be a touchy situation. Secretary Tyler had no specific mandates for the visiting team from the AAUP's Council, save for a desire to see the problem handled broadly, not merely as an issue of faculty suspension or dismissal. Tyler drafted some talking points and dispatched a copy of the association's guidelines for Committee A that, among other things, instructed investigators not to become partisan advocates for aggrieved parties. President Crew assured Chairman Carlson that the AAUP's legal adviser, John M. McGuire of Harvard Law School, would be available if desired. "This case," said Crew, "is probably the most significant one that has yet come before our Association."[26]

Meanwhile, rumors and intrigue permeated the Columbia campus. It was no secret on campus that President Brooks and the dean of the Faculty of Law, James L. Parks, were "at swords' points," a development of long standing. According to Parks, Brooks advised the Executive Board to dismiss everyone involved in the questionnaire business, a fact—if limited to Meyer and DeGraff—borne out by the record. Parks further believed that pressure from Curators Arnold, McDavid, and Blanton prevented the full board's reinstatement of Meyer at least. Also, said Dean Parks, the overwhelming majority of faculty had no confidence in Brooks.[27]

Parks's view mirrored the story making the rounds that a number of curators wanted less severe punishment for faculty involved in the questionnaire but couldn't carry the day. And most faculty doubtless took little pleasure in seeing the curators embarrassed by an investigation, although Jonas Viles told John McCutcheon, "From the outset the two Boards lacked intelligent leadership and effective statements of university ideals." Most faculty thought the sex questionnaire showed little discretion, but that wasn't the issue. The president's role, however, was another story. Brooks's record left questions about his motives and his ability to carry a position for the faculty. Dissatisfaction with the president predated the questionnaire disaster but soon grew widespread. A faculty member who earlier had remarked to a local Bible study class that African characteristics appeared in Caucasians because of race mixing in Europe got no help from Brooks when three members of the Ku Klux Klan demanded his dismissal. In fact, Brooks had requested the faculty member's resignation, only to have it blocked by one of the curators. Doubts arose. In the current crisis, instead of damping down the controversy and running interference against public outrage, Brooks fueled tensions by his intemperate behavior and "sewer sociology" talk. And no compelling reason required sacrifices to the legislative gods in Jefferson City. When economics professor Harry Gunnison Brown told Secretary Tyler that he wondered if Brooks "would protect any of his faculty against any significant outside attack," he doubtless spoke for many of those same people.[28]

It got worse. Winterton Curtis told Henry Crew that he had heard confidentially but reliably that some of the curators were, in Curtis's words, "much annoyed" with Brooks's invitation to the AAUP, and quite suspicious of his motives. More significant, the board felt itself "on trial" and would want to make its case before the investigators. It all looked increasingly formal. "Such a situation would be a remarkable one in view of the

attitude of hostility such a board might assume toward a committee of the
A.A.U.P.," said Curtis. It was a great chance to teach valuable lessons to
the curators, he thought. But despite the invitation from Brooks, an off-
the-record claim by Max Meyer suggested the president may have feared
the coming inquiry. According to Meyer, after the decree of the full board,
but before the AAUP investigating team came to campus, Meyer had been
summoned to the president's office. Brooks talked about the improvements in Meyer's laboratory and asked if he wanted more. No, he didn't,
since improvements had been completed. Well, what about the summer
school teaching that Meyer had been promised but that now, because of
the suspension, had been snatched away? Would Meyer like to teach elsewhere, if Brooks could secure it? The answer might be yes, replied Meyer,
since he had a wife and family to support. Brooks had something else on
his mind—the impending visit of the AAUP investigators. Meyer replied
that he didn't invite them. "Suppose," Meyer recalled Brooks as saying,
"when the investigating committee has arrived in Columbia, I at once
invite them and you to a luncheon at my house. When we then all sit
comfortably around the table, you say suddenly: 'Well, gentlemen, there
is really nothing here to investigate; and you might just as well go home
again by the next train.' Now, if you will do that, it won't be to your dis-
advantage!"[29]

Such a bizarre attempt at bribery, if true (and there is no independent
corroboration), further strengthened the idea that Brooks had been insin-
cere in seeking the association's visit in the first place. It also suggested—
again, if true—that he had no character. Regardless, Carlson's committee
was coming, and a number of faculty pleaded for the availability of transcripts of both curators' hearings. Such openness was in fact promised to
Chairman Carlson by James Goodrich, president of the Board of Curators.
With courtesy and diplomatic polish, Goodrich, a former circuit judge in
Kansas City, pledged complete cooperation from the entire membership,
including providing a transcribed record of the curators' hearing. In return he asked for any official AAUP statement on academic freedom.[30]

Carlson remained busy preparing for the visit of what association president Henry Crew thought was the biggest academic freedom case yet. In
early May he speculated to chapter president Herman Schlundt that in his
opinion—and he acknowledged it was merely his opinion—95 percent of
freshmen who entered the University of Chicago had been exposed to
the issues of the sex questionnaire. The charge of demoralizing the student body formed a significant issue in the Missouri case, and Carlson
wondered if any method existed to determine what situation along that

line obtained at Missouri. He also wanted original questionnaires, as well as interviews and news clippings about the case. Schlundt theorized that Missouri freshmen essentially matched Chicago students in terms of exposure to the pertinent issues but with one stipulation: "if they come from towns where they have the ordinary moving picture shows." In any case, faculty at Missouri were working on the question. Perhaps the dean of men could provide some assistance, as well as the acting dean of women from the previous year, but Schlundt doubted that Bessie Priddy had sufficient student contact to adequately judge.[31]

Meanwhile, Max Meyer got an interesting and unsolicited letter from a surgeon in Seattle who had been intrigued by the questionnaire. Somehow the doctor had acquired a copy, and had it reproduced and then distributed to twenty-six male students and thirty females of varying economic status at the University of Washington—all without the knowledge of the university's regents. In addition, six nurses also had a look at it. Apparently, the surgeon intended to gauge not answers but reaction to the document's efficacy. Out of sixty-two polled, only one male and one female recorded negative responses. "The findings here shown would seem to demonstrate that the younger generation are [sic] seeking scientific sex facts," the doctor told Meyer. "I, for one, am of the opinion that the sensible thing is to give them what they are seeking, since they are better able than are we of the passing generation to appreciate their needs." Meanwhile, such needs weren't appreciated at Oklahoma Baptist University, where a questionnaire reportedly similar to the Missouri edition was quashed by authorities, copies promptly destroyed, and the head of the psychology department and a student assistant dismissed. According to the Associated Press the university's president claimed "the questionnaire was not fit to be distributed in any school."[32]

Was the Missouri questionnaire a worthy instrument to assess student attitude? The AAUP's legal adviser, John Maguire of Harvard Law School, wanted to get a copy to make sure it wasn't just "bunkum." In some respects, of course, the value of the questionnaire stood aside from the larger issues of free inquiry and the integrity of the university. For better or worse, what Max Meyer later called the "third trial in this crazy affair" was about to begin. The visiting committee was ready, and the university had pledged its cooperation. Documents would be plentiful, and the roster of witnesses extensive. But one set of documents wouldn't be available for the itinerant investigators. Several weeks earlier, acting on orders from the Board of Curators, Secretary Leslie Cowan took the questionnaires from the university vault and, with two witnesses looking on, cast them into the furnace at the power plant, getting singed in the process.[33] It was a sad spectacle. Instead of supplying primary data for a harmless term paper in a sociology class or finding lodging in an archives for a later generation's better understanding of the Jazz Age, two hundred or so questionnaires on matters of the heart, all but a couple sincerely completed by midwestern university students, went up in smoke.

7

What Really Happened

> ... students as a whole appreciate and endorse a liberal and frank attitude toward the problems in life, as they do toward anything else.
>
> —Glenn Degner, junior, University of Missouri,
> May 18, 1929, AAUP Hearing, AAUPP

> It is a problem of the younger generation, and we have to face it.
>
> —Alice Sonnenschein, senior, University of
> Missouri, May 18, 1929, AAUP Hearing, AAUPP

Lefevre Hall on the campus of the University of Missouri provided an ironic setting for the hearings of the American Association of University Professors on the sex questionnaire scandal. The accommodating structure, built in 1913, stood five blocks or so from Jesse Hall and took its name from the late zoologist George Lefevre, who had come to Missouri in 1899. Joined two years later by fellow zoologist W. C. Curtis, and the year after that by chemist Herman Schlundt, the Richard Jesse trio would have been an impressive addition to any faculty. In time, all three had buildings named for them. Before Lefevre died in early 1923, he enjoyed a national standing in his discipline and a local reputation for campus leadership and brilliant classroom teaching.[1] It isn't difficult to imagine that he would have approved the goings-on in his building.

Lefevre's onetime colleague, Herman Schlundt, the popular chemistry professor who also headed the local chapter of the AAUP, spent many hours preparing to host the association's investigating team, which was scheduled to arrive in May. He hoped to lodge them in the downtown Tiger Hotel, rooms all in a row, and looked to have other members of the local affiliate, as he told Chairman A. J. Carlson, "welcome you in a quiet way." He also dispatched documents, lined up several witnesses, and took care of other details before the visitors arrived. Apparently, Percy Bordwell wasn't scheduled to arrive by train from the University of Iowa until early Friday morning, May 17. Nonetheless, that same day, when the committee settled into Room 215 in Lefevre Hall on Missouri's "White" or East Campus at 9 A.M., all members of the visiting team, including Carlson's colleague from Chicago, L. L. Thurstone, were present. So also was Howard Lang, the same court reporter employed by the Board of Curators in April.[2]

For one of the most challenging cases in its fourteen-year history, the American Association of University Professors had selected an exceptionally able and balanced visiting team. A native of San Francisco, Percy Bordwell had earned an undergraduate degree at the University of California before the turn of the century, but had gone east for bachelor's and masters degrees in law at Columbia University in New York. He also earned a Ph.D. there in 1908, the same year he published *The Law of War between Belligerents*. He practiced law in New York City prior to teaching, ironically, at the University of Missouri from 1906 to 1910. In the latter year Bordwell became Professor of Law at the University of Iowa, where at the time of his visit to Columbia he was acting dean of the law school. An AAUP veteran, he had served on the Committee on Organization as well as on one of the association's first committees that investigated an alleged violation of academic freedom, at the University of Colorado back in 1915. A family man, a Republican, and an Episcopalian, Bordwell had even seen overseas duty with the U.S. Army in the Great War.

Joining Bordwell on the AAUP's visiting team, psychologist Louis L. Thurstone was a man of numerous talents, having taught engineering at the University of Minnesota and even having served as a laboratory assistant for Thomas Edison before the war. While teaching at Carnegie Institute of Technology, he took a Ph.D. at the University of Chicago in 1917, to which he returned to teach seven years later. Over the course of his long career he maintained a passion for scientific intelligence measurement, worked with the government and the military, and was the driving force behind the founding of the Psychometric Society as well as the journal *Psychometrika*. He also published nine books, one coauthored with his wife, also an academic who, not incidentally, accompanied him to Columbia.

Rounding out the visiting committee was its chairman, Anton Julius Carlson, one of the nation's outstanding scientists. In fact, Carlson's brilliant work in physiology took him to the top of his profession. He learned biology and hard work as a boy tending sheep in his native Sweden. At sixteen, he migrated to the United States, worked as a carpenter in Chicago, and saved up for tuition at Augustana College in Rock Island, Illinois. He anticipated a life in the Lutheran clergy and, in fact, pastored briefly in Montana, but switched to an academic career at fairly new Stanford University in California. He earned the Ph.D. in 1903, got a Carnegie fellowship, and worked at the biologist's center-of-the-universe in Woods Hole, Massachusetts, starting in 1904, the same year he got a teaching job at the University of Chicago. He stayed at Chicago for the rest of his long life. Known as "Ajax" to generations of loyal students, some of whom made their own ground-breaking contributions in science, Carlson found few things physiological that didn't interest him—heart, stomach, liver, nervous system, whatever. In heavy Swedish brogue, his classic and oft-mimicked interrogative, "Vot iss de effidence?" could both intimidate students and encourage experimentation. His 1916 book, *The Control of Hunger in Health and Disease,* became a classic, and in 1941 he landed on the cover of *Time,* which deemed him the "Scientist's Scientist," as well as "the most colorful figure among U.S. scientists." Not bad for the immigrant shepherd boy. Carlson, along with Bordwell and Thurstone, were well prepared to investigate a simmering academic freedom issue that involved a so-called scientific questionnaire at the University of Missouri.[3]

2

At the opening of the hearing on Friday morning, Jack Blanton from the Board of Curators and Professor James Harvey Rogers from the local AAUP chapter joined the trio of investigators. This was new ground for both parties, and the probing of each side by the other began. Chairman Carlson noted the judicial nature of the committee and that its report to the AAUP would eventually lead to the association's official report. That would have been a normal procedure which wouldn't have changed the problem at the university. But Carlson held out the hope of short-circuiting the whole business by offering an olive branch in the form of a "friendly suggestion" to Blanton, who served as a member of both the executive and full boards. What suggestion was that? "Is there a way in which the Committee might help to remedy what looks like, on the basis of the evidence, which might help to remedy an unfortunate and possibly unjust situation?" Blanton: "I can think of none at this time."

The "friendly suggestion" was actually a brash gambit by the investigators, since not all the evidence had been collected, at least not by them, and Carlson, for one, had not even finished reading the curators' transcript. Then a minor but telling glitch developed when Blanton clashed with Carlson over Blanton's insistence that his colleague George Willson and President Stratton Brooks join him in a unified interview. Willson's presence was fine with Carlson, but not Brooks. He'd be interviewed separately. Shortly after the substantive hearing commenced, Willson joined them.

Initial sparring over whether the visitors had already arrived at a conclusion favorable to Meyer and DeGraff ultimately gave way to debate over academic freedom and its definition. Dean Bordwell likened academic freedom's development to common law, a case-to-case evolution. Sharp definitions proved elusive. Willson had the idea that the students' lack of maturity might justify proscription of such freedom and that, in any case, freedom of studying and teaching were two different things. And randomly sending out questionnaires to those with no connection to the class was something else altogether.

Chairman Carlson raised the inevitable touchstone issue of the questionnaire's scientific validity or, more particularly, the curators' ability to judge same. Blanton claimed they never intended to do so, but the crudity of the document gave them such latitude. Willson, more reflective, claimed no scientific pretensions but was stuck on the questionnaire's infamous question three, which asked women whether their male relationships were limited more by religious views, fear of pregnancy, disease, social recriminations, or their own pride, and so on. Willson thought it required no scientific mind to object to the propriety of the indiscriminate dispatch of questionnaires to unsuspecting women not otherwise engaged in the study of sociology or psychology, and who didn't care to be probed on venereal disease and their relationships with men and the like. Maybe someone taking sociology might have de facto agreed to be open to such things, but not young, underage females studying French, history, or music. Questions about childhood sex play indiscriminately thrown at such individuals seemed out of bounds. Willson, a thirty-eight-year-old family man with two children, a St. Louis attorney, a Missouri graduate, and closely associated with the institution for two decades, believed, as he told the investigators, he "ought to be able to form some opinion whether it is proper for young women who come here, under the protection of the Board here to be interrogated and probed and prodded with that question.

'Would you quit associating with a married woman on learning that she engaged in extra-marital sexual activities?' I don't believe it requires the test tube and retort and Bunsen burner of the laboratory to pass on that question."

Curator George Willson was a reasonable man, and by his understanding that was a reasonable concern. But were these young females so innocent of any exposure to such issues as he claimed? He wouldn't have been surprised to find that all female recipients of the questionnaire had no understanding of venereal disease; many males probably didn't know what it meant either. Nor did he think many would have discussed childhood sex play. But what if the vast majority had already been exposed to such matters? Would that make a difference? Not to Blanton. He didn't want such intimate things talked about at all—the less the better. And besides, he cited Meyer's statement to the curators that honest answers would be few.

Blanton was just as emphatic about not being influenced by outside pressures, including the legislature. He had said as much in his newspaper. Curators served without compensation and had no reason at all to bow to pressures. Besides, the "public clamor" included both sides, though Blanton claimed "more noise was made on the other side than on the Board's side." Neither documentary evidence nor reasonable doubt exists to undermine Blanton's outraged claims of innocence in the face of pressure. He believed what he believed. If nothing else, the newspaper business had taught him to resist threats of advertisers and subscribers: "Whenever I get to a point where I am afraid of the legislature or public opinion, that I would come in here and do a deliberate injustice to a faculty member, I will get off the Board and go back to my little newspaper office where I can preserve my self respect. I think that is the position every member of this Board would take."

The exchange between the curators and the visitors dominated the morning but produced little except to highlight their differences. Blanton as much as admitted that no transgression of any specific university code had occurred in the questionnaire's circulation, but was bothered by what he thought was dishonesty in its motives, creation, and circulation. But whether the curators possessed competence to pass on the validity of a scientific investigation became the sticking point. Thurstone, at least, agreed the board had authority to govern the propriety of the questionnaire's circulation, but not to judge its scientific validity. And Blanton may have been right about external pressures not having any influence, but what about the dynamics within the board itself? What about the dominance of the strongest and most combative of its membership—McDavid and Blanton? Attorney Leland Hazard later reflected that George Willson had done as much as could be expected of a junior member of the board but actually wasn't all that courageous. The hearing before the visiting investigators revealed Willson as a reasonable gentleman who acknowledged the wide range of available punishment but wanted some deference shown to those charged with defending the institution and making the tough call.

Perhaps the hearing might have produced more substance had more members appeared. Willson apologized for his colleagues' absence, noting illness and pressing business affairs, and assured the visitors that the no-shows didn't result from "indifference."[4]

Following lunch, the afternoon belonged to Professors DeGraff and Meyer. DeGraff didn't have a whole lot that was new. His Family class had pretty much fallen apart after he was replaced by Howard Jensen, not through any fault of Jensen, who actually saved the students who remained in the course. The 123 or so students in the course had dwindled to about half that number, and forty-four of those who remained signed the petition to the AAUP calling for an investigation. Perhaps the forty-four were all that showed up that day. DeGraff had given Hobart Mowrer permission to work for graduation with distinction since Meyer had signed off on it. Mowrer's committee of four sought out economics instructor Russell Bauder for suggestions because he had been teaching "Labor Problems." Even though the first three questions seemed aloof from the committee's topic on the economic emancipation of women, DeGraff thought that was fine since Mowrer had this other thing going on with Meyer. After everything began to break open, DeGraff said he and Mowrer met in the professor's office on Sunday morning, March 17. Mowrer explained that the first three questions bore relevance to the rest, and that he had intended to incorporate all eleven into his Family paper. That, too, was fine with DeGraff.

But what about the propriety issue? Should those first three questions have been sent out? Didn't it occur to DeGraff? No, he said, it didn't. Except for the dean of men, Albert Heckel, he had more personal contact with students than anybody else on campus. "The students come to me with all manner of problems and a good many of their problems are the problems of just the nature stated in the three questions," he explained. "For that reason, I knew that the information that those questions would bring forth would help me personally in answering some of the problems which those students are repeatedly bringing up in one form or another. I didn't give it any thought of impropriety at all." DeGraff reasoned that all students had familiarity with biology, having had some kind of natural science in the freshman year. Here it was the second semester, so who wouldn't know something about the issues on the questionnaire?

The Mowrer group thought the shotgun approach was the most representative, a good point for sure. DeGraff admitted it was a mistake, not, apparently, because it wasn't scientific, but because of the furor it caused. In any case, he talked to a bunch of students who had filled out the questionnaire. "Some of them had put in three or four hours of serious thought into answering that Questionnaire," he said. "They took a lot of time to work it out. They worked it out sometimes singly and sometimes they worked it out together,—two or three of them together, and so far as I know the matter was taken on [the] part of the student body largely as a matter of course, as a serious attempt to find out something which was going to be to their interest, and they had thought nothing about anything wrong or immoral or of that nature until the accounts came out in the paper and then they began to wonder 'What have I filled out?' " DeGraff thought others regarded the questionnaire "as a joke and put it in the wastebasket and did nothing with it."

Along with the first three questions, the document's preamble about something being wrong with the institution of marriage had also been a stumbling block to critics, including the Executive Board. Aside from its effrontery, the statement seemed to prejudice readers. This was explainable, according to DeGraff. Maybe the wording could have been different, he said, but look around the culture. Rampant divorce, the increasing disintegration of traditional marriage, appeals to social agencies—maybe the foreword said that marriage was a failure to laymen, but not to students. Besides, students probably went straight to the questions, not the foreword.

That may have been a reasonable explanation, but how could a forty-three-year-old sociologist alert to cultural trends not know the volatility of the questionnaire in the larger community? On March 13—Day One of the crisis—oblivious to the forces at work that would destroy his career at Missouri, Professor DeGraff ventured over to the Faculty Club in Tate Hall where tea, fellowship, billiards, and bridge brought professors together. Brooks frequented the club, as did DeGraff. "I had been over there," recalled DeGraff, "and he came out of the big room and we met near the door-way and he said 'What the hell are you trying to do,—ruin the University?' and I said, 'Not that I know of', and he went on with his billiards." A couple of reporters struck up a conversation with DeGraff; he didn't know a thing about the story in the local *Tribune*. He got a copy and that night took it to Charles Ellwood's apartment, thinking his chairman didn't take the paper. DeGraff said Ellwood had already read the story, though Ellwood testified later that he hadn't—a minor point. "We talked the matter over," said DeGraff, "and he made a statement something to the effect,—'If you had talked with me or asked my advice about it, I could have told you that it could not be done because there are some questions in Columbia that you cannot approach'—something to that effect. But we had not been in the habit of talking about courses at all." Ellwood was apparently concerned not about the questionnaire's morality, just its expediency. Ellwood knew very well about such things, in the past having run afoul of the local establishment by offending Presbyterian fundamentalists and, in 1923, over the lynching of James T. Scott. In the latter case, Ed Watson, editor of the *Columbia Daily Tribune,* did not criticize the mobsters who murdered Scott, but lambasted Ellwood when the day following the lynching, Ellwood, responding to a student question in class, criticized the morals of a community that tolerated such things. Watson was evidently part of what the *St. Louis Post-Dispatch* later called Columbia's "home guard."[5]

Max Meyer should have known about the home guard. Why he didn't pay more attention to the politics of the developing questionnaire is a matter of speculation. He told the Executive Board he had been distracted with other things. Stratton Brooks ironically offered something of an excuse for his pressured professor, thinking Meyer had been all involved with planning the meeting of the Southern Society of Philosophy and Psychology scheduled for Columbia in late March, something Meyer himself had cited. Whatever the case, the arguments are plausible but a bit thin. Meyer had seen enough of the questionnaire and even took responsibility for dividing questions 3b and 3c. He seemed to be asleep in the guardhouse.

Also plausible was Meyer's view of how the "Bureau of Personnel Research" got hooked onto the questionnaire. Using the old envelopes of the defunct bureau, which had been used for career guidance some years before, in order to save money on postage seemed logical enough. But was it dishonest to do so, as well as to sign the accompanying cover letter with the same designation? The board had raised the honesty issue, and it *did* look like fraud, as if Mowrer and his committee were either trying to diffuse responsibility or more likely make the whole thing look like an official university operation. According to Meyer, after Mowrer got the envelopes he came back later and proposed using "Bureau of Personnel Research" on the cover letter as well. It was on the envelopes, and besides, wouldn't that be better than simply "Student Committee" or some such made-up title? And it would also likely generate more sober responses from those students who might have otherwise thought it was a hell week stunt or something like that. Of course, why Mowrer and his friends didn't simply spell out in the cover letter what they were doing as part of the Family course remains unclear. In any case, even though Meyer should have seen the explosive potential—and did see it later—he had no objection at the time.

Meyer also thought the questionnaire needed to go out indiscriminately for best scientific results. He believed only a very small percentage of entering students were ignorant of the issues in the document. If they *were* ignorant of such things, females especially, they would probably be in for a shock. In that case, far better to be shocked from a professional document than from older male students where the encounter might be less than healthy.

The investigators wanted to know more about the Executive Board's interest in the subject spoken only in muted tones—Meyer's sex lecture for his Social Psychology class. Meyer said he had been surprised when the two stenographers were excused during the first hearing. What was Meyer going to say, anyway? These were mature women. If McDavid excused them, did he do so because of chivalry or because he wanted the testimony off the record? No one knows for sure, but two months later Meyer pieced together the off-record exchange as best he could for the AAUP committee, including Blanton's alleged hypothetical yet ludicrous remark about a woman giving the sex reflex tabulation to a male friend as an invitation for sex. Meyer wanted the thirteen female members of that class, along with Dorothy Postle, who had also heard the lecture, to appear before the Executive Board. But as he told the AAUP, he "could not even suggest anything because the Chairman suddenly got up out of his chair and said, 'Well, that is all right, we can stop this meeting now and you can go home,' and the President did not say a word and I went up to my office to get my hat and went home and that was the end." The next day Meyer got his notice of termination.

Meyer thought the Executive Board fired him mostly because of the lecture. The whole thing was unlawyerlike, and he thought the secret proceedings probably embarrassed both McDavid and Arnold, the two lawyers among the three executives. "I felt it influenced the decision of the members of the Executive Board," said Meyer, "and at the same time they would not permit anybody to know what had influenced their decision. They wanted to keep that secret. I wanted to have it made clear."

Asked by Chairman Carlson if Brooks had gotten any advice before recommending termination to the Executive Board for himself and DeGraff, Meyer responded,

I would give a double answer to that. First, I would say that I have no information whatsoever that he asked any advice of any faculty member, I have no information; and, secondly, I would say that so far as I have come to know President Brooks during these five [*sic*] years he has been here I don't think he would care to ask for any advice. I think that is contrary to his nature, but that is, of course, a mere inference on my part, drawn from my personal acquaintance with him and his methods. He does not care for faculty advice,— never. He never attends a divisional faculty meeting and when he calls a meeting of the general faculty he generally just tells them to do certain things and if they don't do what he thinks is a good thing to do—he does not take a vote or act in a parliamentary way. He does not even take a vote. He says, "Well, gentleman, let us postpone the action. Some other time we will take it up again."

According to Meyer, in his first year as president Brooks likewise cavalierly dismissed any notion of creating a faculty judicial committee, claiming there existed no need for such a group. While he was president, he allegedly declared, no faculty would be discharged from the university— "that is so unthinkable."[6]

Such behavior seems consistent with Brooks's demeanor. The crude manner in which he reportedly spoke to Harmon DeGraff at the faculty club mirrored the encounter he had with Elmer Ellis when Jonas Viles took the young candidate for a position in the history department to meet him in 1930. Ellis stood on the edge of a long and distinguished career at Missouri, in which he would serve as professor of history, dean of the College of Arts and Science, and finally president. The university library would eventually bear his name. "He was a rather blustery, gruff person," Ellis said of Brooks, "who, when I was introduced, said, 'Well, young man, what do you know about history?' " Ellis might have said "Plenty," but he was a gentleman, something not always true of Brooks. In fact, speaking of gentlemen, one of the final official testimonials of Professor DeGraff on the whole subject of the questionnaire involved his meeting with Brooks the morning after the encounter at the faculty club. In their meeting in Brooks's office on the second day of the scandal, the president "went on to explain to me the two different kinds of sociology," DeGraff told the AAUP visitors. "He has a son in law [*sic*] who is teacher of Sociology in Teachers College in Springfield, and that he had told him there was sociology as such and 'sewer sociology,' and his statement made me exceedingly angry because I inferred from that remark that he was saying that the course in the Family was on the 'sewer sociology' order, though he didn't tell me that." DeGraff added: "That is a situation which does not exist,—and any of my students can tell you that. I took particular pains to inform him of that situation. Then in that night's paper came out an interview with Dr. Brooks in which this same term 'sewer sociology' was used."[7]

DeGraff and Meyer were finished. The committee recessed for supper, resuming at 8 P.M., with Thurstone's wife, Thelma, sitting in on the evening's testimony. Her appearance highlighted the dilemma of the actions of an all-male Board of Curators involving matters of propriety being investigated by an all-male committee. Jonas Viles had wanted a woman on the St. Louis alumni group concerned about the curators' actions, and some members of the AAUP had wanted a female on the investigating team as well. Common prudence seemed to suggest it, and the idea was tossed around the association. Professor E. H. Hollands of the University of Kansas proposed the idea to Secretary Tyler in Washington, an idea echoed by Arthur O. Lovejoy of Johns Hopkins. Herman Schlundt heard of the idea through Frederick Middlebush, and told Tyler "the addition of a woman would be a very desirable element in the membership of the committee." In the end, for unclear practical considerations, no woman joined the group, though Henry Crew and Chairman Carlson suggested that Thurstone's wife accompany the others to Columbia. Thelma Thurstone taught social psychology—also at the University of Chicago—and became something of a consolation as an unofficial adjunct. However, some objectivity may have been compromised, as she was not only a graduate of the University of Missouri but also a former student of Max Meyer.[8]

The investigators, along with Mrs. Thurstone, spent the evening listening to five pillars of Missouri's faculty, James Harvey Rogers, Winterton C. Curtis, Herman Schlundt, Harry G. Brown, and Edwin B. Branson. Rogers said he had gotten involved in the dispute because he feared official reaction given the response in the case of the sociology instructor who had run afoul of the Ku Klux Klan. Although Rogers didn't go into all the details, most faculty could easily recall the notorious affair involving Herbert Blumer, who had been an All-American tackle during his student days at Missouri. Exceptionally bright, Blumer immediately became an instructor in sociology at Missouri after finishing a master's degree in 1922, but stirred up a hornet's nest after he spoke to Miss Burrall's Bible Class Leadership group in January 1925 on "the Negro Problem." While he said he planned no ethical remonstrance nor solution regarding the "problem" but simply its presentation, his address included a tightly reasoned and articulated argument against racism, a plea to see black contributions to America, and, among other things, a declaration that the white race had characteristics of other races, including some among his audience. A reporter from the *Columbia Missourian* was in the crowd and, according to Blumer, didn't get the story quite right. Rumors and gossip filled in the rest. The Klan, powerful in Missouri and other states at that time, went to work, burning a cross in front of Blumer's house on Paquin Street and demanding his dismissal from the faculty. Ed Watson at the *Columbia Daily Tribune* did his part as well, attacking the rival *Missourian* for reporting on the speech ("disseminating matter and expressions that cannot but create ill feeling and dissension"), ridiculing Blumer as foolish and lacking common sense, and suggesting that some might call the Department of Sociology "the department of balderdash and near socialism." Nowhere did Watson criticize the Klan for its attempted intimidation of a twenty-four-year-old instructor. (A year earlier, Watson had mildly criticized the Klan while defending the *Tribune*'s decision to accept its advertising for an upcoming Klan lecture.) For his part, Brooks evidently teetered on the matter, impressed by the Klan's demonstration. Blumer resigned, but soon changed his mind, probably because of faculty support. In fact, a committee of nine Missouri faculty, chaired by Herman Schlundt, was quickly appointed by the local chapter of the AAUP to look into possible academic freedom violations. Blumer ended up going on leave at the end of the year anyway, taking a similar position at the University of Chicago, from which he received a Ph.D. in 1928. (A brilliant career awaited, including national leadership in his discipline; Berkeley's sociology department became one of the most distinguished in the nation during his tenure as chairman in the 1950s and 1960s.)[9]

Meanwhile, if Brooks's response to the Blumer affair wasn't frightening enough, Rogers now feared "that this Questionnaire, which had received considerable publicity, might lead to something of the same sort." His fears were assuaged, he said, at the meeting of numerous faculty, all full professors, on the evening of March 18, the night before the meeting of the Executive Board. The whole idea that someone would be fired because of the questionnaire was beyond the pale, simply "preposterous." That same night, Jonas Viles, one of the group, reported that he had been playing cards and chatting with Brooks and was confident the president understood the issues. But dark talk arose about "something else," namely Meyer's sex lecture tabulation. That was another matter, an academic matter. The group, which met at the home of the Dean of Engineering E. J. McCaustland, authorized Professors Rogers and Branson to see the president before the Executive Board met on the afternoon of March 19 and suggest that perhaps the AAUP could provide an opinion on the issue. The pair did so the next morning and got the impression from Brooks—at least Rogers did—that nothing drastic was in the offing. If such seemed imminent, Brooks would call for faculty to explain that position to the Executive Board. Rogers told the AAUP committee that he had been "much relieved."

Such relief was ignorant bliss. Rogers told the investigators that two days later, about noon, a student told him of the firings by the Executive Board. Rogers hurried to Branson's office, Branson called Brooks, and Brooks told them and others to come to his office. Brooks explained that he not only concurred with the Executive Board's decision but also agreed with it. "He talked, as I recall, further with regard to the Max Meyer Questionnaire [sex lecture tabulation] and spoke of it as something that simply could not get into publicity," said Rogers. "He used the words, 'It would simply blow the lid off the University.'" Meyer's sex lecture tabulation had been supposedly settled and closed between Meyer and the president. But the issue got a new and virulent lease on life when the questionnaire surfaced scarcely more than a week later.

Branson testified that he was mystified by Brooks's agreement with the Executive Board since at the first meeting with the president on March 19 he got the impression that the worst case for DeGraff would be his loss of the Family class. According to Branson, at the postmortem meeting in the president's office the next day, Harry Brown raised the possibility of mass resignations from the faculty, maybe thirty or forty. Brooks announced that if that were the case, such "resignations will be accepted at once." Branson asked, " 'You realize, do you not, Mr. President, that this is going to be a serious matter in getting men to come to the University of Missouri?' 'Do you ever expect to be able to get another such psychologist?' The reply was, 'I don't want one like the present one.' He was a little heated up at the time,—that is as I recall it." Rogers added that "His words, as I recall it, [were] 'I don't want another like this one.'"[10]

Between the Executive Board's meeting in March and the meeting of the full board in April, the president appeared to soften his attitude toward the dismissals. Branson repeatedly warned Brooks of how serious this would be in the larger academic community. During a meeting with about seventeen or eighteen concerned faculty, Brooks claimed Meyer couldn't be tried on the sex lecture tabulation because it involved the principle of freedom of teaching. Branson had been unsuccessful in changing Brooks's mind on the Executive Board's decision, but Rogers thought as time went on the president had moved slightly toward the faculty position. Unlike his colleagues, Harry Brown was not surprised at the Executive Board's decision. The case of the Klan and the Bible class lecture showed that Brooks feared the public more than a bunch of worked-up professors.

Brown also thought Brooks remained consistently opposed to the faculty position even though the president became convinced that the sex lecture tabulation was innocuous. Still, according to Brown, the president feared public opinion should it get out.

Such opinion could readily be distorted by rumors, and Columbia became a veritable rumor mill in the spring of 1929. Things that filled a gossip's day, things spoken of in hushed tones but spoken of nonetheless, things obscene—such things made the rounds in Columbia, including, apparently, Meyer's alleged use of manikins in his graphic classroom instruction. Then there was the one about Meyer and DeGraff wanting to use the questionnaire to compile an "easy girls" roster. W. C. Curtis told the AAUP that on the Thursday after the Executive Board's decision a group of ten faculty met at Branson's house and that "there was some gossip all over the campus to the effect that there was something terrible back of this and if we only knew what it was that we would understand the justification for the Board's action." Well, said Curtis, the group at Branson's house knew Meyer was incapable of such things and so commissioned their own professional review of the point at issue. Viles tried and failed to get Brooks to give him a copy of the sex lecture tabulation, so Branson ended up acquiring one from a student. When the concerned faculty met the following night, again at Professor Branson's house, the document was carefully reviewed, some men even declaring that "if they had daughters in the university" such information would be helpful. At that same meeting Curtis and Addison Gulick, professor of physiological chemistry—two reputable scientists—were asked to develop a position for the group for presentation to the full Board of Curators.[11]

Before the meeting of the full board, Brooks met with a group of concerned faculty opposed to the action of the Executive Board. Ironically, that meeting took place in the same room in Lefevre Hall where W. C. Curtis now described it to the AAUP investigators:

> The President . . . talked about the Questionnaire. He got up talking and was standing there by the corner of the table and [Addison] Gulick and I had been raising the question between ourselves in whispers as to whether he should get out without saying anything about the Meyer situation, because we thought it was infamous for this malicious gossip to be going about the campus; and just as he was ready to go Gulick said, "Isn't there something else, Mr. President?" and I think Gulick said a further thing,—again, I am not recalling his exact words,—"There is so much gossip about the campus and there are reasons to believe that some of

it emanates from your office." I don't remember that the President replied to that, but Gulick was congratulated after the meeting for having said that to him.

According to Curtis, Brooks had every expectation that, barring a reversal of the Executive Board's dismissals, the AAUP would launch its investigation. Perhaps he thought he could get ahead of the investigation by inviting it himself. That's how his mind worked, thought Curtis. Brooks even lavished praise on the activist faculty members who made a positive impression on the full board about Meyer's Social Psychology course, but Curtis, for one, suspected the president's duplicity in the matter, believing "he was making a jump for the winning horse in the faculty thinking that would strengthen his position in the Board with an element that was unfriendly to him. That is a hunch. I was not impressed with his seeming candor."

Nor was Professor Rogers impressed with the underground rumor campaign against Meyer. Incensed by the malicious talk about a morally upright colleague, Rogers stood ready to spill his frustration when he appeared before the full board on April 6, but refrained only because his nervous colleagues cautioned against it. Curtis added that his wife had been in the company of numerous other women, apparently on some outing, and one of the women, a gossip, said her husband had heard something about Meyer and DeGraff "too terrible" to tell even her, but that if it was known to the faculty dissenters they would understand the board's decision. Curtis and Rogers thought the president's loose mouth was behind much of the gossip and even contemplated going to the press or in some way shielding their faculty colleague from such smears. Ultimately, they decided to wait for the cleansing that an AAUP investigation would bring. Professor Branson had an alternate view, lifting part of the blame from Brooks for much of the rumormongering, and claiming "there are all sorts of scandalous things floating around town." But Thelma Thurstone had her own view: "I heard in Chicago a rumor about this syllabus and manikins and so on and it came from the President's office," she said. "I could tell where it came from."

Branson even argued that the rumors hadn't quit, that a week or so earlier a faculty colleague had told him a couple of stories about DeGraff. As he had been doing, Branson checked the veracity of the rumors, in this case with students who had been DeGraff's students, and found them groundless. Still, the talk persisted. Brooks in fact seemed to waver on DeGraff, defaming him in private conversation. Curtis told the investigators he thought that Brooks's ploy was that Meyer "is too big a proposition for him to defame but DeGraff isn't and he can put innuendoes upon DeGraff that he would not dare to put on Mr. Meyer." Herman Schlundt remembered being in the president's office when Brooks said that even without the questionnaire business DeGraff might not have been renewed for another year. For some unclear reason, Brooks claimed DeGraff had been a negative influence on campus, a statement utterly and totally at odds with the views of those who knew him. On the other hand, Brooks also spoke highly of his impact on students, and that if he could be spared in the current crisis, that he would be "safe" and might even evolve into "another Daddy Defoe," a reference to Luther M. Defoe, a popular professor in the engineering school who in nearly four decades at Mizzou had become something of a dependable father-confessor to troubled students.[12]

After recessing on Friday night, the investigators were back the next morning, ready for a protracted session with President Brooks. When the stenographer's notes were transcribed, Brooks's testimony dominated nearly a fourth of the hearing, though he was only one of twenty-five witnesses. Of course, investigators Carlson, Thurstone, and Bordwell had already had an earful about the president and doubtless had formed prejudiced opinions about his behavior. In fact, they had pored over documentary material relative to the case for two weeks prior to their arrival in Columbia. But these were professional men, and Bordwell, the law dean from Iowa, knew all about testimony and judicial procedure. With exhibits in front of them, including transcripts from both meetings of the curators, the early questioning ranged over the origins of the public phase of the questionnaire controversy and the president's use of the terms "damn fool idea," "sewer sociology," or "sewer psychology," and about Meyer's Social Psychology lecture, whether academic freedom issues were presented to the curators, and whether Brooks had talked to the press before talking to Meyer and DeGraff. Brooks's memory of chronology and specifics understandably wavered a bit given the rush of events and press coverage during those hectic days in March.

The air in Lefevre Hall quickly grew tense. Brooks didn't like being on the hot seat. Chairman Carlson asked him about his statements to the curators regarding the questionnaire's propriety or scientific worth. Brooks said he had always maintained that the questionnaire had no scientific validity, that it "did not have a scintilla of basis as a scientific investigation, that it was impossible for it to collect any facts that had a scientific result, and had no purpose behind it to collect those facts and could not by anybody who had any knowledge of scientific methods be defended as a scientific act."

"Q. You made this statement to the Board without having had a conference with Professor Meyer or DeGraff?

"A. No, I would not say that,—

"Q. In connection with the Questionnaire?

"A. No, I would not say that exactly, but I would feel perfectly free to talk to them about it.

"Dean Bordwell: Q. How do you know it had no scientific purpose?

"A. Because I know the history and origin and why it was written.

"The Chairman: Q. Do you want the Committee to understand that you had no recollection of having had any conference either with Meyer or DeGraff—

"A. I have told you two or three times, sir, that I do not remember the details of that conference and, frankly, I didn't come here to discuss the details of that conference.

"Q. Well, that isn't a detail—

"A. Listen here, a minute, to me. I have come to discuss with you whether this Questionnaire is scientific or not, and I am not interested in the rest of it. That one thing, I want your answer to.

"Q. You mean, in this meeting?

"A. No, when your Committee gets around to it. So far as the rest of the phases are concerned, I am not so sure I want to have anything with,—I don't care to have your opinion on it or to be a witness on it.

"Q. But we are very anxious to have your statements of fact. Mr. President, you asked the officers of the Association for the investigation, and you promised them your support in the investigation, and I hope you will give us all the aid that you can."

Despite the testiness, Brooks tried to explain why the questionnaire stood outside scientific inquiry. Brooks outlined the method of DeGraff's Family class, how the various groups worked up a topic, gathered materials, and so on. Some groups employed the questionnaire method and dispatched a limited number of mimeographed copies dealing with one subject or another to a small target group. But Mowrer had bigger aims. He wanted to ready himself for a civil service exam in Michigan and needed material on data tabulation; he also contemplated an article for a *Harpers*-type magazine along with material for graduation with distinction and then for possible graduate work. Brooks figured Mowrer inserted his own sex-related questions into the economic emancipation of women questionnaire and that both Meyer and DeGraff each thought the other was monitoring the thing.

But Dean Bordwell protested that it could still have scientific value. Brooks wanted to know if Bordwell really thought that an undergraduate "would be able to make any real application of that in solving sociological difficulties of life." And besides, the foreword to the questionnaire was highly prejudicial about "something seriously wrong with the traditional system of marriage" and so on. Brooks had a reasonable point and a reasonable objection, which the committee didn't seem to want to grant, but the problem with Brooks was that he didn't even want the issues discussed among students. "When you put into the minds of these folks that there is a grave doubt as to the present marriage system," he said, "and then ask these people that particular question, what reaction will you get?—what tendency are you likely to get?

> "[Carlson] Q. The Committee can't answer that question.
> "A. No, that is a rhetorical question.
> "Q. Well, we would like to have your answer?
> "A. It inevitably tends to immorality, immediately.
> "Q. Immediately?
> "A. We will see by the questions the succession that leads to it.
> "Q. Would you say that reading the same question in fiction, in a magazine article, or seeing the same problem presented on the stage or in the movie, would get the same effect?
> "A. I doubt if you will find in fiction that particular combination, quite so. Secondly, whether that were true or not, does not become a justification for a University, *in charge of the morality of thousands of young people,* to participate in it. [Italics added.]
> "Q. I wish you, Mr. Brooks, would answer my question, if you can,—if you care to.
> "A. My answer is that in none of my experience,—and I read a good deal of fiction and see a good many movies,—I have never once seen anything that put those two things so definitely before a young girl, with the request that she think of them and write an opinion, on it. Undoubtedly, they leave some effect upon their minds."

Percy Bordwell asked Brooks if Dean Priddy had told him that the questionnaire produced "immorality."

"No," Brooks said, "we won't say 'immorality,' but tendencies to immorality." Brooks apparently thought the university exerted a sort of in loco parentis authority over its students, a common practice. But once that assumption was exercised, all manner of difficulties could arise. For Brooks that meant that even discussion of such topics needed to be circumscribed. He had gotten a report from Dean Bessie Leach Priddy about student discussions around campus in the wake of the questionnaire's distribution. Chattering about unprecedented subjects in sororities and boardinghouses upset some of the women and, of course, their chaperons, some of whom had refused to give the questionnaires to the women "on account of the effect they thought they might have." And then there were all those letters from parents. "This is a basic principle of life," said Brooks, "—that if you begin to think about a thing you are more likely to do it than if you don't think about it. If you talk about it, you increase the likelihood of doing it; and insofar as these younger students are concerned there is no question at all in the mind of anybody who knows anything about young people in college that this particular thing starts a very dangerous thing in college.

> "[The Chairman] Q Would you say that thinking and talking, or discussing, about murder in the University community would lead to murder?
> "A. Yes.
> "Q. On the part of those who discuss it?
> "A. On the part of some of them.
> "Q. And thinking or talking about stealing would lead to stealing?
> "A. No cashier of a bank ever ran away with the money because he just happened to think of it that afternoon."

Reading and thinking about theft, according to Brooks, left the hypothetical cashier primed for the right temptation. Same thing with these students, he said.

Such talk left Professor Thurstone incredulous. "President Brooks," he asked, "do we understand you to assume that if a boy and girl in the University sit down to discuss whether they as citizens would endorse trial marriage or denounce it,—would you assume that when a boy and girl in the University sit down and discuss trial marriage, possible advantages and possible disadvantages, that that conversation is necessarily immoral?

> "A. No.
> "Q. Well, that is listed in your report from the Dean of Women as a sample of immorality. I am taking that as one example. The same question might be asked about the other—
> "A. No. They discussed the entire Questionnaire, not that particular question.

"Q. Well, take any other one. Is it necessarily immoral for a boy
and a girl in the University to sit down and discuss the ethics and
merits or demerits of these proposals?

"A. The discussion is not immoral, but the fact that they do discuss it with each other creates the human conditions that tend very
rapidly to it."

That line of questioning betrayed the wide breech between the administration and the investigators. But on the matter of Meyer's sex lecture,
there *seemed* to be some agreement. If Brooks could not defend the questionnaire as a scientifically valid document, he had no problem seeing
Meyer's Social Psychology lecture as a matter of academic freedom.
Brooks thought Meyer's tabulation of the bodily reflexes seemed "unnecessarily detailed" but defended the whole lecture as scientific and certainly appropriate for its narrow target audience. It couldn't be restricted
any more than certain anatomical discussions in the medical school. He
repeated what everyone seemed to know, that is, that the whole sex lecture matter had been concluded and seemed closed when the questionnaire issue revived it. Neither the Executive Board nor the full board
would likely have known anything about it if Brooks had not brought
it up, but he defended the necessity of doing so as part of his job in the
protection of the university. After all, some big-shot had the information
and it could have created difficulty if the general public had discovered
it. Whether one of Meyer's students had been offended or whether her
father somehow got the document containing the tabulation is unclear,
but it was out there just the same. Frank McDavid, the lawyer who had
been greatly offended by the tabulation, had moved to exclude the matter
from the Executive Board's consideration and had so insisted again in the
meeting of the full board a few weeks later. Brooks didn't think it affected
the outcome in either meeting but acknowledged that no one could know
if it lingered in the back of the minds of the curators.

Dean Bordwell pressed the matter of the origins of the wild rumors
about something so awful that explained the Executive Board's decision.
The suggestions about the rumors' origins, he said, pointed to the president's office. Brooks deflected the suggestion, and said rumors flew
around town, and that even his barber was a great source for outrageous
tales.

Did Brooks expect such testimony could so lightly dismiss the suspicion of his involvement? Whatever the source, the president told the investigators that "There has never been the slightest inference or discus-

sion of any evidence tending to support anything of that sort. That is not at all in question."

Despite such confidence in the moral character of his two professors, Brooks stood steadfastly for absolute dismissal of both of them. Normally, the curators would act on some recommendation of the president, but in this case, McDavid thought they had formed their own view and would simply record whether or not the president concurred. He did. In fact, Brooks told the investigators that he thought that the executives' original decision for termination of both was better than the full board's mere suspension of Meyer. And Brooks swore that his views were based solely on the questionnaire, not on the sex lecture tabulation. Actually, the president seemed also to suggest that Meyer's pursuit of psychology had been too narrow—not illegitimate, just narrow—and that the department should be broader, to include more than just a behaviorist approach. Even Mowrer later said he thought Meyer's style seemed to preclude his sharing authority with others in the department, that he wanted to do things his way, essentially by himself. Brooks said he even advised his daughter, a student at Smith College, to take Meyer when she enrolled at Missouri. Brooks was not wrong in his estimate of Meyer's narrow focus, and the fact that the president wanted a broadened psychology department seemed quite legitimate. Perhaps such views influenced his desire for Meyer's total dismissal rather than merely a gross misjudgment in the questionnaire business. Comparisons to Galileo were unwarranted, said Brooks. Some of the finest scientific research in the country involving sex education was going on at Missouri. Brooks pointed to Edgar Allen, professor of anatomy, and even Winterton C. Curtis in zoology as examples, perhaps not seeing the irony of including Curtis, one of the staunchest defenders of the deposed professors.

If Brooks maintained that the decision of the Executive Board was proper—and he recalled that lawyers Mercer Arnold and Frank McDavid believed the firings could be achieved only by action of the full board—he defended Hobart Mowrer and his integrity. The president's interaction with Mowrer was a bit complicated. Mowrer had complained in early May that without his knowledge an entry had been made on his official record that he could not be readmitted to the university until he had first met with President Brooks. He evidently made the discovery when requesting that a copy of his transcripts be either given to him or sent out. Mowrer claimed that the portion of his record so inscribed was both permanent and public, that no due process had been followed in placing it there, and that it constituted, inferentially, a defamation against him.

He wanted the inscription removed. Soon thereafter, Mowrer found that Brooks himself had ordered the notation on his record and, upon meeting with him, asked why and by what authority such action was taken. Brooks readily complied with removing the notation and explained, as Mowrer related it later, "that the reason he had had this entry made was that if I ever wanted to be readmitted to the University of Missouri, he wanted to have a 'serious talk' with me. I assured him that I had no intention of reentering the University, but that if he felt that I had so conducted myself to be in need of his moral advice, I should be very glad to have it. He retorted in substantially these words: 'If you don't intend to try to reenter this school, it is none of my business what you do; but if you ever come back here again, then I shall have something to say to you.' I thanked Dr. Brooks for his kindness and excused myself." Meyer forwarded Mowrer's updated statement to Professor Thurstone at Chicago before the hearings began, telling him, "Mr. Mowrer got so disgusted with the injustice he felt had been done to him that immediately on being informed of having been deposed [from his psychology assistantship], he severed his connection with the University entirely."[13]

Chairman Carlson asked Brooks for help in clearing up a small matter of the records of two students, Hobart Mowrer and one other, a reference to Howell Williams, a member of Mowrer's Family committee. A notation had shown up on Williams's record also. Brooks explained the informal method he sometimes employed that helped keep "the frivolities of youth" off the student's permanent transcript. The disciplinary code had been reworked since Brooks's arrival so that the dean of men could not expel a student but could recommend to the student that he withdraw. If the student complied, then a note was made on his record that before readmittance he had to first see the dean of men. Appeals could be made to a Discipline Committee, of which the dean wasn't a member, but such appeals were rare, occurring once or twice a year. When the student did seek readmission, he would confer with the dean, promise better behavior, and the newspapers were kept out of it. The penciled notation could then be erased.

Mowrer's case was a bit different. According to Brooks, the Executive Board wanted to expel him from the university but Brooks protested, citing the approval of his major professor, his class professor, and three others who had seen the notorious questionnaire. The president's shield didn't extend to Mowrer's assistantship, which was unique to the Department of Psychology. In every other case in the university, an assistantship was granted through the university, but in Meyer's case—and only in Meyer's case—he paid his assistants by the hour. Mowrer lost his

job. Then, when Mowrer sought out Brooks about the whys and where-
fores of the notation, Brooks had no problem complying with the request
to have the notation removed. "He said he wanted to talk to me about
it and I said, 'I have no relation with you whatever. You, yourself, asked
to withdraw from the University. The Registrar will send your card, that
you were here so long and voluntarily withdrew on a certain date. If you
don't want to reenter the University, we have nothing to discuss; and if
you want to reenter, I will have a conversation with you about it.' That
is all that happened until now. That is a common record put on there on
students that look temporarily to be undesirable, and it was put on there
in pencil so as not to be permanent." As for Howell Williams, he hadn't
actually followed through on his intention to withdraw, so the issue was
moot. (Privately, Brooks was much harsher on Mowrer. To an Oklahoman,
he claimed that "Boiled down to its essential facts, a shrewd student desiring to collect material for the purpose of writing sensational articles
to be sold to magazines, was slick enough to get the professors to give
the affair the appearance of official university control." He added: "Our
difficulty is that the whole affair is too dirty to stand publication even as
a matter of defense.")

Perhaps the most remarkable thing about the statement of Mowrer before the hearing, and the testimony of the president during the hearing,
is that they were essentially the same. But the committee wanted to know
about the issue of Mowrer's dishonesty with regard to the "Bureau of
Personnel Research." "Oh, there is nothing to that," said Brooks emphatically. He explained the now-familiar story of Meyer's so-called bureau,
which was created in 1925 to facilitate testing and advising of personnel and the like. It proved to be a headache, and the whole bureau was
scrapped. Brooks claimed no dishonesty was intended in the use of the
left-over envelopes bearing the name; it was just bad judgment and that
was all. Not Meyer, nor DeGraff or Mowrer, were guilty of anything along
those lines, and any dishonesty was not an issue at all. Various discrepancies in testimony from one hearing to another were also typical and
very minor, according to Brooks. That could happen to anyone. Besides,
in Meyer's case, as the president pointed out, Meyer had been involved
in the meeting of the Southern Society of Philosophy and Psychology and
could easily have been distracted.

Brooks had been generous. Seizing on the "Bureau" issue could have le-
gitimately worked in his favor, since Mowrer's use of both the envelopes
and the title might reasonably have been viewed as deception, even if
only a minor one. Unfortunately, such generosity did not extend to the
punishment accorded Meyer and DeGraff. Brooks said he was fine with

the way things turned out, with Meyer's dismissal reduced to a one-year suspension. But he still thought the best interests of the university would be served by starting fresh, with a brand-new person in Meyer's place. Just who would want such a position under the circumstances is another matter. But that was beside the point now, and Brooks said he wanted to do his best to carry out the decision of the curators, and that meant, he said, "getting behind Mr. Meyer and doing everything in the world to put him in fine shape." Brooks added, "There has been no personal antagonism of any kind between us and he is still a professor in the University."[14]

Meyer's bitterness belied Brooks's happy face. The very day after the AAUP hearings, Meyer replied to an admiring former student that Brooks had been less than forthcoming with the curators. The president "intentionally, maliciously and dishonorably withheld from them the information which the members of the Board ought to have had," he complained, "and misguided them in order to serve his selfish purposes and to strengthen his position in the state by playing himself up as a pillar of society and as the watchful protector of the morals of the youth of the state. Therefore he called DeGraff a 'sewer-sociologist' and me a 'sewer-psychologist.'" He looked to the day when the state would be "rid of such a characterless servant."[15]

As the clock ticked toward the noon break, Brooks revisited the issue of the questionnaire's scientific validity, or rather what he thought was its lack of such validity. It was the rise-or-fall issue to each side. Could a governing board judge such things, not merely propriety but rather scientific worthiness? It's what Brooks had early in his testimony claimed he had "come to discuss." Could it be possible that Brooks really didn't regard the questionnaire as scientific, and thought the professional organization would vindicate him? It bothered him, he told the investigators, to have his university classed with Tennessee, to have his professors embarrassed. He knew Winterton Curtis didn't want to face his scientific colleagues at Woods Hole in the summer. But Brooks claimed the faculty would be "more comfortable" if the questionnaire were found unscientific, and that potential faculty could more easily be lured to the university. The president's incredible spin on the whole scientific issue was that the status of the University of Missouri would be enhanced by declaring the questionnaire pseudoscience and thus proceeding with the valid, nationally recognized research that was going on all over campus. The image of Missouri as "pre-Victorian" could impact such research. To Brooks this was not a matter of academic freedom, but of maintaining the integrity of true science. The legislature hardly ever funded research, he said, and he feared losing men of national repute who were tempted by eight-thousand-dollar jobs; other schools—Wisconsin, Illinois, Michigan, and others—offered one thousand to fifteen hundred dollars more per year. Missouri was out beating the bushes for research grants and had shown marked success. But this questionnaire was not scientific, and the world needed to know that. No foundation, said Brooks, would "give money to a Board that does not understand the problems of academic freedom and scientific research; and I want to impress upon you that the University of Missouri is largely lying in your hands in this and if I have been too strenuous in insisting that this particular Questionnaire has not a justifiable defense, I give you that background."

Brooks pinned his case on the questionnaire's lack of scientific basis, and on his view that a professional organization such as the American Association of University Professors could help settle it. "That is the real problem and the reason you are here," said Brooks, "and I didn't ask the board first,—you are the only people that can answer that question. If I am wrong, and you answer the question that this was an interference with academic freedom, our fat is all in the fire."

Such passionate testimony was impressive, but Chairman Carlson seemed a bit incredulous. "Mr. Brooks, just a minute," he interjected, "—as to the report of the Committee: I am a scientist, I hope. Mr. Thurstone is a scientist, I know. Mr. Bordwell is a good legal mind. There are two other members of the Committee who are not here but who will go over the evidence before the final report comes out. So far as I am concerned, we will be influenced only by facts if we can get them. We will endeavor not to do anybody injustice. It will be an objective and a fearless report." But Carlson said he had read newspaper accounts from Missouri and elsewhere, and "the ridicule appearing in those statements," he said, "comes not from the Questionnaire but from the action of the Board on the Questionnaire, taken at your recommendation." Carlson added: "In other words . . . the criticism and ridicule in the minds of national boards and scientific and university men everywhere is not going to the question of the scientific value, the indiscretion, the silliness, and so forth, of the Questionnaire, but on the basis of the serious and apparently precipitate action of the Executive Board in the matter. I am speaking personally, and not as a Committee."[16]

Carlson might just as well have been speaking for the committee, and, indeed, for the academic community in general. The president's best defense, spirited as it was, had clearly fallen short. In fact, it was ludicrous. After lunch and into the evening, the rest of the testimony from more than a dozen witnesses was merely mop-up.

Hobart Mowrer was up first. He explained that the origins of the questionnaire actually reached back a couple of years to when he took a psychology course under Professor Meyer that used as the class textbook *Social Psychology,* coauthored by Meyer and Professor Knight Dunlap of Johns Hopkins University. The class piqued Mowrer's interest in social purpose, psychology, and sexual morality, but not until DeGraff's class in the Family did he have the opportunity to pursue his ideas. He didn't know DeGraff's procedure when he signed up, but the class required term papers on some sociological subject, to be completed by committees of four students each. Mowrer thought it over and in a lengthy statement proposed inquiring into "the economic emancipation of women" that resulted from the changes from an agrarian to an industrial order. He wanted to look into such emancipation on society's ideas of sexual morality, family stability, and marriage itself.

DeGraff found the topic worthy but edited it down to manageable size. Mowrer rounded up three colleagues, who then looked into possible sources and finally rejected a mere rehash of secondary materials in favor of primary information gained from their fellow students. Such material would be subjective and opinion-based, but since opinion impacted behavior the student-generated data would be of value. Mowrer's committee rejected case studies and personal interviews in favor of the questionnaire method, an option increasing in favor among the social sciences. Believing a thousand such questionnaires were required for valid sampling, the project then faced the very real problem of financing, something estimated at between fifty and one hundred dollars. Mowrer didn't think his colleagues should have to ante up such funds, especially since it was his ball and he was running with it. He wrote the cover letter, or most of it anyway; it was essentially Mowrer's document. DeGraff suggested financing from the sociology honor society, but in the end Mowrer thought if he financed the project he could claim ownership of the material, which might be used as part of his proposed master's work under Meyer the next year. Or perhaps he could offer the research to a psychology journal or work up an article for H. L. Mencken's *American Mercury* or *Harpers* or some other such magazine, an idea DeGraff thought worthwhile. In any case, he could use the material as he chose, but only, as he said later, "within the bounds of propriety."

President Brooks had distorted the publishing idea beyond all reality, said Mowrer, that Mowrer wanted to see his name on some sensational article or perhaps for money. Though he didn't blame Brooks, Mowrer said the same distortion occurred over using the magic number of a thousand questionnaires because such was required by the civil service examination in Detroit to demonstrate proficiency in statistics. The project was well in hand before Mowrer ever heard of the civil service exam; that whole thing was peripheral. Nor was the propriety of the questionnaire raised by any of his colleagues or professors. Alberta Davis, if she did object, didn't do so vigorously.

After the publicity broke, Mowrer, at Jesse Wrench's suggestion, went to see Brooks, found him not in, but told his secretary that he stood ready to return if the president wanted to see him. Mowrer heard nothing until the summons to the Executive Board hearing. Meanwhile, DeGraff had told Mowrer that Brooks wanted the completed questionnaires, now numbering about two hundred, to be turned in to Leslie Cowan, secretary to the Board of Curators. Thinking it was some kind of order from the president, Mowrer decided he would refuse, knowing it might mean his dismissal from the university. The young student seemed quite clear about his rights in the matter, believing that the demand constituted confiscation of his private property. That same day, Meyer told Mowrer that it was merely a request that the documents be stored for their temporary safety, as Mowrer recalled it, "to prevent some over-ambitious newspaper reporter from stealing them from my desk or otherwise securing them and then writing some big scare story." Mowrer turned the completed questionnaires over to Cowan and they went in the university's vault, only to be retrieved and destroyed on the orders of the curators.

Chairman Carlson wanted to know if Mowrer contemplated legal action. Mowrer consulted Meyer, as he often did in important matters, and Meyer suggested he talk it over with James L. Parks, dean of the university's law school. Parks, who held Brooks in low regard, harbored some doubt about Mowrer's ability to legally retrieve the fifty-three dollars lost on the project. Pragmatically, with so many sympathetic alumni on Mowrer's side, Parks urged him not to pursue the matter, so he didn't.[17]

Jay William Hudson, professor of philosophy and a Harvard Ph.D. who had been at Missouri since 1908, followed Mowrer in the hearing but offered little help. Not particularly active in the case beyond his alleged abortive involvement in an early petition supporting the administration, he sought out Brooks the day before the meeting of the full Board of Curators. He had always maintained the questionnaire was unscientific and out of line, something he found almost universal among the faculty, but before the meeting of the board on April 6, he gradually came to regard the dismissals as excessive—a view reinforced by conversations with professional colleagues elsewhere during a trip east. But he deferred to Brooks, embarrassingly so ("I knew that the President was wiser than I"), lauding the president's judgment while deprecating his own, and speaking of

Brooks as "a kindly man" with the welfare of the university foremost in his mind.[18]

If the welfare of the university was paramount, that left little protection for real or imagined injustices to faculty. No intervention came from Frederick M. Tisdel, a professor of English and dean of the College of Arts and Science, who was virtually a nonparticipant. Never having presided over a dismissal during his tenure, he was reduced, perhaps through no fault of his own, to recommending to Brooks that both Meyer and DeGraff be suspended only until the fall semester. But Brooks's style of administration meant that he never even asked Dean Tisdel for a recommendation; the dean had to volunteer it. Before the meeting of the Executive Board, however, Tisdel had conferred with Charles Ellwood, who chaired the department of sociology, about not reappointing DeGraff for 1929–1930 "largely" because of the questionnaire. At the time, neither contemplated DeGraff's dismissal. Why Tisdel and Ellwood discussed not reappointing DeGraff essentially because of the current controversy and then Tisdel suggesting to Brooks that he and Meyer merely be suspended until fall is both incongruous and unclear.[19]

Regardless, Ellwood told the investigators that he and President Brooks talked over the matter several times and that Brooks said repeatedly that he wanted to save Meyer and DeGraff. Maybe they could get away with a reprimand. But Brooks claimed he didn't know the board's view, and apparently feared the petition demanding dismissal that was circulating downtown. Ellwood also wanted to save DeGraff, knowing his value as an instructor. Chairman Carlson asked: "You do not ascribe any moral turpitude or sex laxity in connection with DeGraff?" Ellwood's answer: "None at all, no, no, that is absurd."

Ellwood claimed the president "was overwhelmed from various sources with immediate demands that these men be dismissed," and that he had taken measures to save his two beleaguered professors. Carlson wanted to know what measures, something Ellwood didn't feel free to provide. All right, then what about the all-important issue of scientific validity?

> "Q. Do you consider the Questionnaire was reprehensible?
> "A. I consider that it was unwise.
> "Q. Unwise from what point of view?
> "A. Both from the scientific point of view and from the popular point of view.
> "Q. Why from a scientific point of view?

"A. Because it is a well known maxim among social investigators that a questionnaire in order to get worthwhile scientific results has to be very simple and very brief, which this questionnaire was not. Secondly, that it should not deal with a subject concerning which people have too many prejudices; and thirdly, that it should not be such as to involve too subjective action. This questionnaire is open to scientific criticism on all those grounds, and had I seen it I would have given those criticisms.

Such talk left Professor Thurstone with obvious questions. "Suppose a questionnaire is prepared whose purpose is to describe existing prejudices,—if that is what you want to call them,—

"A. Yes.

"Q. How can you attain your purpose of describing existing superstitions or prejudices or notions without asking directly about the content of those prejudices? If you want to know what the distribution of attitude is on trial marriage, how are you going to describe the public opinion about trial marriage without asking people for their opinions about trial marriage,—to take that as an example?

"A. When the prejudice is an ingrained one, and part of the mores, it is advisable to direct such questions to the parties who entertain these prejudices in an emotional way, because no proper responses will be given under such circumstances. If parties can be found who look at these prejudices with the minimum of emotion, it is all right to direct your question to them.

"Q. Your answer would be that if you want to describe the ideas about the sex code as they exist in the student population in the University of Missouri, that investigation simply cannot be called upon because there is a great deal of affect on the subject,—is that your answer?"

"A. I think I agree with you except that I would say that certain selected persons who have given this thing some thought and who discounted their emotional reaction might be counted on.

"Q. You are changing your group?

"A. Yes, sir.

"Q. This is a very fundamental question.

"A. Yes. I want to make one other criticism and that is, while I am not a behaviorist, it is a very great surprise to me that behaviorists should put questions which involve such emotional subjectivity as these questions did."[20]

Dorothy Postle, the young instructor who Meyer seemed to be groom-
ing for a permanent spot in the department, followed Ellwood. She had
been on the faculty only since February and had limited contact with students, but had found none offended by the questionnaire. She had taught
in high school for a couple of years and believed students there had been
exposed to the issues on the questionnaires.

Four female students echoed Postle's low-key response. Janis Rowell,
a freshman from Denver, Colorado, hadn't gotten a questionnaire herself, but a girl where she lived and some of her sorority sisters in Alpha
Gamma Delta had received copies. Carlson asked her if she had heard of
any "actual moral injury" because of the questionnaire.

> "A. No. Of course the Questionnaire was absolutely the only
> topic of discussion for a long time here and it was discussed ev-
> erywhere between boys and girls, even, and the idea of any uni-
> versity student being morally injured was laughed at by all the
> students. That seemed to be more among the parents, or some-
> thing like that,—absolutely their own idea."
> "Q. You say the discussion was quite general?"
> "A. It was absolutely the only topic of discussion."
> "Q. After the publicity, or before?"
> "A. Well, of course it began to be discussed before the publicity,
> but when so much publicity was given—
> "Q. Yes, we understand that,—it was even discussed among fac-
> ulty members, afterwards. Was this discussion before the public-
> ity, on the whole, objective and serious, or frivolous?
> "A. No, that was what was interesting to me,—it was entirely
> serious. Everyone that I came in contact with thought it was a good
> thing, and were interested in the results that could be obtained."

Rowell hadn't had biology, zoology, or physiology in high school but
had taken zoology at Missouri, and no one she talked to had been shocked
by the questionnaire. Occasionally, some student might say it was "terrible," but they weren't shocked. A fellow freshman, Blessing Lippman
from Minnesota, had read the copies of both male and female versions
of the questionnaire on the morning the story broke, then got hers later
in the mail. There was nothing new in it as far as she was concerned. It
turned out that one of her close friends had gotten a copy several days
before, filled it out and mailed it in, and had said nothing to Lippman
about it until after the publicity erupted. That was indicative of the lack
of shock, since, as Lippman told it, "we tell each other everything."

Carlson's question was routine: Any "moral injury" inflicted on coeds?

"I should think that it would have just the other effect," replied Lippman. "It has always been the theory in our family that the more things are above-board the less chance there is of any immorality, and I think it is more likely to have that effect,—at least, on freshmen."

Rowell's fellow students took the issues of the questionnaire seriously, and those she talked to answered honestly. They discussed various viewpoints, she said, "and there wasn't a thing smutty in it or dirty at all, I don't think." What went on among Rowell's friends seemed to describe the interactions of a healthy university campus. Was that also true of healthy families? Blessing Lippman said her family was open with one another. Lucille Dorff's family seemed the same way. Dorff, from Dallas, Texas, and a member of DeGraff's Family class as well as a student leader in the protest against the firings, hadn't heard much criticism of the questionnaire, perhaps, as she said, because she "was rather wrapped up in the affair." Dorff discussed the questionnaire with her mother, a divorcée, who didn't see what the fuss was about. Neither did her younger brother, who read about it in the press. Her brother was "not very liberal minded, either," she said, "—he is a very unsophisticated little boy, and he said, 'Lucille, we talk about things like that at high school,'—he has just finished high school. He said, 'I don't see why the University should be much excited about that.'"

Alice Sonnenschein, a senior from St. Louis, didn't see anything she hadn't seen before, whether in sociology texts or in newspapers or magazines. Those things were discussed all the time, she said. Forbidden items stirred interest all the more. The only person shocked by the questionnaire cited by Sonnenschein was "an old maid Instructor here who was shocked considerably, but she was very much interested in getting the students' point of view." Sonnenschein was so upset about the reaction to the questionnaire that the unnamed "old maid" said nothing. Later, said Sonnenschein, the instructor had changed her view and "realized it was only her Victorian attitude that caused her to become shocked. She really had not let herself think about the thing, and if she had, as we younger folks had been doing, she would not have been, I think. Her universe of discourse, as Dr. DeGraff would say, was limited,—we discuss those things with the boys we go with and with the girls we go with." Obviously, the uproar revealed a gap that separated students' views from the general public. "These people out in the state have not thought about the things that they—even if they did think about them, they never have really been honest with themselves. If they thought—if I were engaged to a person who would do so and so, I would break my engagement,—maybe they have thought about it in their hearts but never had the nerve to come out and talk about it; but with the progress of the human race and becoming more highly educated, we don't fear to talk about such things; whereas it is our problem and they never have voiced those things."

Despite youthful precociousness, Sonnenschein had identified the wide gap between the Victorians and those of her generation who thought— and spoke—differently. Here was a university with a president who didn't want such things discussed, presiding over a student body that included those who were determined to do so. Sonnenschein thought the answers would have been valuable, and Janis Rowell added that her boyfriend said the questionnaire was a good thing because it stimulated thought. "It is a problem of the younger generation," she said, "and we have to face it."

Noting the four young women appearing before the committee, Professor Thurstone asked if it would be easy to produce four female students who had been offended by the questionnaire and resented having it thrust on them. Dorff replied she had asked Ruth Garth, head of the Presbyterian Student Center, to send up a dozen women to testify, without regard to their views of the questionnaire. Inclement weather had precluded Garth from contacting them, but Garth said that, in her personal view, none of them would testify to being shocked unless somehow pressured to do so. Dorff claimed everyone wondered what their folks would think, "but so many have parents who are apt to control their thoughts and some of them would say they didn't want to do anything until they asked their dad and mother." A bunch of them, Dorff's sorority sisters, took the document home at the Easter break and talked it over; while some parents opposed the questionnaire, most didn't.

Dean Bordwell wanted to know about the sorority that had opposed the questionnaire. Oh yes, said Dorff, Chi Omega. Here was the story on that one. It turned out, according to Dorff, "that a local preacher who has a daughter in it or had some connection with it,—he went out and said he thought that [it] would be a fine and Gospel thing for that sorority to vote against it and the majority of the girls had not seen the Questionnaire and the next day there was such a big wave of condemnation and discussion among other people that they had to reverse themselves, in order to remain on campus,—almost."

Thurstone asked, "Are you pretty sure about your statement that any or most of the girls in the sorority had not seen the Questionnaire at the time they voted their disapproval?

"A I talked to several girls who are members of that sorority and they said that was what happened."

Three male students appeared next. The story was the same—no surprises in the questionnaire. Jack Turner, a junior in journalism who had called for the AAUP investigation back in April, had lived in Missouri for several years but had been born and had gotten his early education in Texas. He didn't have biology in high school—it wasn't taught—but he had been born on a Texas farm where "one runs across such things as sex and breeding . . . and I worked a while with the Proctor & Gamble crew over Texas and we got onto those things." A member of DeGraff's class, Turner had heard about the questionnaire since the committees seemed to know what the others were doing. The conversation about it was serious. Turner was reasonably well acquainted on campus, and he didn't find any shock either. Of course, in rare exceptions, Turner heard about those who thought it was inappropriate and wouldn't have wanted their mother or sister to read it. But when the publicity arose, those who talked to Turner thought the newspapers took "a very silly attitude" in the matter. At his fraternity house, copies of the questionnaire that had been put aside indifferently disappeared after the story hit the news. As a group, he thought his fellow students at Mizzou were "clean-minded" and that there wasn't enough in the questionnaire to get worked up about.

Marion Dry, a senior, thought the same thing. In fact, he'd gotten a copy of the questionnaire, laid it on his desk for a day or so, and then filled it out after discussing it with a friend. Chairman Carlson asked candidly: "Did the reading of the Questionnaire and thinking of the answers stimulate your eroticism?"

"No," said Dry, "I am sure it didn't. There are too many other things so much more forceful, that would do that." He detected a change in the tone of discussion after the publicity arose. The guys treated it seriously until then, after which it became something of a joke. "Many people would laugh about all the commotion and say that it was foolish," he said, "that the Questionnaire was harmless,—I should not say it was flippant, no, but the seriousness of it all decreased after the publicity." The issues in the first three questions were certainly not foreign to fraternity house bull sessions.

Glenn Degner, a junior from Minnesota, had a similar reaction. He first heard about the questionnaire at lunch one day and wasn't offended by it but thought its methodology might not produce anything of value. Having no interest in psychology or sociology, he believed personal interviews would have been better than a questionnaire. He heard responses from others that were both serious and flippant. "There is always, of course, a certain element that gets a kick out of a traveling salesman's joke,—most everyone does,—and I know several boys who answered and answered the thing very seriously,—not several, but some,—half a dozen, probably." One Catholic fellow he knew objected to it, thinking the issues were out of bounds. But on the whole, most had no problem with the questionnaire, "at least those students who have done any reading and given any thought to the modern attitude toward life, as opposed to the fundamentalist attitude." Degner, who would be the next student government president, knew his generation was different. "I believe very few students can belong in the University and still escape that new philosophy and new attitude," he said, "and that the students as a whole appreciate and endorse a liberal and frank attitude toward the problems of life, as they do toward anything else."[21]

After the investigating committee recalled Professor Edwin Branson to go over his meetings with President Brooks, they interviewed Dean Bessie Leach Priddy about her relationship with the questionnaire and her views of it. She rehearsed how some women students had first brought the document to her attention, how some felt uncomfortable about it, and how it was discussed at dinner tables among both men and women. At first Priddy heard plenty of criticism of the questionnaire, but she too noticed the shift in student attitude after the penalties were announced. Nobody wanted such punishments for Meyer or DeGraff. Too bad the public had butted into the affair, they thought. She found many who objected to the mixed company discussions prompted by the questionnaire. "One girl said to me that she objected to having men leer at her and ask her if she had answered her Questionnaire yet." Maybe the questionnaire didn't lead to illicit sex, said Priddy, but it certainly increased discussion and openness about sexual matters. Incredibly, some chaperons even tried to forbid discussion of the matter at the dinner table. How far would such maternalism go at a state university? Carlson asked Priddy if such chaperons had "a standing rule that when boys call on girls in their sororities they must not discuss matters of sex?" "Oh, Lord, no," replied Priddy, "—it is not supposed that they do, that is all. That is hardly a subject for social conversation between unmarried people."[22]

Dean Priddy was excused and the hearing was over—about twenty hours of testimony. As the campus prepared for final exams and graduation—graduation for more than seven hundred students, but not Hobart Mowrer—the investigators from the American Association of University Professors withdrew to gather their thoughts, mull over what they had seen and heard, and prepare their official report. Would this be an open-and-shut case of academic injustice? The trio of investigators seemed to lean in that direction, but they were all professionals. At the heart of the matter seemed to be competing pressures for academic freedom, the validity of a particular and allegedly scientific enterprise, the ability of a governing board to judge such validity, and the propriety of disseminating intimate matters to a general student community.

If the questionnaire was deemed scientific, then could the Board of Curators deny the propriety of scientific investigation? This was purportedly science, not titillation, but if titillation occurred, that constituted the price of such scientific inquiry. In fact, such a trade-off figured in Judge Augustus Hand's favorable decision in the Mary Ware Dennett federal obscenity case. The task of the university was to teach, conduct research, and perform community service, and if the curators failed here, so did the concept of the university.

Lurking in the shadows was the muted testimony about Max Meyer's sex lecture. What role had it played so far? Meyer never insisted he had to give that brief lecture. He had lived long enough to know one didn't always get what one wanted. He seemed prepared to forgo a perfectly fine lecture, reviewed by other faculty, other scientists, all for peace with a skittish administration and a portion of the unknowing public. But far from defending his faculty, the president of the university exacerbated the problem. In fact, as Meyer claimed years later, the problem had been the president's "double-tonguedness." After being called to the president's office, Meyer was told by Brooks, "Please send me a written explanation of your teaching *so that I can defend you before the Board,* since some citizens are suspicious of you." The truth had to creep over the minds of increasing numbers of those who saw him in operation that Brooks was in over his head, that limited vision and narrow temperament, perhaps even duplicity, had finally crippled his administration.[23]

3

Whatever the ruling generation or guardians of public morals thought of the questionnaire, students at the University of Missouri had already made up their minds. At the end of the year, Mizzou's student annual, the *Savitar,* captured the niceties of student life in 1929. It deemed the university "the foremost institution of higher learning in the Middlewest." Along with the usual photographs that chronicled the life of a state university—its athletic victories and defeats, its dances and social life, its endless faces looking out from student clubs, societies, and the like, the yearbook couldn't overlook the centerpiece of the spring semester. A facsimile of the questionnaire's cover letter appeared in the advertising section, and along with rush week, homecoming, and football, the questionnaire made the top-eighteen list of why the year had been a scholastic success. If Chi Omega got anonymous kudos for its protest of the questionnaire ("It is inspiring to hear this reaffirmation of the accepted high ideals of our society"), the yearbook still thought it detected material for satirist H. L. Mencken's *American Mercury*. "Once again," it said, "the Inquisition has failed to save humanity from the pitfalls of thought. This relic institution exists in Tennessee, in Arkansas, and—alas—in Missouri. We look forward to its overthrow within the passing of another century." The *Savitar* even tried crude poetry:

> Men still believe in monkeys in the State of Tennessee;
> In Arkansas an Old King Cole still yells for his fiddlers three;
> And now Missouri, hitherto the land of mules and pork,
> Has just confirmed its strong belief in the good old-fashioned stork.

Such imagery also played in the yearbook's parody of Aesop's fable. "You see it was like this: The student body at Missouri was not unusual. Never had the question of sex been discussed by students; everyone was reluctant to mention this subtle, mysterious word at bull sessions, or elsewhere. Everyone believed in the stork."

But a wolf was about to upset the tranquility of the student flock. "His name was DeGraff." Of course, the wolf had to put on sheep's clothing.

> In a short time he became popular—very popular—with the students and co-eds, and he was a guest at every dance and party. Being an unusual individual, he had grasped the student's viewpoint; he saw things as did the student; and he understood student problems. DeGraff loved the students. Impelled by the realization of the needs of student education and moved by his unselfish feeling toward those students, he contributed a new course to the Department of Sociology. It was called "The Family."
> THE ATTACK.
> Time came for the preparation of term papers in the course, and one of the student groups, headed by Mowrer, found it needed actual facts for the proper preparation of its subject. A questionnaire was drawn up to be circulated among men and women at Mizzou—under the guise of RESEARCH. Four or five hundred boys and co-eds answered the questionnaire, had returned it, and had forgotten all about it. Some ten or twelve days slipped by. Then things began to happen.

The wolf was of course exposed. Parents soon got involved, and newspapers splashed the story far and wide.

Then, inhabitants of the Ozark Hills heard of the scandalous affair and sent ultimatums to their representatives in the legislature.

THE FLOCK IS SAVED.

The executive committee of the Board met—it had to. All involved in the circulation of the questionnaire were called in and interviewed. The Board considered public opinion and released DeGraff, Max Meyer, and Mowrer. Once again peace and quiet reign on Francis Quadrangle. Sex has been abolished and the students' faith in the stork has been reaffirmed.

Thus endeth the fable.

In listing the "Rushing Point" for each of the forty-three Greek fraternities and sororities, the *Savitar* had the usual innocuous points: Sigma Chi's scholarship, Alpha Delta Pi's "fastest cook in town," Phi Mu's "Just watch us grow," and Zeta Tau Alpha's yearbook beauty queen, Eleanor Coulter, along with so many others the meanings of which were soon lost in time (Alpha Tau Omega's "There's room for you in our orchestra"). But everyone understood that the nice columns at the Gamma Phi Beta house, where Mary Ellen Hubbard was a sister, "make good necking screens," and doubtless the Tri-Delts might not have wanted their *real* rushing point to be "Dean Priddy is a Delta girl." Others clearly made sport of the spring controversy. "Rushing Point" for Chi Omega: "We believe in the stork." For Lambda Chi Alpha: "Oh, yes, one of our boys wrote the questionnaire."[24]

8

"Facts Are Stubborn Things"

> The frankness on sex matters that has characterized the
> generation that has grown up since the war . . . is something
> foreign to many of the older generation.
>   —Percy Bordwell, May 22, 1929, AAUP Hearing, AAUPP

> We will endeavor not to do anybody injustice. It will be
> an objective and a fearless report.
>   —A. J. Carlson, May 18, 1929, AAUP Hearing, AAUPP

U.S. Route 40 cut horizontally across Missouri from St. Louis to Kansas City, with Columbia nearly halfway in between. West of Columbia, the road crossed the Missouri River and left the low hills and valley to traverse the prairie uplands all the way to Kansas City. In June 1929, Louis L. Thurstone, professor of psychology at the University of Chicago and one of the investigators for the American Association of University Professors, drove along that route on his way to Los Angeles, nearly two thousand miles away. He stopped in Columbia and telephoned Herman Schlundt, professor of chemistry at the University of Missouri and president of the local chapter of the AAUP. The pair discussed the preliminary report of the investigation into the sex questionnaire controversy that had scandalized the university, the state, and the academic community nationwide. Leslie Cowan, secretary to the Board of Curators, was about to take the train to Kansas City, and Schlundt suggested he ride with Thurstone and his wife. They all agreed.

The trip to Kansas City provided an opportunity for Thurstone to get to know Cowan better, but he wasn't prepared for the bombshell the curators' secretary dropped on him. As Thurstone's automobile trundled across middle Missouri, Cowan confidentially declared that the Board of Curators had decided to fire Professor Max Meyer not for his involvement in the infamous questionnaire with its intimate inquiry into the private lives of Missouri students, but rather for his physiology lecture to a bunch of females in his Social Psychology class. To believe Cowan, the curators hashed the matter over, decided to dismiss Meyer for the lecture, then planned to cover it up. "They did not dare give the sex lecture as the reason so they decided to publish the questionnaire as the reason," Thurstone recalled Cowan as telling him. The debate didn't make it into the minutes of the curators, and Cowan was told not to divulge the proceedings. According to Thurstone, Cowan first broached the topic. Why Cowan would divulge such information, if it was true, is subject to speculation (justice for Meyer, undermining of Brooks, or whatever), but it's virtually impossible to believe Thurstone invented the exchange. It's also difficult to believe that Cowan made up the story or that honorable men would engage in gross prevarication. But was Cowan, and Thurstone for that matter, referring to duplicity by the three-man Executive Board or to the full board? After all, the Executive Board dismissed Meyer but the full board later merely suspended him; evidence suggests that the reference was to the action of the Executive Board. But a real cover-up? Did the lecture really play a part in the board's decision and, if so, how much? Was it a matter of nuance or perhaps exaggeration? In any case, the Thurstones dropped Cowan off in Kansas City and headed on to California, where shortly after their arrival, Louis Thurstone promptly wrote to committee chairman A. J. Carlson back in Chicago about the bizarre conversation.

Thurstone had even more news from Kansas City. While in town, he spoke with Leland Hazard, the attorney who had represented Meyer and DeGraff. Hazard's new role was apparently unofficial, but he was working with those in Kansas City attempting to raise money for Meyer. Yet his relationship with the AAUP committee was, as he told Judge James Goodrich, "as an alumnus desiring to do something, if possible, to prevent a bad situation from becoming worse." Hazard now posed a question to Thurstone: would the AAUP investigators be willing to purge their final official report of any criticism of the university in return for the dismissal of President Brooks by the Board of Curators? The bizarre became even more so. Politics and pragmatism, never far from any proceeding involving the public, became staples of the process even as they jostled with absolute principles and those who espoused them.[1]

Between the Columbia visit by the AAUP investigating team in May and Thurstone's western trip in June, the committee had been busily working on its report. A lot was at stake, including the reputation of the University of Missouri, the integrity and influence of the youthful American Association of University Professors, and, of course, the lives and reputations of many individuals touched directly or indirectly by the controversy sparked by a sociology questionnaire. Within two days of the close of the hearing in Columbia, Carlson reported the essentials of the visit to Secretary Tyler in Washington. The three-member visiting team developed a consensus on the basics of the case and "essential apparent culpabilities." The feeling at the university, held most likely by the concerned core faculty, favored an early response by the AAUP, which Carlson hoped could be developed within ten days, then dispatched quietly and without publicity to Brooks and the curators. "What I have in mind," said an optimistic Carlson, "is that such a preliminary report, if presented early, might help to partly undo injustices." All, of course, was subject to the wishes of the association. But there was a nagging rumor that Carlson wanted Tyler to clarify. When President Brooks met in Washington with Tyler and a number of other AAUP members shortly after the Board of Curators meeting in April, did he really say that he had done all in his power to prevent the termination of DeGraff and Meyer? Though Carlson was too guarded and professional to say so, based on the evidence, such would have constituted a falsehood. He thought the committee should know if such a representation was made by Brooks, "as that will help to evaluate some of the phases of the evidence obtained at Missouri."[2]

Apparently, that rumor was floating around, since not only had Leland Hazard heard it but so also had Judge James Goodrich, president of the Board of Curators, who wanted to know the particulars. Tyler told Carlson he couldn't confirm the rumor that Brooks had said he tried everything in his power to stop the firings, but had the "impression . . . that he said he used his influence in favor of modifying the original verdict." That impression was later confirmed by two others present at the Washington meeting. Carlson, in turn, told Hazard that Tyler's recollection stood at odds with not only the curators' minutes but also the president's testimony before the investigating committee. As an added twist, according to the testimony of Professors James Rogers and Edwin Branson, Brooks had told them a few hours before the meeting of the Executive Board that he didn't expect any dramatic action by the curators; in fact, Rogers recalled, as he said in his testimony, "that if drastic action were contemplated he would like to have certain members of the faculty come in and explain the faculty position . . . because he would like to get that position before the Executive Board in case the situation seemed dangerous." Professor Harry Brown, who wasn't present that morning, had told the committee that "the men who went before him had the distinct impression that he [Brooks] was friendly and would avoid drastic action if he could." As it turned out, none of the faculty was called in, but Dean Walter Williams was invited to present the faculty view, though his testimony failed to appear in the minutes of the Executive Board meeting. According to Brooks's testimony before the AAUP investigators, Williams's "presentation was very skilful [sic] and very effective, and he is very influential with the Board." Even though Dean Williams, out of town, never testified before the investigators, he responded in writing to Carlson's inquiry about Brooks's request to him, and about some of his testimony before the Executive Board. Williams said he told the curators that Meyer's dismissal would injure the university, that academics would regard such action as infringement on the freedom to research and teach, and that, in any case, the punishment was too harsh. Further, the Missouri faculty would not approve the action, while the public would be divided but that the majority would be opposed. Recruitment of faculty would be damaged and the image of the university would suffer. Williams said he urged the group to defer any action to the full board. "It should be noted," he said, "that the Executive Board had definitely agreed upon its decision before I was asked to appear before it, or at least before I did appear before it. My appearance came at the close of the sessions of the Executive Board. While I was present, copies of the formal announcement of the Board's action were handed to the members to be delivered to representatives of the press." The evidence was growing that Brooks was either overwhelmed by a board that placed little confidence in him, or that he was a liar, or both.[3]

Tyler's mere "impression" of Brooks's remark disappointed attorney Leland Hazard, since he hoped for a stronger statement confirming the president's duplicity. Two curators knew of the rumor and thought it significant. Hazard wanted some word from others at the Washington meeting that might be ethically passed to the curators, who were scheduled to meet on June 8, though the date was later moved. Rumors also circulated—perhaps more of a hope—that the Board of Curators might oust Brooks at that meeting, though Hazard was doubtful.[4]

2

Meanwhile, the preliminary report took shape. Within a few days of arriving back in Iowa, Percy Bordwell dispatched his views to Carlson, tersely outlining in less than three pages things known and unknown.

"Public clamor demanded victims and this was echoed in the legislature," wrote Bordwell. "Unfortunately, President Brooks responded to
this clamor instead of standing out against it." Brooks also got harsh criticism for his role in renewing the sex lecture controversy and helping "to
fan the flames which he ought to have tried to quench." It undoubtedly
influenced the Executive Board's action, though how much remained uncertain. Excusing the stenographers prompted rumors about "something
else 'too terrible' to mention"—"the rumors that for a time prevailed did
a great injustice to two high-minded and honorable men." Several days
later Thurstone finished his report. Stretching fourteen pages, including
recommendations, the document constituted a model of its kind, demon-
strating extraordinary skill in use of language and in its cogent and tightly
argued rehearsal and interpretation of the Missouri controversy. In carefully reasoned prose, Thurstone dismantled each accusation leveled at
the questionnaire or its perpetrators, including that it was shocking, a
stimulus to immorality, fraudulent, and lacked any scientific validity. He
concluded with dramatic and unprecedented recommendations that included blacklisting the University of Missouri and prohibiting from membership in the association any new faculty who took a position there.
Further, restoration of the university to the AAUP's good graces could
be achieved only by waiting ten years or rectifying the damage done
to Meyer and DeGraff. Most likely, Carlson made use of both drafts in
the preliminary report, though deleting Thurstone's recommendations.
Those recommendations stimulated considerable debate within the association and significant portions of Thurstone's brilliant draft eventually
wound up in the final published report. The investigating team leveled
its harshest criticism at President Brooks for his role in exacerbating the
affair, but also suggested the negative role played by the supposedly off-
the-table lecture by Max Meyer. Still, reflecting Carlson's optimism and
earnest desire for a happy ending, the document held out hope for correction of injustices and the restoration of Missouri's good name.[5]

Lots of people awaited the preliminary results. None was more anxious
for the report than Harmon DeGraff, now out of a job and with a cloud
of doubt hanging over his future in academia. Without knowing when
the report would be ready or what it would say, yet aware that colleges
would look askance at his candidacy for any open faculty positions, he
asked Carlson if the merits of his case might warrant a letter from him
assuaging fears of potential employers. Possessing both professionalism
and humanity, Carlson wrote that the evidence pointed only to DeGraff's
"lack of foresight" under the circumstances prevalent in 1929. "To dismiss
a professor on such a basis is clearly rank injustice," he said. "There is

no charge against you as to personal character, ability or loyalty to the institution."[6]

The twenty-one-page preliminary report got rave reviews. Harvard Law School's John Maguire, who also served as adviser to the AAUP, got a look at an early draft and liked what he saw. "If the final report maintains this standard of excellence," he told Secretary Tyler, "it will be a very valuable document for us." Evidently, Maguire examined an early draft, which at that point contained Thurstone's recommendations. He was dubious about the penalty phase of the report but on second thought, as he told Tyler, "we must put both our feet down hard sometime in order to wake people up." His hesitancy about choosing the Missouri case stemmed largely from "the fairness and courtesy" shown the investigators by university officials.[7]

The "final" preliminary report was ready for the Board of Curators' meeting in Kansas City on June 15 and Carlson dispatched a copy to appropriate parties, all without publicity. As if holding his breath, Carlson told Secretary Tyler, "If any correction of the injustice at Missouri is to be done at once, the report had to reach the Curators by today. We will have to watch the outcome." The next day he told Leland Hazard, another recipient of the document, that they hoped the curators would "find a way to correct an error and the injustice done so that the preparation of our final report will have a different ring."[8]

Copies also went to Herman Schlundt, president of the local AAUP affiliate, and to Meyer and DeGraff. The response was effusive. Meyer thought it was "a perfect statement of the essential facts," and Schlundt praised it as "a 'corker.'" The report needed no changes, and Schlundt thought the ultimate version would constitute "a classic contribution to the advance of education in our state, and probably far beyond the boundaries of our state." He added, "I wish that you could have heard some of the complimentary remarks that the men made when the report was read." Schlundt's colleague who had played such a positive role in the controversy, W. C. Curtis, also praised the report, claiming "your statements have a forthrightness that gives one renewed confidence in our profession." DeGraff, waiting in the wings, had a big personal stake in the ultimate outcome, including financial considerations. As an assistant professor, he had been on a year-to-year contract and part of his salary had been denied, a perceived injustice cited in the report. He liked the report, but beyond all that, he asked a small favor of Carlson: could the final draft include the fact that students from his Family class had called for the AAUP investigation, not just Brooks and several faculty. (DeGraff had long been emotional about his students' loyalty. His Family class had

given him an engraved gold medallion of some sort, with "In Appreciation" on one side, and "To Dr. DeGraff from His Family" on the other. As
a bachelor without close family, his affection was real.)[9]

If Thurstone had been the most articulate in drafting his response to the
Missouri crisis, he also provoked debate within the AAUP for his proposed recommendations, including blackballing the University of Missouri unless Meyer and DeGraff were reinstated along with proper financial restitution. Percy Bordwell, the law dean from Iowa, opposed
sanctions because they would constitute ex post facto action; further, they
would punish the university instead of the culpable individual; and, finally, that the task of the committee was "to find facts and to fix the blame
but not to administer such punishment." Nor did he think the association
competent to inflict punishment. In fairness, Thurstone had proposed recommended sanctions, not expecting the committee to carry them out.

For his part, Carlson liked the principle of the recommendations, but
knew it was a major decision that only the association could make. Beyond that, he pondered the incongruity of the association indirectly pun-
ishing its own members for the sins of an institution's president and governing board but thought it would please the association's militant "left
wing." He talked informally with several colleagues in Chicago, and
they—especially younger ones—were tired of toothless responses to
transgressions. In fact, he worried "the older heads" leading the association were "reluctant to sanction anything with real teeth in it." Secretary
Tyler thought Thurstone's proposals constituted "a rather radical change
of policy on the part of the Association as I do not infer that the University
of Missouri is more blameworthy than various other institutions where
we have made investigations." He wondered if the committee thought
Missouri's sins were more grievous than others or if the time had simply arrived to get tough with offenders. And another important AAUP
member, William B. Munro of Harvard, on sabbatical in Pasadena, California, also urged caution. "I trust that the Council will act conservatively
in adopting the suggestions of Professor Thurstone which accompany this
report. There is no doubt in my mind that president Brooks and the Curators of the University of Missouri acted unjustly; on the other hand it
is a rather serious matter to blacklist an important state institution in the
way that Professor Thurstone suggests."[10]

One potentially affected colleague was Missouri's zoologist Winterton
Curtis, who thought the time *had* come. He told Carlson that while he
loved the report, he took "no satisfaction" about its criticism of his university where he had labored all his life. But loyalty to professional ideals
was strong and he had long believed the association needed to do more

than simply record the facts of administrative injustices. "Until we can put some real teeth in our criticisms we shall not accomplish much," he said. "The time is ripe for this sort of thing and having believed it should be done I can argue for it with all the better grace when it is against my own institution." He believed faculty involvement would serve the university well in time to come by giving confidence to potential faculty recruits. At the same time he told AAUP President Henry Crew that Thurstone's recommendations were mild and that he wanted the association to "do something with more punch to it than mere statements of fact that are soon forgotten." The AAUP was "acknowledged to be a pretty innocuous organization and always will be, unless we begin doing things like this which Professor Thurstone proposes."[11]

Regardless of how the preliminary report was received by its natural friends, the big question was how it would play with the curators. Attorney Leland Hazard, a shrewd and effective advocate, tried to smooth the way. Just before the meeting of the curators in Kansas City in mid-June, Hazard had some explosive information for James Goodrich. He told Goodrich he had been in Columbia during the visit of the AAUP investigators, having gone there to talk with his client Max Meyer about his summer school contract and to tell him that friends in Kansas City had raised funds to cover his lost summer stipend. While in town, Hazard also spoke with the investigators, taking credit for recommending that they issue a preliminary statement with the obvious intention of trying to repair the damage before issuing a final report. Then, in June, Hazard went to Chicago on legal business and while there visited with Chairman Carlson, who showed him the preliminary report. Given the facts of the case, he said he told Carlson that the University of Missouri would never make progress under Brooks's administration, not simply because of his views of the questionnaire, but also because he lacked integrity and judgment. Carlson's interest, said Hazard, was the good of the university rather than simply a derogatory report; a change in the presidency would signal sufficient optimism to justify withholding that report. "This information," Hazard told Goodrich, "placed upon me a serious responsibility which I am discharging by giving the information to you."

The nimble attorney who always seemed to be in the right place at the right time had another card to play. He told Judge Goodrich that he understood that in a case like Missouri's the AAUP investigating committee would make recommendations that included blacklisting the affected institution and denying membership to new faculty members. "I am advised," he confided, "not by the Committee but upon competent academic authority, that the result of such action taken by the Executive Council of the Association upon the recommendation of the Committee is usually as follows. No man of any standing in his field will accept a place in such a University. Younger men, who have not yet attained their standing, will in some cases not be deterred, but the better young men will have regard for the situation, and will be inclined not to accept appointments as instructors." Ousting Brooks could prevent such disaster.[12]

Such intrigue appeared to edge toward blackmail. The skilled attorney apparently didn't know the inaccuracy of his veiled threat. At that very moment the AAUP was agonizing over the bold idea of sanctions, something it hadn't imposed before. Still, Hazard sent Carlson a copy of his letter to Goodrich and kept him apprised of what was going on, even asking if his statements were accurate. As it turned out, the Board of Curators didn't put their full attention on the AAUP issue at its meeting in mid-June. The agenda focused on plans for the new athletic fieldhouse, later named for Chester L. Brewer, Missouri's athletic director. But the curators did give a cursory review of the preliminary report and Carlson's accompanying letter. They expected to give the report their attention at the next board meeting but in the meantime wanted a copy of the AAUP transcript along with clarification about Brooks's now-infamous remark to the AAUP officials in Washington about how he had used his influence to mitigate Meyer's termination. Was there a transcript of those proceedings, Goodrich wondered? Letters? Oral testimony? Further, the curators wanted to know exactly what the AAUP committee meant by, as the preliminary report stated, "its willingness to be of any possible service" regarding the university's predicament.[13]

Fully apprised of the inner workings of the board, Hazard told Carlson that Goodrich would be asking about the Brooks remark, and that summer interruptions might well delay things until fall. Hazard counted "four friendly members" on the board, one of whom was influential but who would be out of the loop at the next meeting. According to Hazard, all four thought Brooks had to go and seemed quite interested in knowing what the AAUP committee required to settle the whole matter amicably. Hazard added: "Since the Board seems particularly interested in the Presidents [sic] statement in Washington, it might be well to satisfy their desire for the original evidence. The President denied the statement at the recent Board meeting. I am informed that the session was not at all comfortable for him." W. C. Curtis didn't have the inside information Hazard did, but told Carlson that Brooks had returned from the Kansas City meeting "in an apparently perturbed state of mind and very 'anxious to please' at least one member of our group who presented other business."[14]

While things seemed to be closing in on Brooks, it was clear that his dismissal would not satisfy the injustice to Meyer and DeGraff. Professor Thurstone had told Hazard as much when he stopped in Kansas City on his way to California in June. Hazard passed that information on to the "friendly" four curators. Then, after hundreds of miles to ponder the whole matter, Thurstone arrived in California with his view unchanged. He told Carlson that it might serve the University of Missouri well if Brooks was dumped in exchange for a muted AAUP report, but that wasn't their assignment. The committee's task, he argued, had been to look into the firings of Meyer and DeGraff, and canning Brooks wouldn't undo the injustice done to them. The Brooks business was a wholly other issue. In that, of course, Carlson concurred.[15]

The problem of what Brooks said or didn't say at the Washington meeting with the AAUP wouldn't go away. The Board of Curators obviously saw the crucial implications. Though Judge Goodrich noted that Brooks emphatically denied making such remarks about trying to modify the verdict of the curators, he doggedly pursued the matter, asking Carlson if independent letters from those at the April meeting could be sent directly to him, for distribution to the full board, containing their recollections of what the president had said. Within weeks, several had done so, and their impressions pointed to Brooks's duplicity. Carlson chortled to Leland Hazard that one of the letters, from a lawyer no less, "was particularly clear and specific." Henry Crew didn't really want the AAUP to get in the middle of a potential squabble between a university president and the governing board, but that's where the association found itself.[16] Of course, what the curators would do with the information was anybody's guess.

Meanwhile, events conspired to delay the disposition of the controversy. In fact, one prominent Missouri alumnus, a Kansas City physician active in the campaign to overturn the curators' decision, warned Chairman Carlson what he was up against. The four attorneys on the board were "trained and skilled in the art of delaying justice," the alumnus told Carlson. "The method is to wear down the opponent by any excuse for delay in reaching a decision—side-step, zig-zag, procrastinate or anything else that will take more time. Some of these Board members are past masters in this art." Take Judge Goodrich, for example, "a most skillful gentleman in circumlocution, who can and will always tell you much in personal conversation, but nothing in writing; who has the reputation of being a strong man, but whose judicial mind allows him to do nothing unless the evidence is presented by some one else in a judicial way; who never leads an unpopular cause, but who joins if the social

pressure upon him is made strong enough; who never assumes a responsibility unless there is popular credit attached; this is the man who refused
to officially receive Mr. Hazard's letter explaining what your committee
meant by its preliminary report, after you so generously, kindly and co-
operatively had hastened to send said report to the Board in time for its
meeting in June." According to the alumnus, Goodrich looked to delay
things until his European trip, knowing also that fellow curator Milton
Tootle's summertime bout with hay fever would soon send him north.
Allegedly, Tootle, who enjoyed wide respect for his cultural refinement
and whom Goodrich regarded highly for his business abilities, had long
known Brooks needed to be replaced.[17]

But McDavid and Blanton were stumbling blocks, each possessing a
strong personality, both very outspoken and very sure of their views, and
both members of the Executive Board that had set the process in motion
back in March. If nothing else, Frank McDavid was the true believer, probably the least pragmatic among the curators. Son of a Presbyterian minister, he was a churchman all his life. He taught school and read law in
Illinois before he and his mentor came to the Missouri Ozarks well before
the turn of the century. Representing Springfield in the state senate in the
Progressive era, McDavid earned notice as an orator, and helped bring
both the court of appeals and the state teachers college to his adopted
hometown. He remained a loyal Democrat, serving as state convention
chairman in 1908 and 1920, and as a national delegate in 1928. Ironically,
Republican Governor Arthur Hyde put him on the university's Board of
Curators in 1921. He was a community builder, a hard worker in the public's interest, a valued member of society who believed in Victorian role
and order. Along with his colleague Jack Blanton, McDavid sensed that
they were holding back the night of social dislocation. As a newspaperman, Blanton resisted the urge of many talented young men to escape to
the bright lights of big-city dailies. Paris, Missouri, was his home and the
Monroe County Appeal, a weekly founded by his father in the nineteenth
century, was his paper. A civic builder, he prided himself on his brief editorials, "Hints by the Horse Editor," all of which suggested satisfaction
with the virtues of rural life at a time when rural-urban splits were most
palpable and pronounced in American life.

It would, however, be a mistake to see the conflict in rural-urban terms
alone. For a time in the 1920s, such phenomena as the Ku Klux Klan, Prohibition, and religious fundamentalism commanded great support not
merely in the crossroads and villages of America, but in the great cities
and metropolitan areas as well. Nor was it regional. Such issues, as one
scholar has argued, were "psychic and not purely geographic in charac-

ter." One need only count the large number of New York and other eastern and Yankee-state license plates on cars crowding into the nation's capital for the infamous forty-thousand-strong-yet-almost-last-gasp Klan march down Pennsylvania Avenue in August 1925. If the alienated artists and writers of the Lost Generation escaped to their garrets on the Left Bank in Paris or to the Algonquin Hotel in New York, to what refuge would the alienated from the heartland flee? Whatever else they were, the Klan, fundamentalist religion, and Prohibition became weapons in the culture wars of the 1920s. Prohibition, in fact, proved quite successful in reducing alcohol consumption, maybe by as much as half, and related diseases also dropped during the decade. And in the developing culture war over the 1929 questionnaire crisis in Missouri, Stratton Brooks's mailbag also showed little if any regional pattern. Alienated Victorians, such as Jack Blanton and Frank McDavid, were present in small-town Missouri and in the oft-ridiculed Ozarks, but they could also be found in St. Louis and Kansas City. Regardless of their origin, Blanton and McDavid constituted a formidable pair to uphold virtuous society against the Philistine assault.[18]

James Goodrich would do anything to keep from offending them. McDavid was among the most senior in age, "fine-hearted, chivalrous," said Carlson's informant, "but completely out of step and full of harsh overtones when he tries to adjust himself to the advances in ethics in sex matters—hard-headed, belligerent, never changing his mind when once determined upon his course—this is the Chairman of the Executive Committee of the Board of Curators." A rumor floated briefly suggesting he contemplated resignation after taking heat for his dogmatism, but that didn't sound like him. He was in it for the long haul. Maybe instead there would be strength in numbers. George Willson and A. A. Speer, along with Milton Tootle of course, were open and fair-minded men; even H. W. Lenox, who usually sat in silence, appeared ready to see Brooks depart. But they had no courage. And all probably knew that Brooks could publicly posture as the martyr who had tried valiantly to save the morals of the university's youth. The curators needed "the iron hand in the velvet glove" approach, all without antagonizing them into defiance, which would do great injustice to all concerned.[19]

The well-meaning alumnus might have seemed a prophet. Within days, Judge Goodrich announced to Carlson that the AAUP transcript was much larger than he had expected, that he'd be leaving for Europe in late July, and that Milton Tootle would soon leave for his summer home on Mackinac Island in Michigan. Others would also likely be out of the loop. Could the whole business be carried over until fall, perhaps October?

It was just a suggestion. Incidentally, Brooks was on vacation also, and when he'd be back Goodrich didn't know.[20]

Carlson was learning what he was up against. He had thought the preliminary report would have been sufficient to prompt appropriate action on the part of the Board of Curators. Evidently, the board had insufficient courage or character to do what would seem right to most reasonable observers. But the AAUP was in a difficult spot. Carlson wanted to get the final report on this weary mess to the printers in August for early publication in the fall. But he probably knew the association wouldn't include Thurstone's draconian penalties, and unless his committee just huffed and puffed, there was little it could do but go forward in the hope that something might break. He sincerely wanted justice for the aggrieved professors and minimal damage to the university's reputation.[21]

If this required gamesmanship, Carlson was prepared to gamble. Laying his cards on the table, he told Goodrich that the committee was moving forward and whatever the curators were going to do they should do now. There might be a little wiggle room if the board provided informal assurances that justice to Meyer and DeGraff would be forthcoming. "Since our hearing at the University information has come to us confidentially, that is, in such a way that we cannot use it officially in our report, which places the action of the Executive Board in an even more unfavorable light than the official testimony and records indicate. The plain inference from this disclosure is, of course, that the members of the Executive Board and the President are standing together for mutual protection on what, I believe, most men would regard as an indefensible act. I assure you, Mr. Goodrich, that our Committee is at your service in anything that we can possibly do in restoring the good name of the great University of Missouri." He'd love to write as the final report, he said, that the Board of Curators reversed the injustice. Case closed.

While Goodrich pondered that, Carlson played another card. His committee had commissioned the University of Chicago Graduate School of Library Science to investigate the relative exposure of high school and college students to things sexual in present and classic literature. He'd seen some of the results so far, and it wasn't going to look good for the board's position. Finally, he told Goodrich flatly that he had reviewed the transcript of the hearing before the full board again and as he prepared the final committee report he pointed out "that the only objection raised by the members of the Board of Curators to Prof. Meyer's lecture at this hearing was raised by Mr. McDavid and that was that the language used by Prof. Meyer in this lecture was too beautiful, and yet, Mr. Goodrich, that was the lecture on which Prof. Meyer was actually dismissed."[22]

The same day he confronted Goodrich by letter, Carlson left for Oregon to attend the convention of the American Medical Association. He'd be back in mid-July if the curators wanted him to come to Missouri. In his absence, Leland Hazard also tried to push the curators into action. He told Curator George Willson, a highly regarded and fair-minded gentleman, that while the AAUP hearing showed that Willson and Thurstone agreed on the board's ability to judge the social expediency of the questionnaire, they were still far apart on the question of the board's competence to judge its scientific validity. Willson evidently placed greater significance than warranted on the social expediency issue. But the problem remained that the Executive Board had publicly adjudged the curators competent in the matter of scientific worthiness and the full board had wholly incorporated that statement into its public release. A collision between the curators and the professors' association was coming. It might all be avoided by reinstating Meyer along with some "salary adjustments." Some curators were making conciliatory rumblings, but the board hadn't done enough to justify the AAUP holding back its final report.

Somewhere in the mix, Brooks had to go. Lots of alumni knew that, just like they knew that he had been elevated beyond his competence. And everybody seemed to know Brooks was responsible for other university misfortunes before the questionnaire had ever surfaced. The university had simply languished under his tenure. But even Hazard knew politics prevented removing Brooks and at the same time restoring Meyer and DeGraff. The two simply couldn't happen simultaneously. Perhaps symbolic of the university's troubles, Dean Frederick Tisdel had reportedly cast a wide canvass in search of a replacement for Meyer, "but his letters were treated as a joke."[23]

The curators, by design or happenstance, were proving artful in delay. Goodrich told Carlson in early July that he couldn't figure why several board members had not responded to his university queries on other business unless they were simply out of town. When the curators finally met on July 13 and still felt unprepared to move on the AAUP's preliminary report, Goodrich proposed a meeting in St. Louis somewhere down the line between Carlson and several members of the board. Back from Oregon, Carlson was eager to meet, and told Goodrich he was heading for Michigan but stood "ready to disrupt any vacation plans that I have if I can be of service in the matter before us." Privately, he wasn't so sanguine, telling Hazard that "If I suspect that there might be some tricks back of it, I shall endeavor to have Mr. Bordwell with me. He has, of course, much more experience than I have in such matters."[24]

3

Not only did the curators have continuing questions about Brooks's veracity at the infamous Washington meeting with the AAUP in April, but they also were now concerned that he had not fully advised them about salary adjustments of the deposed men. The laws of Missouri may have permitted the board to halt DeGraff's salary at the point of termination, but the AAUP had always concerned itself with fairness and justice, not the permissibility of the law. Goodrich claimed the statute hadn't figured in the board's action and wanted information about salary practices in such cases at other universities. He thought Brooks, more familiar with such things, would have provided advice along those lines, but apparently he hadn't. Carlson saw that Goodrich got information about Northwestern and Illinois at Urbana-Champaign, as well as about his own University of Chicago. The latter revealed that university regulations permitted termination only for misconduct or incompetence, only two of which had occurred since 1913, and both of those were clear cases of misconduct. Chicago thus had no parallel situation to that of Missouri. Whether intending to tweak Goodrich or not, Carlson concluded that "Profs. Meyer and DeGraff could not have been suspended or dismissed under the University of Chicago statutes."[25]

When in late July Carlson still hadn't heard from George Willson about a proposed meeting in St. Louis, he figured there would be no useful purpose even if a meeting were held. With a truncated board, and with its president off to Europe, what could be achieved? He chided Goodrich for not quoting their correspondence fully on Brooks's alleged Washington remarks and criticized the board for either misunderstanding or misconstruing the AAUP's question to Brooks about salary adjustments of terminated faculty. He wished Goodrich well in Europe but said he couldn't close his letter "without expressing my profound regret that the Board so far has been unable or unwilling to act on the essential issue of our preliminary report."[26]

After Willson gathered five curators, the meeting in St. Louis finally came off on August 10. With Goodrich in Europe, nothing official would likely occur. Bordwell, doubting the meeting's efficacy, came nonetheless. McDavid wound up chairing the meeting, which turned out to be a probe by the curators to find their least painful way to satisfy the AAUP. Blanton wanted to know if the association would accept full salary adjustments and Meyer's return to full status on January 1, which Carlson reportedly rejected. Ultimately, the mask came off and McDavid asked pointedly what action by the board would suffice. Before McDavid and two others had to leave, they all agreed Bordwell and Carlson would prepare a memo on that very question and submit it to the remaining members, George Willson and A. A. Speer, the thoughtful banker from Jefferson City. Couched in nice words, the memo said nothing new: affirm the moral integrity of the two professors and reinstate them to as near as possible before the crisis arose; and, as a face-saver to the board, as Carlson was frank to admit to AAUP colleagues, the curators could restate their view that the questionnaire had been inappropriate and poorly handled and that future such issues should be handled in line with their recommendation back in April. Sensing conciliation on the part of the curators, Bordwell and Carlson agreed to delay the final report until after the meeting of the full board in late September. Speer and Willson even wanted the AAUP investigating committee to appear at that meeting and Willson concluded by declaring to the visitors, "You gentlemen have accomplished more today than you realize."[27]

Were Bordwell and Carlson innocents abroad, or did events justify optimism? For one thing, Brooks hadn't appeared at the meeting and evidence was piling up against him about his likely duplicity. Carlson exulted to DeGraff, exiled back in Mason City, Iowa, that things looked good and that the vindicating report would likely appear in the association's October *Bulletin*. DeGraff wasn't so sanguine, telling Leland Hazard that he wouldn't believe anything till he saw it.[28]

DeGraff waited all summer for any word about his status. Since he was on annual appointment and had been terminated, the university paid him only the balance of seven-ninths of his salary. Brooks had promised an adjustment, but none was forthcoming. He returned the check, hoping for full payment, all the more since he faced additional financial obligation for surgery in July. His biggest problem, however, was finding a future somewhere else. Brooks tried to help, writing a glowing recommendation to the president of the College of Puget Sound in Tacoma, Washington, which had a vacancy. The ousted professor "has conducted his class work excellently," said Brooks, and "is also very popular with the student body." Unfortunately, the questionnaire constituted "a grave lapse of judgment" and "has undoubtedly impaired his usefulness as a teacher in Missouri where the whole affair was given very wide publicity." DeGraff's morals were never questioned and Brooks was sure he could be put to good use elsewhere.

Actually, the letter was a testimony to Brooks's sad failure as a leader and protector of his faculty. Puget Sound was interested but had two other candidates, so DeGraff held out little hope. In fact, he'd had some opportunities, but each time the questionnaire issue loomed large. One college president told him he had no concern himself but feared parental reaction. Depressed, DeGraff shared information with only a very few friends, and as summer ebbed away, a gifted teacher looking to keep body and soul together contemplated getting into some other kind of work. Litigation against the university would generate more publicity than DeGraff wanted, and he held that option only as "a last resort."[29]

Maybe DeGraff could at least get the balance of his salary. Hazard's sleuthing revealed that with the exception of A. A. Speer, Blanton figured the curators would go no further than salary adjustments and early reinstatement of Meyer. At least they seemed to be leaning that direction, and some curators had told Hazard as much. Once again, however, the curators pushed the September meeting to October 5 because of a conflict with the convention of the Missouri Bar Association (four of the curators were lawyers). Hope mixed with skepticism, but Carlson, the loyal soldier, stood ready to appear at that meeting if invited. In late September, Meyer's potential salary adjustment made front-page reading in the *Kansas City Star,* and Hazard, with good contacts, probably including Goodrich himself, thought Brooks might be ousted at the October 5 meeting.

The prospects were dazzling. Judge Goodrich, fresh from Europe, hadn't worked out any details of such sweeping changes and feared that the appearance of Carlson's committee would confuse matters. In the event the board asked Brooks for his resignation, the martyred president would have a talking point. The board apparently wanted the AAUP to give it more time to dispose of the problem of Meyer and DeGraff. If in fact the AAUP withheld its damaging report and the board reversed itself, then, as Secretary Tyler told Carlson, "that action would be in itself a rather eloquent report." Carlson thought so too, because the Missouri case would be the first as far as he knew where the AAUP had "been actually instrumental in remedying a serious wrong." Leland Hazard was also hopeful and had gone out on a limb in seeming to encourage patience on the association's part. "Of course," as he told Carlson, "if the next meeting passes without any action whatever on any angle of the case we will certainly be forced to the conclusion that we are not being dealt with frankly by the Board. Thus far I personally have tried to believe that the whole situation has simply suffered from the inability of nine men to act expeditiously." He added: "The next meeting will certainly be a test of whether I have been right or wrong in that assumption."[30]

He was wrong, even if it was not immediately apparent. Actually, when the board met on October 5, it didn't reach any conclusions, or so it appeared. After all, Milton Tootle was still on vacation and H. W. Lenox was ill. Brooks and Cowan had been excluded from the executive session, and Goodrich wouldn't say what went on. Hazard had the impression Goodrich would talk with Brooks about the president's resignation. Goodrich, who told Hazard that he thought the curators in St. Louis had been empowered to reach a deal, gracefully and deferentially promised Chairman Carlson that the matter would be decided once and for all at the next board meeting on October 25. Hazard was in on the deal, perhaps to help smooth things over. Goodrich even asked him to remain in his Kansas City office while he dictated a letter to Carlson. Hazard was embarrassed, as any reasonable person would have been, since he had held out hope for a happy ending. He wouldn't even ask Carlson to wait any further, though it seemed clear he was in it for the duration. Winterton Curtis and his concerned colleagues on the Columbia campus thought the association might well err on the side of caution by holding back its report to see what happened. Everyone remained hopeful.[31]

Once again, Carlson exhibited grace and professional decorum. He betrayed no personal ego, and sincerely would have wanted to withhold the report if doing so would produce justice. But he was no fool and felt badly that the delay in publishing the final report might have cost DeGraff an academic appointment for the current year. However, consistent with the wishes of the committee "to be helpful rather than cause embarrassment," he told Judge Goodrich, "we prefer the delay until October 25 on your definite assurance that action in the matter of Professor Meyer and Professor DeGraff will be taken at that time and that we will be speedily advised of the action taken." As an added emphasis, he quoted Secretary Tyler's letter, perhaps as a veiled warning: "As I wrote Professor Crew," Tyler had written to Carlson, "I think it desirable that the trustees should not merely do the right thing by Professor Meyer and Professor DeGraff but that they should also define their future policy in an acceptable manner if they ask us to relieve them from publicity." That prompted some sparring over the meaning of Tyler's statement in addition to the salary issue. In regard to the Tyler statement, Carlson warned pointedly: "With the action of the Board as it now stands, the kind of report and the kind of recommendation that the committee will have to make will, I am sorry to say, be very injurious to the standing of the University." To W. C. Curtis back in Columbia he confided that his committee had delayed only in anticipation of a favorable disposition by the curators. If after all the interchange, he said, the curators failed to "do the right thing" then "that merely adds another paragraph to the serious situation and responsibilities of the trustees."[32]

In the end, the curators didn't do the right thing, at least not according to Carlson and others who had held their breath for so long. Once the curators had approved Judge Goodrich's draft of their views, a formal statement was dispatched to Carlson. Commencing thus, "With a sincere realization of the seriousness of the responsibility resting upon us . . ." the statement droned on for several pages of articulate and dignified prose, the summation of which was that the curators held firm on the suspension and dismissal of the two professors along with a reaffirmation of the impropriety of the questionnaire. The board intended no formal reply to the AAUP's preliminary report, but did so nonetheless. A number of curators, said the statement, had met with representatives of the AAUP committee "with the hope that some action might be taken which would result in saving the University of Missouri from possible harm and injury if the preliminary report should become final, and the suggested punishment be visited upon the University." Those curators, as well as their colleagues, sincerely desired "to prevent further harm to the University on account of this most regrettable episode."

The board did make a sincere, if ineffective, concession on the crucial issue of the board's ability to judge the questionnaire's scientific validity. The curators were prepared to forgo "any reference" as to the document's scientific worthiness "and at the same time concede that there apparently exists a basis among scientific men for denying to our Board the right to pass upon or express an opinion concerning this phase of the controversy." But granting all that wouldn't change the results since the problem of propriety remained. On that issue the board would not yield, dissenting from the preliminary report's claim that the AAUP investigators found no such "impropriety or indecency." The board claimed its views on that issue stood in harmony with those "of a vast majority of the people of this State and of the patrons of the University." The board's statement graciously acknowledged "the most pleasant nature" of its relationship with the investigating committee and regretted the impasse.

On the positive side, the board saw a brighter day. "Our correspondence and contracts have been helpful in many respects and have given us a keener appreciation of the principles involved in the doctrine of academic freedom. Our Board feels that it now has an understanding of this doctrine, and that our action which was influenced solely by the manifest social impropriety of the questionnaire, does not encroach upon the principles of academic freedom." The AAUP could rest assured, said the curators, that those principles would not be violated at the University of Missouri. Further, the board looked to establish regulations and procedures for dealing with such issues in the future. "It is our purpose to shortly give serious and earnest consideration to this subject and to freely consult with the members of the faculty of the University of Missouri, to the end that these regulations, when formulated and promulgated, will be in strict accord with the principles of fairness and justice, and in conformity with similar regulations of the better Universities of this country."[33]

That was it. All the hopes in Columbia and within the American Association of University Professors were dashed. The curators' motivations are difficult to assess—from defiance, ego, and arrogance, to lack of courage or sincere commitment to principle—but for whatever reason the hardliners on the board had carried the day. Professor Curtis had some information, perhaps a leak from the curators' meeting, "that the Board came near to reversing its position." Brooks had engaged in "double-dealing," said Curtis, and the curators had "stultified themselves" and probably deserved even more censure. But now the issue was closed and he saw no reason for not publishing the AAUP report. Curtis thought it was "for the good of an institution's soul to receive merited criticism." Resigned to going forward with the final report, Chairman Carlson, clearly disappointed, noted the promise of new regulations at Missouri, but felt he had been hoodwinked. He opposed Goodrich's suggestion of further dialogue after the report was issued and told his colleagues, "I am now convinced that they are not sincere in this delay that they have repeatedly sought." He even allowed an uncharacteristic spasm of bitterness: "Considering the dilatory tactics and insincerity of the Board of Curators in this matter," he said, "I submit for your further consideration that Dr. Thurstone's recommendations substantially be made a part of the final report."[34]

Fortunately, the "soul" of the University of Missouri was neither its president nor its governing board. The student body and an exceptionally able faculty, along with the traditions of ninety years, could not be disregarded in assessing the virtues or faults of a university. Regardless, final or not, communication between Goodrich and Carlson continued. The chairman quoted back to Goodrich that part of the board's statement which implied impending punishment, asking where such an assumption of any penalties came from: "To my knowledge there is no such statement direct or implied in the preliminary report and unless you can point out the same, I will kindly ask you to authorize the deletion of the quoted paragraph." Of course, there was no such implication in the preliminary report, but Goodrich had obviously gotten such ideas from Thurstone's proposed recommendations, which had been floated by Leland Hazard. Goodrich would provide his source if Carlson desired, but he recited the proposed sanctions with clarity: blacklisting for a significant period and ineligibility of new Missouri faculty for AAUP membership. "I am sure that action of this character," said Goodrich, "would be very harmful to our University."[35]

One member of the board who feared just such a development wasn't happy at all. A. A. Speer, president of the First National Bank in Jefferson City and the oldest member of the board, agonized over the decision. He acknowledged Goodrich's statement as accurate, but regretted his own vote back in April. Decent and sensitive, Speer didn't like the unwarranted language employed by the board in its April statement. Nor did he like the board's handling of the salary issue, nor its evaluating the scientific worthiness of the questionnaire. Respectful of the university's scientists and of scientists generally, Speer noted their criticism of the board's action, in addition to that of some of the state's press. Now the professors' association was about to do the same thing: "I will greatly regret if our University should suffer such criticism." The loss of good faculty would likely worsen. Unfortunately, Speer unburdened himself confidentially, having voted for something he didn't like, a decent man too timid or too pragmatic, deferring to stronger personalities on the board. It was all the more ironic that this member most senior in age saw the cultural trend more clearly than some or all of his younger colleagues. Unscientific constituents of the university failed to see the "scientific values in such discussions [raised by the questionnaire]" lamented Speer, "and are not in harmony with the present progressive trend of thought on such questions. They live in the memory and social habits of their own school days. These people, I realize, are vastly in the majority."[36]

Carlson's militancy, which wavered over time, emboldened Thurstone to encourage "some drastic action." He favored transfer of governance from trustees to faculties. "We have the power," he exulted. "It is simply a question whether we have the 'guts' to use it." (Committee member John Gray, who liked Thurstone's proposals, had called the management of higher education by laymen a "barbarous system.") Incredibly, Thurstone wanted the committee's report to recommend that the AAUP "suggest" that professional scholarly organizations deny membership to faculty who accept appointments at institutions blacklisted by the AAUP. "If only three or four of the scientific societies should adopt such a rule, it would practically cripple the University of Missouri in three years."[37]

Such recklessness had few supporters. The question of penalties got a hearing but went nowhere, at least not then. The American Association of University Professors was no radical group, and its governing council, which had to approve Carlson's committee report, rejected Thurstone's unprecedented proposals. They never had Dean Bordwell's approval, who thought penalties were beyond the association's purview. Bordwell favored instead the cleansing light of the facts, which he wanted published as soon as possible. President Henry Crew liked some "teeth" too, but thought Thurstone a bit impetuous—that ten years down the line Thurstone would be happier with the results as they were. "Facts are stubborn things," said Crew, "and the administrative authorities of the University of Missouri will feel the facts of this report for some years to come." Secretary Tyler was of the same mind, believing Thurstone "perhaps underestimates the moral effect of such a report. It is one of the most severe we have ever published and ought, I believe, to open the eyes of any person considering any appointment at the University."

Though defeated for the moment, Thurstone had raised an important and perhaps inevitable issue, and he still carried the torch for penalties, with rejoinders for several of the criticisms. "You know that the Association is taken for a rather impotent body," he complained to Tyler. That's why it couldn't attract thousands more members among the professoriate. And moral force notwithstanding, justice was still being denied to the affected professors. "It seems high time that the progression of reports of the Association that are dignified and polite and impotent," he said, "be discontinued in favor of action that is more positive and constructive in its force."

Secretary Tyler, moderate in tone and socially quite conservative, saw a difference of opinion as to what constituted the essential point of the association. The goal wasn't necessarily justice for this professor or that, he thought. "I conceive our fundamental aim to be the definition and maintenance of higher standards, and that the crucial question is not what an institution has done with a particular individual, but how it behaves, or tends to behave in its future relations with the profession; that our reports have exerted a substantial preventive influence seems to be sufficiently indicated by the rather general reluctance of administrative officers to be reported by our committees and by their apparent willingness to answer our requests for information in cases which do not in general lead to formal investigations." And in this case, Tyler didn't want President Brooks to worm his way into a sort of martyrdom, that is, that "he and the university were common victims of persecution by us."

Tyler also had a significant point. The whole issue of tenure was still in its formative stages, and progress and uniformity were slow; the association, in fact, had tried to persuade the accrediting agencies, themselves only a generation or so old, to look not merely to an institution's tangible resources but also to its posture on tenure and related issues. Unfortunately, Tyler could report no progress. He was right. To be a trail-blazer in

a cross-disciplinary professional organization required patience and gentlemanly forbearance, qualities Tyler often exhibited.[38]

Even without penalties attached to the report, the editing process proved a bit cumbersome. Those authorized to offer comments and sign off
on the document were in institutions across the nation. The council had
voted to send the draft to the AAUP's Committee A on Academic Freedom and Tenure, largely because the prime issues in the Missouri case involved those issues pertinent to that committee, and in part to distribute
responsibility. Tyler suggested air mail for delivery on the West Coast,
with replies by the same method or by telegraph. Further, the crowded
contents for the December and January issues of the *Bulletin*, the latter
of which was largely devoted to a registry, suggested waiting until the
February issue. Preprints could be circulated in December. Carlson also
got a little advice from President Henry Crew, who didn't want the report too long or its essence overwhelmed by detail. That had happened
to reports in the past, and Crew wanted this one read by the membership,
most of whom were, he believed, "eagerly awaiting."[39]

The final draft came together. Since Carlson thought the curators had
evaded the key issue of the case, that is, academic freedom in research
and teaching along with tenure security, he strengthened that area of the
final draft. Bordwell and Thurstone signed off on the report. Schlundt,
who met with Carlson in Chicago in November, also approved. Carlson also conferred with Leland Hazard, who was "thoroughly familiar
with the conditions in Missouri and with the devious paths of the Board
of Curators." John Gray, the lone member of the committee who didn't
visit Columbia, also approved the report, but wanted alterations in the
treatment of Brooks's April appearance before the council in Washington.
Gray had been present at that meeting, the importance and precise reporting of which remained pesky items. Gray felt Brooks had been "badly
frightened" at that meeting and wanted to get the council members to
think he wasn't responsible for the curators' action and that he believed
the punishment was too severe—all without saying so specifically. Carlson was happy to see the process coming to an end. The Missouri case
was "flagrant and serious," he said, and he wanted more coercive substance in the report. But he also wanted a unanimous report, and Bordwell didn't want sanctions included. "Personally," he told his colleagues
almost wearily, "I have already spent more time on this futile effort than
I can well afford, but in view of this I am also anxious that the report may
serve its maximum usefulness."[40]

One by one, several members of Committee A on Academic Freedom
and Tenure, chaired by Professor A. L. Wheeler of Princeton University,

responded favorably to the draft. These were leaders in American higher education and in the professions. To George Adams in philosophy at Berkeley, the report was "admirable"; Arthur O. Lovejoy at Johns Hopkins thought the same; Richard Tolman at Cal Tech also approved, as did Herbert Goodrich, dean of the Law School at Penn, who deemed the piece "very strong . . . well expressed, moderate in tone, but clear as to its conclusions." To George Roberts of Purdue University, it was "a very good piece of work," while Professor A. M. Kidd at Berkeley's School of Jurisprudence found the draft "refreshing," and "a standard for social science research which I hope will be maintained." He wondered, reasonably enough, whether such a questionnaire should be distributed when the state legislature pondered the university's financial support, "if, as may well be known, the members of the state legislature belong to an older and benighted generation." Frederick Padelford, dean of the Graduate School at the University of Washington, also approved the report, but thought it didn't consider the misjudgment of the professors who oversaw the preparation of a clearly partisan preamble. Chairman Wheeler also didn't think much of the questionnaire or the professors' judgment. But those were social science issues best left alone. The recurring problem of what Brooks said or didn't say at the AAUP headquarters in Washington in April bothered Committee A member Ulysses Weatherly of Indiana University. The investigating committee, he thought, had sort of left Brooks out to dry on that issue, leaving "the implication of possible falsity without definitely deciding one way or the other." In the end, he was generous with his colleagues: "But I assume that the committee, knowing all the facts, used its best judgment in a difficult situation,—and I know something of the ways of university presidents." Did the committee know all the facts? Perhaps J. H. Gray's earlier estimation of Brooks's motives would have to suffice: "I think he consciously tried to mislead us on the part he took at the time."[41]

Also serious were legal issues broached by another member of Committee A, Edward L. Thurstone, professor of law at Harvard (not to be confused with L. L. Thurstone of Chicago). He and John Maguire, a colleague at Harvard Law School who also served as legal adviser to the association, talked about the possibilities of litigation over the issuance of the report. The report "contains a vigorous criticism of President Brooks and also of the Board of Curators," said Thurstone, "and it implies that in the opinion of the Committee, President Brooks has not proper qualifications for the position of President of a State University. It also accuses President Brooks of equivocation and double dealing. Of course, such charges unless founded on truth would be libelous, and unless the statements contained in the Report are true or are what is known as 'privileged state-ments' or 'fair criticism,' the persons submitting the Report and proba-bly all those who have had a hand in its publication (this would include the officers and members of Committee A to whom the Report has been submitted) might be sued for libel by President Brooks and perhaps by several members of the Board of Curators of the University of Missouri." Maguire and Thurstone didn't think that would happen, but warned it could. They figured Dean Bordwell took all that into account during the preparation of the report. Truth was the best antidote to libel, and even a falsehood or mere criticism reasonably given could help mount a defense, but once something got in court anything could happen, especially given the dozens of jurisdictions and the wide broadcast of the statements con-tained in the report. Regardless, like a soldier steeling himself for battle, Thurstone wanted to go forward. "In view of the public advantage to be derived from the publication of this Report," he wrote, "I, for one, am quite willing to stand the risk of being sued and of a possible judgment against myself. I suppose that if such a suit were brought, the Association would be willing to defray all expenses of defending the suit although I do not believe that there is any legal obligation upon the Association to do so."[42]

Tyler thought the views of Thurstone and Maguire merited close atten-tion, but that the association needed to defer to Percy Bordwell, the legal man on Carlson's investigating committee. In fact, Bordwell, like his Har-vard colleagues, didn't think there was much danger. "The more likely thing to happen in the way of legal proceedings," he told Secretary Tyler on December 12, "would be to have the report suppressed because of the publication of the questionnaire. In the course of the discussion with the Board Mr. Blanton repeatedly expressed the opinion that it wouldn't be allowed through the mails." For his part, Tyler didn't think Brooks or the curators could get much mileage out of a lawsuit. He told President Crew that John Dewey, the association's first president, "once remarked that a law suit of that kind would be an excellent thing for the Association, but I don't myself feel quite so enthusiastic on the subject." Bordwell seemed to be in Dewey's camp. He didn't know if Brooks or the curators had tipped their hand about possible legal action, but if they had he thought it would be "pure bluff." As a matter of fact, the association would really be im-potent if it couldn't make such a report. "If they want to try the question out," he said boldly, "this would be as good a time as any to try it out."[43]

A. J. Carlson, the point man for the report, on which potential lawsuits might rest, knew the risks. He read over Ed Thurstone's analysis. He was ready. "I can assure you, the Council and members of Committee A," he told a number of his colleagues, "that most scrupulous care has been taken in all of the statements of fact. There is no exaggeration, I believe, either in the comments or conclusions. I believe the Association must, in justice to itself and the principles involved, publish the report and meet whatever consequences may follow. To do otherwise, it seems to me, will completely paralyze the Association's efforts for the establishment of freedom of research and teaching and the security of tenure in the University." He stood ready for any lawsuit, he said, and would pay for his part of his defense himself if the association wouldn't.[44]

John Maguire may not have feared a significant likelihood of a libel lawsuit, but he and some colleagues remained concerned about the use of the mails. Was Jack Blanton right about the U.S. postal service halting distribution of any document sent through the mails containing the infamous questionnaire? The American Association of University Professors was preparing to mail its February *Bulletin* containing that questionnaire addressed not only to its membership but also to libraries and various complimentary recipients across the nation. Reminiscent of nineteenth-century anti-slavery materials that ran afoul of the postal service, the issue of late had been Victorian notions of what was obscene or morally proper for handling by postal authorities. To head off any interference, Professor Maguire asked the assistance of a friendly contact in the Department of Justice in Washington. "We do not want to do anything underhanded and therefore think that the problem ought to be presented to the Postoffice Department promptly and openly," he wrote. "Our feeling is that this report combines the characteristics of a professional inquiry and of a judicial finding. It seems like the decision of a court upon a sociological and moral question. It cannot be justly appraised unless accompanied by a reprint of the questionnaire." If right and ethical, and Maguire was sensitive to those issues, would he take up the matter with the authorities and get a favorable ruling?[45]

That a professional body feared possible censorship by postal authorities is a barometer of societal norms in the Jazz Age culture wars. In any case, after numerous delays, the February *Bulletin* finally went in the mail, preceded by a press release that roundly criticized President Brooks and, in particular, the Board of Curators for its "clear breach of the principles of freedom of teaching and research and security of tenure in the university."[46]

The laudatory reviews of the draft of Carlson's report within the association were well deserved. The thirty-four-page document was a standard of excellence for such things—pointed, clear, concise, the text uncluttered—the sort of thing President Crew had hoped would be widely read. Appendices carried the preamble and female version of the questionnaire in full, along with the April decree of the Board of Curators, extracts of correspondence, mostly between Carlson and Goodrich, the bulk of Goodrich's report on the board meeting of October 25, and samples of editorial comment from the *Columbia Daily Tribune, Kansas City Star, St. Louis Globe-Democrat,* and *St. Louis Post-Dispatch.* The report quickly rehearsed the events of the case, the actions of the Executive Board and the full board, the procedure of the investigating committee in taking testimony, the hoped-for rapprochement between members of the board and members of Carlson's committee in St. Louis in August, and the board's ultimate decision in October to stand by its earlier verdict. The report also included the formal charges against Meyer and DeGraff—the questionnaire's potential to prompt sexual immorality among students; its shocking of students, especially women; its lack of scientific value; and that it "tended to create the condition that it is alleged to correct." In the evidence section, the report challenged each of the allegations, noting that the latter charge was "clearly a misconception," since nothing could be construed that the questionnaire tried to correct anything. The moral integrity of those involved had not been officially questioned by anyone; in fact, it was above reproach.

Nor had any evidence been produced that immorality resulted from the circulation of the document. Perhaps the authorities might have suppressed the questionnaire had they had advance knowledge of it, but that would have been all. Here the report bore Percy Bordwell's stamp: "The frankness on sex matters that has characterized the generation that has grown up since the war . . . is something foreign to many of the older generation, but the questionnaire seems to have shocked Mr. Gentry and those who signed his petition and some others, including President Brooks and some of the members of the Board of Curators." In fact, even Missouri high school students were acquainted with issues in the questionnaire—Brooks, Dean Priddy, and the students themselves so testified. Unless briefly calling attention to these issues produced immorality, then no harm was done. "The leading students, men and women, appearing before the Committee," said the report, "were unanimous on the point that the capacity of the questionnaire to arouse eroticism is nothing in comparison to many factors of the environment in normal daily life. Professor DeGraff testified that as a student adviser he had been frequently consulted by students about the very issues that are raised in this questionnaire concerning the sex code and the moral ideals that are also involved in engagement and marriage. The students testified that these problems of the sex code of morals, engagement, and marriage, are frequently discussed frankly, not only in the fraternity and sorority houses but also by the girls with their boy friends."

The investigators thought it "strange" that the board regarded some of the recipients of the questionnaire as too sensitive and immature to possess views on the subjects it discussed. Nearly all were of legal age for marriage. They did have convictions about society's moral code and they discussed them. They "have access to books and magazine articles by the hundreds which deal with the social institutions of betrothal, marriage, fidelity, birth control, divorce, and other aspects of *our sexual code*" [emphasis added]. To bolster the report's contention in this regard—indeed, to point out the obvious—the investigating committee had asked the Graduate Library School at the University of Chicago to survey young people's potential exposure to sexual issues in popular culture. The results of the inquiry, supervised by Professor Douglas Waples, made interesting reading: Of 152 novels, 208 motion pictures, and 212 stage plays—all current— the depiction "of unconventional sex situations (illegitimates, seduction, cohabitation, promiscuity, premarital relations, extra-marital relations, divorce, etc.)" totaled 38 percent for novels, 29 percent for movies, and 29 percent for plays. Conventional sexual situations were similar: novels, 31 percent; movies, 42 percent; and plays, 29 percent. The rest remained "Unclassified." The study, concluded the report, provided "a quantitative confirmation of what every informed person knows: namely the preponderance of sex situations, conventional and unconventional, in current fiction, plays, and pictures. It is the impression and opinion of the Committee that the students in the University of Missouri do not differ essentially from students in other universities in their contacts with this phase of modern life."[47]

Not only did the report validate the questionnaire method, but it also noted that what was decent and what was not might rest on *"intent"* and *"circumstances."* "Not so many years ago," it argued, "many people in this country considered knee-length skirts or a one-piece bathing suit indecent apparel for women. Today the same apparel is considered indecent by very few people. Whose standards of decency shall be used as the criterion? Scientific investigation would be paralyzed if required to wait for unanimity of opinion on questions of social propriety."

The report did sustain some of the criticism of this particular questionnaire's prejudicial and sophomoric qualities. It might have been worded less offensively, or given only to advanced students. The questionnaire had been a problem for most everyone. Doubtless most if not all of the faculty at Missouri had a problem with the wording, structure, propriety, or other aspects of the document. So did others. And so would others within the AAUP after the report had been circulated around the nation. Even Secretary Tyler had told A. L. Wheeler, chairman of Committee A, that he was "personally conservative enough to sympathize in a measure with parental objectors who feel that indiscriminate circulation of such a document among freshmen girls tends not to make them immoral but to make them think and talk too much in that particular line." But Tyler understood the difference between propriety and the larger issue.[48] So did Committee A, and so did the investigators. Still, the report carried a footnote on page 1: "In approving the publication of the report the Committee on Academic Freedom and Tenure expresses no opinion on the value of the questionnaire procedure, deeming this a question for the judgment of specialists in the field concerned."

The larger issue, of course, remained that of the freedom of teaching and research, and in this particular case, the competence of the Board of Curators—or any governing board for that matter—to assess the validity of scientific investigation. Such inquiries proceeded "in all reputable universities" despite questions of validity, which, by the way, "has never been established by any legal procedure or by the dictates of any board." Engagement, marriage, and family rested "largely on a code governing sex conduct. Conduct which complies with this code is called moral. The explicit formulation of this code we call our ideals." Investigation of these institutions required asking people things, and the questionnaire, while "not so satisfactory a fact-gathering device as the instruments of the older sciences," was a legitimate method, perhaps the only one, for learning people's attitudes toward right and wrong. Even the three most offensive questions were appropriate for inquiry. The final report incorporated major portions of Thurstone's preliminary draft, including the section on the history of scientific inquiry and its tormentors: how Galileo's work had offended Pope Urban; how in France, Charles V, and, in England, Charles IV banned equipment required for chemical processes; how Priestley's equipment and library were destroyed by a Birmingham mob, with the approval of Anglican clergy; and so on. Of late the problem in science was evolution. "Now social science has its turn so that factual inquiry about the social institutions that are based on our sex code simply must not be made in some parts of the world because they offend the taboos of the generation that is passing." Even if Thurstone and the report stretched a bit to place a poorly crafted questionnaire in the company of Galileo and the others, the point remained unshakable that the document was a flawed but serious attempt to uncover attitudes about social issues among university students.

The report also scored Brooks's intemperate criticism of the questionnaire and his as well as the Executive Board's failure to place it in its educational context. The Missouri press also left the state's citizens without full understanding, never printing the whole questionnaire. Brooks was also criticized for the unfairness of the salary issue. The report further itemized what seemed to be Brooks's duplicity to the faculty, to members of the AAUP Council in Washington in April, along with the conflict between Brooks's testimony to Carlson's committee and Walter Williams's letter of May 24. "This serious discrepancy between the testimony of President Brooks and Dean Williams on a salient point," said the report, "must be judged in the light of other discrepancies and evasions in President Brooks' testimony in this case." It was clear to the investigators, as it had been to Leland Hazard. But they were gentlemen and professionals, loathe to utter the word: Stratton Brooks appeared to be a liar.

In more than one phase of the report, the committee addressed the problem that constituted the ultimate significance of the controversy. The president's view that the action of the board constituted no unwarranted infringement on teaching and research was simply at odds with the facts. "The two professors," said the report, "were severely disciplined because the Board disapproved this type of teaching and research. By this action the Board of Curators served notice on the faculty of the University of Missouri that the Board has and may exercise the right of dismissal of any member of the faculty whose teaching and research does not conform to the undeclared standards of the Board. There is little freedom of teaching and research in a university governed by such principles, particularly when important actions touching freedom of teaching and research are taken without, or against, competent faculty advice, and guided by a president who does not seem to understand the real functions of a university."

What about the infamous sex lecture, spoken by the unknowing only in hushed tones, something "too terrible" to mention? The investigating committee believed Meyer's lecture on the physiology of sex figured in his suspension and briefly recited some of the history of that unnecessary and unfortunate distraction. It had been a closed issue, eventually peer reviewed, and was "nothing more than proved physiology." President Brooks even claimed that disciplining Meyer because of the lecture would indeed impair academic freedom. But the Executive Board merely verbally reprimanded Jesse Wrench and Russell Bauder, while Meyer had been fired. It was "difficult for experienced men to escape the conclusion that Professor Meyer was suspended partly, if not mainly, because of the sex lecture in his course in Social Psychology. It is going to be difficult

for experienced men to accept as true that a professor of national standing and nearly thirty years' efficient service in the University was suspended without pay solely because he failed to take steps to suppress a
questionnaire in a department not his own" just because he misjudged
public opinion.

The essential point of tenure security and academic freedom lay at the
heart of the whole matter. "This is the issue between the Board and the
Association that must now go before the higher court of informed public
opinion," said the report. The board's suggestion in its response to the
preliminary report that it now understood these issues and that the AAUP
need not be concerned about future violations "carry neither weight nor
conviction, in the face of the failure to do justice to Professor Meyer and
Professor DeGraff."

The report concluded that the university should expect a certain sen-
sitivity on the part of the faculty when approaching societal taboos. At
the same time, the faculty should expect appropriate defense by university authorities, a clear failing by the president and the board in this case;
also, there should be some parallel between offenses and punishment;
and finally, faculty standing at Missouri was tenuous, especially so in
light of recent developments, and sufficiently so to attract serious concern
from academics in general as well as from the professional associations.
The concluding statement was Leland Hazard's suggestion: "Under the
present administration the University of Missouri is not an institution
where scholars may go and work with the assurance of the freedom in
teaching and research, and the security of tenure granted in the ranking
universities of the country."

Despite Professor Thurstone's best efforts, the report contained neither
sanctions nor recommendations. The association wasn't ready yet. Also
missing from the report was Meyer's allegation about Brooks's bribery
attempt. Although the investigating committee knew about it, the claim
had no independent verification. Besides, it might only have obscured
the larger issue. Brooks's alleged threat against the activist professors—
among the finest on campus—also didn't appear in the report. "If I win
this fight," Brooks reportedly told Leslie Cowan, "the 17 professors
will go."[49]

The difficult part for the AAUP was over. But how would the report
be received in the profession, on the campus, in the boardroom, and in
Missouri? Reporters had "somewhat besieged" the association's national
office in Washington for news as early as December. Eventually, preprints
of the report were dispatched to 150 newspapers in Missouri, and many

more were distributed by the local chapter president, Herman Schlundt, and of course, copies went to Judge Goodrich in Kansas City. Even Floyd Shoemaker, builder of the archives at the State Historical Society of Missouri, got a copy.[50] But anyone who thought the report of the investigating committee constituted the last word on the subject, or that the matter was now closed, or that normality would now return to the administration and faculty of the University of Missouri, would have been dead wrong.

9

Denouement

> . . . the whole situation is impossible and cannot go on indefinitely; in other words I think there will be a story sometime.
>
> —Jonas Viles, March 4, 1930, Viles-Hosmer Family Papers

In January 1930, Ed Watson, editor of the *Columbia Daily Tribune*, looked over the press release announcing the report of the American Association of University Professors condemning Stratton Brooks and the Board of Curators of the University of Missouri and offered a terse assessment: "The judgment of the pedagogues be damned." Or, that's what Watson said was the "verdict" of the good folks of the state of Missouri. Back in March 1929, Watson's outraged editorial lambasting the sex questionnaire had started the long parade of printed comment in the culture war over what was education and what was obscenity. So it was fitting he'd have something to say after so many gallons of ink had been spilled examining every angle of the scandal. And Watson had lost little of his passion. The questionnaire was still "vulgar, lecherous" and "low down," but now the AAUP investigators were "four high-browed and muchly degreed members of the intelligentsia" whose views deserved no respect. The only mistake by the university authorities, he said, was not dumping Max Meyer permanently.[1]

Watson may well have spoken for much of Missouri. Winterton Curtis, Missouri's reputable zoologist, told Chairman A. J. Carlson that the state's newspapers appeared mostly hostile to the early news of the report, but he thought reaction might have been better had news editors had the whole document, copies of which were sent later to 150 papers. The *St.*

Louis Globe-Democrat calmly supported the decision of the curators, as did the *Kansas City Star,* as did, less generously, Jack Blanton's *Monroe County Appeal,* which mislabeled the AAUP and deemed it "the labor union of the educational world." No surprise there. True, the association had its defenders, including the always-loyal *St. Louis Post-Dispatch,* whose cartoonist, Daniel Fitzpatrick, drew another ionic column on Mizzou's Quad and labeled it the AAUP report. The paper condemned "Brooks and his fellow witch burners" along with "the howling pack which drove Prof. Meyer into exile" and so on. "We knew that Missouri would not be happy when the judgment came," said the paper, "and we urged the State University to right itself." Just give Meyer his job back and encourage him in the future to consider parents' sensibilities. But the university wouldn't do it. "It held out in the stiff-necked fashion characteristic of ignorance," said the paper, "and so landed in the public stocks."[2]

Print media from Boston to Spokane also revisited the issue. Alabama's *Birmingham News* defended the report, as did Topeka's *Daily Capital,* which saw "no difference at bottom between the obscurantism of the President Brookses and the laws of Tennessee, both being actuated by fear of knowledge." That's what happened when education got its financial support from "politicians or millionaires." The liberal *New Republic* later claimed, "The situation is precisely as if a board of trustees should forbid certain experiments in chemistry because they might introduce doubt as to the reality of transsubstantiation." The magazine added: "The report . . . makes clear that the Board of Curators was led throughout the entire episode by their man on the job, President Stratton D. Brooks, whose course was marked by the tortuousness and evasion which in college too often marks the administration of the presidential office." But critics, including the *New York World, Boston Traveler, Kansas City Star,* and *Philadelphia Record,* outnumbered the supporters. The *Detroit Free Press* thought a good part of such questionnaires were "inspired by vulgar and not over clean and rather morbid curiosity," and dismissed much of the AAUP report as "little more than a package of 'blah.' "[3]

President Brooks's mailbag also seemed to vindicate Ed Watson's judgment. The people stood ready to damn the pedagogues. A southwest Missouri school superintendent heard no dissenters among his colleagues, all of whom supported Brooks. Having read the morning newspaper, one St. Louis clergyman noted "the evil monster has bobbed up again" and looked to Brooks, as did so many others, to see it through to the end. One Seneca resident, in southwest Missouri, told Brooks, "Many of us have a none to [sic] high opinion of the Association of University Professors, and for that matter of theorists in general. Too many of them seem to be rather too closely affiliated with communist and socialist activities." He added that communists were insinuating themselves into American education. "I have heard people question the advisability of sending their children to certain coleges [sic] and universities for that reason, at least until the children are less impressionable." Chivalry would have required another supporter to deal effectively with the questionnaire's author had his daughter been a recipient. Upset by the AAUP's report, he was not narrow-minded, he said, but still saw "a limit to the vicious pruriency of sociological 'scholars,' and you and your associates sounded a wholesome call for a return to decency." A Sedalia resident—"Your unlearned friend"—thought along the same lines: "When America puts self expression and Personal Liberty (or License) above the [sanctity] of the American Home and above the teachings of the Bible then America will crumble like Rome of old."

The president's support was hardly limited to the "unlearned." A judge of the U.S. Circuit Court of Appeals in Kansas City supported Brooks, called Carlson's committee "radically progressive," and criticized turning "extremists and zealots in sociology, religion and politics loose upon students of acutely impressionable age." Supporters also included the St. Joseph county agent, the Marshall physician, ministers from Warrensburg and Poplar Bluff, and so on—and from beyond Missouri as well, among them the state school superintendent of Michigan. Albert Bushnell Hart, the legendary Professor of Government Emeritus at Harvard, read the lengthy story in the *Boston Herald* and told Brooks he knew him too well to doubt he would have acted inappropriately. Not surprisingly, Brooks picked up endorsements of several college presidents and other academics, including a professor at the University of Buffalo, who lauded him for his stand against "the growing evil of indecent questionnaires masking under the fair name of scientific research." Another supporter at the University of Alabama School of Medicine was a graduate "of 'Old Mizzou' " and had studied with A. J. Carlson at Chicago. He told Brooks the questionnaire's author "must have been senile [or] a pervert." There was an occasional critic, but not many. One Fulton parent who wouldn't send his kids "to a university that acts in a childish way on such matters," later changed his mind and apologized after he heard Brooks speak at an American Legion dinner. And a pastor concluded a series of transdenominational meetings in Moberly by publicly criticizing the report and defending Brooks and the curators. "Unquestionably," he said, "the tendency of university life is away from the family altar and the church."[4]

2

If an unrepentant Brooks took comfort in wide support, all was not well back home. What little moral capital he had with the curators going into the controversy in the spring of 1929 had been exhausted. A look at his mail would have convinced anyone who doubted that Brooks might have postured, as Meyer later described it, "as the savior of the morals of the young people of the state," but it wasn't to be. As AAUP President Henry Crew had said, facts were stubborn things, and the association's report, despite its many critics, stood as a serious indictment against an administration that failed to grasp the fundamentals of a university. It took no genius to know that the Brooks administration, bereft of significant contributions in the advancement of education either on the campus or in the state, had been a failure. He had joined a fine university in 1923 with a recent heritage of outstanding leadership, plus a faculty—some with national reputations—that most universities would be fortunate to call their own. He had done little to inspire a lackluster Board of Curators and a recalcitrant legislature, neither of which, despite some good and able men, possessed exemplary vision. The decade called for extraordinary skill, but none appeared. In sum, the University of Missouri was a less reputable place in 1930 than when Brooks had arrived seven years before.

Talk of Brooks's ouster, dormant for several months, now revived. Charles Ellwood, who had founded modern sociology at Missouri, resigned in January, heading for greener pastures and a better salary at Duke University. Even Jack Blanton was sorry to see him go. That was soon followed by the resignation of James Harvey Rogers, an internationally renowned economist and one of the bright lights of the Missouri faculty since his arrival in 1916 and who had been very active in the questionnaire controversy. He was off to Yale, his alma mater, and his departure was bitter. Unfortunately, their leaving followed a train of departures, a manifestation of faculty discontent. Others were rumored to be ready to go.[5]

How much operating room existed for presidential discretion is unclear, but it was probably a great deal more than President Brooks exercised. W. C. Curtis later claimed that had the president "wished and if he had had the sense to do so, he could have snuffed out the whole matter in the first three or four hours and nothing would have come of it." A few months before his death in 1930, President Emeritus J. Carleton Jones, whose outstanding service as chief executive had been matched by his later fund-raising for the Memorial Union and Stadium, told Walter Williams, "The tempest could have been stilled by the quiet words of a few wise leaders!" Some on the faculty thought Brooks had seized the questionnaire issue to grab public attention and shore up his slipping position with the Board of Curators. Back in 1924, Walter Williams noted that he was personally likable and had won plaudits statewide with a call for "higher moral standards." Over time, of course, that couldn't make up for deficits in educational vision or condescension to faculty. In the 1929 crisis, had Brooks stood firm on the integrity of research and teaching, the impact of the controversy surely would have been lessened, but Curtis's view may have been a bit too optimistic. Even the majority floor leader of Missouri's Fifty-Fifth General Assembly told Jack Blanton confidentially that, with two daughters in the university, his "little quiet personal investigation" had uncovered "at least one sexual pervert" involved in the questionnaire. Who that was he didn't say. While he was "somewhat disgusted at the talk about freedom of teaching," he had opposed legislative intervention when the questionnaire controversy arose. "However," he said, "if no action had been taken I think that it would then have become the duty of the legislature to have made its own investigation." And if that wasn't frightening enough, C. M. Buford, the buffoonish legislator from Ellington who had barged into the curators' hearing back in April, seemed immune to the implications of James Harvey Rogers leaving for Yale. Were there any more professors like that who think the questionnaire was a good idea? The sooner they're gone, he told Brooks, the better. He still argued that it was illegal to print or mail the questionnaire. All that pointed up a fatal deficit in Brooks's leadership. He had been, said Curtis later in retirement, "by all means the most incompetent president the University of Missouri ever had in the period with which I am familiar."[6]

The departure of Rogers highlighted the ongoing problem in Brooks's administration. Rogers excoriated the loss of academic freedom guarded so scrupulously under prior regimes, and claimed that "the spirit of the thing" had prompted his resignation. But there was more to it. Returning from the East Coast at the end of February, President Brooks cavalierly dismissed the resignation, claiming he knew Rogers would leave as soon as a spot at Yale opened up. Stanford University had wanted him, Brooks told the press, and so had Harvard's business school. Rogers had refused them both, waiting instead for the call to Yale. Brooks suggested it was a bit disingenuous for Rogers to now claim he was leaving because of recent developments. (Brooks's public references to Stanford and Harvard outraged Fred Middlebush, dean of the School of Business and Public Administration, who had told the president about those offers in the first place. "I had always been under the impression, Dr. Brooks, that such communications were confidential at least in so far as the names of the institutions were concerned and I regret that these institutions were mentioned in the press accounts. That places us in a very embarrassing position.")

Brooks may have been right about Rogers's posturing, but if so, he missed the larger issue of the subliminal and growing discontent with his own administration. Nothing was new here. Brooks had been criticized for years for lack of democracy in dealing with faculty, for his high-profile sixty-seven-thousand-dollar renovation of the president's house on Francis Quadrangle, and even, by petty critics, for not socializing locally as a president should. Further, he had been losing curator support, including that of Mercer Arnold, the Ozark attorney. Arnold, who deeply and sincerely loved the university, hated the loss of good faculty, and told Walter Williams in 1928 that his own shaping by outstanding faculty in his days at the university thirty years earlier had made a great impact on his life. "We can't replace with brick and stone men like these," he said, "or like some of the men we have recently lost, and any price we are able to pay is not too much to pay, if it keeps such men at Missouri." Arnold feared loyalty to the president sometimes overrode the best interests of the university; at the same time, however, Brooks had never really won over those who, back in 1923, wanted a president with a more impressive résumé. One newsman with close ties to the selection process that year, who had publicly favored Walter Williams for president, thought Brooks's selection was a blunder, knowing of "his lusterless career" back in Oklahoma. Within months of Brooks's inauguration, rumors that all was not well reached Frank Thilly, the philosophy professor Woodrow Wilson had lured to Princeton and who then had gone to Cornell. The thrust of the rumors, Thilly told Walter Williams in early 1924, was that Brooks treated the faculty "like little school-boys." Williams, always fair, replied that Brooks hadn't been in place long enough to firm up lasting impressions, but, yes, some feared he had little educational vision, and, yes, some of his lectures to the professors had been a bit high-schoolish. The situation never really did get much better—Brooks had been a polarizing figure for years and had done nothing to heal the breach in a divided faculty.[7]

The curators, of course, had promptly issued a lengthy statement to the press in January defending their action and denying any infringement on academic freedom. But the whole mess had sapped the energy of just about everyone. John D. McCutcheon, the prominent St. Louis alumnus also active in the controversy since the beginning, read about the AAUP report in the *Chicago Tribune* on the train returning to St. Louis. He liked what he saw. A week later he got into an angry debate at lunch with several alumni, including curator George Willson, who, as McCutcheon told Jonas Viles, "of course tried desperately to justify the board's action." Pressure against Brooks also mounted on the other side of the state. Rabbi Samuel S. Mayerberg, of Kansas City's Temple B'Nai Jehudah, had recently arrived in Kansas City from Ohio, and had thrown himself into liberal causes. He would shortly take on the infamously corrupt Pendergast machine in his adopted hometown and within a decade sound a clarion call about the Nazi danger in Europe. But now he focused on President Brooks and the goings-on at Missouri's flagship university. Along with other liberal clergy, he called for Brooks's departure. In a letter to Judge Goodrich, a copy of which Mayerberg gave to the *Kansas City Star*, he demanded an investigation of the stifling fear among the faculty—"mental terror" he called it—that had resulted in the lamentable resignation of James Harvey Rogers. If no investigation was forthcoming, he would call on Governor Henry Caulfield to appoint a panel to look into the matter. One reporter for the *Star*, eager for a story, told Jonas Viles that Mayerberg was "the kind of man who will do it. He is liberal minded, and his position is such that he has a large and influential following—particularly if this paper gets behind him."[8]

"Who is this man Mayerberg[?]" said Brooks when shown the newspaper story of the rabbi's letter. He'd welcome an investigation, he said. As for Governor Caulfield, he wasn't interested in any investigation, as he said in a statement to the press. Further, even though he thought the punishment in the questionnaire business was a bit stern, he had confidence in the curators. He saw no reason for faculty to be uneasy, and one incident was insufficient "to cause members of the faculty to feel any mental restraint in any *proper* educational research." Jonas Viles knew an investigation wouldn't get anywhere, as if the campus hadn't seen enough of them. "The Faculty here is tense and on edge," he told the inquiring reporter for the *Star* privately, "not so much from fear of danger to any individual (tho what happened to M[e]yer might happen to any) as from fear of some further mistakes which will still further injure the standing of the University and make it an almost impossible place for some of us." Viles actually thought the university had become "one of the safest places in the country as far as getting fired is concerned. The Board would be extremely cautious in accepting any recommendation for drastic action."[9]

Viles may have been right about faculty safety, but "drastic action" awaited President Brooks. Rumblings about his departure grew louder during March, even as a group of local ministers rallied to his side. The curators met in Columbia on March 18, decided unanimously not to review the questionnaire verdict of the previous year, and interviewed faculty and deans about the charges of unrest swirling around the campus. According to W. C. Curtis, he and Schlundt were the only faculty interviewed because Brooks, having been sent home in the morning, "not being able to stand it any longer, came over to his office and was told by the Curators that they wanted his resignation." The curators refused to publicly comment on Brooks's potential resignation, and Brooks himself told the Associated Press he knew nothing about it. Meanwhile, the *St. Louis Post-Dispatch* claimed Brooks would be gone before the end of the day, or at least very shortly. Rabbi Mayerberg told the press he knew of fourteen unnamed faculty ready to quit if Brooks didn't go. The curators wound up going home with Brooks still in his job. But by the end of the month, the *New York Times* reported that he'd soon be out. Citing damage to the institution by the ongoing saga, the *Times* reported that some predicted the way out of the mess was Brooks's resignation, regardless of who was right. The paper even reported that Walter Williams was slated for the presidency, but that he "smiles and says he expects to go to Buenos Aires next year on a leave of absence. Dr. Brooks is making no admissions that he intends to resign." [10]

Brooks resisted to the end. Apparently weary of the controversies, the curators urged his resignation. Shortly before the board met in early April, Brooks went to see Jack Blanton in Paris, Missouri. "He seemed in great mental stress," recalled Blanton much later. "I told him that he was in the hands of a hostile Board and advised him to resign, which advice he refused to follow." On the eve of the board's meeting on April 5, the curators closeted themselves at a Columbia hotel, carrying over their discussion to campus the following morning. While several of them, including Goodrich, Speer, and probably McDavid, tried to talk Brooks into quitting, others sat around in Leslie Cowan's office in Jesse Hall making light talk over prospects for Mizzou football, the nice weather, and Ozarks bass fishing. Nothing worked. The full board then met officially, and after several hours, with only Milton Tootle absent, fired Brooks outright.

In its unanimous resolution, the board claimed the sex questionnaire played no role in the ouster, not even indirectly. In fact, the board again reaffirmed its decision of the previous year. Nor did political considerations have a part, as, according to the board, they never had in any issue. The board also explicitly found no evidence "of 'mental' or 'mortal' terror" in the faculty. "However," read the resolution, "the Board does find that the relations between President Brooks and the members of this Board, and the relations of President Brooks with the faculty of the University have created and brought about a situation in the University which has impelled the members of this Board to declare, as they now do, that the welfare of the University requires that the term of Dr. Brooks as President of the University should end." The board, which always wanted to lift itself above the turmoil of the street, claimed that its actions were "in spite of, rather than because of, the activities of certain groups who seem interested chiefly in changing our action on the questionnaire, and with those views on that subject this Board can not agree." In reality, Brooks's ouster consummated the quiet work over a couple of years on the part of some of the curators, including Mercer Arnold and others.[11]

The curators gave its fired president a benefit or two, something it refused to give Harmon DeGraff. Brooks would give up his active role as president on June 5, with Walter Williams, to no one's surprise, replacing him as acting president until December 31, when Brooks would be out permanently and Williams would take the presidency outright. There was no search committee, no national canvass for a new president, just rule by fiat. Fortunately, Williams was a perfect choice. He embodied integrity, was familiar with the university's situation, and enjoyed not only the confidence of the board but also the loyalty and respect of the faculty, as well as widespread admiration throughout the state and nation. Williams, in fact, had been a candidate for the presidency in 1923 but was passed over in favor of Brooks. Had he been selected instead, would the questionnaire crisis have been resolved earlier and better? One influential Williams supporter, Bart B. Howard, editorial writer for the *Post-Dispatch,* told him in the midst of the crisis back in 1929: "You could have done great things for Missouri as president of the State University. It is a damned shame you didn't have the chance." As it turned out, Williams would now get that opportunity.

As for Brooks, he told the press he liked Columbia and planned to stay in town if he could arrange to do so. Herman Schlundt told AAUP Secretary Tyler that the faculty was upbeat after Brooks's removal. In his valedictory to the faculty in May, even his critics could be generous. "It is the code of the sea that the captain must go down with his ship," Brooks told them. "It is not, however, necessary that the ship go down when the captain is lost. There is always the first mate ready to navigate the ship, and behind him still other mates in line." He urged the faculty to put aside differences and move the university forward. He had come to the university a bit reluctantly, he said, drawn by the challenge of improving the gross underfunding by the state. He cited achievements, not failures, and, in the end, received a great ovation. Around the state, talk made the rounds about a run for governor two years hence, the sort of spasmodic reaction expected in such cases. Nothing came of it.[12]

3

While Brooks was navigating his last turbulent semester at the helm, Max Meyer returned to active faculty status, his year of penance having expired. Sixty or so of his colleagues, including deans or assistant deans of seven university divisions and a couple of former deans of women, threw a dinner for him at the Tiger Hotel—"an impressive ovation," said Addison Gulick. Unfortunately, Meyer was neither repentant nor humble, perhaps in part because of the humiliation of a frankly difficult year for him and his family. He hadn't wanted to immerse himself in litigation with the curators and had voluntarily forfeited his contract for summer school and accepted an offer to conduct research on acoustic teaching of congenitally deaf people at the Central Institute for the Deaf in St. Louis. The institute had a nice facility but paid little. Fortunately, Rabbi Mayerberg in Kansas City had organized a fund for Meyer that, with the support of friends and former students, eventually totaled twelve hundred dollars, a tidy sum—but one that didn't approach the lost wages of a full professor. While the negotiations between Carlson's committee and the curators dragged on, Meyer got an unexpected offer in August to teach for a semester at the University of Chile. In fact, as he was departing he ran into Percy Bordwell in St. Louis, who was in town for the negotiating session with the curators and wondered what it was all about. On board ship in the Caribbean, he wrote Leland Hazard that he had headed for Chile not for the money but "simply as a scientific missionary" and that the appointment's five-hundred-dollar stipend would not cover his round-trip fare. He wanted to be "useful," he said, and carried along the instruments he had used in St. Louis for demonstration in Chile. At the same time, he puzzled over the board's failure "to see that the man whom they have put into the presidency of the University is a dishonest person. However, his method of personal approach is so pleasing, that it took me, too, a long, long time, before I convinced myself that he was a characterless person. Besides," he added, "being a school superintendent is the worst possible preparation for being a University President."[13]

During the lean times back home, Meyer's wife, Stella, constantly worried about family finances, including impending taxes she had to pay. About the time of the Wall Street stock market crash, she got a letter from Max asking for four hundred dollars to pay his return fare. She told Rabbi

Mayerberg that a local bank where she sought a loan insulted her, "as if my husband were a fugitive from justice, or something of the sort, and would probably never come back." Her brother in Florida had been financially ruined by a recent hurricane and couldn't help. Alerted to the problem by Leland Hazard that the Meyers needed about two thousand to twenty-five hundred dollars to carry them until his reinstatement at the University of Missouri, A. J. Carlson tried to generate some money through the Julius Rosenwald Fund in Chicago. No end of worthy projects had been funded by Rosenwald's philanthropy. Carlson explained that Meyer's suspension "was one of the most flagrant cases of injustice that has occurred in an American University in recent years." He added: "If I had the money I would supply it myself because the matter is not small from the point of view of Prof. Meyer and his family." Evidently, just like the hoped-for reinstatement in January, nothing was forthcoming.[14]

Professor Carlson's generosity of spirit was not matched by the Board of Curators, which had callously deprived a twenty-nine-year veteran of the faculty—and his family—of needed resources. Likewise DeGraff, as Meyer bitterly recalled it, "was summarily dismissed exactly as a day laborer by some employer is told he need not come next morning." Secretary Tyler thought the whole thing over Meyer's finances was sad. "It is a shame," he told Carlson, "that the curators should not raise the necessary funds themselves."[15]

Shame indeed. Of course, nobody wanted the report of the American Association of University Professors more than Harmon O. DeGraff. He had waited since spring for his anticipated vindication. Meanwhile, at the last minute, he had gotten a position teaching sociology and economics at Superior State Teachers College in Wisconsin. He kept the news fairly quiet, not wishing to upset pending changes in salary adjustments or possibly even reinstatement at Missouri. Nor did he want publicity in Wisconsin, where the local press had noted his name on the roster of new faculty. One reporter, who turned out to have a heart, wanted an interview, but DeGraff dissuaded him and publicity was avoided. By November, he had just about ruled out a lawsuit, knowing the odds were clearly in favor of a Board of Curators loaded with politicians, lawyers, and newspapermen who could shape opinion. Considering the time, energy, costs of litigation, and perhaps worst of all, the renewed publicity a lawsuit would entail, DeGraff pretty much decided it was a lost cause. He would be out the balance of his salary plus summer school—a total of $872. At least he and Meyer would be vindicated in the academic world.[16]

If the curators betrayed little sense of humanity or moral obligation to the two professors, maybe the AAUP could help, or at least that's what some members had in mind. The Missouri case had not only proved one of the most significant in the history of the American Association of University Professors but also had prompted internal debates, including the one over penalties as well as over establishment of a fund for its members suffering injustice at the hands of university governing authorities. The proposal for such a fund originated with Professor R. W. Gerard, a junior member of the physiology department at the University of Chicago. Carlson thought it a splendid idea, asked Gerard to work it up, and thought the details would be no problem. Leland Hazard had even told Carlson that if such a fund existed, he, having no children, would name it in his will. Gerard argued that the interest of younger members of the association felt "luke warm," believing the organization had been ineffective in carrying out its worthy goals. He was aware of the arguments against "unionization," but claimed that a pool funded by dues, contributions, and so on would raise spirits and produce effective results with administrators. If an investigating team found no warrant in a dismissal, the fund would carry the affected member for a year or until he was employed elsewhere. If the administrative authorities rejected the report, others at the institution would be encouraged to leave and then supported, as funds permitted, by the AAUP. Blacklisted institutions would then be off-limits to AAUP members until the problem had been remedied.[17]

Gerard's proposal was linked to Louis Thurstone's sanction recommendations and presented in part to the AAUP's governing council in November 1929, and then, in December, to the annual convention of the membership. Both matters were thrashed out and rejected, but relevant documents remained available for circulation among council members, chapter officers, and others who wanted to see them. Fears of "trade union" methods and "class war," along with concern for lost professional prestige and other concerns, outweighed sympathy for the proposals. For example, Berkeley's A. M. Kidd, a former chairman of Committee A, argued that the number of cases referred to the Academic Freedom and Tenure Committee was small, and that progress under the old moral suasion system had been working. "Most of the institutions, especially the better ones, observe our rules scrupulously," he argued. "The violations come usually from small denominational colleges, pressed with financial and other difficulties, western agricultural colleges and expanding normal schools whose governing boards have not yet been taken out of politics." In fact, most of what the association wanted in freedom and tenure had been realized because university presidents had perceived Committee A's fairness. A case like the University of Missouri was rare. Maybe ad hoc contributions for "exceptional cases of wrongful dismissal" would be appropriate instead. Professor U. G. Weatherly of Indiana University, a member of Committee A since its beginning, thought such militancy would wreck the association's judicial nature, and Professor Ernest Bernbaum of the University of Illinois didn't like the "blacklisting" idea at all. When the association became "an organization of professors who have no regard for the consensus of opinion among educated men, or for ill-natured soreheads, its doom is sealed." He believed the AAUP was "trying to pass gradually from an old and intolerable status of professors to a new and rational status. Such a transition requires time and coolness," he said. "During the transitional period there are bound to be regrettable but unavoidable cases of individuals who will suffer because the old regime is still strong."[18]

Most of the AAUP's gentlemanly and rational leadership wanted no part of militancy or trade union practices. But change was coming. The next year, following problems in the higher educational institutions in Mississippi, the annual convention passed a resolution that excluded them from the association's "eligible list," a sort of embryonic censuring procedure. The 1931 annual convention got even tougher, developing a " 'non-recommended' list"; by 1936 that list became "censured institutions," with the names of offending institutions published in the association's *Bulletin* beginning in 1938. In 1940, the AAUP published a mature statement of academic freedom, something which, in time, became a watchword in American education. If there were abuses on both sides, that was the price a free society paid for its commitment to the freedom of research, teaching, and learning.[19]

None of that meant much to Max Meyer in the spring of 1930. He might have basked in the sympathy and goodwill of his colleagues and students following his return to active duty. He chose to squander it instead. In February, even before his official return, he warmed up with a speech to Alpha Pi Zeta, the honorary social science fraternity that long before he had helped organize in part to foster an inquisitive spirit among students. Ignorance sustained social taboos, he said, some of which had outlived their usefulness. In a scarcely veiled reference to his own situation, Meyer said that the social scientist who challenged such taboos stood in danger of martyrdom from the ignorant mob. But the university was the place for original thought, though he encouraged patience because societal transformation required more than one generation.

So far, so good. But ten days after his reinstatement, Meyer showed up at the convention of the Southern Society of Philosophy and Psychology at the Andrew Jackson Hotel in Nashville and delivered his out-going presidential speech to the after-dinner crowd. Meyer's fellow social scientists were treated not to a scholarly appraisal of his latest auditory findings, or to some insight into their shared disciplines, but rather to an eyebrow-raising diatribe of how he ran afoul of an outrageous cast of characters back in Missouri who proved his undoing and that of Professor DeGraff. One could pick out familiar figures: the editor of the *Columbia Daily Tribune*; a country editor who called the AAUP "a labor union"; the self-disclosed noncollege-educated inquisitor on the Executive Board; North Todd Gentry and his petition; but mostly, a dishonest, rumormongering president who whipped up the backwater of the state to shore up his shaky regime and then tried to bribe him. The speech was breathtaking. He talked about the Inquisition and ignorance and hypocrisy. True, tucked away in the address were nuggets of worth, including the legitimacy of his Social Psychology lecture and Meyer's overall thesis that it was "dangerous business to be a teacher of a social science." But that night in Nashville the internationally renowned psychologist's address, laden with sarcasm and bitter wit, seemed worlds away from anything presidential or distinguished.[20]

Of course, it took little time for Meyer's spleen-venting to reach the eyes and ears of the curators back home, and everyone else. It had been "a psychological moment," chortled the *Tribune*'s Ed Watson. The campus and the state, which had barely absorbed the ouster of President Brooks, now were abuzz with new speculation. The other shoe dropped quickly. Judge Goodrich scrambled to get a copy of the speech, asking President Brooks to secure one. Brooks, already out of the picture, had no interest in the subject and said so to both Goodrich and Meyer. Brooks frankly told Meyer that anything to do with the Nashville speech was all the curators' doing and that he, Brooks, had nothing to do with it. Curator Frank McDavid was offended by the speech, and honestly believed the board had been fair with Meyer—certainly more lenient than he had wanted. Still, he didn't want his resentment to get the best of him, or to hurt the university. At the same time, he didn't want the board to appear weak, as if they had caved in to Meyer's supporters.

President-designate Walter Williams thought Meyer had crossed the line and that his usefulness to the university was exhausted. But in the interests of the university and in fairness to Meyer he counseled caution and delay. He quietly worked with Meyer's friends, trying to persuade him to resign. But Williams knew the larger issue was the long-term relationship between the faculty and governing officials. The Board of Curators agreed with Williams, and called a meeting for May 2 at the Muehlebach Hotel in Kansas City to decide what do about the most recent episode in the endless saga. Optimistic faculty, elated over Brooks's impending departure, stood ready to work with the board, which had asked for an elected faculty committee—informally known as "the Group"—to help develop plans for meeting personnel crises in the future. For all practical purposes, the Group more formally replaced those who had tried to work with the authorities after the questionnaire crisis began. Unfortunately, Meyer's lack of judgment came at a bad time, doubly so since the Group and the board had not yet formulated any guidelines.

Alarmed, the Group's nineteen faculty members, which included some of the usual activists desperate to spare the university more injury, pleaded with the board not to take disciplinary action until guidelines had been developed. Of course, technically speaking, the Group spoke only for themselves, though their input would be valuable to a board earnestly seeking to emulate procedures prevalent in other universities.[21]

Even though disciplinary procedures were not yet in place, the curators moved cautiously at their meeting in Kansas City. Meyer, no longer under suspension, was entitled to legal representation and a hearing, which they scheduled for May 16. Sensitive to "star chamber" charges—something noted in Meyer's speech—some curators hinted that the hearing might welcome members of the press. Of course, Meyer actually wasn't charged with anything yet, but the board's resolution passed on May 2—filled with whereas this and whereas that—said that the board couldn't ignore Meyer's Nashville speech since it had been noised all over the state and had injured the university. The board wanted to see if discipline was warranted. Mercer Arnold and A. A. Speer weren't at the Muehlebach meeting, and Blanton and McDavid, objects of scorn in Meyer's speech, said nothing and recused themselves from the vote. However, just *who* had told the board the university might have been damaged by Meyer's remarks wasn't made clear.[22]

Few, if any, defended Meyer's intemperate remarks in Nashville. His attorney, Leland Hazard, was in Chicago and met with A. J. Carlson, who had done so much for Meyer's vindication. After reading Meyer's speech, Carlson told AAUP Secretary Tyler back in Washington, "What he said is essentially all on record and it was true, but he used some adjectives that were bound to be irritating in Missouri at the present time of high tension." Another professor told Tyler that a colleague who had heard the speech said Meyer had used tactless language fully aware of the presence of the Associated Press. He added that others who had known the Meyers decades before said nothing had changed. As he reported it to Tyler, "He was then as tactless and without any vestige of common sense as he is today." Those were the kind, he lamented, that needed rescuing by the association. A former colleague of Meyer's, now teaching at

Stanford, acknowledged Meyer's "very poor judgment and worse taste" to Fred Middlebush, but said, "The time has come to call a halt and let bygones be bygones." That was the view of an anonymous Columbian who wrote Judge Goodrich with nothing much good to say about the Nashville speech but who urged mercy and restraint before dispatching a man with three decades of service. Another critic of the speech, Judge Robert F. Walker, a Missouri alumnus and a justice of the state supreme court, wrote a scathing letter to the board—apparently released to the Associated Press—censuring Meyer's speech and reopening all the old issues of obscenity, use of the mails, and dangers to Missouri's youth.[23]

If Walker's statements offered no real help to the authorities in finding a way out of the mess, one of Meyer's colleagues at Missouri, Winterton C. Curtis, tried his own hand. Curtis agonized over the university's future. He respected Meyer's mind and achievements, even if Meyer had exasperated him. Curtis met with Goodrich just prior to the hearing on May 16 and left a statement of his views with the judge. He was thinking of the good of the university, he said, not Meyer, and he certainly didn't approve of Meyer's speech. But Curtis knew why Meyer had said what he said in Nashville. He had been "the victim of slanderous rumors," said Curtis, and he wanted to defend himself. Brooks had handled the whole questionnaire business badly. Everybody knew that. And surprisingly, Frank McDavid had said that curators shouldn't have to handle such things— something they all thought as well. But Curtis pleaded for the university. Financially, the school had suffered for years because of underfunding, and even though the new State Survey Commission appointed to look into state institutions had recommended increases, it was doubtful the university would get them. On top of that, the AAUP report had probably upset Goodrich, but Curtis defended it. The report had gone through the approval process and had "been taken seriously in academic circles." Added Curtis: "And now comes Nashville." Meyer's friends were upset, including Curtis—"angry beyond all reason," he said—but on reflection he understood why Meyer had done it. But if personalities got in the way, the institution would suffer. If the board disciplined Meyer, he said, some would claim "it was because he told the truth," and with that on top of the AAUP report, the university would be condemned for a long time. Of course, Curtis had looked at the opposite view, that after the negative report the school's reputation could hardly get any worse. "No one can say dogmatically what will be best," concluded Curtis. "I have urged the course of action indicated because of my faith that there are situations in which only generosity and forbearance can turn the tables and bring victory from defeat."[24]

For his part, Meyer didn't like the vagueness of the charges against him. Technically, of course, the curators' resolution made no official charge at all, just that the board had been informed that Meyer may have done something in his Nashville speech to injure the university. Talk of insubordination seemed to stretch the point, as if the curators were reaching for something official to hang on the beleaguered professor. Presumably, Meyer may have been insubordinate in talking publicly and negatively about an issue the board regarded as closed. But for all of Meyer's faults, and they were many, he had been smeared mercilessly, and the charges had gone unanswered. Years later Meyer defended his Nashville remarks because of the innuendo in and out of the country that he was a degenerate and a pervert, and that a generous Board of Curators had simply hid that from the public. He believed the curators, some of them at least, had nurtured that view. "I saw no way out of this ruinous persecution," he said, "except by telling the public that the Full Board had never found me guilty of any sexual immorality."

Meyer was right, of course, but he did much more than that in Nashville. Still, it seemed that fairness dictated that the administration assure the public and the profession that there was no moral indictment against Professor Meyer. But it hadn't done that, and so a year of bottled-up frustration cut loose one night in Nashville. That was pretty much what Meyer said publicly a few days before his formal hearing, and it would constitute part of his defense. Goodrich had let Meyer know that if the board did find insubordination, it might make a difference if his Nashville remarks were "intentional or premeditated."[25]

Premeditated? Meyer told Leslie Cowan that his speech was indeed premeditated, but whether any "insubordination" was intentional might have been something quite different. At the two-day hearing commencing on May 16, Meyer's case wasn't helped by the unearthing of a March 8 letter he sent to Rabbi Samuel Mayerberg, his benefactor, in which Meyer, well before his Nashville speech, outlined his plans to use the forum as an exposé of the whole miserable questionnaire episode. His Alpha Pi Zeta speech in February had been only a rehearsal for the real thing. In his Nashville speech, he said he intended to name names, to call curators Blanton and McDavid "mentally unfit" for the positions they held. (In a later letter he called Blanton "senile.") He would dare them to fire him permanently. A follow-up letter to Mayerberg seemed to take back his intention of challenging the governing authorities, and Meyer explained that he had only been joking about being fired.

Whatever Meyer really intended, the correspondence suggested a man virtually out of control. But the anger was explainable, and at the hearing

Meyer sternly defended his attack on Blanton and McDavid since they had been behind his ouster and disgrace. Who would vindicate him? The board had closed the sex questionnaire issue, so appealing to the curators seemed hopeless. Justice demanded that the curators publicly declare that Meyer had not written or fostered the questionnaire; that he had never been charged with immoral teaching; that he had never been charged with seduction or abuse of his position in the university; and that his controversial "syllabus" and lecture on the physiology of sex had been judged scientifically sound by professionals. After all, Meyer produced harshly critical editorials from Ohio—where he had been scheduled to teach summer school at Ohio State University—even comparing him to a faculty member who had murdered a student there. Such rumors of moral leprosy even followed him to Chile, made him an outcast there, and damaged his work at the university in Santiago. The heavy punishment inflicted by the curators in 1929 lent credibility to wild tales about his lack of moral fitness. Meyer even showed the curators a letter he had written to Bruce Blevins, editor of the *New Republic*, after his dismissal by the Executive Board back in March 1929. He told Blevins not to be too hard on the university administration, which had been in bondage to the legislature, and that the low intellect of a considerable part of that body and their constituents had required action of some sort. If Blevins wanted to place blame, Meyer told him, place it there, and with a local editor whose competition with the journalism school's paper caused him to interfere in university business, and with locals who didn't know science when they saw it. "It is the petition of these business men which makes it impossible for me to live in this stinking town any longer. I could make up for mutual misunderstandings. But to remove the University from a town of Babbitts is, of course, impossible."[26]

Meyer had planned the whole thing, but never to injure the university, only to vindicate himself, his family, and the university's reputation. He also hoped to advance the cause of science. Among the curators, only McDavid and Blanton had been singled out for scorn. McDavid had argued that Meyer had "made the subject of sex too attractive," and of course the whole sex lecture got hashed over again. "It was quite impossible for Senator McDavid to make a rational decision," Meyer testified. "He gave me the impression he thought sex was ugly. There should be no mystery in sex. Every mystery excites the imagination far more than a plain statement of anatomical facts. Women who are unmarried who intend to go into professional work, and who have reached the age of 16, must have some kind of sex education if they have not already had it. These women should not have to seek experimental information."[27]

At times, the atmosphere in the hearing room became tense and heated. On the first day of the hearing, Jack Blanton asked to be excused from the active participation, and for much of the first afternoon sat in the hearing room reading newspapers. McDavid felt no such need, taking part in the questioning. On day two, in a discussion on the "mentally unfit" charge, McDavid, according to the *St. Louis Post-Dispatch,* shouted questions at Meyer, claiming, "I care nothing about what Dr. Meyer thinks of me." Blanton retorted, "That goes for me, too." It was unseemly behavior for gentlemen. The end hardly came soon enough, and after two days with Meyer in the dock for more than dozen hours, the curators made no decision and adjourned until May 26.

Undoubtedly exhausted, Meyer threw in the towel. When the curators resumed, they had his letter, offered by his attorney Leland Hazard, asking to be relieved of his professorship, along with apologies all around including those to Blanton and McDavid. He had been a man humiliated and besieged, he said. Now he wanted to end the whole mess and asked to be given a research appointment so he could continue his work at the Central Institute for the Deaf in St. Louis. He wanted to develop instruments to help educate congenitally deaf children, and to assemble material for "a comprehensive treatise on the Psychology of the Deaf Child—a subject upon which there is at present no comprehensive work in existence." He wanted no royalties or remuneration from the scientific devices he had developed. "To give to the deaf-born power to speak as persons who hear is in my opinion a distinct social contribution," Meyer said. "These instruments need to be perfected and their use explained and extended among teachers of the deaf."[28]

Meyer had offered the curators a way out, which, after deliberating much of the day in Leslie Cowan's office and at the Tiger Hotel, they decided to accept, or most of it anyway. By 8 P.M. the board issued its statement, offered by A. A. Speer, seconded by Milton Tootle, and passed unanimously. Meyer lost his tenure as professor of psychology, such as it was, and was named research professor of psychology for a year so he could work on the projects he had underway at the Central Institute for the Deaf. The curators believed such work would "be of inestimable value" for Missouri's deaf children as well as afford the university a chance for public service. The board took a parting shot at Meyer's Nashville speech, but thought that all things considered, the university would be best served by the action it took. And, after all, they said the university's welfare was what they had wanted all along.

Now that the curators had registered their displeasure with Meyer's speech, what about an official public statement clearing Professor Meyer of the rumors and innuendoes that had plagued him for more than a year? Would there be any statement saying he wasn't a pervert after all? A petition started out among faculty calling for the board to do just that, as well as asking Meyer to recant his nasty remarks about the curators. Meyer had done that. The board, however, said nothing.[29]

Meyer, of course, was no pervert. Far from it. Once upon a time his life had been consumed, he said during his exile in Chile, "in sexless problems of the physiology of hearing and seeing" when his world collapsed over a silly questionnaire. But if he wasn't a pervert, that didn't mean others weren't, at least as he saw it. After the questionnaire business had blown up and the spring semester concluded, the University of Missouri had "two strange resignations" in mid-1929, one the director of personnel for undisclosed reasons, the other from someone in the art department for allegedly "admitted homosexual practices." Meyer had his suspicions about the director of personnel. Over the years, the dean of women had occasionally asked Meyer "for advice on cases of neurotic-restless girls who failed in their studies." Meyer loathed such sessions, thought them "distasteful," but complied anyway. A year before the questionnaire fiasco, when one young woman failed to show up for an appointment, Meyer reported the no-show to the dean, who told him that the director of personnel claimed that such interviews were within his portfolio. The young woman had gone to him instead. Said Meyer: "I gave my thankful prayers to God for the relief." Meyer obviously thought improprieties of some sort developed between the personnel director and one or more of the women, eventually leading to his quiet resignation. "Not a single girl can say that I ever pried into her intimate life," he told A. J. Carlson near the end of 1929. "I regard psychoanalysis as an absurdity and leave it to Freudians and Catholic priests."[30]

Epilogue

"So Far from Columbia"

> Out here, so far from Columbia, we are not able to tell
> what it is all about.
> —Illinois resident to Stratton Brooks, April 2, 1929, UMPOP

> Some day the whole story can be told.
> —*Missouri Alumnus*, December 1952

E dna St. Vincent Millay came to the University of Missouri to read
some of her poetry and verse the year following the sex questionnaire scandal. The women's organizations were fortunate to get the
Pulitzer Prize winner, and her bisexuality and alcoholism were probably
unknown to her attentive listeners in Jesse Auditorium. In her writing
and lifestyle, bohemian Millay flaunted a titillating naughtiness that vi-
cariously appealed to students not ready to cross the line. She may have
been from Greenwich Village, but "Bowery parties" at Mizzou were ruled
off-limits by the dean.

Otherwise, the parties looked the same, the agriculture school's Barnwarmin' moved to the new Brewer Fieldhouse, the alumni came back
home in the fall, and the football team went 5–2–1 but, most important,
beat Kansas by a single point. Delta Gamma must have set a pinning
record, Chi Omega boosted their grades so they could have dances again,
but the sisters of Alpha Gamma Delta didn't pay their light bill so they
threw a dance by candlelight. Jesse Wrench, the good chaperon, did his
best to light up darkened corners, though the *Savitar* goodnaturedly wondered if he'd get invited again. Some sororities got new houses that year,
including Phi Mu. The story was that since the new house didn't have

window shades when the sorority moved in, the guys from adjacent Sigma Epsilon got no sleep for two weeks. And Zeta Tau Alpha's new house was so far away it was a wonder they could make their early classes. Except that they were "nice girls," the *Savitar* saw blackmailing possibilities of those who passed the Zeta house while sneaking out to Jefferson City or the quarry—a partying and necking hang-out. Tennessee Williams also came to Mizzou that year—as a student; his playwright career lay ahead. True, studying psychology was a mess that year—only two courses were offered that fall—and Professor Max Meyer stirred up old controversies by damning the curators in Nashville; and, true, there was discontent among the faculty until President Brooks was fired by a board tired of it all. But mostly, Mizzou was trying to get back to normal. Said the *Savitar:* "Couples wandering about the campus, arm in arm, rainy days in April, the May Fete, baseball, girls in new clothes, a queen for the season. That is spring at Missouri."[1]

Unfortunately, some things would never be normal again. Missouri and the nation slipped into the Great Depression and the university struggled to survive drastic cutbacks, as did their counterparts everywhere. President Walter Williams, in poor health, left the presidency in July 1935 and died a few weeks later, replaced by Frederick Middlebush, who served nearly two decades, the longest administration in the university's history. Mizzou did its part in World War II, bringing uniforms and military training to campus; then the "G.I. Bill" ballooned postwar enrollments. The campus tried to keep pace, adding classrooms, residence halls, and other new facilities, including a major enlargement to Jesse Auditorium. Jellying faded from campus slang, the Board of Curators slowly changed composition—though Blanton and McDavid hung on till the 1940s—and the sex questionnaire receded into distant memory. It was still close enough in 1939, however, that Jonas Viles, in his *Centennial History* of the university, couldn't say much, only that the whole thing "revealed the inadequacy of the [Brooks] administration."[2]

There were no outrageous rogues in the questionnaire story, just a mix of pragmatists and true believers, some a bit devious perhaps, but all showing human nature. And despite their many contributions, it's hard to call all of their behavior honorable. As for Stratton Brooks, after his firing, he became not Missouri's governor but rather the executive secretary of the Order of DeMolay in Kansas City, seemed happy at it, and died of a cerebral thrombosis at his home in January 1949. Frank McDavid became board chairman in the early 1930s but always had difficulty adjusting to changing times, including his hesitancy about his party's embrace of the New Deal. Upon reflection, he thought Brooks's ouster had been too drastic but likely had no regrets about DeGraff or Meyer. At the time of all the nasty business of firing the president, McDavid told Walter Williams that he didn't have anything against Brooks personally, just that "the complaints came to me from so many quarters that I could not ignore them, and my own contact with him in the meetings of the Executive Board gave me the impression that he was impatient of the restraints put upon him by that body of men." Further, McDavid had been deeply disturbed by the departures of a number of able faculty, including law dean James P. McBaine, who left for Berkeley in 1928, and dean of education M. G. Neale, who left for the presidency of the University of Idaho after that. McDavid was sorry about it all, but Brooks just had to go. In any case, McDavid remained a Missouri booster and ardent Tiger football fan. When he died at his home in Springfield at seventy-nine in April 1943 the eulogies were many and glowing, including those which extolled his great kindness and integrity. Fifteen years later a residence hall at the university bore his name.[3]

McDavid's chief coprosecutor in the questionnaire scandal, Jack Blanton, rotated off the board in the 1940s, but never thought about retiring from his beloved *Monroe County Appeal*. He became the quintessential and much-celebrated country editor, a fount of earthy wisdom. Featured in *Country Gentleman, Saturday Evening Post,* and *Time,* he began his popular and endearing serialized reminiscences, "When I Was a Boy," in the *St. Louis Globe-Democrat* in 1950. When retired dean and history professor Frank Stephens, busily writing his administrative history of the University of Missouri in the early 1950s, got stuck on the Brooks firing—given the sparse paper trail in official university documents—he sought help from Blanton. The question for Stephens in 1953 was the same others had had nearly a quarter of a century before: what was the *real* reason for Brooks's ouster? Blanton offered little help, repeating the shopworn fiction that the firing "had no connection whatever" to the questionnaire business. It was all about some publicly unspecified insubordination on the president's part, said Blanton, along with faculty discontent and piled-up complaints. "A little diplomacy on his [Brooks] part could have saved the Executive Board, of which I was a member, from all the trouble and embarrassment incident to the making of a mountain out of that molehill."[4]

Such bald revisionism is, of course, belied by the stark record that indicts Blanton for the same offense. Nonetheless, a little more than a year later, the country editor was eulogized far and wide when he died at age eighty-five shortly after filing his last editorial in January 1955. The eulogies were a celebration of common sense but, in many ways, unwittingly, of untutored intelligence.[5]

The visiting AAUP team also continued their respective careers. Percy Bordwell taught at Iowa, including another stint as acting dean of the Law School, until his retirement in 1948. By no means finished, he taught full-time at Rutgers for a few years in the 1950s, was honored in his old age, and died in Iowa City in 1970 at age ninety-two. Louis L. Thurstone served in numerous learned groups, including as president of the American Psychological Association in the early 1930s. Ever the militant, he didn't let the Meyer issue drop, trying unsuccessfully to bully Missouri President Walter Williams into paying Professor Meyer a salary in 1933 when the university couldn't and wouldn't do it, and repeatedly nudging his colleagues to help get a pension for the aging professor or assist him in some way. In 1938, Thurstone became Charles F. Gray Distinguished Service Professor at Chicago, where he continued until his retirement fifteen years later. Meanwhile, he published *Vectors of Mind* in 1935 and *Multiple Factor Analysis* in 1947. After retirement from Chicago, he became research professor at the University of North Carolina and directed the Psychometric Laboratory in Chapel Hill, as well as serving as visiting professor at the University of Stockholm. When he died in September 1955, at age sixty-eight, the world lost a significant contributor to quantitative psychology.

Thurstone's colleague, Anton J. Carlson, also continued at the University of Chicago, even past his emeritus status in 1940. During the 1930s he opposed Chicago's young president, Robert Maynard Hutchins, in what he thought was Hutchins's low view of scientific education. "Three hundred years ago," Carlson was quoted as saying in his characteristic Swedish accent, "Hutchins vould haf been a monk in a monastery. I don't belief in retreating from de vorld; I belief in staying in it and mastering it." "Ajax," as he was affectionately known, also got involved in the America First movement of isolation before World War II, but he was most noted for his scientific achievements. *Time* celebrated him more than once, including a cover story in February 1941, calling him the "Scientist's Scientist." His infamous interrogative, "Vot iss de effidence?" said *Time*, "has launched a thousand experiments." For his seventy-fifth birthday in January 1950, hundreds of his friends, admirers, and former students lauded him with a bound volume of tributes, some bearing letterheads from prestigious hospitals and universities around the nation. The old scientist, a good and decent man, died in Chicago in September 1956 at age eighty-one.[6]

Whither the other major players in the drama? Editor Ed Watson of the *Columbia Daily Tribune,* whose biting editorials fostered controversy for decades, died in 1937 at age seventy. Aside from his reputed alcoholism— Max Meyer called him "the drinker"—his critics claimed he skewered the university when he could because the Journalism School published the rival *Columbia Missourian.* According to Hobart Mowrer, "The questionnaire played right into his hands." Watson's venom may have been directed less toward the university than the rival paper, which he vilified more than once, calling it "the campus sheet," "notoriously unreliable," and run "by aliens who have no interest in Columbia." The "youngsters" who reported for the paper had to "unlearn" a good deal of what they were taught at the J-School, said Watson. His editorial outrage proved selective, however, lambasting Charles Ellwood and the *Missourian* when they criticized community morals for tolerating a lynching, and doing the same to Herbert Blumer, the young instructor whose lecture violated local racial taboos and earned him a burning cross in his yard. So it should have been no surprise when a twenty-two-year-old also earned his outrage for asking a few intimate questions of innocent girls at the university. But Watson's editorials had no outrage for the mobsters who murdered James Scott, nor for those who said they sometimes approved mob violence, nor for Klansmen who tried to intimidate a young instructor.

Herman Schlundt also died in 1937, a month after Watson, though his memory among admiring students long outlived him. "To many of us," remembered one classroom veteran, "he was the most inspiring teacher we ever encountered. His chemistry lectures held everyone spellbound." Judge James Goodrich left the presidency in the early 1930s after heading the Board of Curators for more than a decade. The Missouri graduate always wanted to do the right thing for his alma mater, but was ill-served by the university president the curators had hired. When he died in Kansas City in October 1952, he left a distinguished record in banking and the law. Leslie Cowan, secretary to the Board of Curators, continued in that role for another quarter century, accruing more influence during the presidency of Frederick Middlebush. He even added the role of vice-president for business operations in 1944. Elmer Ellis, Middlebush's successor as president in the mid-1950s who had come up through the ranks since joining the history faculty in 1930, thought well of Cowan's service but believed he had usurped authority and was occasionally devious. His alleged leaking of secrets was probably true, though it's not clear that was the sort of thing Ellis had in mind. As a condition of his taking the presidency, Ellis insisted that Cowan give up one of his roles. Cowan, who had pretty much devoted his life to the university, gave up being board secretary in 1954, and retired from business operations in 1956, though he continued to serve as appraiser for university real estate after that. Critical of the school's leadership late in his life, he died in Columbia in 1974 at age eighty-six.

Winterton C. Curtis became dean of the College of Arts and Science in 1940 and served until his retirement six years later. The curators, he thought, had never held anything against the activist members of the faculty, himself included, for their role in the Meyer business. In fact, it seemed to earn them greater respect. Frank McDavid, for example, even suggested Curtis's name as a faculty representative to the presidential search committee for a successor to Walter Williams. Curtis, however, didn't have much respect for Jay William Hudson, with whom he had words over Hudson's role in the questionnaire affair. Regardless, Curtis enjoyed life in Columbia for another twenty years after his retirement, lucid until the end at age ninety in June 1966. In the decade or so before his death, he reminisced about his days in Dayton, Tennessee, about his friendship and correspondence with attorney Clarence Darrow, about the university and his scientific work, and about being diagnosed with Hodgkin's disease in 1924. His diagnosis was confirmed by physicians from the Mayo Clinic—their first such case—and by others at Johns Hopkins and Northwestern. Son of a Congregational minister but apparently agnostic to the end, Curtis concerned himself with neither Heaven nor Hell and lived four decades past his death sentence. Today, buildings bearing the names of Curtis, Schlundt, and LeFevre, who had died in 1923, all stand proximate to one another on Mizzou's "White Campus." To one familiar with their namesakes' careers, they are like large monuments in a cemetery, except that they are mute but living testimonials to three gifted scientists who once brought distinction to the university.[7]

Another nonbeliever was Leland Hazard, the young Kansas City liberal lawyer, student of Veblen, part-Harvard, all-Mizzou, who tried to defend his clients in the worst of times. His defense put him on the front pages frequently in those days, and in the years following he remained a reformer in a city corrupted by machine politics. He left his old law firm in the 1930s, hung out his own shingle, but soon had an offer to become general counsel for Pittsburgh Plate Glass in Pennsylvania (he also became vice-president and a director). It was a change and a challenge, but lucrative. Active in civic betterment affairs in Pittsburgh and Allegheny County as he had been back in Kansas City, his work also brought him face-to-face and shoulder-to-shoulder with big-shots in industry, the New Deal, and in wartime Washington. He and his wife traveled widely in later years, collected art, and never gave up advancing liberal causes. Full of energy and never out of ideas, retirement age brought changes, not rocking chairs. For years, he taught "Ideas and the Changing Environment" at Carnegie-Mellon while remaining for a time a director and consultant to Pittsburgh Plate Glass. He proudly carried a gold watch some Missouri faculty gave him for his performance in the Meyer affair. He even found time to write his memoirs—including a section on the great sex questionnaire scandal—a chronicle of an active life stilled only by death at eighty-seven in 1980.[8]

After leaving Missouri, the fired Harmon DeGraff went north. After a sad nail-biting summer seeking employment, his popularity as a teacher may have helped him land the offer from the teachers college in Superior, Wisconsin. His appointment, however, turned out to be a port in a storm, and the following year he joined the faculty of the University of Akron, in Ohio. There he did what he did best, and, as at Missouri, won the hearts of his students. When sociology split from economics soon after his arrival, DeGraff became chairman of the department, helping it grow to one of Akron's largest by the time he retired in 1951. "Doc" was popular as ever among students, "a sweet, kind soul" among his peers. A bachelor to the end, he lived a spartan life at the local YMCA. He took pride in his former Akron students, who constituted about 50 percent of Summit County's social workers. There may not have been a Hobart Mowrer among them, but no matter. DeGraff, like Mowrer, was people-oriented. His post-retirement career included counseling at Ohio's Summit County Juvenile Court and guiding marriage partners teetering on separation or divorce. He also logged service as a deacon at a local church and on the boards of the YMCA and Goodwill Industries. He retired from his second career in 1964 and died three years later at age eighty-one, leaving no close relatives—only thousands of grateful students.[9]

Also grateful were those who fit Jesse Wrench into their collegiate experience. The beloved chaperon and student advocate, who performed reasonably well in the questionnaire scandal, remained a fixture at the university for another generation. A frequent feature in the *Savitar* or *Missouri Alumnus*, Wrench yielded to mandatory retirement at age seventy in 1953, but wasn't allowed to go quietly. The state legislature acknowledged him as symbolizing the university and commended him, along with other things, for having bucked tradition in declaring his views and affecting "his own distinctive mode of attire." At one of Jesse's last pep rallies, according to a student who was there, the whole thing was a bit slow until he noted the lights burning in the library. " 'The trouble with this school is that there are too many people over there who ought to come over here.

If they won't come to us, we'll go to them!' And with that, he started a snake dance down the street right through the library."[10]

Wrench's wife, Jane, his partner in chaperoning and entertaining students over the years, was in on a student plan to serenade the retiring professor during final exam week in May 1953. Concerned about his health—Wrench had already suffered a heart attack—she asked another history faculty wife, Louise Atherton, if she and her husband Lewis could come over after dinner on the appointed evening and, without letting on why they were there, to linger until after the students departed, "just in case she needed help with J. E." The event commanded the attention of *Time*, which recorded the goings-on for the nation: "At the University of Missouri one night last week," it reported on June 1, "some 500 students stood outside a small, red brick house yelling their heads off: 'We want Monkey Wrench! We want Monkey Wrench!' Finally a white-goateed man appeared in his doorway, waving his arms and nodding his head. After more than 40 years teaching history, Professor Jesse E. Wrench, 70, was retiring and his students had come to pay their respects. 'My gosh,' said he, 'I don't know why you're honoring me. All I've done is to have fun all my life.' " "As generations of Mizzou men well know," said *Time*, "the professor was only telling the truth." Lewis Atherton, Wrench's colleague, whose own stellar association with the university commenced in the mid-1920s, had been a teaching assistant under Wrench in 1929–1930, and later returned for more than half a century on the faculty, was on hand that night. Lyrically, he recorded what he had seen: "It turned out to be an ideal spring night with a full moon," remembered Atherton, "a perfect backdrop for the performance of . . . [the] students and a small band of instrumental musicians who played and sang the traditional Missouri pep songs and other Missouri favorites. When J. E. stepped forth to thank the group, his silver hair shining in the moonlight, the performance became an actual realization of all the myths of the favorite college professor and the typical student body that audiences have always recognized as being nothing more than an impossible version of the never-never land. But for the Wrenches it materialized and it was a fitting tribute to both of them."

In the mythical 1950s of innocuous panty raids and sudsy college life, that memorable night might have seemed a million miles from 1929. But the supposed rebellion of the twenties and the supposed innocent conformity of the fifties may have been closer than the layers of myth and stereotype have allowed. No matter. Few, if any, of the hundreds of students who serenaded Professor Wrench had been alive during the great scandal. According to *Time*, the students "showered him with scrolls, letters, a gold watch and a plaque. [The Student Government Association gave the watch; the chain was from the Association of Women Students.] Then, suddenly, the fun was over. 'This is all very nice,' said Monkey Wrench, 'but all of you ought to be home studying for exams.' With that, he led one last cheer and shook hands all around." The old professor died in Columbia more than five years later at age seventy-six. At a memorial in the student union, Dean Thomas Brady eulogized his former teacher and colleague who had opened new worlds for him, and who had generously given of himself without ever asking anything in return. "In an age when too many think only of themselves," he said, "his shining example should make us all wish to be nobler men." [11]

No one's life was more impacted by the questionnaire scandal than that of Max Meyer. His dismissal by the Executive Board, then the suspension by the full board, then the disaster in Nashville led to his appointment as research professor through the Central Institute for the Deaf in St. Louis in 1930. The curators extended it for another year, after which he got an appointment at the struggling University of Miami in Coral Gables, Florida. There he taught and conducted research on deaf children who would have had no instruction at all without him. But Miami, which went into financial receivership in 1932, paid Meyer nothing save perhaps for a summer session or so, and he had to cobble finances together where he could get them just to keep body and soul together. He lived in near destitute conditions, for a while sharing a place in Florida with his brother-in-law who didn't work much, but mostly he lived by himself in humble quarters. Fortunately, he was not a complainer about such things, and had few aspirations for his own comfort. To make matters worse, his left arm was severely injured by a burglar who broke into his house in the summer of 1934. Though the intruder was later apprehended and executed by the state of Florida for an even more heinous crime, Meyer didn't get medical attention because he couldn't pay for it. [12]

The University of Missouri, first under Walter Williams and then under his successor Frederick Middlebush, might have done more for Meyer if the curators would have approved, but the economic depression seemed to preclude any real assistance. Still, the curators placed him on leave without pay for several years after 1932. But he wouldn't qualify for a small pension from the Carnegie Foundation for the Advancement of Teaching until he reached retirement age in 1938. Established in 1909, Carnegie pensions were an economic salvation for higher educational institutions that had no pension programs at all; at the same time, their existence, meager as it was, may have precluded universities from developing their own earlier than they did. Faculty at the University of

Missouri—which had long been approved for inclusion in the Carnegie program—tried and failed in the 1920s to develop a pension plan acceptable to the curators. Little was achieved until a state plan became effective in 1940, only to be obviated by a federal program in the 1950s. In reality, few Missouri faculty qualified for a Carnegie pension, but Meyer was one of them.[13]

Meanwhile, several people tried to help Meyer in any way possible. Former colleagues at Missouri, notably W. C. Curtis, tried unsuccessfully to find suitable employment. The American Psychological Association wanted to get him a pension, perhaps goaded by Louis Thurstone, its new president. Alumni wrote letters to the curators in his behalf. Thomas Edison, Helen Keller, and others, including Gallaudet College for the Deaf in Washington, got letters from Meyer's friends trying to generate employment or funding for his research with the deaf. Nothing worked. Times were hard, funding was scarce, and, besides, Max Meyer seemed to be past his prime, an aging eccentric. Somehow, Meyer managed to build his own place in Florida rather cheaply. With all five children on their own, he wanted his wife, still back in Columbia, to join him there. Stella had other plans. In 1937, she filed for divorce, which he didn't contest; the legal grounds were "mutual desertion." The marriage had lasted more than thirty years but had been anything but idyllic. Max and Stella were both independent, rather stubborn, and certainly intelligent (she had been elected to Phi Beta Kappa). Anybody who knew anything at all about the two of them knew that Meyer was hard to live with. But every story had two sides. Though she had stood loyally by his side through the questionnaire crisis, their marriage had been dysfunctional for decades. She had announced after the birth of their fifth child in August 1914 that she was sexually frigid, that she would never again be intimate with her husband, and that she had gotten married only because she wanted five kids. Not only did they sleep in separate beds after that, but even on different floors in their commodious house back in Columbia. It was a strange marriage. After the divorce, Stella remained in Columbia, teaching at Christian College. She died in 1957.[14]

Eventually, Meyer retired from his largely shadow appointment at Miami. But his passionate commitment to hearing theory and work with the deaf continued. From his late seventies to early eighties, Meyer kept publishing, with ten audition articles scattered equally between the *American Journal of Psychology* and the *Journal of the Acoustical Society of America*. He lamented that acousticians had turned their interests to hi-fi and television to the exclusion of everything else, something he deemed a "fad" destined to "fade out." At eighty-nine, he became the oldest member of the American Psychological Association, and two years later he demonstrated his cochlea model at the Acoustical Society and the Southern Society for Philosophy and Psychology.

Though self-effacing, Meyer never could accept criticism, whether from his family or from professionals who evaluated his work. Still, some thought his pioneering work had never received proper credit, including Professor Erwin Esper at the University of Washington. Covering nearly a dozen years beginning in the mid-fifties, Esper gathered numerous opinions from those in the profession who knew Meyer, eventually producing a pair of intellectual-biographical articles in the 1960s. Meyer told his old student Hobart Mowrer that he couldn't understand why Esper was interested. After all, said Meyer, he hadn't originated any of the divisions within the discipline and he didn't even consider himself a psychologist anymore. Harvard's Edwin Boring, with whom Meyer had exchanged letters and viewpoints over the years, and who could be as cantankerous as his pen pal, told Esper he had heard virtually nothing favorable about Meyer in half a century. Boring claimed Meyer "seemed unwilling to let his peers judge his theory or to take into consideration his own chances of error." But jealousies and egos marked academic research, and Edwin Boring had his share; one Florida State scholar, John Paul Nafe, told Esper to pretty much ignore the Harvard-MIT crowd. Much was also made of Meyer's "Teutonic temperament," as one colleague called it. Meyer made breakthroughs before his departure from the University of Missouri, but spent much of the remainder of his life defending his old auditory theories that were superseded by new ones. To those who grew up in the later era, "Meyer's theories," as one scientist recalled, "have always seemed quaintly outdated to me." One scientist who knew Meyer and read one of Esper's articles prior to publication told him: "I was especially pleased to note that you made no attempt to paint him as anything different from what he is—a misunderstood, crotchety, badly treated, delightful, brilliant old man."[15]

For many of Meyer's old students, none of that mattered. A profile of him in the *Missouri Alumnus* in December 1952 revived memories among former students and provided a clue as to the old professor's whereabouts. One longtime Kansas City physician claimed the story "reminds many of your old students the great debt we owe you." After all, Meyer had started them out "in their mental maturity." Ironically, Meyer discouraged promising psychology students from staying at Missouri for graduate study. Albert Weiss did, and had a brilliant and productive career cut short only by early death. Meyer seemed to know some of his own liabilities, and never really wanted to share his department at Missouri.

Dorothy Postle (later Marquis), the young instructor who Meyer thought was brilliant, came on in the spring of 1929, but spent her career at Michigan, not Missouri. Hobart Mowrer had been lured into psychology by his own depression, had gotten inspired by Max Meyer, but learned the discipline from others. Regardless, the revived Department of Psychology at Missouri invited Meyer to return to celebrate the half-century of the founding of its psychology laboratory. He declined, citing poor health. In old age, he remained as philosophical as ever, taking life as it came. Despite many travails in his adopted country, he thought himself lucky to have left Germany so long before. After all, he missed two world wars and the Hitler regime, which might easily have sent him to a death camp. He had been baptized a Lutheran back in Germany, he told Erwin Esper, and had even studied theology and sang in a Calvinist church. But now he was an agnostic who trusted in himself, not in God.

For a long while, save for a watch dog, Meyer lived alone in his little place in Florida. He had five kids, twelve grandchildren, and two great-grandchildren, but few ever came to see him. It hadn't been a warm family. Active in a pathetic sort of way nearly to the end, Meyer moved in with a kind daughter and perhaps kinder son-in-law in Virginia. When the family moved to Long Island, New York, he looked forward to his new surroundings. Unfortunately, he suffered a broken hip, seemed to recover, but then wound up in a Long Island nursing home and, finally, a hospital. He died there on March 14, 1967. He was ninety-three.[16]

While some of Meyer's contraptions wound up in the Smithsonian Institution, his old student Hobart Mowrer was providing something of a living legacy. Mowrer's life, in fact, proved in some ways the most spectacular of all those involved in the questionnaire and its backwash. When young Orval Hobart Mowrer got on the train and left Missouri, he left not only his widowed mother and a pinned girlfriend he would never marry but also the widening waves of the questionnaire scandal. As he said later, "Rarely has a university alumnus left his alma mater with less honor than I did in June of 1929."

That summer, shortly after he began graduate school in psychology at Johns Hopkins in Baltimore, he fell into an "agitated depression" that put him in the city's Memorial Hospital. A well-regarded physician told him pointedly that he was "in a typical depression," that such was part of his constitution, that his condition would worsen and become "more frequent" as he aged, and that he would simply have to live with it. The doctor was essentially right. The psychology books at Mowrer's hospital bedside interested him not at all, and when he recovered sufficiently to leave, with no desire or stamina for graduate school, he went to New York to get a job on some steamer for ports unknown. But the United States teetered on the threshold of the Great Depression, and already unemployment and a decline in tourism beset the maritime economy. The steamer idea was out. Mowrer returned to Baltimore, began graduate school in the fall of 1929, and got into psychoanalysis, a new field filled with promise. It did him no good; in fact, he felt worse, not helped by the five dollars per session. He hid his condition, told friends he suffered "heart trouble," and feared that continuing the useless psychoanalysis might blow his cover.

Better days lay ahead. He eventually recovered, immersed himself in graduate studies, and fell in love with Willie Mae Cook, a fellow student whom he married in 1931. Willie Mae, or Molly, as she was known, had been a sister of Alpha Gamma Delta and a Phi Beta Kappa graduate of the University of Georgia's class of 1927. She became not only a professional colleague but a refuge in Mowrer's personal turmoil as well. Also, the University of Missouri, under the new Walter Williams administration, generously *gave* him sufficient hours for an A.B. degree before he finished the Ph.D. in 1932, completing his dissertation on "The Modification of Nystagmus by Means of Repetition." In the Great Depression, academic positions were few, so he went to Northwestern University on a National Research Council Fellowship, while Molly, who had finished her own Ph.D. in 1931, stayed at Johns Hopkins as instructor. He "toughed-out" another bout of depression in the summer of 1933, took another research fellowship at Princeton for the new academic year, and went to Yale in 1934 on a Sterling Research Fellowship. Molly joined him there the following year, and Hobart's fellowship grew into a joint staff position in Yale's department of psychology and the Institute of Human Relations. While in New Haven, he tried psychoanalysis again—this time for three years—with unclear results.

Despite recurring depression, Mowrer found happiness with Molly and their growing family, which eventually included a son and two daughters, and in professional success in research and well-regarded publications. The latter led to a joint appointment in psychology and graduate education at Harvard in 1940, with brief service in World War II in the Office of Strategic Services assessing the psychological fortitude of those slated for special and dangerous wartime service. Mowrer felt hypocritical, knowing those on whom he passed judgment were superior psychologically to himself.

Mowrer eventually looked back on his first youthful bout with depression as an attack of conscience for some undisclosed adolescent sexual perversion. By his own account, the guilt he carried robbed him of the joy of living and led down some bizarre paths, including, at the behest of Dr. Hanns Sachs, a Freud associate with whom he underwent another try at psychoanalysis, blaming his mother for inadequacies on her part. Further, his first two psychoanalysts claimed, despite what Mowrer called his "irresponsible sexuality," that he was sexually repressed; Mowrer's inference "that a little extra-marital sex might be 'therapeutic' for me" led to infidelity after nine years of happy marriage. The result was disastrous. Ultimately, his long wallowing in the slough of Freudianism with its theories of superegos and sexual repression led to disillusionment and swearing off psychoanalysis altogether. In 1945, he finally confessed *all* his sins to Molly, who, though hurt, proved forgiving and supportive. "From a strictly 'therapeutic' point of view," he said decades later, "that 'hour of truth' with my wife did more to heal and release me from neurotic bondage than all the professional 'help' I had previously received." No analyst had ever even hinted at such a course. In his own professional work, Mowrer became convinced of an honest autobiographical or "self-disclosure" approach to healing; in fact, he became the acknowledged progenitor of "integrity therapy." [17]

Mowrer's self-disclosure seemed to lead to eight years of tranquility. During the 1940s he resisted inquiries from Louisiana State University and New York University for chairmanships, but he finally left Harvard in 1948, lured away by the University of Illinois as research professor of psychology. He continued to climb in the profession. Election to the Council of Representatives of the American Psychological Association was a preamble to his election to the APA's Board of Directors and to the presidency of two divisions—Clinical Psychological, and Personality and Social Psychology—and ultimately, in 1953, to the presidency of the American Psychological Association itself. Scores of published papers were interspersed with a number of important books, including *Frustration and Aggression* coauthored in 1939, *Learning Theory and Personality Dynamics* and three volumes of *Patterns of Modern Living*, all in 1950, and *Psychotherapy—Theory and Research* and *Learning Theory and Symbolic Processes* a decade later. Much more was still to come. Unfortunately, he suffered his worst psychological collapse in the summer and fall of 1953, commencing even as he traveled to California for summer teaching at Berkeley. Checking into a Chicago mental facility, he became suicidal, lost touch with reality, and suffered the psychotic torments of deep depression. Return to reality left him thinking he would be professionally disgraced, his family destroyed, and that he was generally finished— "through"—he called it later. Grateful for the kindness and patience of the professionals at the hospital, Mowrer was astonished at the action of his colleagues, who elected him to the APA presidency anyway, and with the notice that he would appear in *Who's Who*.[18]

Fortunately, he soon recovered and resumed his professional activities. In 1956, the Alumni Association and the College of Arts and Science at his old alma mater, the University of Missouri, invited him to return to speak during Arts and Science Week, at which he would receive one of the first three Citations of Merit in the school's history. The idea was to inspire undergraduates with the achievements of Missouri grads who had distinguished themselves in life. Mowrer's attitude when he learned of the impending honor typified his genuine humility, likely nurtured in part by his bouts with the hellish side of life. He asked his friend Fred McKinney, a distinguished psychologist who had been at Missouri for twenty-five years, if he had heard correctly. "Do me a favor, will you, Fred?" he asked. "If there's some mistake about this, just let me know. If not, then sort of take me in hand and give me a 'briefing' for the big event!" Mowrer, a self-effacing genius who had been associated with some of the most prestigious academic institutions in the nation and whose colleagues had elevated him to the pinnacle of his profession, grew wistful about returning to Mizzou, the place of both victory and defeat so long before. "I am, of course," he told McKinney, "very grateful for this honor—and, I may say, a little sentimental about it all."[19]

He enjoyed his exile's return. To eager undergraduates at his alma mater he spoke on "Psychology, Then and Now" and reminisced about his undergraduate days, his fascination with Max Meyer and the aura he created, and how after his first year on campus, as he put it, "the thought never so much as entered my head that I would or could be anything but a psychologist."[20]

Max Meyer, long exiled in Florida, reminisced a bit himself that same year, telling his former student they were "co-victims of that insanity which once struck the president and curators of the University of Missouri," a place he had not visited in nearly a quarter century. He long before had absolved the curators ("a crazed board," he once told Erwin Esper). Back in 1932 he had told Winterton Curtis that Brooks had set them up, that they had fallen in the president's trap. "That they were unnecessarily stubborn afterwards is human nature," he said. "We are all that way." Now, in 1956, referring to the rising Civil Rights movement, Meyer noted that the problems of Missouri in the questionnaire scandal weren't exactly the same, but were "analogous to the insanity which at present is striking the campuses of the Universities of Alabama and Mississippi. Mankind," he told Mowrer, "is still far from deserving to be called 'homo sapiens.'"[21]

Mowrer also had occasion to reflect on his long-ago run-in with university authorities and midwestern Victorianism. He often "cringed" at the thought of that "sophomoric" preamble he had written for the questionnaire. His part in the whole deal was "pretty silly," he thought, though maybe not so bad given his youth at the time. Mowrer had no problem taking responsibility for all manner of personal transgressions, but decades after the questionnaire fiasco, he still thought his elders could have done better. He wondered why Meyer and other faculty members didn't have that reaction then. In 1962, he told Leland Hazard, then working on his memoirs wherein Meyer appeared victimized in a clear academic freedom issue, that he, Mowrer, was approaching the age Meyer had been at the time of that project, and believed he would respond differently if the situation had been presented to him. Mowrer didn't think Meyer showed much maturity in the matter, the same deficiency that eventually wrecked his marriage. He wasn't out to trash his old mentor, whom he had regarded, along with Knight Dunlap at Johns Hopkins, with a sort of "youthful veneration," but he sensed that Hazard was making a heroic figure of Meyer, something Mowrer didn't think had merit. He and Molly had visited Meyer in Florida in 1956 and found him his exasperating old self. To Erwin Esper, then working on Meyer's intellectual biography, Mowrer claimed Meyer had always been something of a "Prussian." He was also a seriously flawed human being—stubborn, hard to be around, and, as always, "perilously close to paranoia." It was a wonder that he never fell apart. Mowrer had warm feelings for his old professor—he was even a bit protective of him—but he didn't think the curators had been entirely at fault. Still later, Mowrer said he believed the questionnaire "was poorly constructed scientifically and involved bad judgment, but the 'reaction' that occurred was all out of proportion to the facts of the case."[22]

After Mowrer's psychotic breakdown in 1953, he gave formal religion another look. He and his family took instruction and joined a Presbyterian church near the Illinois campus and, despite its benefits, discovered that much of Christendom's clergy, seminary professors, and even local membership had "accepted Freud" the way an earlier culture had counseled the acceptance of Christ. His thirty-year hiatus from religion since his freshman year in college had left him unaware of both what he regarded as the church's disastrous embrace of Freud and also the evangelical revival that had been underway in earnest since the 1940s. The former, to Mowrer, suggested the church's "decline and desperation" and was "a sad reflection on its discernment and competence." But Mowrer's reading in the history of Christianity revealed the therapeutic value of the early Church's *koinonia* group confession and restitution for sin. For "creedal" reasons he left the Presbyterian church in the mid-1960s, disdained easy or cheap grace, but developed an "integrity therapy" of confession. Owning up to one's transgressions was a basis for healing and atonement. In 1959, the American Psychological Association was treated to what *Time* called "a soul-searching symposium entitled 'The Role of the Concept of Sin in Psychotherapy,'" wherein "famed Researcher O. Hobart Mowrer" damned a Freudian straw-man and claimed that future therapy would "take guilt, confession and expiation seriously and will involve programs of action rather than mere groping for 'insight.'" Later, he rejected justification by faith whether espoused by St. Paul, Martin Luther, or John Calvin, views that showed up in *The Crisis in Psychiatry and Religion* in 1961.

Though Mowrer became internationally acclaimed for his self-help integrity therapy approach, and believed deeply in its efficacy, by the early 1970s he became less sanguine about the movement's longevity. In sum and over his lifetime, Mowrer's work seemed to be all over the psychological map. He wandered from physiological psychology early on, to psychology of learning, then psychology of languages, and then psychotherapy. But whether it was personality dynamics, spatial orientation, learning theory, or integrity therapy, it all added up, said one colleague, to "a coherent search for mental health and a theoretical formula for it."[23] Ironically, the anticipated magazine article on the attitudes of his fellow undergraduate students never saw print, but more than two hundred publications eventually carried his name, including several important books. None could know when he prowled Jesse Hall that the work he started under Professor Meyer would take him to the pinnacle of his profession and make him one of the premier psychologists of the middle of the twentieth century—the boy from Unionville whose father hoped that one day he might be a university man.

Mowrer retired from the University of Illinois in 1975, yet still published and retained great interest in life and the world. Long celebrated and written about in the profession and noted in the press, the anchors of his life remained what they had always been—Molly and their three children. The kids were already established in their own lives. Molly, however, suffered health problems, "primarily cardiovascular," he wrote later, "resulting first in serious heart insufficiencies and then in a stroke, which largely incapacitated the left side of her body but impaired her good mind and engaging personality very little. It was still a great joy to be with her; and when, in the early morning of March 5, 1979, she died peacefully in her sleep, something inexpressibly precious went out of my life."[24]

Mowrer published a bit after that and took pleasure in his garden, but looked at the world with sad pessimism. The best days for the world seemed past, juxtaposed against his own "particularly happy childhood" marked by role and order and his own useful life. He had come a long way since those days in Jesse Hall. This decent and self-effacing man would gladly have given up his bouts with depression but knew they had helped define his career and even some of his profession. He recalled a boyhood story that every dog needed some fleas to remind him that he was a dog. That was life. But now he felt that ill health threatened to drain his resources and deprive his children of a tangible legacy. He had long contemplated death by suicide but had resisted, knowing he was needed and that he would recover from depression. Three years after Molly's death, Mowrer believed his usefulness had been exhausted. In June 1982, at age seventy-five, he ended his life.[25]

2

Meanwhile, Mowrer's alma mater put the embarrassment behind it and reached upwards in academics, eventually boasting Research I status and gaggles of National Merit Scholars. Columbia became rated among the most livable cities in the nation. Victorian buildings on the Quad, subject of demolition talk in the 1960s, got put on the National Register of Historic Places in 1974, and the infamous columns, dating from 1843, became one of the most visited tourist spots in the state. The Columbia campus and that of the School of Mines at Rolla were joined by schools in St. Louis and Kansas City to make a four-campus university in 1963; buildings proliferated, curricula were modernized, and student enrollments swelled to more than forty thousand at all four sites. Students coming to Columbia from all fifty states and more than a hundred foreign countries could choose from among more than 250 degree programs.[26]

If some things about college life remained the same, others changed. Nationally, the Jazz Age yielded to Depression-era Swing. Elizabeth Eldridge observed the college scene in the *Saturday Evening Post* in 1937 and found that students still jellied at Mizzou "with both parties consciously priding themselves on making the drink last as long as possible without overt dawdling." But she claimed that students nationwide in 1937 had declared "Joe College" of the 1920s dead and gone. The raccoon coat also disappeared, as did the tie and jacket. But the guys still migrated to the cute clothes-and-date-conscious females as in the days of "the candid-kneed, boyish-figured flapper of the F. Scott Fitzgerald era." And while female students still couldn't go into frat houses unchaperoned, the guys, always on the lookout for potential new dates, still made themselves at home in the sorority houses. The supposed "New Seriousness" of the Depression-era college student was also belied by the great numbers who knew nothing of the Spanish Civil War or of Mussolini's aggression in Abyssinia. Nor had the bull session changed much—in sororities it centered on men, marriage, and kids. Nothing was new there. At the frat house the bull still focused on women, marriage, and money-making, along, of course, with the meaning of life. The slang changed slightly. "Once upon a time you 'spooned,'" noted Eldridge, "then you 'petted,' after that you 'necked'—still the most widely used term—but now you may 'smooch' or 'perch,' or, reaching the heights of college argot, you may 'pitch and sling woo.'"

That same year, *Life* surveyed the American college experience and stopped in Columbia for a look. "Smack in the centre of Missouri and of the U.S.A. lies the University of Missouri with its 6000 students," chortled *Life*. It was not as big as Ohio State or California, nor so progressive as Wisconsin or so liberal as Minnesota. It had, after all, a "southern tradition" that made it a conservative place. "Otherwise," said *Life*, "Missouri is the typical State university. Since it is a land-grant school, under the controlling eye of politicians who demand practical results, its students learn by doing things." They ran the *Columbia Missourian* and the university farm, marched every Wednesday on the Quad in required military education, and jellied at Gaebler's Black and Gold. It was the Depression, but the guys still gave up daytime corduroys for jackets and slacks in the evening. Greeks dominated social life on campus as usual and some sororities seemed snootier than ever. But the old Bible Class started by Miss Burrall was the biggest in the world, or so they said.[27]

A dozen years later, *Life* visited Mizzou again, this time developing a cover story comparing a public university with, of all places, Smith College, the private woman's school that had its own questionnaire scandal a quarter of a century before. Stratton Brooks's daughter had even gone to Smith. At Missouri, Greeks still dominated, students still danced and drank cokes and beer, and still hung out at the rock quarry for Sunday afternoon swimming. They also jellied around campus, but not for much longer. The magazine compared Jane Stone, a Chi Omega at Missouri, with Janet Trowbridge at Smith. "They represented two sides of a good argument," claimed *Life*; "Jane believes that only at a coed college like Missouri can she get a rounded education for living as well as thinking. She thinks woman's colleges like Smith are stuffy. Janet believes that a woman's college is the only place for a real education and that coed institutions like Missouri are just date factories." *Life* added: "Either Jane or Janet could be right—educators have never been able to agree."[28]

Jane Stone had a full social life at Mizzou at midcentury and said she would die before being caught on campus in blue jeans. Change was coming, but it didn't have much to do with the "modern youth" of the 1920s. In 1967, *Look* stopped in Columbia, not to visit Gaebler's or the columns on the Quad, but rather to have a look at the drug scene at Missouri, a port-of-call for an itinerant dealer on his rounds of midwestern universities. College life in the late 1960s was light-years from anything the campus or the nation had seen. A confluence of social and political streams produced a river of change unknown in the celebration of youth in the 1920s or in the stereotypical conformity of the 1950s. None of the stereotypes fit any of those decades perfectly, but the arguments in the late sixties were not over permission to leave town or Dean Priddy's requirements for chaperons, nor even about a sex questionnaire. Now the loudest debates were global—about war, civil rights, alienation, politics, and liberation; and about a countercultural and often drug-skewered rejection of middle-class values. At home there was plenty of argument about free speech and curricula. While shifts in American culture trace to the 1920s and even earlier, the exponential changes date from a later generation. As late as 1960, a University of Kansas couple, missing late at night from their respective dorm rooms, was taken into custody after police found them in a motel in town. The young man was expelled for the balance of the term. But change was coming, and in loco parentis at colleges and universities declined rapidly after the mid-1960s.[29] A few years later, the University of Missouri debated long and hard before granting male-female intervisitation in university housing.

Hobart Mowrer's fellow students in the 1920s were just ahead of the leading edge of *The Greatest Generation*, much acclaimed for enduring a depression, winning a world war, and raising families. But the university students of the 1920s were in the generation that Franklin Roosevelt in 1936 claimed had "a rendezvous with destiny." They also endured the Great Depression, fought World War II, and some of them, for better or worse, begat members of the "Baby Boom" generation. They had little in common with rebellious youths later in the century, or with the coarsening of American culture, the blatant loss of shame, and the decline of any semblance of role and order. Such profane developments trace not from the culture wars of the 1920s, but to the complicated changing American society most notable since World War II. The seeds of a genuine counterculture in the 1960s, fertilized by general prosperity and attendant youthful alienation, drug abuse, and lots of other things, and catalyzed by an anti-war movement, produced an ugly harvest decades later. Will Hays, the movie monitor who made sure America's middle class kept coming back to neighborhood theaters, would never be welcomed in Hollywood again, but never was he needed so much. Cultural decay was complemented by the rise of speech codes on university campuses and in society in general. Curricula were now dictated by counter-cultural political pressures every bit as great as the remnants of Victorianism decades before; at the same time, free inquiry struggled against stifling anti-intellectual "thought police" as debilitating as societal restraints in the 1920s. In fact, despite the alienated writers and the moral adjustments of college students, the 1920s never witnessed a serious and sustained challenge to the concept of standards, or of absolute truth itself. One limited questionnaire given to sixty college students, as well as to parents, grandparents, and others in the 1920s seemed to suggest that the students decided issues on a more pragmatic basis than their elders. But the study acknowledged that that's what the students said, not necessarily what they really did, and that twenty years down the line, they might respond the same as their parents. In reality, tradition's mortal enemies—sin without guilt, loss of shame, the elevation of the base and the decline of the noble, and much more—lay far in the future.

In time, of course, the sex questionnaire scandal "that figuratively shook the Columns" was largely forgotten. It got passing mention here and there in a historical article or book, or in a Sunday feature story. But students at Mizzou during that raucous period likely never forgot the experience. One 1927 journalism graduate recalled her own involvement with the questionnaire six decades later: "Hidden among my keepsakes all these years," she said, "is a now yellowed copy of the questionnaire that reached St. Louis, where on the evening of April 12 [1929], the young man I was then dating slipped it to me, folded just as it is to this day. Bob and I never discussed its specific content—heavens no! Had I shown it to my elderly spinster landladies, the shock might have robbed me of my $5-a-week third floor room." "By today's standards," she added, "the questions on sexual relationships and marriage that threatened to wreck a state university in '29 are so tame that my 8-year-old great granddaughter could take some of them in stride."[30]

The point was well taken. But to the declining Victorian generation in the 1920s, the moral foundation of American culture was under mortal assault. Honorable men and women conscientiously and understandably decried the destruction of the passing order. Even showing moving pictures on Sunday by the end of the decade was a shock to cultural conservatives. For those opposed to Sunday movies, said a columnist in the

Missouri Student in 1929, "It must seem that the bottom has fallen out of everything. They have had to stand by to see the acceptance of bobbed hair, sockless men, rouged lips, short skirts, summer furs, women smoking, the Charleston, girls saying 'dam.' [*sic*] The coming of Sunday shows must be looked on as the last straw to this civilization; these people must be somewhat shattered and without hope for the present generation."

The sex questionnaire fiasco at the University of Missouri simply pointed up the growing fissure in American culture. While the predicted eclipse of marriage fortunately never happened, the collision of change and continuity in the 1920s was real, perhaps even inevitable; the moral letdown after the war had also been real; attitudinal shifts were palpable. Perhaps the questionnaire was a flawed attempt by the rising generation to come to terms with modern life, bolstered by the brashness of the sociological enterprise that it naively thought might guide the way. But if the Victorians were going to build a backfire against growing change, they needed to build it further back on safer, more rational ground. Their negative response, like the imposition of Prohibition, noble in intent, was a heavy-handed attempt to enforce homogeneity on an increasingly pluralistic culture. The same was true of Progressive efforts to maintain a uniform morality in a fragmenting society. H. L. Mencken's oft-cited Puritan-bashing was really an attack on Victorian culture. Whether Puritan or Victorian, both demanded something the twentieth century wouldn't or couldn't accept.

The chairman of Cornell University's Board of Trustees, Frank Hiscock, lamented early in the 1920s that all things once held unshakable were now under assault, the sort of thing that F. Scott Fitzgerald fantasized about in era-defining fiction. Nothing seemed firm anymore, said Hiscock. Universities were attacked for using academic freedom to protect radicals and visionaries who would destroy democratic government and free enterprise. "I think," he said, "that this accusation is greatly exaggerated." Hiscock might have added social liberals to the mix, those who challenged Victorian concepts of home and family and held strange notions about marriage, divorce, and women's place in society. In 1926, the *St. Louis Post-Dispatch*, the paper that would prove most friendly to the kids in the questionnaire scandal, turned the whole argument on its head, claiming that it was not "flaming youth" which produced social change, but their parents, the face-lifted flapper and the old guy who "puts on a Kollege-Kut dinner-jacket and goes out to learn the Charleston." "The jazz palaces and gin mills are supported by men and women in the roaring forties, the fatuous fifties and the naughty sixties," claimed the paper. It added: "Many a daughter has learned to smoke cigarettes from her charming mother. Many a boy has been encouraged by his papa to become a flask-toter. Who get the divorces?" The *Post-Dispatch* exaggerated, of course. The truth was that society often saw radical "flaming youth" fomenting cultural revolution where there were only "modern youth" challenging social constraints. Charges of "moral laxity" and vice of one sort or another mixed with positive claims that "The old prudery is giving way to frankness," and that "Victorian idealism was a soft, cowardly way out."

Hedonistic retreat from Wilsonian ideals may have been real among some Americans, but rumors of wild rebellion in the culture wars of the decade were often just that—rumors. One cultural observer noted in 1927 that "the youthful generation is probably without historic parallel," and that they had rejected a phony good-versus-evil approach to life, looking instead for "a morality pure and undefiled." That was slightly silly, but it *was* true that the kids of the Jazz Age created something of a new moral code—not Victorian, but not hostile to tradition's moral values either. They weren't as wild as everyone thought.

That was the plea of Washington University's *Student Life* during the heated questionnaire debate in 1929. The paper complained that the ruling generation always looked for evidence of the irresponsible rebellion of youth, and pleaded with the authorities to leave their sister institution alone. It was more stereotype than reality. When the decade was over, the *Missouri Student* complained that even though women were coming alive at the university, they hadn't "attained their rightful place on this campus." The newspaper thought that the university should be a leader in change but was actually "one of the last bulwarks of medievalism to go down before the modern women's crusade for equality. But anyone familiar with the situation on this campus must admit that it is still a Man's School." Maybe that was partly because men outnumbered women two to one, but it was also because tradition yet reigned, double standards and all. Tradition lived, robust, to see society through depression and war. After all, the 1920s undermined not tradition, just the last vestiges of the Victorians' world. And at the end of the 1920s regrets were few. Maybe Hobart Mowrer's friends who were young and filled with energy and expectation in that exciting decade would agree with him, that maybe his assessment of his own life applied to them and their generation as well. "Not long ago," Mowrer wrote at the end of his life, "someone asked me, if I could live my life over again, in what ways would I like to change it. Half-facetiously, I said I wouldn't change it in the slightest detail—I would be too afraid I wouldn't be so lucky."[31]

Abbreviations

AAUP   American Association of University Professors

AAUPP   American Association of University Professors Papers, now housed in the Special Collections Department, Gelman Library, The George Washington University, Washington, D.C.

AP   Associated Press

BP   Edwin Bayer Branson Papers, Western Historical Manuscript Collection, Ellis Library, University of Missouri-Columbia

CP   Winterton Conway Curtis Papers, Western Historical Manuscript Collection, Ellis Library, University of Missouri-Columbia

EP   Erwin Esper Papers, Special Collections, Main Library, University of Washington, Seattle

GP   North Todd Gentry Papers, Western Historical Manuscript Collection, Ellis Library, University of Missouri-Columbia

GNPP   George N. Peek Papers, Western Historical Manuscript Collection, Ellis Library, University of Missouri-Columbia

LEAP   Lewis E. Atherton Papers, Western Historical Manuscript Collection, Ellis Library, University of Missouri-Columbia

MP   O. Hobart Mowrer Papers, Archives, Main Library, University of Illinois, Urbana-Champaign

SCELUM   Special Collections, Ellis Library, University of Missouri-Columbia

SCMLUI	Special Collections, Main Library, University of Iowa, Iowa City
SCRLUC	Special Collections, Regenstein Library, University of Chicago
SLWP	Sara Lockwood Williams Papers, Western Historical Manuscript Collection, Ellis Library, University of Missouri-Columbia
SP	Frank Fletcher Stephens Papers, Western Historical Manuscript Collection, Ellis Library, University of Missouri-Columbia
TC	Peter Tamony Collection, Western Historical Manuscript Collection, Ellis Library, University of Missouri-Columbia
UMBCR	University of Missouri Board of Curators Records, Western Historical Manuscript Collection, Ellis Library, University of Missouri-Columbia
UMPOP	University of Missouri President's Office Papers, Western Historical Manuscript Collection, Ellis Library, University of Missouri-Columbia
UMSBPAR	University of Missouri School of Business and Public Administration Records, Western Historical Manuscript Collection, Ellis Library, University of Missouri-Columbia
UP	United Press
VHFP	Viles-Hosmer Family Papers, Western Historical Manuscript Collection, Ellis Library, University of Missouri-Columbia
WP	Jesse E. Wrench Papers, Western Historical Manuscript Collection, Ellis Library, University of Missouri-Columbia

Notes

Preface

1. Lewis Erenberg, *Steppin' Out: New York Nightlife and the Transformation of American Culture, 1890–1930* (Chicago: University of Chicago Press, 1981), 234 (quote); see also Henry F. May, *The End of American Innocence: A Study of the First Years of Our Own Time, 1912–1917* (1959; reprt., Chicago: Quadrangle Books, Inc., 1964; see review excerpts on back cover of the latter); William Leuchtenburg, *The Perils of Prosperity, 1914–1932* (1958; 2d ed., Chicago: University of Chicago Press, 1993), 157–77; Thomas Hine, *The Rise and Fall of the American Teenager* (New York: Avon Books, 1999); see also Frederick Lewis Allen, *Only Yesterday: An Informal History of the 1920's;* Paul Carter, *Another Part of the Twenties* (New York: Columbia University Press, 1977); Stanley Coben, *Rebellion against Victorianism: The Impetus for Cultural Change in 1920s America* (New York: Oxford University Press, 1991); Ann Douglas, *Terrible Honesty: Mongrel Manhattan in the 1920s* (New York: Farrar, Straus, and Giroux, 1995); Lynn Dumenil, "Re-Shifting Perspectives on the 1920s: Recent Trends in Social and Cultural History," in John Earl Haynes, ed., *Calvin Coolidge and the Coolidge Era: Essays on the History of the 1920s* (Washington, D.C.: Library of Congress, 1998), 63–96; Lynn Dumenil, *The Modern Temper: American Culture and Society in the 1920s* (New York: Hill and Wang, 1995); Dorothy M. Brown, *Setting a Course: American Women in the 1920s* (Boston: Twayne, 1987); Charles Eagles, "Urban-Rural Conflict in the 1920s: A Historiographical Assessment," *Historian* 49 (November 1986): 26–48; Lewis Erenberg, *Swingin' the Dream: Big Band Jazz and the Rebirth of American Culture* (Chicago: University of Chicago Press, 1998); Paula Fass, *The Damned and the Beautiful: American Youth in the 1920's* (New York: Oxford University Press, 1977; paperback, 1979); Ellis Hawley, *The Great War and the Search for a Modern Order, A History of the American People and Their Institutions, 1917–1933* (New York: St. Martin's Press, 1979); Don S. Kirschner, "Conflicts and Politics in the 1920's: Historiography and Prospects," *Mid-America* 48 (October 1966): 219–33; Estelle B. Freedman, "The New Woman: Changing Views of Women in the 1920s," *Journal of American History* 61 (September 1974): 372–93; Daniel J. Leab, "Coolidge, Hays, and 1920s Movies: Some Aspects of Image and Reality," in Haynes, ed., *Calvin Coolidge and the Coolidge Era,* 97–131; Lawrence W. Levine, "Progress and Nostalgia: The Self Image of the Nineteen Twenties," in *The Unpredictable Past: Explorations in American Cultural History* (New York: Oxford University Press, 1993), 189–205; Henry F. May, "Shifting Perspectives on the 1920's," *Mississippi Valley Historical Review* 43 (December

1956): 405–27; Roderick Nash, *The Nervous Generation: American Thought, 1917–1930* (1970; reprt., Chicago: Ivan R. Dee, 1990); Burl Noggle, "The Twenties: A New Historiographical Frontier," *Journal of American History* 53 (September 1966): 299–314; Geoffrey Perrett, *America in the Twenties: A History* (New York: Touchstone Book by Simon and Schuster, 1982).

2. Fass, *The Damned and the Beautiful*, 376 (quote); Allen, *Only Yesterday*, 81–89.

3. See Levine, "Progress and Nostalgia," 189–205.

4. Peter Gay, *Pleasure Wars: Victoria to Freud* (New York and London: Oxford University Press, 1998), 20–23.

5. Coben, *Rebellion against Victorianism*, 158.

6. See ibid.

1. "A Filthy Questionnaire"

1. Priddy testimony, AAUP Hearing, AAUP; Priddy to Brooks, March 13, 1929, UMPOP; see return envelope in UMPOP.

2. *Columbia Daily Tribune*, March 13, 1929, UMPOP.

2. Rumors of Sex

1. Brooks to Charles O. Wright, March 27, 1929, UMPOP; see Brooks testimony, AAUP Hearing, AAUPP; see also Priddy to Brooks, March 13, 1929, UMPOP; *Columbia Daily Tribune*, March 13, 1929; *Kansas City Star*, March 14, 1929; *St. Louis Globe Democrat*, March 14, 1929; Brooks to Isaac H. Lionberger, March 15, 1929, UMPOP; Brooks testimony, AAUP Hearing, AAUPP; *St. Louis Globe Democrat* (?) n.d., AAUP. Brooks later said he had no remembrance of using the terms "sewer sociology" or "sewer psychology" in interviews. Brooks testimony, AAUP Hearing, AAUPP.

2. *Kansas City Star*, March 14, 1929, UMPOP; *St. Louis Globe-Democrat*, n.d., AAUPP, including reprint in unidentified newspaper; *Sikeston Standard*, March 19, 1929, UMPOP.

3. *Columbia Evening Missourian*, March 15, 1929; *St. Louis Globe Democrat*, March 15, 1929; *Kansas City Times*, March 15, 1929 (quote); H. G. C. Baldry to Brooks, March 15, 1929; Anonymous to Gentry, March 16, 1929, UMPOP.

4. *Missouri Alumnus*, June 1928; see also Gentry, How to Hold the Young People in Sunday, unpublished address, April 1903, Gentry Papers, 49; *Columbia Daily Tribune*, October 27, 1923.

5. Gentry to V. C. Rose, Jr., December 6, 1928 (copy); Gentry to T. S. Mosby, November 19, 1928; Gentry to Leslie Rudolph, November 19, 1928, GP. During the questionnaire scandal a wild accusation surfaced that the furor was part of a conspiracy to embarrass Brooks and replace him as president with former governor Baker, a close Gentry friend and ally. Gentry would then become dean of the university's law school. But such conspiracies were out of character for Gentry, and even Brooks privately dismissed such talk as "wholly gossip." Newspaper clipping, n.d., AAUPP; Brooks to Robert S. Clough, April 1, 1929, UMPOP.

6. Newspaper clippings, n.d. (datelined March 16), AAUPP; T. C. Owen to Gentry, March 22, 1929; E. L. Hobart to Gentry, March 22, 1929; Mary Phillips to Gentry, March 24, 1929; G. W. Sneed to Brooks, March 22, 1929; Ralph W. Wilson to Gentry, March 18, 1929; see John R. Hall to Gentry, March 18, 1929 (Hall claimed he had "much data" about socialist, communist, and other groups who were attacking the family); Clifford Moore to Gentry, March 18, 1929; Margaret N. McCluer to Gentry, March 20, 1929; see numerous other relevant communications, all in GP.

7. Brooks testimony, AAUP Hearing ("publicity" quote), 111–12, AAUPP; *St. Louis Globe Democrat*, March 15, 1929, UMPOP. Referring to the lecture and its cancellation, one constituent told North Todd Gentry, "Have we not enough parasitical lecturers and reformers here without importing them?" Anonymous to Gentry, March 16, 1929, UMPOP. *Columbia Evening Missourian*, March 15, 1929; *St. Louis Globe Democrat*, March 15, 1929, UMPOP; newspaper clipping, n.d., AAUPP.

8. Congratulatory letter to Brooks, March 14, 1929; Supporter to Brooks, March 14, 1929; 1909 Alumnus to Brooks, March 18, 1929, UMPOP.

9. Circuit Court Judge to Brooks, March 15, 1929; St. Louisan to Brooks, March 15, 1929, UMPOP; see also St. Louisan to Gentry, March 18, 1929, GP; Postmaster to Brooks, March 15, 1929; telegram, *Mexico Ledger* editor to Brooks, March 16, 1929, UMPOP.

10. *Kansas City Star*, March 16, 1929; *St. Louis Post-Dispatch*, March 17, 1929, UMPOP; see also newspaper clipping (datelined March 16, 1929), AAUPP.

11. Crank to Brooks, March 16, 1929, UMPOP.

12. *Fort Scott Tribune-Monitor* editor to Brooks, March 16, 1929, with clipping from *Fort Scott Tribune-Monitor*, March 16, 1929, and enclosed questionnaire; Brooks to *Fort Scott Tribune-Monitor* Editor, March 26, 1929, UMPOP. Missouri's questionnaire, Brooks told the editor, was "so much more indecent than the one you attached as to make yours seem very mild indeed."

13. See copies of the questionnaire in UMPOP; original in BP; see also *Bulletin of the American Association of University Professors* 16 (February 1930): 163–66.

14. *Columbia Daily Tribune*, March 13, 1929; Priddy to Brooks, March 13, 1929, UMPOP.

15. *St. Louis Globe Democrat*, March 14, 1929, UMPOP; Brooks testimony, AAUP Hearing, AAUPP.

16. *St. Louis Globe-Democrat*, March 15, 16, 1929, UMPOP; March 16, 1929, also in AAUPP; see also newspaper clipping (UP story, datelined March 14, 1929), AAUPP.

17. Sedalia Attorney (with handwritten notations to Gentry) to Williams, March 18, 1929; Williams to Sedalia Attorney, March 19, 1929, GP; *Kansas City Star* (?), March 21, 1929, UMPOP. The *Kansas City Times* scored Jones for his behavior: "There should be no ulterior consideration, such as has been thoughtlessly projected into the case by Chairman Jones." Editorial reproduced in *Columbia Missourian*, March n.d., 1929, UMPOP; Kirk Jones to Editor, *Globe-Democrat*, n.d. (March 15, 1929); *St. Louis (Daily) Globe-Democrat*, two copies in two different editions, one n.d., one March 20, 1929, AAUPP.

18. *Columbia Evening Missourian*, March 18, 1929, UMPOP; unidentified copy also in AAUPP; *St. Louis Star*, March 19, 1929 (all quotes except last two), UMPOP; see also *St. Louis Globe-Democrat*, n.d., dateline March 18 (also "all worked up"

quote), AAUPP; *St. Louis Post Dispatch*, March 19, 1929, UMPOP; newspaper clipping, AP story datelined March 19 (last two quotes), AAUPP; see other relevant newspaper clippings in AAUPP.

19. James H. Jones, *Alfred C. Kinsey: A Public/Private Life* (New York: W. W. Norton, 1997), 43, 232; May, *The End of American Innocence*, 182, 373, 376; Ben Lindsey and Wainwright Evans, *The Revolt of Modern Youth* (1925; reprt., Seattle: University of Washington Press, 1973, Introduction by Charles E. Larsen), 1–8; Ben Lindsey and Wainwright Evans, *The Companionate Marriage* (New York: Boni and Liveright, 1927); in all or most of his writings, the undereducated Lindsey provided substance while others provided the prose. See *Debate between Judge Ben Lindsey and G. C. Brewer on "Companionate Marriage,"* Memphis Auditorium, April 2, 1928 (Cincinnati: The Christian Leader Corporation, 1928); *Judge Ben B. Lindsey on The Child—The Movie—and Censorship* (New York: Motion Picture Producers and Distributors of America, Inc., n.d.); see also Ben Lindsey, "An Answer to the Critics of the Companionate Marriage," June 5, 1929, "Foreword" from an edition of Lindsey and Evans, *The Companionate Marriage*, and taken partly from *Outlook*, April 28, 1929 (copy in Pamphlet Collections, Duke University Library); Fass, *The Damned and the Beautiful*, 31–34, 38–40, 42; Perrett, *America in the Twenties*, 160; Gilman M. Ostrander, *American Civilization in the First Machine Age, 1890–1940* (New York: Harper and Row, 1970), 252–53.

20. Newspaper clippings, one n.d., one March 20, 1929 (Lindsey quotes); two newspaper clippings, n.d. (datelined March 16, 1929, both UP), AAUPP.

21. 1921 Alumnus to Brooks, March 18, 1929; Kansas City Critic to Brooks, March 18, 1929; Journalism School Grad to Brooks, March 17, 1929, UMPOP.

22. Kansas City Couple to Brooks, March 18, 1929, UMPOP; Richard Kirkendall, *A History of Missouri, Volume V, 1919 to 1953* (Columbia: University of Missouri Press, 1986), 110–11; Linda Brown-Kubisch and Christine Montgomery, "Show Me Missouri History: Celebrating the Century Part 2," *Missouri Historical Review* 94 (April 2000): 318; *Bulletin of the American Association of University Professors* 16 (March 1930): 226–44; Kansas City School Principal to Brooks, March 18, 1929, UMPOP; Charles W. Saylor to Editor of the *Post-Dispatch*, n.d., AAUPP; Kansas City Physician to Brooks, March 19, 1929 ("mole hill" quote); 1912 Alumnus to Brooks, March 18, 1929; John D. McCutcheon to Brooks, March 18, 1929 (St. Louis alumni), UMPOP; see copy of McCutcheon letter also in VHFP.

23. Clay County Alumni President to Brooks, March 16, 1929; Kansas City Woman to Brooks, March 17, 1929; Telegram, Parent to Brooks, March 17, 1929; Tulsa Editor to Brooks, March 19, 1929, UMPOP; see also other relevant supportive letters and telegrams in UMPOP.

24. *St. Louis Post-Dispatch*, March 17, 1929; *St. Louis Globe-Democrat*, March 17, 1929, *St. Louis Star*, March 19, 1929, and other relevant newspaper clippings in UMPOP and AAUPP; Cole testimony, Executive Committee Hearing; *Kansas City Star*, March 16 (17?), 1929 ("right to petition" quote); *St. Louis Post-Dispatch*, March 18, 1929, UMPOP.

25. *St. Louis Post-Dispatch*, March 18, 1929, UMPOP (slightly different edition datelined March 18 and presumably published March 19 in AAUPP); see also *Columbia Evening Missourian*, March 18, 1929, UMPOP.

26. *Columbia Daily Tribune*, March 18, 1929; newspaper clipping, UP story, n.d. (datelined March 18), AAUPP; see also James and Vera Olson, *The University of*

Missouri: An Illustrated History (Columbia: University of Missouri Press, 1988), 56–57, 61; *Missouri Student*, March 19, 1929, AAUPP; John Beahler, "A Sense of Place," *Mizzou* (spring 2001): 19.

27. DeGraff to Brooks, March 15, 1929; *St. Louis Post-Dispatch*, March 18, 1929; Jensen to Brooks, March 19, 1929, UMPOP; *St. Louis Post-Dispatch*, n.d. (datelined March 18), AAUPP. Jensen excoriated the press for its "direct violation of the ethical code upon which the press prides itself." The press had made no attempt to contact him, he said. In the final analysis, all a teacher had was a hard-earned reputation, and the paper's inclusion of him constituted what Jensen called "newspaper sabotage upon my property rights in my professional standing as ruthless as any that can be committed with dynamite." He asked Brooks to review correspondence from others about his professional standing, part of which, in justice to himself, he thought should be put before the curators. Jensen to Brooks, March 18, 1929, UMPOP.

28. *St. Louis Post-Dispatch*, March 18, 1929, UMPOP; newspaper clipping, n.d. (datelined March 18); "Curators Favor Firing Teachers Aiding Sex Quiz," newspaper clipping, n.d. (datelined March 19; McDavid quote); newspaper clippings; synopsis of Executive Board Meeting, n.d, (March 1929), AAUPP; see Frank Stephens to "Dear Blonda," March 15, 1929, SP, 3599; and letter from numerous faculty members to curators and president, April 3, 1929, BP; and relevant letters in VHFP.

29. DeGraff Personal and Professional Data, Training Summary, and numerous recommendations including that by Scott E. W. Bedford, August 19, 1926, AAUPP.

30. *Columbia Daily Tribune*, March 20, 1929; Alberta Davis Interview, March 17, 1929; Mary Ellen Hubbard Interview, March 15, 1929 (both apparently by Bessie Leach Priddy), UMPOP; newspaper clipping, n.d. (last two quotes), AAUPP.

31. *Columbia Daily Tribune*, March 20, 1929; *Kansas City Star*, March 16, 1929; *St. Louis Star*, March 19, 1929, UMPOP; Eva B. Hansl, "What About the Children?" *Harpers* 154 (January 1927): 220–27; DeGraff personnel material, AAUPP; Mowrer testimony; Howell testimony, Executive Committee Hearing (student quote), UMPOP; *Missouri Student*, September 25, 1928, SCELUM; newspaper clipping, n.d., AAUPP.

32. Student testimony, Executive Committee Hearing, UMPOP.

33. *Columbia Daily Tribune*, March 18, 1929, AAUPP; *Columbia Evening Missourian*, March 18, 1929, UMPOP (also unidentified clipping of same in AAUPP); For Jesse Hall and Francis Quadrangle, see Pamela Ann Miner, "Like a Phoenix: The Creation of Francis Quadrangle," *Missouri Historical Review* 84 (October 1984): 42–62; *100 Years on the Quad: A Francis Quadrangle Centennial Calendar for 1995* (Columbia, n.d.); and *A Walking Tour of Francis Quadrangle* (Columbia, n.d.).

34. Hobart Mowrer, AAUP Hearing, AAUPP; Meyer to Brooks, March 13, 1929; *Columbia Daily Tribune*, March 20, 1929, UMPOP.

35. Critic to H. J. Blanton, March 25, 1929; newspaper clipping, n.d. (datelined March 11, 1929?; "Boy" and "Some take" quotes), UMPOP; *Time* (June 1, 1953): 44; see Ginny Glass, "Jesse Wrench: Beloved Oddball," *Missouri Alumnus* (winter 1989): 24–26. The author encountered the latter Wrench anecdote in the 1960s; see Lewis E. Atherton, untitled tribute to Jane Wrench, n.d., AP; Graduate Student to Editor, *Missouri Student*, September 28, 1926, SCELUM; Les Jackson, "Grand

Old Man of Missouri," *Missouri Showme,* n.d. (ca. May 1953), 13–14, 22, 29, copy in WP.

36. Bauder testimony, Executive Board Hearing, UMPOP; see DeGraff to Brooks, March 15, 1929, UMPOP.

3. "Jellying" at Mizzou

1. Walker also claimed it couldn't burn because of its beer-saturated wood. He was wrong. Already closed to make room for a new alumni center, the Shack went up in flames in November 1988. Karen Worley, "Flames Spark Shack Memories," *Missouri Alumnus* (spring 1989): 15–17; Paul Hoemann, "The Class of '38: A Bunch of Lively Survivors," *Missouri Alumnus* (summer 1988): 13–15; Albert C. Andrews (MA '48) to editor, editor's note, Galen K. Longenecker (JD '32) to editor, *Missouri Alumnus* (summer 1989): 4, 6; Madeline A. Stewart (AB '33) to editor, *Missouri Alumnus* (spring 1990): 6; Doine Williams, Editor's Note, *Missouri Alumnus* (October 1944) ("night spot" quote); "Big Missouri," *Life* (June 7, 1937): 34; Elizabeth Eldridge, "Sheepskin Deep," *Saturday Evening Post* (February 20, 1937): 7 (" 'jelly' skillfully" quote); see "Campus Legend: It's An Old Missouri Custom," *College Years* (spring 1939): 49; Damon Runyon, "Brighter Side," *San Francisco Examiner,* May 16, 1939; *Down Beat* (February 1939): 24, last three in TC (also includes *Life* and *Saturday Evening Post*); Douglas, *Terrible Honesty,* 101, 357, 557; Virginia Carter, "University of Missouri Slang," *American Speech* 6 (February 1931): 203–6.

2. *Savitar,* 1920s; *Missouri: A Guide to the "Show Me" State* (New York: Duell, Sloan and Pearce, 1941; reprt., *Missouri: The WPA Guide to the "Show Me" State,* St. Louis: Missouri Historical Society Press, 1998), 207–15; Henry Sullivan Williams, "The Development of the Negro Public School System in Missouri," *Journal of Negro History* 5 (April 1920): 137–65.

3. *Savitar,* 1920s; *Missouri Student,* September 21, 1926 ("galaxy of automobiles" quote), October 30, 1928; E. W. S. to Editor, September 27, 1927 (senior quote), SCELUM; *Missouri Traditions* (visitor brochure, Columbia, n.d.); Edith Matzke, "A Study of the Voluntary Health Program of the Women Students of the University of Missouri," *Journal of Social Hygiene* 10 (February 1924): 89–101; "Around the Columns," n.d. (1925), copy in SP; *Columbia Daily Tribune,* August 4, October 4 ("back home" and last quote), November 9, 1923.

4. *Savitar,* 1921; Allen, *Only Yesterday,* 77, 80; on Mencken, see Hawley, *The Great War and the Search for a Modern Order,* 138.

5. *Savitar,* 1920s; "Gray Towers" to Editor, *Missouri Student,* May 10, 1927 ("average University of Missouri girl" quote), SCELUM; *Missouri: A Guide to the "Show Me" State,* 213; Galen K. Longenecker to Editor, *Missouri Alumnus* (summer 1989): 4; *St. Louis Post-Dispatch,* n.d. ("novelty" quote), AAUPP; *New York Times,* May 19, 1929; Helen Lefkowitz Horowitz, *Campus Life: Undergraduate Cultures from the End of the Eighteenth Century to the Present* (New York: Alfred A. Knopf, 1987), 208; Fass, *The Damned and the Beautiful,* 197–98, 229–30, 290; *New York Times,* February 4, 5 (Heckel quote), 6, 1926; *Columbia Daily Tribune,* February 4, 5, 6, 8, 1926.

6. *Missouri Student,* October 16, 1926; September 20, 1927; "Haig and Haig"

to Editor, *Missouri Student*, October 4, 1927; "A Book Worm" to Editor, *Missouri Student*, November 29, 1927, SCELUM.

7. *Missouri Student*, October 18, 1927; "Aunt Susie" to Editor, *Missouri Student*, October 25, 1927, SCELUM.

8. Untitled, unsigned statement of former student, n.d. (1929), AAUPP.

9. Fass, *The Damned and the Beautiful*, 79, 262; Allen, *Only Yesterday*, 78–79; Robert S. Lynd and Helen M. Lynd, *Middletown: A Study in American Culture* (New York: Harvest Book, Harcourt Brace and Company, 1929, 1957), 112; Beth Bailey, *From Front Porch to Back Seat: Courtship in Twentieth-Century America* (Baltimore: Johns Hopkins University Press, 1988), 13–14; Harvey Green, *The Light of the Home: An Intimate View of the Lives of Women in Victorian America* (New York: Pantheon Books, 1983), 10–13; *Columbia Daily Tribune*, February 5, 1926; *New York Times*, April 8, 1929; "An Acquittal of the College Girl," *Literary Digest* (March 30, 1929): 28, also contained in newspaper clipping, n.d. (April 3, 1929), AAUPP; Stuart A. Rice, "Undergraduate Attitudes Toward Marriage and Children," *Mental Hygiene* 13 (October, 1929): 788–93; "A. Nonemus" to Editor, *Missouri Student*, December 6, 1927; *Missouri Student*, January 17, 1928; "A Boy" to Editor, *Missouri Student*, January 22, 1929; "Another Boy" to Editor, *Missouri Student*, January 29, 1929; "A Girl" to Editor, *Missouri Student*, February 5, 1929, SCELUM.

10. Curtis memoir draft, CP.

11. O. H. Mowrer, *Abnormal Reactions or Actions? (An Autobiographical Answer)* (Dubuque, IA: Wm. C. Brown Company, 1966), 2–13; Mowrer testimony, AAUP Hearing, AAUPP; *Unionville Republican*, March 24, 1920; September 30, 1925; *Kansas City Star*, n.d. (March 1929), UMPOP; on the Scopes trial, see Hawley, *The Great War and the Search for a Modern Order*, 149; Edward J. Larson, *Summer for the Gods: The Scopes Trial and the Continuing Debate over Science and Religion* (Cambridge, Mass.: Harvard University Press, 1997); Paul Conkin, *When All the Gods Trembled: Darwin, Scopes, and American Intellectuals* (Lanham, Md.: Rowman and Littlefield Publishers, Inc., 1998); and Ray Ginger, *Six Days or Forever? Tennessee v. John Thomas Scopes* (Boston, 1958; reprt., Chicago: Quadrangle Books, Inc., 1969); Dumenil, *The Modern Temper*, 187–91.

12. Glenn Babb, "History of the University," *Savitar*, 1914, 35–41; Jonas Viles, *The University of Missouri: A Centennial History* (Columbia: University of Missouri, 1939), 3–218; Frank F. Stephens, *History of the University of Missouri* (Columbia: University of Missouri Press, 1962), 263–321; Curtis, Missouri: Mother of the West, typed, unpublished manuscript (December 1954), CP.

13. Lawrence O. Christensen, "Presidents and the Presidency," *Missouri Historical Review* 84 (October 1989): 31; John C. Weaver, "Footsteps in the Corridors behind Us," *Missouri Historical Review* 62 (April 1968): 230–34; Miner, "Like a Phoenix," 42–62; Stephens, *History*, 325–85; Viles, *Centennial History*, 219–61; Olson and Olson, *The University of Missouri*, 29–47; see also North Todd Gentry, Viles's History of the University of Missouri, n.d., typed twenty-seven-page unpublished manuscript critiquing Viles, *Centennial History*, GP.

14. Stephens, *History*, 378; Olson and Olson, *University of Missouri*, 35–37, 45; the institution's name underwent a name change in 1901 when the board approved the official title "University of Missouri" from the old "University of the State of Missouri." Stephens, *History*, 381; Beahler, "A Sense of Place," 19.

15. Meyer to Mowrer, 1956, MP; Viles, *Centennial History,* 250–52; 259–60; Curtis, Missouri: Mother of the West, CP; see also Ronald T. Farrar, *A Creed for My Profession: Walter Williams, Journalist to the World* (Columbia: University of Missouri Press, 1998), 119; and V. V. Masterson, *The Katy Railroad and the Last Frontier* (Norman, Okla., 1952; reprt., Columbia: University of Missouri Press, 1978), 269; Eldridge, "Sheepskin Deep," 88 ("rah-rah" quote).

16. Stephens, *History,* 383–84; Viles, *Centennial History,* 258, 260, 261; Frank Thilly to Walter Williams, February 5, 1924, SLWP; Meyer to Stratton Brooks, November 15, 1925, UMPOP; Frank Stephens, Conversation with Dr. Loeb, nineteen-page typed manuscript, n.d., SP.

17. Viles, *Centennial History,* 261–66 (quote on 261); Stephens, *History,* 386–493; for Hill's conflict with the faculty see Gentry, Viles's History of the University of Missouri, GP; Olson and Olson, *University of Missouri,* 50.

18. "A Chinese Memoir of the University of Missouri, 1920–1923," translated by David R. Knechtges and annotated by Lewis O. Saum, *Missouri Historical Review* 77 (January 1983): 189–207.

19. *New York Times,* April 30, 1923 (quote); July 14, 1923; January 1, March 16, December 19, 1924; August 8, 1925; (National) Association for the Advancement of Colored People to the editor of the *New York Times,* July 22, 1923; *Columbia Daily Tribune,* April 21, 23, 26, 27, 28, 30; May 2, 3, 4, 8, 1923; Robert L. Zangrando, *The NAACP Crusade against Lynching, 1909–1950* (Philadelphia: Temple University Press, 1980), 6; *Columbia Daily Tribune,* July 6, 7, 9, 10, 11, 12, 14, 24, 1923. For a review of the efforts of Republican Congressmen Leonidas C. Dyer of St. Louis pushed to secure federal anti-lynching legislation in 1923, see *New York Times,* July 2, October 7, 1923; and Zangrando, *Crusade against Lynching,* 78–80.

20. Stephens, *History;* 509–23; Olson and Olson, *University of Missouri,* 56–61.

21. House underwent renovation, see Stephens, *History,* 527n1 and *St. Louis Post-Dispatch,* January 23, 1926, cited therein; *Columbia Daily Tribune,* May 8, 1923.

22. "Exercises at the Inauguration of Stratton Duluth Brooks as President of the University of Missouri," *University of Missouri Bulletin* 24 (1923): 6–12, 26–30, quote on page 12, copy in UMPOP; see also Stephens, *History,* 494.

23. Viles, *Centennial History,* 266–67 (quotes); Stephens, *History,* 490–529; Lawrence O. Christensen calls Brooks's tenure "generally lackluster." Christensen, "Presidents and the Presidency," 33.

24. Stephens, *History,* 360; Viles, *Centennial History,* 271–72.

25. Leland Hazard, *Attorney for the Situation* (Pittsburgh: Carnegie-Mellon University Press, 1975), 103 (quote); Esper, "Max Meyer in America," 3; on Meyer's difficulties with Stumpf and on his intellectual relationship to Max Planck, MP; see Boring to Meyer, June 19, 1951; A. A. Roback to Meyer, January 28, 1963, EP.

26. Curtis recollections of Meyer, n.d. (March 13, 1966), (see Fred McKinney to Esper, March 14, 1966), EP; Esper, Max Meyer in America, 9, 12, fn 6, MP.

27. Esper, "Max Meyer in America," 12, MP; O. H. Mowrer, "The Present State of Behaviorism, Part 1," *Education* 97 (fall 1976): 5; Esper, "Max Meyer in America," fn 7, MP.

28. Meyer to Mowrer, 1956; Esper, "Max Meyer in America," 26–27, MP; Dorothy Meyer Schiller, Recollections of Max F. Meyer, unpublished typed eight-page manuscript; Esper to W. C. Curtis, July 30, 1966; see also numerous family letters to Esper in the 1960s as well as Mary Paxton Keeley to Erwin Esper (two),

n.d.; and August 16, 1966; Sophie Ottens to Esper, April 21, 1966, and numerous other relevant letters in EP.

29. Esper, "Max Meyer in America," 30, 35, MP; see Robert S. Daniel, "Fred McKinney (1908–1981)," *American Psychologist* 38 (November 1983): 1245–46; see William H. Lichte to Erwin Esper, November 24, 1965; see also John Paul Nafe to Esper, November 9, 1965, EP. After observing Meyer decades later, Nafe told Esper, "He is abrupt, perhaps a bit cantankerous, contemptuous of ignorance behind pretence of knowledge. But he is a gentleman and a scholar." See also Meyer to Edwin G. Boring, January 14, 1928, EP; apparently, other such letters were dispatched to various academic psychologists. For Boring's rebuff, see Boring to Meyer, January 21, 1928, EP. Nonetheless, Meyer was sufficiently encouraged from others to move forward on the proposal. See Meyer to Boring, March 6, 1928, EP.

30. Mowrer to Esper, June 17, 1957 (last quote), EP; Mowrer, "Psychology, Then and Now," unpublished manuscript of a paper read at the University of Missouri, December 1956 (Extracts) ("upper-story" quote), MP; see Curtis recollections of Meyer, n.d. (March 13, 1966); Fred McKinney to Esper, March 14, 1966; and Dorothy Schiller, Recollections of Max F. Meyer, August 1967, EP.

31. Guy Forshey in Sunday Magazine of the *St. Louis Post-Dispatch,* April 21, 1929, quoted in Esper, "Max Meyer in America," 28, MP.

32. Otis declared that the research associated with the questionnaire "doubtless would have gone unnoticed in any unthrottled university in the world." He added, "[O]ne cannot help recalling the instance of Socrates, who was condemned to drink the hemlock because it was charged that he, whom Plato called 'the best and wisest man who ever lived['], was 'corrupting the youth of Athens.' " *Kansas City Star,* March 21, 1929, UMPOP; partially quoted in Esper, "Max Meyer in America," 29; 30, MP; see letters about Meyer between Farnsworth and Erwin Esper in the 1960s in EP.

33. Dorothy Postle Marquis to Erwin Esper, June 20, 1957, EP; also quoted in Esper, "Max Meyer in America," 29 (Postle quote on p. 30; Smith quote on p. 29), MP.

34. Mowrer to Esper, June 17, 1957 ("behaviorist" anecdote; see also Mowrer, "Present State of Behaviorism," 5); Esper, "Max Meyer in America," 34, MP; Curtis recollections of Meyer, n.d. (March 13, 1966) (see Fred McKinney to Esper, March 14, 1966), EP; Stephens, *History,* 357–58, 581, 588.

35. Charles Ellwood, "A History of the Department of Sociology in the University of Missouri," thirty-seven-page typed manuscript, n.d. (1927; all quotes); see also Ellwood to Brooks, August 8, 1927, UMPOP; Coben, *Rebellion against Victorianism,* 56.

36. Newspaper clipping, n.d. (1929); H. B. to Editor of the *St. Louis Star,* n.d. (bicycle club quotes), AAUPP; C. E. W. Smith to North Todd Gentry, March 17, 1929; Margaret McCluer to Gentry, March 20, 1929; L. A. Tatum to Gentry, April 22, 1929 (and enclosure), 49 (Gentry Papers); Ralph Easley to Stratton Brooks, March 16, 1929, UMPOP; Helen Lefkowitz Horowitz, *Alma Mater: Design and Experience in the Women's Colleges from Their Nineteenth Century Beginnings to the 1930s* (New York: Alfred A. Knopf, 1985), 282; *New York Times,* May 22, 1927 ("lowdown" quote); February 7, 1928 (alumni letter); February 8, 1928 ("Sodoms" quote).

37. Ellwood, History, UMPOP.

4. Inquisition

1. *St. Louis Star,* March 19, 1929, UMPOP; *Columbia Missourian,* March 19, 1929; *Columbia Daily Tribune* (?), March 19, 1929, AAUPP.

2. Paul C. Nagel, *Missouri: A History* (Lawrence: University Press of Kansas, 1977 reprint), 15–20, 72–77; R. Douglas Hurt, *Agriculture and Slavery in Missouri's Little Dixie* (Columbia: University of Missouri Press, 1992); Richard E. Oglesby, *Manuel Lisa and the Opening of the Missouri Fur Trade* (Norman: University of Oklahoma Press, 1963); Robert K. Gilmore, *Ozark Baptizings, Hangings, and Other Diversions: Theatrical Folkways of Rural Missouri, 1885–1910* (Norman: University of Oklahoma Press, 1984); V. V. Masterson, *The Katy Railroad and the Last Frontier* (Norman, Okla., 1952; reprt., Columbia: University of Missouri Press, 1978); Lawrence O. Christensen and Gary R. Kremer, *A History of Missouri, Volume IV, 1875 to 1919* (Columbia: University of Missouri, 1997); Kirkendall, *History of Missouri, 1919 to 1953;* Lewis E. Atherton, *The Frontier Merchant in Mid-America* (Columbia: University of Missouri Press, 1971); Atherton, "James and Robert Aull—A Frontier Missouri Mercantile Firm," *Missouri Historical Review* 30 (October 1935): 3–27; *WPA Guide to the "Show Me" State."*

3. *St. Louis Star,* March 19, 1929, UMPOP; *Columbia Missourian,* March 19, 1929; *Columbia Daily Tribune* (?), March 19, 1929, AAUPP.

4. Synopses of Executive Board Hearing, AAUPP; Gentry testimony; Cole testimony, Executive Board Hearing, UMPOP.

5. Heiken testimony, Executive Board Hearing, UMPOP.

6. Dorff testimony, ibid.

7. Turner testimony, ibid.

8. Mowrer testimony, ibid.

9. Williams testimony, ibid.

10. Davis testimony, ibid.

11. Ferguson testimony, ibid.

12. Bauder testimony, ibid.

13. Postle testimony, ibid.

14. Wrench testimony, ibid.

15. DeGraff testimony, ibid; William Leuchtenburg, *The Perils of Prosperity, 1914–1932* (1958; 2d ed., Chicago: University of Chicago Press, 1993), 163; Hawley, *The Great War and the Search for a Modern Order,* 137; Lynd and Lynd, *Middletown,* 123, 127–28, 133, 142, 211; *Nation* (January 16, 1929): 59 ("honesty" quote); (March 6, 1929): 273 ("temerity" quote); Colleen McDannell, "Parlor Piety: The Home as Sacred Space in Protestant America," in Jessica H. Foy and Thomas J. Schlereth, eds., *American Home Life, 1880–1930: A Social History of Spaces and Services* (Knoxville: University of Tennessee Press, 1992), 174; Arthur Garfield Hays, "Companionate Divorce," *Nation* (April 10, 1929): 420–21; Larson, *Summer for the Gods,* 68–69; Charles W. Wood, "What is Happening to Marriage?" *Nation* (March 20, 1929): 341–44; Perrett, *America in the Twenties,* 160, 162, 172, 200; Henry Noble MacCracken, "Parents and Daughters: A College President on the American Family," *Harpers* 154 (March 1927): 454; Allen, *Only Yesterday,* 87, 100 (quote). See also Dorothy Dunbar Bromley, "Civilized Divorce," *Nation* (May 22, 1929): 608–9; newspaper clipping, n.d. (*What Is Wrong with Marriage?* material; latter part of Watson's quote), AAUPP; Hamilton and Macgowan, *What Is Wrong with Mar-*

riage? (New York: A & C Boni, 1929), 307–8 (Watson's quotes on xiii-xiv).

16. DeGraff testimony, Executive Board Hearing, UMPOP.

17. *Columbia Missourian*, March 20, 1929, UMPOP; *St. Louis Post-Dispatch*, n.d. (datelined March 20, 1929); newspaper clipping, n.d., AP story (datelined March 19, 1929), AAUPP.

18. Max F. Meyer, Anti Evolution, then Anti Social Science, and What Next?— "The Folks Say: Damn the Pedagogs," presidential address to the Southern Society of Philosophy and Psychology, April 18, 1930, Nashville, Tennessee, UMPOP.

19. Meyer testimony, Executive Board Hearing; *Kansas City Star*, March 20, 1929; Meyer, Anti Evolution, then Anti Social Science, and What Next? (last three quotes), UMPOP.

20. Synopses of Executive Board Hearing, AAUPP; Meyer testimony, Executive Board Hearing, UMPOP.

21. *Columbia Daily Tribune*, March 29, 1929, UMPOP; see Leslie Cowan to Mowrer, March 20, 1929, and copies of Executive Board order in MP and AAUPP.

5. "Tallow Candles"

1. *Columbia Daily Tribune*, March 20, 1929; *Kansas City Star*, March 20, 1929, UMPOP; newspaper clipping, n.d., March 20, 1929, AAUPP.

2. *St. Louis Star*, n.d. (datelined March 21, 1929); newspaper clipping, AP story, n.d. (datelined March 20, 1929); *St. Louis Times*, March 21, 1929, "MU STUDENTS BACK OUSTED TEACHERS: ENTIRE BODY MEETS TO PROTEST ACTION ON SEX INQUIRY," AAUPP; *Kansas City Star*, March 21, 1929, UMPOP.

3. Other potential resignations had been mentioned, including that of Jonas Viles. *St. Louis Star*, March 21, 1929 (second Wrench quote); newspaper clipping, n.d. ("medieval injustice" quote with photo of Dorff); see also newspaper clipping, UP story, n.d. (datelined March 21, 1929), AAUPP; newspaper clipping (*Kansas City Star*?), n.d. (datelined March 20, 1929; first quote); newspaper clipping, n.d. ("veteran history professor" quote); *Columbia Missourian*, March 21, 1929, UMPOP.

4. *St. Louis Post-Dispatch*, April 3[?], 1929 (contains samples of editorials); *Baltimore Sun*, March 26, 1929, AAUPP; *Kansas City Star*, March 21, 1929; *St. Louis Post-Dispatch*, March 21, 1929, UMPOP; *Nation* (April 12, 1929): 412.

5. Philadelphian to Brooks, March 24, 1929; Seattle Alumnus to Brooks, March 21, 1929; Father of female student to Brooks, March 22, 1929; Hannibal Businessman to Brooks, March 30, 1929; Liberty Mother to Executive Board of Curators, March 20, 1929; Sedalia Father to Brooks, March 21, 1929; Circuit Court Judge to Brooks, March 21, 1929; Kansas City Attorney to McDavid, March 26, 1929; Clergyman to Brooks, March 25, 1929; Kansas City Attorney to McDavid, March 26, 1929; Kansas Citian to Brooks, April 2, 1929; Moberly Pastor to Brooks, April 3, 1929; R. L. Davidson to Brooks, March 21, 1929, UMPOP; "A friend of the University" to Gentry, April 3, 1929, Gentry Papers.

6. Illinois Father to Brooks, March 21, 1929; Phi Beta Kappa to Brooks, March 22, 1929, UMPOP.

7. Alumnus to Brooks, March 22, 1929; Former Student to Brooks, March 20, 1929; Villager to Brooks, March 21, 1929; Kansas City Critic to Brooks, April 5,

1929; St. Louis Critic to Board of Curators, March 21, 1929; St. Louis School Principal to Board of Curators, March 21, 1929, UMPOP; *St. Louis Post-Dispatch,* March 21, 1929, AAUPP; W. L., California Alumnus, to Brooks, March 25, 1929; see also George Johnson to Board of Curators, March 25, 1929, UMPOP.

8. Newspaper clipping, UP story, n.d. (datelined March 22, 1929); newspaper clipping, AP story, n.d. (datelined March 22, 1929), AAUPP; telegram, Dakan to Brooks, March 26, 1929, Brooks to Dakan, March 27, 1929; Dakan to Brooks, April 1, 1929, UMPOP.

9. McCutcheon to Brooks (copy to Board of Curators), March 18, 1929, UMPOP (copy also in VHFP); McCutcheon to Viles, March 22, 26, 1929; Viles to McCutcheon, March 23, 1929, VHFP.

10. Viles to McCutcheon, March 23 ("have in mind" quote), April 2, 1929 ("sprung" quote), VHFP.

11. McCutcheon to Viles, March 26, 1929, VHFP; McAfee to Goodrich, March 26, 1929; McAfee to Brooks, March 28, 1929, UMPOP; Sixteen faculty members to President and Board of Curators, April 3, 1929, Branson Papers; copy also in UMPOP.

12. Newspaper clipping (*Star,* datelined March 23, 1929), AAUPP; Stephens to "Dear Carrie and All," March 24, 1929, SP, 3599.

13. *Columbia Missourian,* n.d., UP story (datelined March 22, 1929 [Queen quotes]); *Baltimore Sun,* March 26, 1929, AAUPP.

14. Meyer to Brooks, March 22 (first quote), April 11, 1928, March 11, 1929; Brooks to Meyer, March 23, 1928; Program, Twenty-Fourth Annual Meeting of the Southern Society for Philosophy and Psychology, University of Missouri, Columbia, Mo., Friday and Saturday, March 29 and 30, 1929; Meyer to "My dear Colleague," March 6, 1929, UMPOP.

15. Meyer to Brooks, March 20 and 22 (second quote), 1929; Brooks to Meyer, March 21, 1929 (first quote); Meyer to Editor, *Columbia Missourian,* March 22, 1929; Brooks to Thomas Bowen, March 22, 1929; Program, Twenty-Fourth Annual Meeting of the Southern Society for Philosophy and Psychology; *St. Louis Globe Democrat,* March 30, 1929 (AP quote), UMPOP. See also *Columbia Daily Tribune,* March 30, 1929, UMPOP. Decades later, one psychologist who was not in the profession at the time of the Lexington meeting reflected on Meyer's association with the society in 1929 and 1965: "I believe that the Southern Society then, as now, honored Dr. Meyer by electing him its president as the result of his scientific contributions and, as with any scientific organization, did not concern itself with his personal life." D. R. Kenshalo to Erwin Esper, October 21, 1965, EP.

16. Brooks testimony, AAUP Hearing, AAUPP; Loeb to Middlebush, March 23, 1929, UMSBPAR.

17. W. B. Munro, "Message from President Munro," AAUP *Bulletin* 16 (February 1930): 142; *St. Louis Globe-Democrat,* April 2, 1929 ("trade union" quote), UMPOP; AAUP *Bulletin* 1 (December 1915); 2 (March 1916): 34; Livingston Farrand to John Dewey, July 9, 1915, AAUP *Bulletin* 2 (April 1916): 34–35, 46; 2 (May 1916): 1–57; 10 (February 1924): 9; 10 (April 1924): 21–68; Robert C. Brooks (from *Science and Society*) in 10 (October 1924): 24–28 ("British constitution" and "casual laborer" quotes on p. 25); Frank Thilly, "The American Association of University Professors," *American Review* 3 (March 1925): 200; see also other issues of the AAUP *Bulletin,* vols. 3–16 for several academic freedom cases.

18. *New Republic* (May 28, 1924), reproduced in AAUP *Bulletin* 10 (October 1924): 11–15; A. O. Leuschner to Editors, *New Republic* (October 6, 1924): 15 ("facts" quote), 16; see also Arthur O. Lovejoy to Editor, *New Republic*, n.d., 16–18 (first letter is to the Editors, second to the Editor).

19. Munro, "Message from President Munro," AAUP *Bulletin* 16 (February 1930): 142; 2 (March 1916): 13; *Bulletin* 15 (January 1929): 10–61; Thilly, "American Association of University Professors," 202.

20. Warren to Tyler, March 23, 1929, AAUPP.

21. Faris to Quincy Wright, March 23, 1929, AAUPP.

22. Lovejoy to Tyler, March 23, 27 (containing quote), 1929; Tyler to Lovejoy, March 26, 1929; telegram, Tyler to Herman Schlundt, March 26, 1929 (copy); Tyler to Fairclough, March 26, 1929; see also Henry Crew letter (to Tyler and Fairclough), March 28, 1929 (copy), AAUPP.

23. Schlundt to Tyler, March 27, 1929; see Tyler to Schlundt, March 29, 1929, AAUPP.

24. Henry Crew to Tyler and Fairclough, March 28, 1929 (copy), AAUPP.

25. *St. Louis Globe-Democrat*, April 2, 1929, UMPOP.

26. *Kansas City Star*, March 21, 1929 ("can't be helped" quote); *Columbia Missourian*, March 20, 1929, UMPOP; March 23, 1929, AAUPP; *Columbia Daily Tribune*, March 20, 1929 ("die" quote), UMPOP; newspaper clipping, n.d. (also "die" quote), AAUPP. "The idea that I could return to Germany as a university professor never entered my mind," said Meyer much later. "I knew that I was too insignificant a creature to be accepted in Germany as the holder of such a position. And the same is true for America." Meyer to Erwin Esper, November 18, 1965, EP.

27. *Kansas City Star*, March 20, 1929 (Mowrer quotes; also elsewhere), UMPOP; Mowrer, *Abnormal Reactions or Actions?* 13 ("unpleasant notoriety" quote); newspaper clippings, n.d. and March 20, 1929, AAUPP.

28. Newspaper clipping, March 20, 1929; *Kansas City Post-Journal* (?), March 24, 1929, AAUPP; W. H. Brown to Brooks and Curators, n.d., UMPOP.

29. *Missouri Student*, March 19, 1929, AAUPP; Priddy to Brooks, March 13, 1929; *Kansas City Star*, March 21, 1929, UMPOP; *Columbia Daily Tribune*, August 4, 1923.

30. *Kansas City Star*, March 21, 1929, UMPOP; Bank President to Brooks, April 3, 1929; Father of male student to Brooks, April 1, 1929, UMPOP.

31. *Kansas City Star*, March 21, 1929, UMPOP; Allen, *Only Yesterday*, 97.

32. *Columbia Missourian*, n.d.; UP story datelined March 22, 1929, AAUPP.

33. *Columbia Missourian*, March 22 (?), 1929 ("Good luck" quote); *Columbia Daily Tribune* (?), March 22, 1929 (DeGraff quotes), AAUPP.

34. *Columbia Daily Tribune* (?), March 22, 1929 (DeGraff quotes); *Baltimore Sun*, March 26, 1929, AAUPP.

35. Newspaper clipping (*Star*, datelined March 23, 1929 ["calm" quote]); *Columbia Daily Tribune* (?), March 22, 1929; *Columbia Missourian*, March 23, 1929, AAUPP; *Kansas City Star*, March 21, 1929; Brooks to Thomas C. Hargis, March 26, 1929, and other such letters, UMPOP.

36. *Missouri Student*, March 26, 1929; *Columbia Missourian*, n.d., and March 23, 1929; *Kansas City Journal Dispatch* (?), March 24, 1929; newspaper clipping, AP story, March 28, 1929 (datelined March 27, 1929 [quotes]), AAUPP.

37. *Columbia Missourian*, n.d., AAUPP and UMPOP.

38. *St. Louis Globe-Democrat*, March 27, 30, 1929, UMPOP and AAUPP; newspaper clipping, two UP stories, March 28, 1929 (datelined March 28, 1929); *Columbia Daily Tribune*, March 28 ("summary action" quote), 29 ("questionnaire is dead" quote), 1929, UMPOP and AAUPP.

39. *St. Louis Globe-Democrat*, April 2, 1929, UMPOP; *Columbia Daily Tribune*, April 3, 1929; see also newspaper clipping, UP story, n.d. (datelined April 1, 1929); *Columbia Daily Tribune*, April 3, 1929; newspaper clipping, AP story, n.d. (datelined April 6, 1929), AAUPP.

40. *Kansas City Star*, March 16, 1929; *Columbia Daily Tribune*, March 28 ("unsophisticated" and "uncensored" quotes), 29, 1929, UMPOP; *St. Louis Post-Dispatch*, March 29, 1929, AAUPP.

41. See, for example, Vivian L. Davis to Registrar, University of Missouri, April 30, 1929; S. L. Hornbeck to Brooks, April 3, 1929; E. L. Hume to Brooks, March 22, 1929; Olaf Moe to Brooks, March 16, 1929; Morris Ernst to University of Missouri, March 18, 1929; J. R. Allen to Brooks, April 3, 1929; and related other letters; *Kansas City Star*, March 24, 1929, UMPOP; see also J. L. Roberts to Gentry, March 19, 1929; A. A. Speer to Gentry, March 18, 30, April 4, 1929; R. F. Walker to Gentry, March 27, 1929; Shelbyville Minister to Gentry, March 18, 1929 ("if the mails" quote); and others; Gentry to Speer, March 31, 1929, Gentry Papers; *Columbia Missourian*, n.d.; *St. Louis Star* (?) March 20, 1929, AAUPP.

42. *Columbia Daily Tribune*, March 20, 1929, UMPOP; newspaper clippings, AP, UP stories and *Kansas City Journal-Post* (?), n.d. (all datelined March 22, 1929), AAUPP.

43. *Kansas City Star*, March 27, 1929, UMPOP.

44. Werner et al. to Goodrich, March 27, 1929 (copy); C. H. Williams to Brooks, March 30, 1929 ("crude and abusive" quote); George Williams to Brooks, March 20 (probably 30), 1929, Louis Hehl to Brooks, March 30, 1929; see numerous and varied newspaper clippings, including *Minneapolis Star, New York Times, St. Louis Post-Dispatch, St. Louis Globe-Democrat, Kansas City Star*, and others, including the *Columbia Daily Tribune*, April 6, 1929 ("cheap political meddling" quote), UMPOP; see also clippings in AAUPP.

45. *Columbia Daily Tribune*, March 29, 1929; *St. Louis Globe-Democrat*, March 30, 1929 (two editions), UMPOP (partial copy of one also in AAUPP); see also newspaper clipping, *The Star* (datelined March 29, 1929), UMPOP.

46. Jefferson City Woman to Brooks, March 16, 1929; Constituent (Maplewood, Missouri) to James Goodrich, H. W. Lenox, A. A. Speer, Charles Ward, George Willson, March 27, 1929, UMPOP; Stephens, *History*, 518, 520.

47. *Baltimore Sun*, March 26, 1929; *Kansas City Star*, March 24, 1929; *Columbia Daily Tribune*, March 25, 1929 ("acclamation" quote); newspaper clipping, March 25, 1929, AAUPP; *St. Louis Globe-Democrat*, April 4, 1929, UMPOP.

48. *Monroe County Appeal*, March 22, 1929; copy also in UMPOP.

49. *Columbia Missourian*, March 22 (?), 1929, AAUPP; *Missouri Student*, March 26, 1929.

6. Up in Smoke

1. Hazard, untitled typed manuscript, n.d. (1962), MP; see also Hazard, *Attorney for the Situation*, 100–101; Hazard to Mowrer, August 31, 1962, MP.

2. Hazard to editor, March 16, 1929, *Columbia Missourian*, n.d., AAUPP.

3. *Kansas City Star*, March 21, 1929, clipping, UMPOP; Hazard, typed manuscript, MP; Hazard, *Attorney for the Situation*, 86, 99 (quotes, including the *Kansas City Star*), 101.

4. Hazard, typed manuscript; Hazard, *Attorney for the Situation*, 101 (quotes).

5. Businessman to President, Board of Curators, April 2, 3, 1929; School Principal to Curators, April 3, 1929; Ten School Men to Curators, March 28, 1929; Medical Doctor to President, Board of Curators, April 5, 1929; telegram, Ohio to Curators, April 6, 1929; petition, fourteen alumni from Schenectady, April 4, 1929; Alumnus in Madison, Wisconsin, to Secretary, Board of Curators, March 27, 1929; Alumnus at Cornell to Curators, April 2, 1929; Superintendent, Jewish Hospital, April 4, 1929; Frank Knight to Curators, April 3, 1929; faculty group to President and Curators, April 3, 1929; also see other relevant material, including Brooks to Curators, April 6, 1929, all in Reel 122, UMBCR.

6. Haupt to Brooks, April 4, 1929, Reel 122, UMBCR.

7. Bertha Witt to Curators, April 1, 1929; Thomas Nelson to Curators, April 5, 1929; Cole to Goodrich, April 4, 1929; Cole to Brooks, April 4, 1929; May Hunt and Grace McDonald to Curators, April 2, 1929; Louise Hess and Violet Gieselman to Curators, April 3, 1929; telegram, Mrs. Otho Matthews to Leslie Cowan, April 5, 1929; Geraldine Blessing D.A.R. Vice-Chairman to President, Executive Board of Curators, April 2, 1929, all in Reel 122, UMBCR.

8. James Goodrich to Leslie Cowan, April 2, 1929; Goodrich to DeGraff, April 2, 1929 (copy, with note that identical letters went to Meyer and Mowrer); DeGraff to Brooks, April 5, 1929; Mowrer to Brooks, April 5, 1929; Meyer to Brooks, April 5, 1929, Reel 122, UMBCR; *Columbia Missourian*, April 6, 1929, UMPOP; newspaper clipping, UP story, n.d. (datelined April 6, 1929), AAUPP; Hazard, *Attorney for the Situation*, 106.

9. *Columbia Missourian*, April 6, 1929; *Kansas City Star*, April 6, 1929; *Columbia Daily Tribune*, April 6, 1929, UMPOP; Minutes of the Board of Curators, April 6, 1929, Reel 122, UMBCR.

10. *Columbia Daily Tribune*, April 5, 1929, AAUPP; Minutes of the Board of Curators, April 6, 1929; M. Slade Kendrick to Curators, April 2, 1929, Reel 122, UMBCR; Ostrander, *American Civilization*, 91–92, 95–97; Perrett, *America in the Twenties*, 160; Helen Lefkowitz Horowitz, "Victoria Woodhull, Anthony Comstock, and Conflict over Sex in the United States in the 1870s," *Journal of American History* 87 (September 2000): 403–34; May, *The End of American Innocence*, 345; Erenberg, *Steppin' Out*, 62; unidentified editorial, n.d. ("kicked out" quote), AAUPP; Hazard, *Attorney for the Situation*, 102–7; *New York Times*, January 15, April 24, 26, 28, May 1, 4, June 13, 1929, March 4, 1930.

11. Hazard, *Attorney for the Situation*, 104, 106 ("easy" quote), 107; AAUP Hearing (all other quotes), AAUPP; Dorothy Postle, Social Psychology Lecture, March 6, 1929, BP; Interview with Miss Dorothy Postle, March 15, 1929 (obviously by Bessie L. Priddy), UMPOP.

12. Memorandum, A. J. Carlson to James Goodrich, August 13, 1929 (copy), AAUPP; see audit of Meyer's sex reflex tabulation by Addison Gulick and Winterton C. Curtis, and endorsed by fifteen additional University of Missouri faculty, March 25, 1929, UMPOP; AAUP Hearing, AAUPP; Hazard, *Attorney for the Situation*, 107–9 (quote on 109); Max Meyer, Lecture for small and advanced class,

composed exclusively of women preparing to be social workers or to direct social work, n.d., AAUPP.

13. Hazard, *Attorney for the Situation*, 109.

14. Newspaper clipping, n.d. ("40 deep" quote); *Kansas City Star* (?), n.d. (datelined April 6, 1929 ["Ozarks" quote]), AAUPP.

15. Larson, *Summer for the Gods*, 22, 186, 270–71; Minutes of the Board of Curators, April 6, 1929, Reel 122, UMBCR; Curtis to H. W. Tyler, April 10, 1929; *St. Louis Globe-Democrat*, April 8, 1929, UMPOP; AAUP Hearing ("refreshed" quote), AAUPP; Hazard, *Attorney for the Situation*, 106. One of at least seven scientists called, Curtis went to Dayton but never took the witness stand. While the prosecution successfully convinced the court to bar the scientists' testimony, written depositions were allowed in the record. Winterton C. Curtis, "The Evolution Debate," in Jerry Tompkins, *D-Days at Dayton: Reflections on the Scopes Trial* (Baton Rouge: Louisiana State University Press, 1965), 74–85; Edward Caudill, Edward Larson, and Jesse Mayshark, *The Scopes Trial: A Photographic History* (Knoxville: University of Tennessee Press, 2000), 47; see also Conkin, *When All the Gods Trembled*.

16. *St. Louis Globe-Democrat*, April 8, 1929, UMPOP; Hazard, *Attorney for the Situation*; Minutes of the Board of Curators, April 7, 1929, Reel 122, UMBCR.

17. Minutes of the Board of Curators, April 7, 1929, Reel 122, UMBCR; Tisdal testimony, AAUP Hearing, AAUPP.

18. Action Taken by the Board of Curators of the University of Missouri, April 7, 1929, AAUPP; *St. Louis Globe-Democrat*, April 8, 1929, UMPOP.

19. *St. Louis Globe-Democrat*, April 7, 1929, UMPOP; *Kansas City Star* (?), n.d. (datelined April 8, 1929); newspaper clipping, n.d., AAUPP.

20. *Kansas City Star* (?), n.d. (datelined April 8, 1929); *St. Louis Globe-Democrat*, April 8, 1929; newspaper clipping, April 8, 1929, AAUPP.

21. Viles to McCutcheon, April 11, 1929, VHFP; *Kansas City Star* (?), n.d. (datelined April 8, 1929); Lovejoy to Tyler, April 5, 1929; Schlundt to Tyler, April 7, 1929; Meyer to A. J. Carlson, December 7, 1929 ("Professors-Union" quote), AAUPP.

22. Telegrams, Gulick to Tyler, April 8, 1929; Rogers to Tyler, April 8, 1929; Turner to Tyler, April 8, 1929; Letter, Dorff, Turner, Davis, and forty others to Tyler, April 10, 1929; Viles to Tyler, April 11, 1929 (copy also in VHFP); see also other relevant material, AAUPP.

23. Telegram, Brooks to Tyler, April 8, 1929; Tyler to Arthur Lovejoy, April 8, 1929; night letter, Tyler to Brooks, April 8, 1929 (also letter of same date); night letter, Tyler to Crew, April 8, 1929; telegram, Crew to Tyler, April 9, 1929; Tyler to Crew, April 11, 1929 (copy); Weiss to Chairman of Committee A, April 10, 1929; Tyler to Crew, April 11, 1929 (copy), AAUPP.

24. Tyler to Crew, April 13, 1929; *St. Louis Post-Dispatch*, April 15, 1929; Curtis to Crew, April 20, 1929; Curtis to Tyler, April 10, 1929, AAUPP; Symes, "What Shall We Tell the Children?" *Harpers* 158 (April 1929): 529–39 (quote on 531).

25. Schlundt to Tyler, April 22, 1929; Warren to Tyler, April 16, 1929; Tyler to J. H. Gray, April 25, 1929; day letter, Tyler to Grave, April 25, 1929; telegram, Grave to Tyler, April 25, 1929 (also quoted in Tyler to Crew, April 25, 1929); Tyler to Dear Professor, April 23, 1929; Crew to Curtis, April 26, 1929; and numerous other relevant communications in AAUP; *St. Louis Post-Dispatch*, April 15, 1929, AAUPP; see also numerous newspaper clippings from various cities in AAUPP.

26. Tyler to Brooks, April 29, 1929 (with copies to others); telegram, Crew to Carlson, April 29, 1929; Tyler to Carlson, April 30, 1929; Tyler to H. C. Warren, April 30, 1929; Schlundt to Lovejoy, May 8, 1929; W. C. Curtis to Crew, May 1, 1929; Tyler to Carlson, April 30, 1929; Tyler to Thurstone, April 30, 1929; Tyler to Bordwell, April 30, 1929; Schlundt to Tyler, May 3, 1929; Schlundt to Carlson, May 3, 1929; telegram, Bordwell to Carlson, May 7, 1929; Crew to Carlson, April 30, 1929; also related materials, and numerous other relevant communications in AAUPP.

27. W. W. Cook to Tyler, May 13, 1929, AAUPP.

28. Viles to McCutcheon, April 11, 1929, VHFP; Brown to Tyler, April 12, 1929, AAUPP.

29. Curtis to Crew, May 1, 1929, AAUPP. Max F. Meyer, Anti Evolution, then Anti Social Science, and What Next? presidential address to the Southern Society of Philosophy and Psychology, UMPOP. Meyer spurned the alleged bribe.

30. Herman Schlundt, W. C. Curtis, E. B. Branson, and J. H. Rogers to Curators, April 23, 1929, Reel 122, UMBCR; Goodrich to Carlson, May 3, 1929, AAUP. Carlson actually wanted transcripts of both hearings, something Goodrich would likely have had no problem providing. Carlson to Goodrich, May 6, 1929; see also Tyler to Goodrich, May 8, 1929; and Carlson to Tyler, May 6, 1929, AAUPP.

31. Carlson to Schlundt, May 6, 1929; Schlundt to Carlson, May 8, 1929, AAUPP.

32. G. Shearman Peterkin, M.D. Surgeon to Meyer, April 29, 1929 (copy), AAUPP. Meyer passed along the copy to L. L. Thurstone, a member of the visiting team. See Meyer to Thurstone, May 6, 1929; newspaper clipping, n.d. (datelined April 25, 1929), AAUPP.

33. Maguire to Tyler, April 9, 1929; *St. Louis Globe-Democrat*, April 10, 1929, UMPOP; newspaper clipping, n.d, AAUPP.

7. What Really Happened

1. Stephens, *History*, 357–58, 513.

2. Schlundt to Carlson, May 8, 1929; telegram, Bordwell to Carlson, May 15, 1929; AAUP Hearing, AAUPP.

3. J. P. Guilford, "Louis Leon Thurstone, 1887–1955," *Biographical Memoirs* 30 (1957): 349–82, copy also in Archival Biographical File, SCRLUC; newspaper clipping, April 6, 1945; "Recent Developments in Guidance," *Guidance Newsletter*, March 1947; Thurstone resume, Archival Biographical File, SCRLUC; see clippings and other material in Percy Bordwell file, SCMLUI; *Who's Who in America*, vol. 25 (Chicago: A. N. Marquis Company, 1948): 253; see "Anton J. Carlson, 1875–1956," *University of Chicago Magazine*, January 1957 (eulogies by Lester L. Dragstedt and Lawrence A. Kimpton), 20–22; Lester L. Dragstedt, "Anton Julius Carlson, January 29, 1875–September 2, 1956," *Biographical Memoirs* 35 (1961): 1–32, copy also in Archival Biographical File, SCRLUC; see also Special Memorial Issue, *Bulletin for Medical Research of the National Society for Medical Research*, November–December 1956; *Time* (February 10, 1941): 44, 46–48; and other material in Anton Julius Carlson, Archival Biographical File, SCRLUC; AAUP *Bulletin* 2 (March 1916): 13; 2 (April 1916): 35; *Who's Who in America*, vol. 15 (Chicago: A. N. Marquis Company, 1928; London: Stanley Paul and Co., 1928), 326, 445.

4. Blanton testimony; Willson testimony, AAUP Hearing, AAUPP; Hazard to Max Meyer, August 31, 1962, MP.

5. DeGraff testimony; Ellwood testimony, AAUP Hearing; AAUPP; *Columbia Daily Tribune,* May 1, 2, 1923; *St. Louis Post-Dispatch,* March 21, 1929, UMPOP.

6. Meyer testimony, Executive Board Hearing, UMPOP; Brooks testimony, AAUP Hearing, AAUPP.

7. Elmer Ellis, *My Road to Emeritus* (Columbia: State Historical Society of Missouri, 1989), 69; DeGraff testimony, AAUP Hearing, AAUPP.

8. Hollands to Tyler (obviously misdated); Tyler to Hollands, May 4, 1929; telegram, Lovejoy to Tyler, April 23, 1929; Schlundt to Tyler, April 29, 1929; Tyler to Schlundt, May 2, 1929; Tyler to Brooks, May 2, 1929; Carlson to Tyler, May 20, 1929; see also Tyler to "Dear Professor," April 23, 1929, AAUPP; Meyer to W. C. Curtis, January 14, 1932, UMPOP; Guilford, "Louis Leon Thurstone, 1887–1955," 351, copy also in Archival Biographical File, SCRLUC.

9. Rogers testimony, AAUP Hearing, AAUPP; Ellwood, History; *Columbia Daily Tribune,* January 30, 31 (quotes), 1925; February 12, 1924; *Columbia Missourian,* January 29, 1925, UMPOP; Blumer to Board of Curators, February 8, 1925 (two of same date); Blumer, Particulars Concerning the Address on the Negro Problem, n.d. (address given January 27, 1925); Brooks to Blumer, February 12, 1925; March 23, 1926; May 12, 1927, UMPOP; University *Bulletins,* 1920s, Persons Being Considered for an Honorary Degree, University of Missouri, December 1966, 3603, LEAP; C. W. Greene to E. B. Branson, February 12, 1925, 2404 Branson Papers; Herbert Blumer, Archival Biographical File, SCRLUC.

10. Rogers testimony; Branson testimony; Brown testimony, AAUP Hearing, AAUPP. Brown himself recalled his saying that he asked Brooks "'. . . what would the Board do if some 20 or 30'—I don't know what number I mentioned,— 'of the well known professors in the institution should say that under the circumstances we can't stay here?' Then he replied 'Their resignations would be accepted at once and I would ask to have them accepted.'" Brown testimony, AAUP Hearing, AAUPP.

11. Branson testimony; Brown testimony; Curtis testimony; AAUP Hearing; AAUPP; Max F. Meyer, Anti Evolution, then Anti Social Science, and What Next? presidential address to the Southern Society of Philosophy and Psychology, UMPOP.

12. Curtis testimony, Schlundt testimony, Rogers testimony, Branson testimony; Mrs. Thurstone testimony, AAUP Hearing, AAUPP; Defoe Hall was later named in the popular professor's honor. Stephens, *History,* 581; see also Viles, *Centennial History,* 196, 197, 240.

13. A. J. Carlson to James E. Goodrich, June 22, 1929, AAUPP. Mowrer to Erwin Esper, June 17, 1957, EP; Brooks testimony; Mowrer testimony, AAUP Hearing, AAUPP; Mowrer to Meyer, May 3, 1929; Meyer to Thurstone, May 8, 1929, including O. H. Mowrer, "A Statement," n.d., AAUPP.

14. Brooks testimony, AAUP Hearing, AAUPP; Brooks to Richard L. Jones, March 26, 1929 ("shrewd" quote), UMPOP.

15. Meyer to Kathryn Steinberg, May 19, 1929, AAUPP.

16. Brooks testimony, ibid.

17. Mowrer testimony, ibid.

18. Hudson testimony, ibid.

19. Tisdel testimony, ibid.

20. Ellwood testimony, ibid.

21. Postle testimony; Rowell testimony; Lippman testimony; Dorff testimony; Sonnenschein testimony; Turner testimony; Dry testimony; Degner testimony, ibid.

22. Branson testimony; Priddy testimony, ibid.

23. Hazard, *Attorney for the Situation*, 104, 106 ("easy" quote); Meyer testimony, AAUP Hearing, AAUPP; Meyer, A Historical Sketch of the Missouri Case, n.d. (1930s) ("double-tonguedness" quote; underscoring in original), AAUPP; *Savitar*, 1930; *Missouri Alumnus*, May 1929, 1.

24. *Savitar*, 1929.

8. "Facts Are Stubborn Things"

1. *WPA Guide to the "Show Me" State*, 338–39, 348; see state map in *Seventh Biennial Report of the State Highway Commission of Missouri* (Jefferson City: State Highway Commission, 1930); Thurstone to Carlson, June 28, 1929; Hazard to Goodrich, June 14, 1929; see also Carlson to Goodrich, July 3, 1929, AAUPP.

2. Carlson to Tyler, May 20, 1929, AAUPP.

3. Hazard to Carlson, May 21, 1929, AAUP. Tyler to Carlson, May 24, 1929 (copy; copies to others); Tyler to Thurstone, May 29, 1929 (copies to others), AAUPP. Rogers testimony; Branson testimony; Brown testimony, AAUP Hearing; Carlson to Hazard, May 27, 1929, AAUPP; Academic Freedom at the University of Missouri, AAUP *Bulletin* 16 (February 1930).

4. Hazard to Carlson, May 31, June 7 (one of two of that date), 1929, AAUPP.

5. See a Preliminary draft evidently edited by Carlson in Carlson (?) to James Goodrich, June 4, 1929; Bordwell to Carlson, May 22, 1929 ("rumors" quote); see L. L. Thurstone, Report on the Missouri Case; University of Missouri, Preliminary Report on the Dismissal of Professor DeGraff and the Suspension of Prof. Meyer, n.d., and other relevant material in AAUPP.

6. DeGraff to Carlson, June 5, 1929; Carlson to DeGraff, June 10, 1929, AAUPP.

7. University of Missouri, Preliminary Report on the Dismissal of Professor DeGraff and the Suspension of Prof. Meyer, n.d.; Maguire to Tyler, June 1, 1929, AAUPP.

8. Carlson to Tyler, June 12, 1929; Carlson to Hazard, June 13, 1929, AAUPP.

9. See Meyer's handwritten notation on a copy of Carlson's letter to Schlundt, June 11, 1929; Schlundt to Carlson, June 14, 1929; Curtis to Carlson, June 24, 1929; DeGraff to Carlson, June 5, 15, 1929, AAUPP. The students' call for an investigation was not acknowledged in the final published report.

10. Bordwell to Carlson, June 15, 1929; Carlson to Hazard, June 13, 1929; Carlson to Crew, June 15, 1929 ("left wing" quote); Carlson to Tyler, July 3, 1929; Carlson to Curtis, July 3, 1929 ("older heads" quote); Tyler to Carlson, June 14, 1929 (copies to others); Munro to Tyler, June 28, 1929, AAUPP.

11. Curtis to Carlson, June 24, July 19, 1929; Curtis to Crew, July 19, 1929; see also Crew to Curtis, July 23, 1929, AAUPP.

12. Hazard to Goodrich, June 14, 1929, AAUP. Three days before, Hazard had told Carlson that he "would like to be sure that I have permission to state to the

curators that those recommendations represent the view of one member of the Committee." Hazard to Carlson, June 14, 1929, AAUPP.

13. Olson and Olson, *University of Missouri*, 41; Hazard to Carlson, June 14, 18, 1929; Goodrich to Carlson, June 17, 1929, AAUPP.

14. Hazard to Carlson, June 18, 1929; Curtis to Carlson, July 19, 1929, AAUPP.

15. Hazard to Carlson, June 18, 1929; Thurstone to Carlson, June 28, 1929; Carlson to Thurstone, July 3, 1929, AAUPP.

16. Goodrich to Carlson, July 17, 1929; Quincy Wright to Goodrich, August 1, 1929; Wright to Carlson, August 1, 1929; Crew to Carlson, August 13, 1929; Carlson to Hazard, August 15, 1929; see also Carlson to J. P. Lichtenberger (copies to others), July 31, AAUPP.

17. Prominent Alumnus I. Anderson to Carlson, June 21, 1929; Goodrich to Carlson, June 25, 1929, AAUPP.

18. *Springfield Leader and Press*, April 13, 1943; copy also in Springfield–Greene County Library, Springfield, Missouri; *Monroe County Appeal*, January 13, 20, 27, 1955; see also *Time* (May 29, 1950): 66–67; Levine, "Progress and Nostalgia," 197–98 ("psychic" quote on 198); Perrett, *America in the Twenties*, 192; *New York Times*, August 6, 7, 8, 1925; see also editorial, July 31, 1925; Douglas, *Terrible Honesty*, 25, 34, 465, 491–92; see also Kirschner, "Conflicts and Politics in the 1920s," 229–30.

19. Prominent Alumnus I. Anderson to Carlson, June 21, 1929, AAUPP.

20. Goodrich to Carlson, June 25, 1929, AAUPP.

21. Carlson to Prominent Alumnus (Anderson), July 3, 1929, AAUPP.

22. Carlson to Goodrich, July 3, 1929, AAUPP.

23. Hazard to Willson, July 5, 1929 (Hazard quoted the "joke" story); Hazard to Carlson, July 10, 1929; Carlson to Goodrich, July 3, 1929, AAUPP.

24. Goodrich to Carlson, July 5, 13, 1929; see Carlson to Tyler, July 16, 1929 (copies to others); Carlson to Goodrich, July 16, 1929; Carlson to Hazard, July 16, 1929, AAUPP.

25. Hazard to Carlson, July 19, 1929; Carlson to Hazard, July 26, 1929; Goodrich to Carlson, July 17, October 24, 1929; Carlson to Goodrich, July 29 (quote), August 12, 1929; Goodrich's secretary to Carlson, August 3, 13, 1929; see also Carlson to Goodrich, October 26, 1929, and other relevant correspondence in AAUPP. Henry Crew had asked his colleague at Northwestern, Thomas Holgate, who had spent many years in administration, to look into the matter of termination and salaries. Holgate recalled only one dismissal—actually ending in resignation—not for misconduct, and in that case the affected instructor still got his salary to the end of the contract period. "It is difficult to conceive of a mistake in judgment, not involving moral conduct, so serious that a Professor must be dismissed during term time and without due process involving a hearing. I am inclined to think that one so dismissed has a valid claim for a salary, not only till the end of the unfinished year but beyond till his relation with the University is severed after due notice." Holgate to Carlson, July 31, 1929, AAUPP.

26. Carlson to Hazard, July 26, 1929; Carlson to Goodrich, July 27, 1929 (appears as a draft), AAUPP.

27. Willson to Carlson, August 1, 1929; telegram, Bordwell to Carlson, August 3, 1929; Goodrich's secretary to John H. Gray, August 9, 1929; Memorandum, Carlson to Crew, Tyler, Bordwell, Thurstone, Maguire, Lovejoy and Gray, n.d.; Hazard to Carlson, August 24, 1929, AAUPP.

28. Carlson to Hazard, August 15, 1929; Hazard to Carlson, August 17, 1929; Carlson to DeGraff, August 17, 1929; DeGraff to Hazard, August 19, 1929, AAUPP.

29. Brooks to Edward H. Todd, July 22, 1929, UMPOP; DeGraff to Leslie Cowan, June 4, July 10, 24, 1929, Reel 122, UMBCR; DeGraff to Carlson, June 16, 1929; De-Graff to Hazard, August 19, 1929 ("resort" quote, copy); see also Edward Todd to AAUP, July 27, 1929; DeGraff to Carlson, August 15, 19, 1929, AAUP. Hazard told Carlson that DeGraff's "case appeals to me as really pathetic." Hazard to Carlson, September 3, 1929, AAUP. Secretary Tyler told the president of the College of Puget Sound that the impending report by the AAUP was "entirely favorable" to DeGraff. Tyler to Todd, September 7, 1929 (copy), AAUPP.

30. Hazard to Carlson, August 24, September 25, 26, October 2 (quote), 1929; Carlson to Hazard, September 28, 1929; Tyler to Carlson, October 2, 1929; Carlson to Tyler, October 4, 1929, AAUPP.

31. Hazard to Carlson, October 12, 15, 1929; W. C. Curtis to Carlson, October 9, 1929; Goodrich to Carlson, October 15, 1929; Curtis to Carlson, October 9, 1929, AAUPP.

32. Carlson to Goodrich, October 16 (first quotes), 21 (next to last quote), 23, 1929; Carlson to Curtis, October 18, 1929; see also Carlson to Hazard, October 17, 1929; Goodrich to Carlson, October 19, 24, 1929, AAUPP.

33. Goodrich to Carlson, October 28, 31 (two), 1929, AAUPP (copy of the Board statement also in Reel 123, UMBCR); see also Goodrich to Cowan, November 5, 1929, Reel 123, UMBCR.

34. Curtis to Carlson, November 5, 1929; memorandum, Carlson to Bordwell, Thurstone, Tyler, and Crew, n.d., AAUPP.

35. Carlson to Goodrich, November 5, 1929; Goodrich to Carlson, November 12, 1929, AAUPP (copy of latter letter also in Reel 123, UMBCR).

36. Speer to Goodrich, October 30, 1929, Reel 123, UMBCR. Though he wrote confidentially to Goodrich, Speer sent a copy to Leslie Cowan, asking his response. Speer to Cowan, November 25, 1929, Reel 123, UMBCR.

37. Thurstone to Carlson, November 6, 1929; Memo, Carlson to Crew, Tyler, Bordwell, Gray, Thurstone, n.d.; Gray to Tyler, August 31, 1929 (copy), AAUPP.

38. Handwritten notes, n.d. (November 9, 1929); excerpts of Council meeting minutes, November 9, 1929; Bordwell to Carlson, November 6, 9, 1929; Crew to Carlson, November 12, 1929; Tyler to Carlson, November 13 ("severe" quote), 1929; Thurstone to Tyler, November 21, 1929; Tyler to Thurstone, November 29, 1929, AAUPP.

39. Tyler to Schlundt, November 26, 1929; see Tyler to Carlson, November 16, 23, 1929; see also Joseph Mayer to Schlundt, November 23, 1929, AAUP. Handwritten notes, n.d. (November 9, 1929); excerpts of Council meeting minutes, November 9, 1929; Tyler to Carlson, November 13, 1929; Crew to Carlson, November 6, 1929 ("eagerly" quote); Tyler to Joseph Mayer, November 19, 1929 (copy of excerpt), AAUPP. Carlson didn't want to send galleys to Brooks and the curators, believing they had seen the essentials already and that the whole issue had been gone over enough. Besides, he thought they wanted delay so the folks back home would forget the matter anyway. Carlson to Tyler, November 21, 1929, AAUPP.

40. Memorandum, Carlson to Crew, Tyler, Bordwell, Thurstone, and Gray, November 11, 1929; Gray to Carlson, November 11, 1929; see Thurstone to

Carlson, November 11, 1929; Memo, Carlson to Crew, Tyler, Bordwell, Gray, Thurstone, n.d. (last two quotes), AAUPP. Whether to publish the whole of the infamous questionnaire produced a minor snag in the editing process. Arthur Wheeler, who chaired Committee A on academic freedom, thought it might be a problem. Gray thought fairness to all concerned dictated the added space and expense required by its publication in toto, and, in fact, Thurstone, ever the militant, wouldn't allow his name on the report without including the questionnaire. Wheeler to Tyler, November 20, 1929; Gray to Tyler, November 20, 1929; Thurstone to Tyler, November 21, 1929; AAUPP.

41. Adams to A. L. Wheeler, December 2, 1929; Kidd to A. L. Wheeler, November 30, 1929; Lovejoy to Wheeler, December 2, 1929; Tolman to Wheeler, December 2, 1929; Goodrich to Wheeler, December 2, 1929; Roberts to Wheeler, December 4, 1929; Padelford to Wheeler, December 5, 1929; Wheeler to Tyler, December 5, 1929; Weatherly to Wheeler, November 30, 1929; Gray to Tyler, August 31, 1929 (copy), AAUPP.

42. Edward Thurstone to Joseph Mayer, December 6, 1929; see also Maguire to Tyler, November 30, December 8, 1929, AAUPP.

43. Tyler to Crew, December 12, 1929; Bordwell to Tyler, December 12 (Bordwell's first quote), 13 (Bordwell's second quote), 1929, AAUPP.

44. Memo, Carlson to Crew, Tyler, Bordwell, Wheeler, and Maguire, n.d. (December 1929), AAUPP.

45. Maguire to John L. O'Brian, December 18, 1929; see also Tyler to Wheeler, December 18, 1929, AAUPP.

46. AAUP press release (draft), December 10, 1929 (actually released January 10, 1930); Carlson to Mayer, December 26, 1929; Kaufman to Mayer, December 19, 1929; see also numerous other relevant materials in AAUPP.

47. "Academic Freedom at the University of Missouri: Report on the Dismissal of Professor DeGraff and the Suspension of Professor Meyer," AAUP *Bulletin;* see also Douglas Waples to Carlson, September 5, 1929 (and accompanying tables), AAUPP.

48. "Academic Freedom at the University of Missouri"; AAUP Hearing; Tyler to Wheeler, November 22, 1929; see *St. Louis Globe-Democrat,* January 11, 1930, AAUPP.

49. "Academic Freedom at the University of Missouri"; Carlson to Crew, Tyler, Bordwell, Thurstone, and Gray, November 11, 1929; Carlson to Tyler, December 21, 1929; Carlson to Tyler, November 15, 1929 ("17 professors" quote), AAUPP.

50. Schlundt to Mayer, November 19, 1929; Hazard to Carlson, November 21, 1929 (with Carlson's handwritten notation); Carlson to Tyler, November 26, 1929; Tyler to Maguire, December 9, 1929; Carlson to Joseph Mayer, December 26, 1929; Schlundt to Mayer, January 12, 1930; Floyd Shoemaker to Mayer, January 11, 1930; Goodrich to Tyler, January 20 (with handwritten notation), February 4, 1930; Tyler to Goodrich, January 23, 1930; Tyler to Shoemaker, January 21, 1930; see also Helen Read to AAUP, January 14, 1930; M. W. Knarr to John H. Gray, January 15, 1930; and other relevant material in AAUPP.

9. Denouement

1. *Columbia Daily Tribune,* January 10, 1930, AAUPP.

2. Curtis to Carlson, January 18, 1930; *St. Louis Globe-Democrat,* January 11, 1930; *St. Louis Post-Dispatch,* January 12, 1930, AAUPP; *Monroe County Appeal,* January 17, 1930.

3. *Literary Digest* (February 1, 1930): 28–29; copy also in AAUPP; *Topeka Daily Capital,* n.d.; *New Republic* (March 26, 1930): 142, AAUPP; *Detroit Free Press,* January 11, 1930; *Boston Traveler,* January 11, 1930; Editor, *Philadelphia Record* to Brooks, March 26, 1930; Brooks to Editor, March 28, 1930, UMPOP.

4. School Superintendent to Brooks, January 15, 1930; Clergyman to Brooks, January 10, 1930; Seneca Resident to Brooks, January 10, 1930; Resident to Brooks, January 10, 1930; Unlearned Friend to Brooks, January 12, 1930; U.S. Circuit Judge to Brooks, January 11, 1930; Hart to Brooks, January 10, 1930; Old Mizzou Graduate to Brooks, March 17, 1930; Fulton parent to Brooks, January 11, February 19, 1930; and other relevant letters in UMPOP; *Moberly Monitor-Index,* January 11, 1930, UMPOP ("Unquestionably" quote).

5. *Monroe County Appeal,* January 17, 1930; see R. M. White to Blanton, March 27, 1930; Addison Wallace to Blanton, March 28, 1930, UMPOP; *St. Louis Post-Dispatch,* January 12, 1930; *Kansas City Star,* n.d. (datelined April 5, 1930), AAUP; George Berry to Viles, n.d. ("Friday," 1930), VHFP; Max F. Meyer, Anti Evolution, then Anti Social Science, and What Next? presidential address to the Southern Society of Philosophy and Psychology, UMPOP.

6. W. E. Freeland to Blanton, March 14, 1930; Buford to Brooks, March 5, 1930, UMPOP; W. C. Curtis, statement on Max Meyer, n.d, EP; Stephens, *History,* 513; Jones to Williams, January 14, 1930; Walter Williams to Frank Thilly, March 18, 1924, SLWP.

7. *New York Times,* March 30, 1930; *Kansas City Star,* March 2, 1930, UMPOP; Middlebush to Brooks, March 3, 1930, UMSBPAR; Bart B. Howard to Williams, April 5, 1929 ("lusterless career" quote), see also attached clipping; Arnold to Williams, June 1, 1928; Thilly to Williams, February 5, 1924; Williams to Thilly, March 18, 1924, SLWP.

8. Statement of the Board of Curators, January 1930, UMPOP; McCutcheon to Viles, January 17, 1930, VHFP; Kirkendall, *History of Missouri, 1919 to 1953,* 112, 155, 241; Hazard, *Attorney for the Situation,* 120–21; George Berry to Viles, n.d. ("Friday", 1930), VHFP; *Kansas City Star,* March 2, 1930 ("mental terror" quote), UMPOP.

9. *Columbia Daily Tribune,* March 6, 1930 (Caulfield quote; emphasis added), *New York Times,* March 30, 1930; *Kansas City Star,* March 2, 1930 ("Who is this man" quote), UMPOP; Viles to Berry, March 4, 1930, VHFP.

10. *Washington Post,* March 19, 1930, AAUPP; *New York Times,* March 30, 1930 (copy also in UMPOP, though misdated); W. C. Curtis, statement on Max Meyer, n.d., EP.

11. Blanton to Frank Stephens, October 20, 1953, SP 3599, *Kansas City Star,* April 6, 1930, AAUPP; Minutes of the Board of Curators, April 5, 1930, Reel 123, UMBCR; Arnold to Walter Williams, April 9, 1930; see also A. A. Speer to Williams, April 9, 1930, SLWP.

12. *Kansas City Star,* April 6, May 23 (?, quotes), 1930, AAUPP; see handwritten notation, Schlundt to Tyler, n.d., on Tyler's letter to Schlundt, February 26, 1930, AAUPP; *Springfield Leader,* June 6, 1930; see other newspaper clippings in Stratton Duluth Brooks, Scrapbooks/Newspaper Clippings, 1923–1930, Series C: 1/11/1, Box 1, University of Missouri Archives, Lewis Hall, Columbia.

13. Gulick to H. M. Parker, March 7, 1930; Gulick to Meyer, June 11, 1930, University of Missouri, Max Meyer Incident Papers; Max F. Meyer, Anti Evolution, then Anti Social Science, and What Next? presidential address to the Southern Society of Philosophy and Psychology, UMPOP; Meyer to Hazard, August 20, 1929 (copy), AAUPP.

14. Stella Meyer to Mayerberg, November 7, 1929 (copy); Carlson to E. R. Embree, November 14, 1929, AAUPP.

15. Max F. Meyer, Anti Evolution, then Anti Social Science, and What Next? presidential address to the Southern Society of Philosophy and Psychology, UMPOP; Tyler to Carlson, November 18, 1929, AAUPP.

16. DeGraff to Carlson, October 18, 1929; November 12, 1929, AAUPP; see also Carlson to DeGraff, October 21, 1929; DeGraff to Joseph Mayer, December 20, 1929, AAUPP; Cowan to DeGraff, December 20, 1929, Reel 122, UMBCR.

17. Memorandum, Carlson to Crew and Tyler, November 1929; R. W. Gerard to Carlson, November 29, 1929, AAUPP.

18. Thurstone-Gerard Proposals, n.d., AAUPP.

19. Jordan E. Kurland to author, March 3, 1998. See also "How Censure Decisions Are Reached," *Chronicle of Higher Education* (June 15, 1988): A18. In March 1930, Thurstone, with apparent support from Chicago colleagues Gerard and Carlson, took the censure proposals to the convention of the Federation of American Societies for Experimental Biology. *Columbia Daily Tribune,* n.d. (datelined March 21, 1930), UMPOP; AAUP *Bulletin* 26 (February 1940): 49–54.

20. *Columbia Missourian,* February 12, 1930; Max F. Meyer, Anti Evolution, then Anti Social Science, and What Next? presidential address to the Southern Society of Philosophy and Psychology; *St. Louis Post-Dispatch,* April 20 (?), 1930, UMPOP.

21. *Columbia Daily Tribune,* n.d. ("psychological moment" quote), UMPOP; Brooks to Meyer, April 22, 1930, UMPOP; McDavid to Williams, April 23, 1930; James Goodrich to Williams, April 24, 1930; Williams to McDavid, April 25, 1930; Williams to Goodrich, April 27, May 29, 1930, SLWP; Group to Board of Curators, April 28, 1930, VHFP; Goodrich to Fred Middlebush, May 28, 1930, UMSBPAR.

22. Minutes of the Board of Curators, May 2, 1930; see also Cowan to Meyer, May 3, 1930, Reel 123, UMBCR; *Kansas City Times,* May 3, 1930, AAUPP.

23. Carlson to Tyler, May 5, 1930; S. A. Mitchell (?) to Tyler, May 17, 1930, AAUPP; T. S. Barclay to Middlebush, April 29, 1930, UMSBPAR; A Most Interested Observer to Goodrich, April 30, 1930, Reel 123, UMBCR. Goodrich wanted Secretary Cowan to find out, if he could, the identity of the author. He also wanted the letter copied and sent to fellow board members. Goodrich to Cowan, May 3, 1930, Reel 123, UMBCR; *Columbia Daily Tribune,* May 12, 1930, UMPOP; see *Kansas City Star,* n.d. (datelined May 12, 1930), AAUPP.

24. Curtis to Goodrich, May 16, 1930, and accompanying statement (May 16, 1930), UMPOP; see Curtis, statement on Max Meyer, n.d., EP; *Missouri Alumnus,* May 1929.

25. *St. Louis Globe-Democrat*, May 14, 1930, UMPOP; see also *Kansas City Star*, May 13, 1930, UMPOP; Goodrich to Meyer, May 7, 1930, Reel 123, UMBCR; Meyer, A Historical Sketch of the Missouri Case, n.d. (1930s) (Meyer quote), AAUPP.

26. Cowan to Goodrich, May 10, 1930; see Goodrich to Cowan, May 3, 1930, CP, Reel 123; *Kansas City Times*, May 17, 1930 ("mentally unfit" quote), AAUPP; *Columbia Daily Tribune*, May 17, 1930 ("senile" and "Babbitts" quotes); *St. Louis Post-Dispatch*, May 18, 1930 (also "senile" quote), UMPOP.

27. *Columbia Daily Tribune*, May 17, 1930; *St. Louis Post-Dispatch*, May 18, 1930 (quotes), UMPOP.

28. *Kansas City Times*, May 17, 1930, AAUP; *St. Louis Post-Dispatch*, May 18, 1930 (quotes), UMPOP; Meyer to Board of Curators, May 26, 1930, Reel 123, UMBCR.

29. Minutes of the Board of Curators, May 26, 1930, Reel 123, UMBCR; newspaper clipping, n.d., AAUPP.

30. Meyer to Carlson, December 7, 1929, AAUPP.

Epilogue. "So Far from Columbia"

1. *Savitar*, 1930; Douglas, *Terrible Honesty*, 498–99; Fass, *The Damned and the Beautiful*, 373; Dumenil, *The Modern Temper*, 155; *Missouri Student*, February 5; September 19, 1929, SCELUM. Tennessee Williams never graduated, but Missouri gave him an honorary degree in 1969. *Mizzou* (winter 1998): 10.

2. See W. J. Shepard to W. C. Curtis, January 21, 1932, UMPOP; W. C. Curtis to H. W. Tyler, June 24, 1932; Curtis to W. W. Cook, November 20, 1934, AAUPP; Viles, *Centennial History*, 267; Farrar, *A Creed for My Profession*, 223; Williams to Curators, September 10, 1934; see also *Columbia Missourian*, September 10, 1934, SLWP.

3. *New York Times*, January 20, 1949; McDavid to Walter Williams, April 9, 1930, SLWP; Jack Blanton to Elmer Ellis, October 15, 1953, SP; Stephens, *History*, 495, 532 (Stephens claimed McBaine left in 1927, though it was actually 1928); *Missouri Student*, April 8, 1928, SCELUM; Theophil Irion, "The School of Education"; and Percy Hogan, "The School of Law," both in Viles, *Centennial History*, 370–71; 442–43; *Springfield Leader and Press*, April 13, 1943 (copy also in Springfield–Greene County Library, Springfield, Missouri); *Missouri Alumnus* 47 (December 1958): 7.

4. *Time* (May 29, 1950): 66–67; *Monroe County Appeal*, January 13, 20, 27, 1955; Blanton to Elmer Ellis, October 15, 1953 (Blanton quotes); Stephens to Blanton, October 19, 1953; Blanton to Stephens, October 20, 1953, SP, 3599. Ellis had written to Blanton on Stephens's behalf.

5. *Monroe County Appeal*, January 13, 20, 27, 1955. Judge James Goodrich, who left the Board in the 1930s, died in Kansas City in October 1952. *Missouri Alumnus* (December 1952): 20.

6. Percy Bordwell file, SCMLUI; *Who's Who in America*, vol. 25 (Chicago: A. N. Marquis Company, 1948), 253; Thurstone to Walter Williams, August 26, 1933 (copy); Williams to Thurstone, August 29, 1933 (copy); see also Herbert Blumer to Williams, July 10, 1933; Williams to Blumer, July 12, 1933 (copy), UMPOP; Thurstone to W. W. Cook, October 23, 1934, and other relevant correspondence in AAUPP; J. P. Guilford, "Louis Leon Thurstone, 1887–1955," *Biographical Memoirs*

30 (1957): 349–82, copy also in Archival Biographical File, SCRLUC; also news-paper clipping, April 6, 1945; "Recent Developments in Guidance"; Thurstone resume, Archival Biographical File, SCRLUC; Lester L. Dragstedt, "Anton Julius Carlson, January 29, 1875–September 2, 1956," *Biographical Memoirs* 35 (1961): 1–32; *Time* (February 10, 1941): 44, 46–48 (quotes on 47–48); April 5, 1948, 49, copies also in Anton Julius Carlson, Archival Biographical File, SCRLUC; Letters Written to Dr. A. J. Carlson by Students and Friends on the Occasion of His Seventy-Fifth Birthday (bound volume, n.d., 1949–1950), Anton Julius Carlson Papers, SCR-LUC; see also William H. McNeill, *Hutchins' University: A Memoir of the University of Chicago, 1929–1950* (Chicago: University of Chicago Press, 1991), 58–59, 91, 100; and copy of an America First speech given by Carlson, n.d., in GNPP.

7. *Columbia Daily Tribune*, July 10, 14 (quotes), 17, September 1, 1923; November 30, December 1, 2, 3, 1937; December 1, 1974; Meyer, A Historical Sketch of the Missouri Case, n.d ("drinker" quote), AAUPP; Leland Hazard claimed that Wat-son's "knowledge—by common repute—of the uses of alcohol was greater than his respect for the academic pursuit of truth." Hazard, *Attorney for the Situation*, 97; Mowrer to Erwin Esper, August 5, 1957 ("played right into his hands" quote), EP; Edwin M. Watson, biographical material, GP; Stephens, *History*, 583; John W. Kennedy to editor of *Missouri Alumnus* (spring 1992): 9 ("spellbound" quote); see also Elizabeth M. Calhoun to editor, *Missouri Alumnus* (summer 1992): 8; *Missouri Alumnus* (December 1952): 20; *Who's Who in America*, vol. 30 (Chicago: A. N. Mar-quis Company, 1958); *Columbia Daily News*, December 1–2, 1974; Ellis, *My Road to Emeritus*, 146–53, 158–59; on Cowan see also Olson and Olson, *The University of Missouri*, 80; Charles McMullin to Erwin Esper, August 3, 1966, EP; Curtis to W. W. Cook, March 18, 1935, AAUPP; further on Curtis, see his letters in EP; also, Curtis, "The Evolution Controversy," 84–85; Curtis, Missouri: Mother of the West, CP. Hudson told Curtis that Brooks couldn't understand why Curtis had been so critical of him, when the president had been good to him. That was true, which Curtis had told the curators. But Curtis said in 1935, "It is one of my regrets in the matter that Brooks, who in certain ways is a likable chap, can never understand that a man whom he has treated well could stand up against him on principle. But after all, that kind of attitude was one of the things the matter with Brooks." Curtis to Cook, March 18, 1935, AAUPP.

8. Hazard, *Attorney for the Situation*; W. C. Curtis, statement on Max Meyer, n.d., EP.

9. *Akron Beacon Journal*, November 24, 1967.

10. Glass, "Jesse Wrench," 24 (first quote), 26 (second quote). Wrench remains a favorite legend. See John Beahler, " 'Be as Young as They Are,' " *Mizzou* (summer 2000): 35–37; see also numerous letters generated by the Wrench story in *Mizzou* (fall 2000): 3–5.

11. Glass, "Jesse Wrench," 24–26; *Time* (June 1, 1953): 43, 44–45; Atherton, unti-tled tribute to Jane Wrench, n.d., LEAP; "Students Say Farewell to Jesse Wrench," *Missouri Alumnus* (June 1953): 4–5, 12, copy of latter in WP; Thomas A. Brady, "Jesse E. Wrench, 1882–1958," *Missouri Alumnus* (November 1958): 36–37.

12. Meyer to W. W. Cook, November 25, 1934; see also numerous relevant cor-respondence in AAUPP. Meyer told the AAUP's General Secretary in 1935: "My educational research proceeds very well;—but under great restrictions due to the enormous financial stress to which I am exposed, almost as in my student days

when I had to study and make a living at the same time, by menial labor." Meyer to W. W. Cook, February 23, 1935, AAUP. Even Meyer's inherited property back in Germany had been ruined by the wild inflation in that country in the early 1920s. Cook to Edwin Patterson, January 15, 1935 (which quotes Meyer), AAUPP.

13. W. C. Curtis to H. H. Tyler, June 24, 1932; Meyer to Tyler, June 18, 1933; Meyer to W. W. Cook, October 13, 1934 (copy), November 1, 1934, AAUPP. Thurstone thought, apparently incorrectly, Missouri could simply declare Meyer retired and thus enable him to begin collecting his Carnegie pension. For his part, Meyer's paranoia worked overtime as he wondered if Frank McDavid, as president of the Board of Curators, was taking "glory in his revenge." Thurstone to Cook, October 23, 1934; Meyer to Cook, October 13, 1934 (copy); but see Memorandum, S. A. Mitchell to Cook, October 30, 1934, AAUPP. W. C. Curtis, an ardent Meyer defender, believed the curators thought they were doing the right thing by keeping Meyer on leave status in the event he obtained employment elsewhere. Nor did he think anyone could pry early retirement funds from the Carnegie Foundation before age sixty-five, save for physical disability. Continuing Meyer at some sort of salary during depressed economic times was simply out of the question. Curtis to Cook, November 20, 1934, AAUPP. On pensions at Missouri, see Stephens, *History*, 585–87, 624n. For Meyer's Carnegie pension, see 529n.

14. Thurstone to H. W. Tyler, June 27, 1932, August 8, October 3, 1933; Thurstone to Joseph Mayer, July 7, 1933; Walter Williams to Meyer, June 9, 1933; H. W. Tyler to Percival Hall, June 21, 1933; Hall to Tyler, June 23, 1933 (copy); Edwin Patterson to W. W. Cook, March 29, 1935, and numerous relevant correspondence in AAUPP, much of it internal; William J. Robbins to Thomas Edison, June 10, 1931; J. V. Miller to Graduate School, University of Missouri, June 18, 1931; Robbins to Helen Keller, June 10, 1931; Curtis to Meyer, January 11, 1932; E. V. Cowdry to Curtis, January 22, 1932, and numerous relevant correspondence in UMPOP. Meyer to Erwin Esper, September 6, 1966, EP. For his part, Meyer absolved the curators of guilt.

15. Meyer to Mowrer, February 26, 1956, MP; Meyer to Boring, November 1, 1955; Meyer to Leo Jacobs, February 16, 1957 ("fad" and "fade out" quotes); Hazard to Meyer, July 13, 1962; Mary Ellen Curtin to Meyer, March 30, 1964; Boring to Esper, October 4, 1965; Nafe to Esper, November 9, 1965, Juergen Tonndorf to Esper, February 17, 1966 ("Teutonic" quote); William H. Lichte to Esper, November 24, 1965; W. A. Van Bergeijk to Esper, February 18, 1966 ("quaintly outdated" quote); Jerry Tobias to Esper, May 18, 1964, August 18, 1966 (last quote); and other relevant material in EP.

16. Isadore Anderson to Meyer, December 23, 1952; Fred McKinney to Esper, October 13, 1965; Meyer to Esper, postcard, n.d. (postmarked June 1964); Meyer to Esper, March 11, 1955; March 27, 1956; June 24, 1964; Mowrer to Esper, June 17, 1957, EP; Meyer to Mowrer, February 26, 1956, MP; J. W. Bridges to Esper, February 21, 1967; Dorothy Schiller to Esper, March 15, 1967, EP. See also numerous other correspondence regarding Meyer in EP.

17. Everett Jackson to Dorothy Schiller, April 12, 1967, EP. Mowrer, *Abnormal Reactions or Actions?* 9–13 ("Rarely" quote on 13); *Champaign-Urbana News-Gazette*, March 6, 1979; Mowrer biography statement, n.d., MP. The circumstances for the awarding of the hours is unclear; a Citation of Merit brochure in 1956 listed the

date of his Missouri degree as 1931. MP. However, a colleague claimed the year was 1932. J. McVicker Hunt, "Orval Hobart Mowrer (1907–1982), *American Psychologist* 39 (August 1984): 912.

18. Mowrer, *Abnormal Reactions or Actions?* 21–22; see Knight Dunlap to Mowrer, January 28, 1941; E. B. Robert to Mowrer, February 5, 1941; Mowrer to Robert, February 12, 1941; William Baer to Mowrer, April 25, 1947; Mowrer to James B. Conant, n.d. (copy); Conant to Mowrer, May 6, 1948, and other relevant material in MP.

19. W. Francis English to Mowrer, November 10, 19, 21, 1956; Mowrer to McKinney, November 15, 1956 (quote); McKinney to Mowrer, November 19, 1956; program and other relevant documents in MP.

20. Mowrer, Psychology, Then and Now; Robert S. Daniel ("Bob") to Mowrer, n.d. ("Saturday"); Mowrer to Daniel, December 14, 1956, MP.

21. Meyer to Curtis, January 13, 1932, UMPOP; Meyer to Esper, March 27, 1956, EP; Meyer to Mowrer, February 26, 1956, MP.

22. Hazard to Mowrer, August 31, 1962; Mowrer to Hazard, September 17, 1962, MP; Mowrer, "Present State of Behaviorism," 6 ("youthful veneration" quote); Mowrer, *Abnormal Reactions or Actions?* 13; Mowrer to Esper, June 17, August 5 ("Prussian" and "paranoia" quotes), 1957; January 21, 1958, EP.

23. Hunt, "Orval Hobart Mowrer," 912 ("coherent search" quote); Mowrer, *Abnormal Reactions or Actions?* 33–39 (first three quotes on 34; "creedal" quote on 38); *Time* (September 14, 1959): 69, copy in MP; Arthur Foster, review of Mowrer, *The Crisis in Psychiatry and Religion* (Princeton, N.J.: Van Nostrand, 1961), *Foundations*, volume unknown (July 1964), 304, MP.

24. Mowrer, *Leaves from Many Seasons: Selected Papers* (New York: Praeger Publishers, 1983), 318 (quote), 327; Hunt, "Orval Hobart Mowrer," 914 (part of quote also).

25. Mowrer, *Leaves from Many Seasons,* 326–27 (quote on 326); Hunt, "Orval Hobart Mowrer," 914; Mowrer, "Autobiography," *Education* 97 (fall 1976): 3.

26. See *MU Tour* (visitor brochure, Columbia, n.d.); University of Missouri admissions material; Olson and Olson, *University of Missouri,* 267; *100 Years on the Quad.*

27. Erenberg, *Swingin' the Dream,* xi–xiv, 3–31; *Life* (June 7, 1937): 32–37, 67 (quotes on 33); Eldridge, "Sheepskin Deep," 7, 85–89 (quotes on 7, 87, 88, 89).

28. "Missouri vs. Smith," *Life* (May 9, 1949): 67–80 (quote on p. 67).

29. Jack Shepherd, "Potheads in Missouri," *Look* (August 8, 1967): 14–16; Beth Bailey, *Sex in the Heartland* (Cambridge, Mass.: Harvard University Press, 1999), 68–69, 81.

30. Tom Brokaw, *The Greatest Generation* (New York: Random House, 1998); Frances Dunlap Herron to editor, *Missouri Alumnus* (winter 1990): 4; see John Leo, *Two Steps Ahead of the Thought Police* (New York: Simon and Schuster, 1994); Alan C. Kors and Harry A. Silverglate, *The Shadow University: The Betrayal of Liberty on America's Campuses* (New York: Free Press, 1998); Alice Anderson and Beatrice Dvorak, "Differences between College Students and Their Elders in Standards of Conduct," *Journal of Abnormal Psychology* 23 (October 1928): 286–92.

31. "Johnny Says" (columnist), *Missouri Student,* October 9, 1929 (Sunday movies quote), SCELUM; AAUP *Bulletin* (February 1923): 33 (Hiscock quote); *Columbia Daily Tribune,* February 9, 1926 (reprint of *St. Louis Post-Dispatch* edi-

torial); Dumenil, *Modern Temper*, 6, 198, 226; May, "Shifting Perspectives on the 1920's," 407; Kirschner, "Conflicts and Politics in the 1920s," 221; see Allen, *Only Yesterday*, 102–5; and Fass, *The Damned and the Beautiful*, 366, 376; Nancy Bristow, *Making Men Moral: Social Engineering During The Great War* (New York: New York University Press, 1996), xvii-xix, 10, 215–18; Avis D. Carlson, "Wanted: A Substitute for Righteousness," *Harpers* 154 (January 1927): 148 (second "moral laxity" quote); Elton Mayo, "Sin with a Capital 'S,'" *Harpers* 154 (April 1927): 545 ("pure and undefiled" quote); *Missouri Student*, February 5, 1930, SCELUM; for a somewhat contrary view, see Coben, *Rebellion against Victorianism*; Mowrer, *Leaves from Many Seasons*, 327–28.

Essay on Sources

The availability of numerous valuable sources make possible a fuller examination of the culture wars of the 1920s. The decade has attracted many able scholars who for years have been correcting the simplistic stereotypes of a complex and dynamic era. There is also some movement away from the Progressive paradigm that viewed the decade in largely negative and crass terms, at best a sort of foil for the New Deal years. Some of the traits of the 1920s, while not untrue, became stereotypes through the otherwise pathbreaking social history of Frederick Lewis Allen, whose *Only Yesterday: An Informal History of the 1920's* became a virtual classic after its publication in 1931. Henry F. May, *The End of American Innocence: A Study of the First Years of Our Own Time, 1912–1917*, advanced the idea of cultural change predating the 1920s and offered an early historiographical assessment in "Shifting Perspectives on the 1920's." But see also Lynn Dumenil, "Re-Shifting Perspectives on the 1920s: Recent Trends in Social and Cultural History," in John Earl Haynes, ed., *Calvin Coolidge and the Coolidge Era: Essays on the History of the 1920s*, 63–96; and Charles Eagles, "Urban-Rural Conflict in the 1920s: A Historiographical Assessment"; Paul Carter, *Another Part of the Twenties*; Stanley Coben, *Rebellion against Victorianism: The Impetus for Cultural Change in 1920s America*; Ann Douglas, *Terrible Honesty: Mongrel Manhattan in the 1920s*; Lynn Dumenil, *The Modern Temper: American Culture and Society in the 1920s*; Lewis Erenberg, *Steppin' Out: New York Nightlife and the Transformation of American Culture, 1890–1930*; Lewis Erenberg, *Swingin' the Dream: Big Band Jazz and the Rebirth of American Culture*; Paula Fass, *The Damned and the Beautiful: American Youth in the 1920's*; Ellis Hawley, *The Great War and the Search for a Modern Order, A History of the American People and Their Institutions, 1917–1933*; Don S. Kirschner, "Conflicts and Politics in the 1920's: Historiography and Prospects"; Daniel J. Leab, "Coolidge, Hays, and 1920s Movies: Some Aspects of Image and Reality," in Haynes, ed., *Calvin Coolidge and the Coolidge Era*, 97–131; William

311

Leuchtenburg, *The Perils of Prosperity, 1914–1932;* Lawrence W. Levine, "Progress and Nostalgia: The Self Image of the Nineteen Twenties," in *The Unpredictable Past: Explorations in American Cultural History;* Roderick Nash, *The Nervous Generation: American Thought, 1917–1930;* Burl Noggle, "The Twenties: A New Historiographical Frontier"; and Geoffrey Perrett, *America in the Twenties: A History.* See also numerous other relevant books cited in the Endnotes.

Such secondary work is supplemented by contemporary discussions of the mores and culture in books and articles published during the 1920s, citations to which are also found in the Endnotes. Whether the discussion was about companionate marriage or allegedly rebellious youth, or divorce, or Victorianism, or whatever, the published material reveals a culture at war with itself, and places Hobart Mowrer's otherwise brash questionnaire firmly in the context of an enticing and raucous decade. Ben Lindsey's books and public debates jostled with fearful editorials, along with pieces in *Harpers* or elsewhere arguing that modern youth culture wasn't so bad after all.

For manuscript sources, the well-developed and well-managed materials at the Western Historical Manuscript Collection in Ellis Library at the University of Missouri in Columbia proved invaluable. Notably, the University of Missouri President's Office Papers were crucial in judging constituent reaction to the questionnaire and providing access to many newspaper clippings; also, the papers of North Todd Gentry and several Missouri faculty, including those of Winterton C. Curtis, Edwin B. Branson, Lewis E. Atherton, Jesse E. Wrench, Frank F. Stephens, and Jonas Viles also proved helpful. Records of the Board of Curators, while not particularly well organized on microfilm, were nonetheless valuable, and those from the School of Business and Public Administration provided insight into Isidor Loeb's and Frederick Middlebush's thoughts. The Sara Lockwood Williams Papers were limited but still helpful on not only Dean Walter Williams but also Curator Mercer Arnold; a small collection, University of Missouri, Max Meyer Incident, also proved valuable. The Peter Tamony Collection, containing an incredible array of slang, provided direction in tracking down the practice of "jellying" at Mizzou.

Ellis Library also housed copies of the university student annual, the *Savitar* (though the author has copies of 1928 and 1929), and Special Collections has copies (some of them quite brittle) of the *Missouri Student,* the campus paper that began in the mid-twenties. Both the annuals and the newspaper allowed valuable insight into collegiate mores during the decade, and the latter even provided a forum for divergent views among students. University catalogs/bulletins, along with the university's web site, were consulted for various factual matters without specific citation.

While there are no Max Meyer papers as such, many relevant documents can be found in Erwin Esper's papers at the University of Washington in Seattle. In constructing an intellectual biography of Meyer, Professor Esper, a noted psychologist, gathered a sizable collection of papers not only originally belonging to Meyer but also those which detailed the thoughts and candid opinions of those who knew Meyer professionally and personally. Included are letters from some of Meyer's children that offered insight into an interesting but not always happy home life. Esper's work later appeared in two journal articles. Hobart Mowrer's papers at the University of Illinois in Urbana-Champaign, while not a particularly large collection, provided valuable understanding into his life and work. Tracking down several of the players in this drama was assisted by the Internet web site Ancestry.com with its link to the Social Security Death Index. Incidentally, though not cited, university catalogs and bulletins may be consulted for information on faculty and class offerings.

Aside from the Western Historical Manuscript Collection at the University of Missouri in Columbia, the most valuable and numerous collection of documents came from the American Association of University Professors in Washington, D.C. While supplemented by the *Bulletin*, which began publishing in 1915, and which shows the development of an outstanding organization, those papers are now housed at the Gelman Library at George Washington University in Washington. The author and his wife were allowed access to them while they were still at the AAUP offices where they had been resting for nearly seven decades. While not organized at the time, the papers were easy to categorize, and included numerous news clippings that both complemented and overlapped those collections at the University of Missouri. Importantly, the AAUP material not only showed how a professional organization went about its cautious investigation of academic freedom matters, including formation of the investigating committee, but also revealed the interaction of outstanding leaders of American higher education in the 1920s. The AAUP impacted the University of Missouri, just as the case impacted and changed the fourteen-year-old agency. Correspondence between leaders of the AAUP and university officials as well as with Leland Hazard, Max Meyer's attorney, provide valuable material available nowhere else. Of course, Hazard's own memoirs, *Attorney for the Situation*, which chronicles a long and busy life, also offers important and occasionally amusing insights into a case the once-young lawyer never forgot.

The sum of the collections noted in this essay or in the Endnotes are another testimony to the value and tedious work of archivists across the nation, without which, along with the work of their colleagues, much of the American experience would simply be lost. Fortunately, this book is a beneficiary of the able work of many of those professionals.

Index

Abyssinia, Mussolini's aggression in, 274
Academic Hall. *See* University of Missouri, Jesse Hall
Adams, George, 227
Addams, Jane, 149
Algonquin Hotel, 215
All Souls Unitarian Church, 68
Allen, Edgar, 187
Allen, Frederick Lewis, 85
Almstedt, Hermann, 53
Alpha Chi Omega, 31, 35
Alpha Delta Pi, 31, 32, 35, 203
Alpha Epsilon Phi, 31
Alpha Phi, 17, 31
Alpha Pi Zeta, 248, 252
Alpha Tau Omega, 35, 203
American Association of University Professors (AAUP), 246–47, 249; history and operation of, 127–29; early involvement in Missouri case, 157–65; investigation and hearing by, 167–200; development of report by, 204–14, 215–34; reaction to report of, 236–39, 241–42, 251; development of, 248; mentioned, 259 302*n40*
American Journal of Psychology, 265
American Journal of Sociology, 62
American Political Science Association, 126
American Psychological Association, 58, 161, 259, 265, 266, 269, 272
American Speech, 29
American University, 160, 162, 246
American War Mothers, 6
Anderson, Isadore, 122
Andrew Jackson Hotel, 248

Arnold, Mercer, 66, 69, 81–82, 87, 102, 141, 153, 156, 163, 175, 187, 241, 244, 250
Associated Press, 13, 116, 126, 136, 137, 139, 141, 165, 243, 250, 251
Atherton, Lewis, 263
Atherton, Louise, 263
Augustana College, 169

Babbitry, 14, 253
"Baby Boom" generation, 275
Baker, Isabel, 133
Baker, Sam A., 5
Barrett, Jesse, 53
Bauder, Russell, 26, 73, 77–78, 90, 172, 233
"Beetle Bailey," 29
Belden, Henry, 50, 124
Bell, Morris Frederick, 23
Benedict, H. Y., 137
Birkhead, L. M., 68
Blackmon, Earl, 67
Blanton, H. J., "Jack," 66, 69, 87, 102, 150, 152, 156, 163, 175, 218, 220, 240, 250, 257; editorials, 143, 237; AAUP hearing and, 169–72; profile of, 214–15; questionnaire not deemed mailable by, 228–29; on Ellwood's resignation, 239; urges Brooks to resign, 243; Meyer's attack on, 252–53; retort to Meyer, 254; explanation of Brooks's firing, 258; later career and death of, 258–59
Blevins, Bruce, 253
Blumer, Herbert, 63, 177–78, 260
Blunderbuss, 137
Bolshevism, 6, 13, 46, 64, 148, 238
Bone, Harry, 6
Boone County, Missouri, 12, 30, 47